Teaching with
The Norton Anthology
of African American Literature

SECOND EDITION

A Guide for Instructors

Teaching with
The Norton Anthology
of African American
Literature

SECOND EDITION

A Guide for Instructors

Joycelyn K. Moody

UNIVERSITY OF WASHINGTON

W • W • NORTON & COMPANY
New York • London

Composition by PennSet, Inc.
Manufacturing by Maple-Vail Book Manufacturing Group.
Book design by Antonina Krass

ISBN 0-393-92468-8 (pbk.)

W. W. Norton & Company, Inc., 500 Fifth Avenue, New York, NY 10110
www.wwnorton.com

W. W. Norton & Company Ltd., Castle House, 75/76 Wells Street,
London W1T 3QT

1 2 3 4 5 6 7 8 9 0

Contents

Acknowledgments

The completion of this guide is due in no small measure to the generosity, collegiality, and professionalism of many people. I am deeply grateful to them all:

- Helen R. Houston and Frances Smith Foster, authors of *Teaching with The Norton Anthology of African American Literature: A Guide for Instructors*, First Edition
- Julia Reidhead, vice president and editor, W. W. Norton & Company
- Erin Dye, editorial assistant, W. W. Norton & Company
- William L. Andrews, E. Maynard Adams Professor of English, University of North Carolina at Chapel Hill

At the University of Washington:

- Richard Dunn, professor and acting chair, Department of English
- Megan Munson and Jewel Rademacher, graduate student research assistants

At the University of Kansas-Edwards Center:

- James Hartman, professor and chair, Department of English
- Sharon Anthony, office of the vice provost
- Lynn Wolz, head librarian—and all of her accommodating staff
- Michelle Bird, building coordinator

At Johnson County Community College in Overland Park, Kansas:

- John Thomson III, assistant dean, Department of English
- Carmaletta Williams, associate professor of English
- Susan McGarvey, director of the Writing Center

Across the country:

- Bertram Ashe, associate professor of English, College of the Holy Cross, Worcester, Massachusetts
- J. Edgar Tidwell, associate professor of English, University of Kansas
- Gary Handwerk, professor of English and comparative literature, University of Washington
- Barbara Neely, Novelist and Friend Extraordinaire, Jamaica Plain, Massachusetts

At home:

- George and Catherine Moody: Thank you for *three* seasons—and a lifetime—of loving support. See what Sam Cooke and Moms Mabley on Mimosa Drive have wrought.
- Clell, Sr., and Clell, Jr.: You know a brighter day is (always) coming.
- And in my heart, Lorraine Martínez: Thank you for enduring patience, power, and clarity.

Teaching with
The Norton Anthology
of African American Literature

SECOND EDITION

A Guide for Instructors

Goals and Key Questions

What this Guide Offers:
- Strategies for designing vigorous and provocative course units in African American literature
- Strategies for thinking through the implications of course design decisions in the teaching of African American literature
- Suggestions for assignments, based on the selections in *The Norton Anthology of African American Literature* (*NAFAM*), to develop students' perspicacity as thinkers, readers, and writers
- Ideas for discussions of individual authors and text selections
- Ideas for exposing students to diverse African American literary styles
- Essay, exam, and discussion questions
- Cross-referenced lists of authors and themes
- Suggestions for using the Audio Companion to teach *NAFAM*
- Lists of (major) publications for authors in *NAFAM*
- Suggestions for developing students' knowledge of the chronology and intersections of African American literary history
- Genre breakdown by authors within literary periods
- List of supplementary multimedia resources
- A bibliography of (teaching) articles and books on *NAFAM* authors and texts

Key Questions to Engage Sudents:
- Why read and study African American literature?
- Why are some African American texts regarded as literature while others are not? Who determines that distinction? On what bases?
- What are the major authors, themes, traditions, conventions, and tropes of African American literature?

3

- What is African American literature *becoming*? What has it *been* becoming?
- What does African American literature illuminate about American literature?
- What is the relationship of African American literature to other American literatures?
- What is the relationship of African American literature to other American ethnic minority literatures?
- What themes, conventions, and traditions does African American literature share with literature by blacks in other African diasporas?
- Can African American literature be produced by persons *not* of African descent?

Key Questions for All *NAFAM* Selections:
- What are the worldviews and cultural values implied in this text? From whence do they seem to emerge?
- How does this author or text conform to or diverge from positions taken up by other texts in the course?
- What statement(s) about ethnic and cultural identity does the text assert? About an African identity cultivated outside Africa? About national identity as an American?

Key Questions about Emotional Issues Related to Teaching African American Literature:
- What are the advantages and disadvantages of providing students with either humor or "the metaphorical veil of 'other people's' . . . beliefs" (Anatol 58) to assuage the uncomfortable feelings that often develop during discussions of race in U.S. classrooms? See Kimberly Nichele Brown, "Useful Anger: Confrontation and Challenge in the Teaching of Gender, Race, and Violence," and Giselle Anatol, " 'Passing/Out' in the Classroom: Eradicating Binaries of Identity," both in *Women Faculty of Color in the White Classroom*, edited by Lucila Vargas.
- Kimberly Brown offers the following: "Because of my classroom experiences, the questions I have sought to answer are as follows: How do I teach students to respect and understand the anger displayed by many African American authors and not reinforce negative stereotypes concerning Blackness? How do I highlight sensitive issues such as gender, race, and violence without making my students feel uncomfortable? And finally, is it possible to teach such topics without causing discomfort?" (90). See Kimberly Nichele Brown, "Useful Anger: Confrontation and Challenge in Teaching Gender, Race, and Violence," in *Women Faculty of Color in the White Classroom*, edited by Lucila Vargas.

Literary Periodization

NAFAM facilitates historical approaches to teaching African American literature with its period introductions and its chronological arrangement of the entries by the authors' birth dates. However, "historical" periods are often defined by extraliterary considerations, and, in course design, they are subject to a variety of priorities, privileges, and practices. Many African American writers included in the anthology lived and wrote across two or more periods specified here; living authors among those whose works are included will undoubtedly be taught in multiple ways. Because authors do not necessarily conform to the dominant patterns and concerns of the period with which they may be identified, and because authors do not consistently reflect the social or aesthetic norms of their day, chronologically arranged periods are probably most useful simply as guides.

While chronological approaches generally group texts into periods, historical approaches consider texts within their contexts. A course structured around a historical perspective may concentrate on the social and political situations at the time when an individual artist was writing or when an artistic movement prevailed. A historical perspective may include biographical information about the writers or data about the impact these texts had when they first appeared or when they were rediscovered.

Furthermore, historical approaches address such questions as the following:

- Why are certain genres—or certain conventions and tropes within a genre—so prevalent? What relationships exist to foster certain conventions at certain times?
- How does African American literature reflect or (cor)respond to the social, political, philosophical, religious, aesthetic, or economic conditions of a historical period?
- How and why are certain writings didactic? How do particular writings or writers attempt to influence the social, political, aesthetic, or economic conditions of their milieu? In retrospect, how effective or influential were these writers?
- What was a particular writer's position within the literary establishments of her or his day? What definition of literature and what aesthetic objectives directed this writer?
- How does a particular writer's work represent, revise, or anticipate the works of other writers past and future?

Suggested Readings for Thematically Organized Courses

Alphabetical Quicklist of Themes

Academic discourses
African Americans outside the United States
African diasporas
Amalgamation and miscegenation/passing
American aesthetics, rhetoric, and polemics
(Thwarted) American dreams
Authenticity and identity
Bondage, imprisonment, incarceration
Civil wars
"Cleo just grinned," or *Resistance*, she wrote
"don't it all come down to e/co/no/mics"
Education and literacy theories
Family
Gender portraits, differences, and/or conflicts
Ghosts and gothicism
Home and heritage
"The Influence of Ancestry": artistic intertextuality
Labor
Literary authority and critical theories

Major authors
Marriage
Migration, exodus, passages
Natural landscapes
Periodical literature
Protest literature
Resisting women
Romantic love
Separation and segregation
Sexual identities
Slave narratives
Southern traditions
Spirits and gods
Trauma—and in some cases recovery
Tricksters and shape-shifters
Urban landscapes
Violence against African Americans
"The Ways of White Folks": blacks define whiteness

This section groups the *NAFAM* selections into themes that can be used to organize or inspire courses in African American literature. Each thematic list of suggested authors and texts is further divided by historical/literary period as defined in the anthology. Courses organized by theme might draw, then, on authors and texts across periods or within periods. In the respective sections of this guide, from "The Vernacular Tradition" through "Literature since 1975," you will also find lists of genres in which *NAFAM* authors of that period are represented. The lists below are arranged in the order given in *NAFAM* for ready periodization and historicity, as well as intertextuality and cross-genre studies.

Academic Discourses

The titles listed below are appropriate for a course that concentrates on specific modes of learning and knowledge or on literary criticism and/or theory, especially as that critical thought emerges from or is developed in academic settings. Some of the texts overtly reference institutions or ideals of higher learning (e.g., Du Bois's "Criteria of Negro Art"), whereas others indirectly invoke the traditional academy. Hurston's "You May Go But This Will Bring You Back," for example, ends with a few minutes of interview with Hurston in her role as amateur learner, informal insider-outsider, and professional cultural anthropologist.

The Vernacular Tradition

SECULAR RHYMES AND SONGS

"You May Go But This Will Bring You Back"

BALLADS

"The Signifying Monkey"

HIP HOP

"The Revolution Will Not Be Televised"
"The Message"
"Don't Believe the Hype"
"The Evil That Men Do"
"Things Done Changed"
"N.Y. State of Mind"

SERMONS

"The Ballot or the Bullet"

FOLKTALES

"Deer Hunting Story"
"How to Write a Letter"
" 'Ah'll Beatcher Makin' Money' "
" 'De Reason Niggers Is Working So Hard' "

Slavery and Freedom

Wheatley:	"To Mæcenas," "To the University of Cambridge," "On Being Brought from Africa to America"
Delany:	*The Condition*
Douglass:	*Narrative of the Life, Life and Times*
Harper:	"Aunt Chloe's Politics," "Learning to Read," "Fancy Etchings," "Woman's Political Future"
Wilson:	*Our Nig*

Reconstruction to the New Negro Renaissance

Grimké:	Journals
Washington:	*Up From Slavery*
Hopkins:	"Famous Men of the Negro Race," "Letter from Cordelia A. Condict"
Wells-Barnett:	*A Red Record*

Du Bois: *The Souls of Black Folk*, "Criteria of Negro Art"
J. Johnson: Preface to *The Book of American Negro Poetry*
Dunbar: "A Cabin Tale"

Harlem Renaissance

Schomburg: "The Negro Digs Up His Past"
Locke: "The New Negro"
McKay: "To the White Fiends"
Larsen: *Quicksand*
Hughes: "Letter to the Academy," "Theme for English B"

Realism, Naturalism, Modernism

Tolson: "An Ex-Judge at the Bar," *Libretto for the Republic of Liberia*
Wright: "Blueprint for Negro Writing," "The Ethics of Living Jim Crow," *Black Boy*
Ellison: "Change the Joke and Slip the Yoke," "The World and the Jug," "Remembering Richard Wright"
Brooks: "Young Heroes"

Black Arts Era

Fuller: "Towards a Black Aesthetic"
Malcolm X: *The Autobiography*
King: "Letter from Birmingham Jail"
Gayle: *The Black Aesthetic*
Lorde: "Poetry Is Not a Luxury"
Jordan: *Civil Wars*
Reed: "Dualism"
Giovanni: "Nikki-Rosa"
Rodgers: "Jesus Was Crucified"

Literature since 1975

Murray: *Train Whistle Guitar*
Marshall: "Reena," "The Making of a Writer"
Kennedy: *A Movie Star Has to Star in Black and White*
Morrison: "Rootedness," "The Site of Memory," "Unspeakable Things Unspoken"
Gaines: "The Sky Is Gray"
Forrest: *There Is a Tree More Ancient Than Eden*
Wideman: *Brothers and Keepers, Damballah*

Walker:	"Women," "In Search of Our Mothers' Gardens," "Everyday Use," "Advancing Luna," *The Color Purple*
Johnson:	"The Education of Mingo"
Naylor:	*The Women of Brewster Place*
Dove:	"History," "Demeter's Prayer to Hades"
Danticat:	*Breath, Eyes, Memory*

African Americans Outside the United States

The texts grouped in this section depict, analyze, and/or allude to African Americans functioning in a milieu outside U.S. national borders or imagining a life outside the United States.

The Vernacular Tradition

THE BLUES

"Beale Street Blues"

SONGS OF SOCIAL CHANGE

"The Backlash Blues"

RHYTHM AND BLUES

"Dancin' in the Street"
"What's Goin' On?"

SERMONS

"The Ballot or the Bullet"

Slavery and Freedom

Delany:	*The Condition*
Garnet:	"An Address to the Slaves of the United States"
Douglass:	*My Bondage and My Freedom, Life and Times*

Reconstruction to the New Negro Renaissance

| Chesnutt: | "The Passing of Grandison" |
| Hopkins: | "Talma Gordon," "Famous Women of the Negro Race" |

Du Bois: "Two Novels"
J. Johnson: *The Autobiography of an Ex-Colored Man*

Harlem Renaissance

Schomburg: "The Negro Digs Up His Past"
Garvey: "Africa for the Africans"
Larsen: *Quicksand*
Brown: "Sam Smiley"
Bontemps: "Nocturne at Bethesda"
Hughes: "Jazz Band in a Parisian Cabaret"

Realism, Naturalism, Modernism

Tolson: "An Ex-Judge at the Bar," *Libretto for the Republic of Liberia*
Wright: "The Man Who Lived Underground"
Hayden: "O Daedalus, Fly Away Home," "A Letter from Phillis Wheatley"
Baldwin: "Stranger in the Village"

Black Arts Era

Evans: "I Am a Black Woman"
Williams: *The Man Who Cried I Am*
Jordan: "Poem about My Rights," "Intifada"
Madhubuti: "The Long Reality"

Literature since 1975

Marshall: "To Da-duh, in Memoriam"
Major: "Round Midnight"
Cliff: "Columba"
Komunyakaa: "February in Sydney," "Facing It"
Shange: "Bocas: A Daughter's Geography"

African Diasporas

The titles listed here are perhaps those most suitable for organizing a course that defines African identities, that deals with people of African descent living within or across multiple African diasporas, or that addresses the African diaspora as a geopolitical state.

The Vernacular Tradition

THE BLUES

"My Handy Man"

SONGS OF SOCIAL CHANGE

"The Backlash Blues"
"Four Women"

JAZZ

"It Don't Mean a Thing (If It Ain't Got That Swing)"
"(What Did I Do to Be So) Black and Blue"
"Parker's Mood"

SERMONS

"The Ballot or the Bullet"

Slavery and Freedom

Hammon:	"An Address to Miss Phillis Wheatley"
Smith:	*Narrative of the Life and Adventures*
Wheatley:	all selections
Walker:	*Appeal in Four Articles*
Garnet:	"An Address to the Slaves of the United States"
Séjour:	"The Mulatto"
Douglass:	*Life and Times*
Harper:	"Ethiopia"

Reconstruction to the New Negro Renaissance

J. Johnson:	"Fifty Years," Preface to *The Book of American Negro Poetry*

Harlem Renaissance

Garvey:	"Africa for the Africans"
McKay:	"Africa," "Enslaved"
Bennett:	"Heritage"
Hughes:	"Jazz Band in a Parisian Cabaret," "Afro-American Fragment," "Negro Servant"
Cullen:	"Heritage"

Realism, Naturalism, Modernism

Tolson:	"A Legend of Versailles," *Libretto for the Republic of Liberia*
Wright:	"The Man Who Lived Underground"
Hayden:	"Middle Passage," "Soledad," "A Letter from Phillis Wheatley"
Brooks:	"Young Heroes"
Baldwin:	"Sonny's Blues"

Black Arts Era

Williams:	*The Man Who Cried I Am*
Lorde:	*Zami*
Jordan:	"Intifada"
Clifton:	"move"

Literature since 1975

Marshall:	"To Da-duh, in Memoriam," "The Making of a Writer"
Kennedy:	*A Movie Star Has to Star in Black and White*
Morrison:	"Unspeakable Things Unspoken"
Wideman:	*Damballah*
Walker:	"In Search of Our Mothers' Gardens"
Wilson:	*Joe Turner's Come and Gone*
Cliff:	all selections
Butler:	"Bloodchild"
Mackey:	"Song of the Andoumboulou: 8"
Shange:	"Bocas: A Daughter's Geography"
Jones:	*Corregidora*
Kincaid:	*Annie John*
Dove:	"Parsley," "The Oriental Ballerina"
Phillips:	*Crossing the River*
Danticat:	*Breath, Eyes, Memory*

Amalgamation and Miscegenation/Passing

The titles here address a range of issues related to mixed-race peoples, to the "mixing" of ethnic groups, to persons passing as members of a race other than the one to which a dominant society has ascribed them, to persons being passed (i.e., people presumed to identify with a racial group to which they in fact do not).

The Vernacular Tradition

SONGS OF SOCIAL CHANGE

"Four Women"

Slavery and Freedom

Brown:	*Clotel*
Séjour:	"The Mulatto"
Harper:	"The Two Offers"
Wilson:	*Our Nig*

Reconstruction to the New Negro Renaissance

Chesnutt:	"The Wife of His Youth"
Hopkins:	"Talma Gordon," "Letter from Cordelia A. Condict"
J. Johnson:	*The Autobiography of an Ex-Colored Man*
F. Johnson:	"The Scarlet Woman"

Harlem Renaissance

Fauset:	*Plum Bun*
McKay:	*Home to Harlem*
Larsen:	*Quicksand*
Toomer:	*Cane*
Brown:	"Slim Greer"
Hughes:	"Mulatto"
Cullen:	"Heritage"

Realism, Naturalism, Modernism

Wright:	"Blueprint for Negro Writing"
Ellison:	"The World and the Jug"
Baldwin:	"Stranger in the Village," "Sonny's Blues"

Black Arts Era

Madhubuti:	"Back Again, Home," "Malcolm Spoke / who listened?"
Rodgers:	"For Sistuhs Wearin' Straight Hair"

Literature since 1975

Kennedy: *A Movie Star Has to Star in Black and White*
Walker: "On Stripping Bark from Myself"
Cliff: "Columba"
Butler: "Bloodchild"
Naylor: *The Women of Brewster Place*

American Aesthetics, Rhetoric, and Polemics

The titles listed below all engage some aspect of argumentation—from theories of rhetorical style and skill (e.g., the vernacular boast-ballad "The Signifying Monkey") to antagonistic statements designed to elicit passionate response from a specified, targeted audience (e.g., Horton's "The Creditor to His Proud Debtor"). In other instances, the texts develop theories and methodologies of rhetorical beauty, power, persuasion, and force (e.g., Ellison's "Prologue" to *Invisible Man*). These texts illustrate African American ideas about *what* to debate as well as *how* to engage.

The Vernacular Tradition

SPIRITUALS

"Go Down, Moses"
"Swing Low, Sweet Chariot"

GOSPEL

"Freedom in the Air"

THE BLUES

"Backwater Blues"
"Trouble in Mind"
"Good Morning Blues"
"Hoochie Coochie"
"My Handy Man"

SECULAR RHYMES AND SONGS

"Promises of Freedom"
"No More Auction Block"

Bᴀʟʟᴀᴅꜱ

"The Signifying Monkey"
"Stackolee"
"Sinking of the *Titanic*"
"Shine and the *Titanic*"

Sᴏɴɢꜱ ᴏꜰ Sᴏᴄɪᴀʟ Cʜᴀɴɢᴇ

"Oh, Freedom"
"Strange Fruit"
"We Shall Overcome"
"The Backlash Blues"
"Four Women"

Jᴀᴢᴢ

"It Don't Mean a Thing (If It Ain't Got That Swing)"
"Parker's Mood"
"(What Did I Do to Be So) Black and Blue?"

Rʜʏᴛʜᴍ ᴀɴᴅ Bʟᴜᴇꜱ

"Respect"
"What's Goin' On?"

Hɪᴘ Hᴏᴘ

"The Revolution Will Not Be Televised"
"The Message"
"Don't Believe the Hype"
"The Evil That Men Do"

Sᴇʀᴍᴏɴꜱ

"I Have a Dream"
"The Ballot or the Bullet"

Fᴏʟᴋᴛᴀʟᴇꜱ

"How to Write a Letter"
"De Reason Niggers Is Working So Hard"
"How Mr. Rabbit Was Too Sharp for Mr. Fox"
"The Awful Fate of Mr. Wolf"

Slavery and Freedom

Wheatley:	"To the University of Cambridge," "On Being Brought from Africa to America," "To the Right Honourable William, Earl of Dartmouth"
Walker:	*Appeal in Four Articles*
Horton:	"The Creditor to His Proud Debtor"
Truth:	"Ar'n't I a Woman?" (both versions)
Stewart:	*Religion and the Pure Principles of Morality*, "Lecture Delivered at the Franklin Hall"
Delany:	*The Condition*
Jacobs:	*Incidents in the Life of a Slave Girl*
Brown:	*Narrative*
Garnet:	"An Address to the Slaves of the United States"
Douglass:	*Narrative of the Life*, "What to the Slave Is the Fourth of July?" *Life and Times*
Whitfield:	"America"
Harper:	"Eliza Harris," "The Slave Mother," "A Double Standard," "Our Greatest Want," "Woman's Political Future"
Wilson:	*Our Nig*

Reconstruction to the New Negro Renaissance

Washington:	*Up From Slavery*
Cooper:	"Womanhood"
Hopkins:	"Famous Women of the Negro Race," "Letter from Cordelia A. Condict"
Wells-Barnett:	*A Red Record*
Du Bois:	"A Litany of Atlanta," *The Souls of Black Folk*, "Criteria of Negro Art," "Two Novels"
Corrothers:	"Paul Laurence Dunbar"
J. Johnson:	"Lift Ev'ry Voice and Sing," "O Black and Unknown Bards," "Fifty Years," "Brothers," *The Autobiography of an Ex-Colored Man*, *The Book of American Negro Poetry*
Dunbar:	"The Colored Soldiers," "An Ante-Bellum Sermon," "We Wear the Mask," "A Cabin Tale," "The Haunted Oak," "Black Samson of Brandywine," "The Poet," "The Fourth of July and Race Outrages"
Dunbar Nelson:	"April Is on the Way"
Braithwaite:	"The House of the Falling Leaves," "Sic Vita," "Quiet Has a Hidden Sound"
F. Johnson:	"Tired," "The Scarlet Woman"

Harlem Renaissance

Spencer:	"Dunbar"
Fauset:	*Plum Bun*
Locke:	*The New Negro*
G. Johnson:	"Lost Illusions"
McKay:	"If We Must Die," "To the White Fiends," "America," "Outcast," "Harlem Runs Wild"
Hurston:	"How It Feels to Be Colored Me," "Characteristics of Negro Expression"
Larsen:	*Quicksand*
Toomer:	*Cane*
Schuyler:	"The Negro-Art Hokum"
Fisher:	"The Caucasian Storms Harlem"
Bonner:	"On Being Young—a Woman—and Colored"
Brown:	"Old Lem"
Bennett:	"Heritage," "Sonnet—2"
Thurman:	*Infants of the Spring*
Bontemps:	"Southern Mansion," "A Summer Tragedy"
Hughes:	"Afro-American Fragment," "Negro Servant," "Christ in Alabama," "Letter to the Academy," "Merry-Go-Round," "Trumpet Player," "Theme for English B," "The Negro Artist and the Racial Mountain"
Cullen:	"Yet Do I Marvel," "Tableau," "Saturday's Child," "Heritage," "To John Keats," "From the Dark Tower"
H. Johnson:	"Poem," "Sonnet to a Negro in Harlem"

Realism, Naturalism, Modernism

Tolson:	"An Ex-Judge at the Bar," "Dark Symphony," *Libretto for the Republic of Liberia*
Wright:	"Blueprint for Negro Writing," "The Ethics of Living Jim Crow," "The Man Who Lived Underground," *Black Boy*
Petry:	all selections
Hayden:	"Homage to the Empress of the Blues," "Middle Passage," "Those Winter Sundays," "Runagate Runagate," "Frederick Douglass," "A Ballad of Remembrance," "El-Hajj Malik El-Shabazz," "A Letter from Phillis Wheatley"
Ellison:	all selections
Walker:	"For My People," "Prophets for a New Day"
Brooks:	"the mother," "Sadie and Maud," "the preacher," "The Children of the Poor," "The Lovers of the Poor,"

| | "The Chicago *Defender*," "Two Dedications," "Young Heroes" |
| Baldwin: | "Everybody's Protest Novel," "Stranger in the Village," "Notes of a Native Son" |

Black Arts Era

Evans:	"Status Symbol"
Fuller:	"Towards a Black Aesthetic"
King:	"Letter from Birmingham Jail"
Malcolm X:	*The Autobiography*
Gayle:	*The Black Aesthetic*
Lorde:	"Coal," "A Litany for Survival," "Poetry Is Not a Luxury"
Baraka:	"Black Art"
Jordan:	"Poem about My Rights," *Civil Wars*
Neal:	"The Black Arts Movement"
Reed:	"Chattanooga," "Neo-Hoodoo Manifesto"
Madhubuti:	"Introduction," "Malcolm Spoke / who listened?" "a poem to complement other poems"
Giovanni:	"For Saundra," "From a Logical Point of View"
Troupe:	"Impressions / of Chicago," "In Texas Grass"
Rodgers:	"Jesus Was Crucified," "For Sistuhs Wearin' Straight Hair"

Literature since 1975

Angelou:	"And Still I Rise"
Marshall:	"Reena," "The Making of a Writer"
Kennedy:	*A Movie Star Has to Star in Black and White*
Morrison:	"Rootedness," "The Site of Memory," "Unspeakable Things Unspoken"
Gaines:	"The Sky Is Gray"
Major:	"Chicago Heat"
Forrest:	*There Is a Tree More Ancient Than Eden*
Wideman:	*Damballah*
Walker:	"Outcast," "On Stripping Bark from Myself," "In Search of Our Mothers' Gardens," "Everyday Use," "Advancing Luna," *The Color Purple*
Wilson:	*Joe Turner's Come and Gone*
Cliff:	"Within the Veil"
Butler:	"Bloodchild"
Komunyakaa:	"February in Sydney"
Mackey:	all selections

Johnson:	"The Education of Mingo"
Shange:	all selections
Jones:	*Corregidora*
Naylor:	*The Women of Brewster Place*
Dove:	"David Walker (1785–1830)," "Receiving the Stigmata," "Daystar," "Mother Love," "Demeter's Prayer to Hades"
Mosley:	"Equal Opportunity"
Mullen:	*Muse & Drudge*
Hemphill:	*Conditions* (xxi and xxiv)
Danticat:	*Breath, Eyes, Memory*
Whitehead:	*John Henry Days*

(Thwarted) American Dreams

The works in this section include texts that address and engage the trope of the American Dream. Many texts here, like Jacobs's *Incidents in the Life of a Slave Girl*, expose the lie of the dream by subverting nationalistic and mythic notions of what constitutes material success and promise in the United States. Others depict (a pursuit of) the American Dream in more literal and straightforward terms, as is the case with Frances E. W. Harper's "The Two Offers." Still others seem now to invoke the trope earnestly, now to taunt rebelliously—that is, they treat the American Dream with both ambiguity and ambivalence.

The Vernacular Tradition

SPIRITUALS

"City Called Heaven"
"I'm a-Rollin'"

GOSPEL

"Freedom in the Air"

THE BLUES

"Good Morning Blues"
"C. C. Rider"
"St. Louis Blues"
"The Hesitating Blues"
"Fine and Mellow"
"Sunnyland"

SECULAR RHYMES AND SONGS

"[We raise de wheat]"
"Me and My Captain"
"Promises of Freedom"

BALLADS

"John Henry"
"Frankie and Johnny"

SONGS OF SOCIAL CHANGE

"Oh, Freedom"
"We Shall Overcome"
"The Backlash Blues"
"Four Women"

RHYTHM AND BLUES

"Living for the City"

HIP HOP

"The Revolution Will Not Be Televised"
"The Message"
"The Evil That Men Do"
"Things Done Changed"
"N.Y. State of Mind"

SERMONS

"Listen, Lord, a Prayer"
"I Have a Dream"
"I've Been to the Mountaintop"
"The Ballot or the Bullet"
"O God of Love, Power and Justice"

FOLKTALES

"How to Write a Letter"
" 'Ah'll Beatcher Makin' Money' "
"A Flying Fool"
"What the Rabbit Learned"

Slavery and Freedom

Smith:	*Narrative of the Life and Adventures*
Terry:	"Bars Fight"
Wheatley:	"To the University of Cambridge," "On Being Brought from Africa to America"
Walker:	*Appeal in Four Articles*
Horton:	"The Lover's Farewell," "On Hearing of the Intention of a Gentleman," "George Moses Horton, Myself"
Truth:	"Ar'n't I a Woman?" (both versions)
Stewart:	*Religion and the Pure Principles of Morality*, "Lecture Delivered at the Franklin Hall"
Delany:	*The Condition*
Jacobs:	*Incidents in the Life of a Slave Girl*
Brown:	*Narrative*
Garnet:	"An Address to the Slaves of the United States"
Keckley:	*Behind the Scenes*
Douglass:	*My Bondage and My Freedom,* "What to the Slave is the Fourth of July?" *Life and Times*
Whitfield:	"America," "Self-Reliance"
Harper:	"Eliza Harris," "The Slave Mother," "The Two Offers," "Our Greatest Want," "Fancy Etchings"
Wilson:	*Our Nig*

Reconstruction to the New Negro Renaissance

Washington:	*Up From Slavery*
Chesnutt:	"The Goophered Grapevine," "The Passing of Grandison," *The Journals*
Hopkins:	"Talma Gordon," "Famous Men of the Negro Race," "Letter from Cordelia A. Condict"
Wells-Barnett:	*A Red Record*
Du Bois:	"The Damnation of Women"
Corrothers:	"The Snapping of the Bow," "At the Closed Gate of Justice," "An Indignation Dinner"
J. Johnson:	"Lift Ev'ry Voice and Sing," "Fifty Years," "Brothers," *The Autobiography of an Ex-Colored Man, The Book of American Negro Poetry*
Dunbar:	"We Wear the Mask," "Little Brown Baby," "Douglass," "The Poet," "The Fourth of July and Race Outrages"
Braithwaite:	"The Watchers," "Turn Me to My Yellow Leaves"
F. Johnson:	"Tired," "The Scarlet Woman"

Harlem Renaissance

Schomburg:	"The Negro Digs Up His Past"
Fauset:	*Plum Bun*
G. Johnson:	"Lost Illusions"
Garvey:	"Africa for the Africans"
McKay:	"Harlem Shadows," "America," "The White House," *Home to Harlem*, "Harlem Runs Wild"
Larsen:	*Quicksand*
Toomer:	*Cane*
Schuyler:	"The Negro-Art Hokum"
Fisher:	all selections
Bonner:	"On Being Young—a Woman—and Colored"
Brown:	"Old Lem"
Bontemps:	"A Black Man Talks of Reaping," "Nocturne at Bethesda," "A Summer Tragedy"
Hughes:	"Dream Deferred," "I, Too," "Negro Servant," "Merry-Go-Round," "Harlem," "Theme for English B"
Cullen:	"Saturday's Child," "The Shroud of Color," "Heritage," "From the Dark Tower"
H. Johnson:	"Invocation"

Realism, Naturalism, Modernism

Tolson:	"Dark Symphony," *Libretto for the Republic of Liberia*, "The Birth of John Henry," "Satchmo"
West:	*The Living Is Easy*
Wright:	all selections
Himes:	"To What Red Hell"
Petry:	all selections
Hayden:	"Homage to the Empress of the Blues," "Middle Passage," "Those Winter Sundays," "Runagate Runagate," "Frederick Douglass," "Mourning Poem for the Queen of Sunday," "Soledad," "El-Hajj Malik El-Shabazz," "A Letter from Phillis Wheatley"
Ellison:	"Richard Wright's Blues," *Invisible Man*, "Change the Joke and Slip the Yoke," "The World and the Jug," "Remembering Richard Wright"
Walker:	"For My People," "For Malcolm X," "Prophets for a New Day"
Brooks:	all selections
Baldwin:	all selections
Hansberry:	*A Raisin in the Sun*

Black Arts Era

Evans:	"Status Symbol"
King:	"Letter from Birmingham Jail"
Gayle:	*The Black Aesthetic*
Lorde:	"Equinox," "A Litany for Survival"
Baraka:	*Dutchman*
Sanchez:	"homecoming," "for our lady"
Spellman:	"Did John's Music Kill Him?"
Jordan:	"Poem about My Rights," *Soldier*
Clifton:	"the lost baby poem," "move"
Cortez:	"How Long Has Trane Been Gone"
Reed:	"Chattanooga"
Harper:	"Deathwatch," "Grandfather"
Madhubuti:	"Back Again, Home," "The Long Reality," "a poem to complement other poems"
Giovanni:	all selections
McPherson:	"A Solo Song: For Doc"
Troupe:	all selections
Rodgers:	"Jesus Was Crucified," "It Is Deep"

Literature since 1975

Angelou:	"Still I Rise"
Marshall:	"Reena," "The Making of a Writer"
Kennedy:	*A Movie Star Has to Star in Black and White*
Morrison:	*Song of Solomon*, "The Site of Memory," "Unspeakable Things Unspoken"
Gaines:	"The Sky Is Gray"
Major:	"Swallow the Lake," "Chicago Heat"
Forrest:	*There Is a Tree More Ancient Than Eden*
Wideman:	*Brothers and Keepers*
Williams:	"Tell Martha Not to Moan"
Walker:	"In Search of Our Mothers' Gardens," "Advancing Luna"
Wilson:	*Joe Turner's Come and Gone*
Cliff:	all selections
Komunyakaa:	"February in Sydney," "Facing It," "Sunday Afternoons"
Mackey:	"Falso Brilhante"
Johnson:	"The Education of Mingo"
Shange:	"Nappy Edges," "Bocas: A Daughter's Geography"
Naylor:	*The Women of Brewster Place*
Dove:	"David Walker (1785–1830)," "The Event," "Daystar,"

	"The Oriental Ballerina"
Mosley:	"Equal Opportunity"
Hemphill:	*Conditions* (xxiv)
Phillips:	*Crossing the River*
Danticat:	*Breath, Eyes, Memory*
Whitehead:	*John Henry Days*

Authenticity and Identity

The texts here are concerned with the significance and "degree" of blackness that a subject embodies. Some purport to measure blackness; others question its measurability, its corporeality, or its substance, arguing that all that gilded gold ain't really black; still others take its materiality as given and celebrate its uniqueness.

The Vernacular Tradition

THE BLUES

"Prove It on Me Blues"
"Trouble in Mind"
"Rock Me, Baby"
"My Handy Man"

SECULAR RHYMES AND SONGS

"Me and My Captain"

BALLADS

"The Signifying Monkey"
"Stackolee"
"Sinking of the *Titanic*"

SONGS OF SOCIAL CHANGE

"Four Women"

JAZZ

"It Don't Mean a Thing (If It Ain't Got That Swing)"
"(What Did I Do to Be So) Black and Blue"
"Parker's Mood"

RHYTHM AND BLUES

"The Tracks of My Tears"
"Dancin' in the Street"
"We're a Winner"

HIP HOP

"Don't Believe the Hype"
"I Ain't No Joke"

SERMONS

"The Ballot or the Bullet"

FOLKTALES

"How to Write a Letter"
" 'De Reason Niggers Is Working So Hard' "
"The Wonderful Tar-Baby Story"
"How Mr. Rabbit Was Too Sharp for Mr. Fox"
"The Awful Fate of Mr. Wolf"

Slavery and Freedom

Hammon:	"An Address to Miss Phillis Wheatley"
Equiano:	*The Interesting Narrative of the Life*
Wheatley:	"To Mæcenas," "To the Right Honourable William, Earl of Dartmouth"
Horton:	"George Moses Horton, Myself"
Truth:	"Ar'n't I a Woman?" (both versions)
Delany:	*The Condition*
Jacobs:	*Incidents in the Life of a Slave Girl*
Brown:	*Narrative*
Séjour:	"The Mulatto"
Keckley:	*Behind the Scenes*
Douglass:	*Narrative of the Life, My Bondage and My Freedom, Life and Times*
Harper:	"Our Greatest Want," "Fancy Etchings"
Wilson:	*Our Nig*

Reconstruction to the New Negro Renaissance

Washington:	*Up From Slavery*
Chesnutt:	all selections
Hopkins:	"Talma Gordon," "Famous Men of the Negro Race," "Letter from Cordelia A. Condict"

Du Bois:	"The Song of the Smoke," *The Souls of Black Folk*, "Two Novels"
J. Johnson:	"O Black and Unknown Bards," "Fifty Years," *The Autobiography of an Ex-Colored Man*
Dunbar:	"The Colored Soldiers," "Ere Sleep Comes Down to Soothe the Weary Eyes," "When Malindy Sings," "We Wear the Mask," "Her Thought and His," "Sympathy," "Black Samson of Brandywine," "The Poet"
Dunbar Nelson:	"Violets" (1895)

Harlem Renaissance

Spencer:	"At the Carnival"
Fauset:	*Plum Bun*
Locke:	*The New Negro*
Garvey:	"Africa for the Africans"
McKay:	"To the White Fiends"
Hurston:	"How It Feels to Be Colored Me," "Characteristics of Negro Expression"
Larsen:	*Quicksand*
Toomer:	*Cane*
Schuyler:	"The Negro-Art Hokum"
Fisher:	all selections
Bonner:	"On Being Young—a Woman—and Colored"
Bennett:	"Heritage," "To a Dark Girl"
Thurman:	*Infants of the Spring*
Bontemps:	"A Black Man Talks of Reaping," "Miracles"
Hughes:	"The Negro Speaks of Rivers," "Mulatto," "Afro-American Fragment," "Negro Servant," "Theme for English B"
Cullen:	"Yet Do I Marvel," "Tableau," "Saturday's Child," "The Shroud of Color," "Heritage"
H. Johnson:	"Poem," "Sonnet to a Negro in Harlem"

Realism, Naturalism, Modernism

Tolson:	"An Ex-Judge at the Bar," "Dark Symphony," "The Birth of John Henry," "Satchmo"
West:	*The Living Is Easy*
Wright:	"Long Black Song," "The Man Who Lived Underground," *Black Boy*
Hayden:	"Homage to the Empress of the Blues," "O Daedalus, Fly Away Home," "Runagate Runagate," "A Ballad of Remembrance," "El-Hajj Malik El-Shabazz," "A Letter from Phillis Wheatley"

Ellison:	all selections
Walker:	"For My People"
Brooks:	"a song in the front yard," "Sadie and Maud," "The Sundays of Satin-Legs Smith," "Maxie Allen," "The Children of the Poor," "The Lovers of the Poor," "We Real Cool," "Young Heroes," *Maud Martha*
Baldwin:	"Stranger in the Village," "Notes of a Native Son," "Sonny's Blues"

Black Arts Era

Evans:	"Status Symbol"
Fuller:	"Towards a Black Aesthetic"
Gayle:	*The Black Aesthetic*
Lorde:	"Coal," "Poetry Is Not a Luxury," *Zami*
Baraka:	"SOS," *Dutchman*
Sanchez:	"for our lady"
Jordan:	*Soldier*, "Poem for Guatemala"
Cortez:	"How Long Has Trane Been Gone"
Neal:	"The Black Arts Movement"
Reed:	"I am a cowboy in the boat of Ra," "Dualism," "Chattanooga," *Mumbo Jumbo*
Harper:	"Dear John, Dear Coltrane"
Madhubuti:	"Back Again, Home," "Introduction," "Malcolm Spoke / who listened?" "a poem to complement other poems"
Giovanni:	"Nikki-Rosa"
Rodgers:	"It Is Deep," "For Sistuhs Wearin' Straight Hair"

Literature since 1975

Murray:	*Train Whistle Guitar*
Marshall:	"The Making of a Writer"
Kennedy:	*A Movie Star Has to Star in Black and White*
Morrison:	all selections
Major:	"Round Midnight"
Wideman:	all selections
Delany:	*Atlantis: Model 1924*
Walker:	"Women," "Outcast," "On Stripping Bark from Myself," "In Search of Our Mothers' Gardens," "Everyday Use," "Advancing Luna," *The Color Purple*
Wilson:	*Joe Turner's Come and Gone*
Cliff:	all selections
Butler:	"Bloodchild"
Komunyakaa:	"Facing It"

Mackey:	"Djbot Baghostus's Run"
Johnson:	"The Education of Mingo"
Shange:	*for colored girls,* "Bocas: A Daughter's Geography"
Jones:	*Corregidora*
Kincaid:	*Annie John*
Naylor:	*The Women of Brewster Place*
Dove:	"Parsley," "Motherhood," "Daystar," "The Oriental Ballerina," "Demeter Mourning," "Demeter's Prayer to Hades"
Mullen:	*Muse & Drudge*
Hemphill:	*Conditions* (xxi)
Phillips:	*Crossing the River*
Whitehead:	*John Henry Days*

Bondage, Imprisonment, Incarceration

Texts developing this theme address African Americans in material, penal, psychological, economic, or social confinement.

The Vernacular Tradition

SPIRITUALS

"Didn't My Lord Deliver Daniel?"

THE BLUES

"Fine and Mellow"

SECULAR RHYMES AND SONGS

"Promises of Freedom"
"No More Auction Block"
"Another Man Done Gone"
"You May Go But This Will Bring You Back"

BALLADS

"Frankie and Johnny"

WORK SONGS

"Go Down, Old Hannah"

SONGS OF SOCIAL CHANGE

"Oh, Freedom"

Rhythm and Blues

"Living for the City"

Hip Hop

"The Message"
"The Evil That Men Do"

Sermons

"I've Been to the Mountaintop"
"The Ballot or the Bullet"

Folktales

"All God's Chillen Had Wings"
"Big Talk"
" 'Member Youse a Nigger"
"Why the Sister in Black Works Hardest"
"Brer Rabbit Tricks Brer Fox Again"
"The Wonderful Tar-Baby Story"
"How Mr. Rabbit Was Too Sharp for Mr. Fox"

Slavery and Freedom

any/all authors and selections

Reconstruction to the New Negro Renaissance

Washington:	*Up From Slavery*
Chesnutt:	"The Passing of Grandison"
Wells-Barnett:	*A Red Record*
Du Bois:	"The Damnation of Women"
Corrothers:	"The Snapping of the Bow"
J. Johnson:	"Fifty Years," "Brothers"
Dunbar:	"An Ante-Bellum Sermon," "We Wear the Mask," "A Cabin Tale," "Sympathy"

Harlem Renaissance

G. Johnson:	"The Heart of a Woman"
Hurston:	"Sweat"
Larsen:	*Quicksand*
Toomer:	*Cane*
Bonner:	"On Being Young—a Woman—and Colored"

Brown:	"Southern Road"
Bontemps:	"A Summer Tragedy"
Hughes:	"Ballad of the Landlord"

Realism, Naturalism, Modernism

West:	*The Living Is Easy*
Wright:	"The Ethics of Living Jim Crow," "Long Black Song," "The Man Who Lived Underground"
Himes:	"To What Red Hell"
Hayden:	"Middle Passage," "Runagate Runagate," "Soledad," "A Letter from Phillis Wheatley"
Ellison:	*Invisible Man*, Chap. 1
Brooks:	"a song in the front yard," "The Rites for Cousin Vit"
Baldwin:	"Going to Meet the Man," "Stranger in the Village," "Sonny's Blues"
Kaufman:	"Grandfather Was Queer, Too," "Jail Poems"

Black Arts Era

Malcolm X:	*The Autobiography*
King:	"Letter from Birmingham Jail"
Knight:	"The Idea of Ancestry," "Hard Rock"
Lorde:	"Coal," "A Litany for Survival," "Poetry Is Not a Luxury," *Zami*
Baraka:	*Dutchman*
Spellman:	"Did John's Music Kill Him?"
Jordan:	"Poem about My Rights," *Soldier*, "Poem for Guatemala," "Intifada"
Reed:	"Dualism"
Troupe:	"Conversation Overheard"

Literature since 1975

Major:	"Chicago Heat"
Wideman:	*Brothers and Keepers*
Wilson:	*Joe Turner's Come and Gone*
Cliff:	"Columba"
Butler:	"Bloodchild"
Komunyakaa:	"Sunday Afternoons"
Jones:	*Corregidora*
Dove:	"Daystar," "The Oriental Ballerina," "Statistic: The Witness"
Mosley:	"Equal Opportunity"

Civil Wars

In addition to the War between the States, *civil war* here connotes national or international disputes that involve or affect African American life and culture. In every instance, its use is both ironic and not.

The Vernacular Tradition

SONGS OF SOCIAL CHANGE

"The Backlash Blues"

RHYTHM AND BLUES

"What's Goin' On?"

Slavery and Freedom

Keckley:	*Behind the Scenes* ("Preface")
Douglass:	*Life and Times*
Whitfield:	"Yes! Strike Again That Sounding String"

Reconstruction to the New Negro Renaissance

J. Johnson:	"Fifty Years"
Dunbar:	"The Colored Soldiers"

Realism, Naturalism, Modernism

Tolson:	"Dark Symphony," "A Legend of Versailles," *Libretto for the Republic of Liberia*
Wright:	"Long Black Song"
Petry:	*The Street*
Hayden:	"Middle Passage"
Ellison:	"Remembering Richard Wright"
Brooks:	"Riot"

Black Arts Era

King:	"Letter from Birmingham Jail"
Gayle:	*The Black Aesthetic*
Lorde:	"Equinox"
Jordan:	"Poem for Guatemala," "Intifada"
Karenga:	"Black Art"

Literature since 1975

Gaines: "The Sky Is Gray"
Komunyakaa: "Facing It"
Shange: "Bocas: A Daughter's Geography"
Dove: "Parsley"

"Cleo just grinned,"* or *Resistance*, She Wrote

Because an African American woman wrote each text listed below, this group can be used to select texts for a course on black women's literature even when the theme is not expressly resistance to sexism, racism, economic inequity, or other forms of dominance or subjugation.

The Vernacular Tradition

THE BLUES

"C. C. Rider"
"Backwater Blues"
"Down-Hearted Blues"
"Prove It on Me Blues"
"St. Louis Blues"
"Fine and Mellow"
"Handy Man"

SECULAR RHYMES AND SONGS

"You May Go But This Will Bring You Back"

BALLADS

"Frankie and Johnny"

SONGS OF SOCIAL CHANGE

"Strange Fruit"
"Four Women"

RHYTHM AND BLUES

"Dancin' in the Street"

HIP HOP

"The Evil That Men Do"

*Title of a chapter in *The Living Is Easy* by Dorothy West.

FOLKTALES

"Why the Sister in Black Works Hardest"

Slavery and Freedom

Wheatley:	all selections
Truth:	"Ar'n't I a Woman?" (both versions)
Stewart:	*Religion and the Pure Principles of Morality*
Jacobs:	*Incidents in the Life of a Slave Girl*
Keckley:	*Behind the Scenes*
Harper:	all selections
Wilson:	*Our Nig*

Reconstruction to the New Negro Renaissance

Cooper:	"Womanhood"
Hopkins:	all selections
Wells-Barnett:	*A Red Record*
Dunbar Nelson:	"Violets" (1895), "I Sit and Sew"

Harlem Renaissance

Grimké:	"Tenebris"
Spencer:	all selections
Fauset:	*Plum Bun*
G. Johnson:	"The Heart of a Woman," "Lost Illusions," "I Want to Die While You Love Me"
Hurston:	"Sweat," *Their Eyes Were Watching God*
Larsen:	*Quicksand*
Bonner:	"On Being Young—a Woman—and Colored"
Bennett:	"Heritage," "To a Dark Girl," "Hatred"
H. Johnson:	"Remember Not"

Realism, Naturalism, Modernism

West:	*The Living Is Easy*
Petry:	all selections
Walker:	"Prophets for a New Day"
Brooks:	all selections

Black Arts Era

Evans:	"I Am a Black Woman"
Lorde:	"Equinox," "A Litany for Survival," "Poetry Is Not a Luxury," *Zami*

Sanchez:	*A Blues Book for Blue Black Magical Women*
Jordan:	"Poem about My Rights," *Civil Wars, Soldier,* "Poem for Guatemala," "Intifada"
Clifton:	"malcolm," "homage to my hips," "wishes for sons"
Bambara:	"Raymond's Run"
Giovanni:	"For Saundra," "Nikki-Rosa," "From a Logical Point of View"
Rodgers:	all selections

Literature since 1975

Angelou:	"Still I Rise," "My Arkansas"
Marshall:	all selections
Morrison:	all selections
Williams:	all selections
Walker:	all selections
Cliff:	all selections
Butler:	"Bloodchild"
Shange:	all selections
Jones:	*Corregidora*
Kincaid:	*Annie John*
Naylor:	*The Women of Brewster Place*
Dove:	"David Walker (1785–1830)," "Parsley," "Receiving the Stigmata," "Motherhood," "Daystar," "The Oriental Ballerina," "Pastoral," "Statistic: The Witness," "Mother Love," "History," "Demeter's Prayer to Hades"
Mullen:	*Muse & Drudge*
Danticat:	*Breath, Eyes, Memory*

"don't it all come down to e/co/no/mics"*

The works here include titles that examine the economic state of black America.

The Vernacular Tradition

SECULAR RHYMES AND SONGS

"[We raise de wheat]"
"No More Auction Block"

---

*"Indianapolis/Summer/1969/Poem" by Sonia Sanchez. This poem is not in the anthology.

BALLADS

"John Henry"

SONGS OF SOCIAL CHANGE

"The Backlash Blues"

RHYTHM AND BLUES

"Living for the City"

HIP HOP

"The Revolution Will Not Be Televised"
"The Message"
"Things Done Changed"

SERMONS

"O God of Love, Power and Justice"
"Elder Eatmore's Sermon on Generosity"

Slavery and Freedom

Smith:	*Narrative of the Life and Adventures*
Horton:	"The Creditor to His Proud Debtor"
Delany:	*The Condition*

Reconstruction to the New Negro Renaissance

Washington:	*Up From Slavery*
Chesnutt:	"The Goophered Grapevine," *The Journals*
Hopkins:	"Talma Gordon," "Famous Men of the Negro Race," "Letter from Cordelia A. Condict"
Wells-Barnett:	*A Red Record*
Du Bois:	"The Damnation of Women"
Corrothers:	"An Indignation Dinner"
J. Johnson:	*The Autobiography of an Ex-Colored Man*
Dunbar:	"Philosophy"
F. Johnson:	"Tired," "The Scarlet Woman"

Harlem Renaissance

McKay:	"Harlem Shadows," *Home to Harlem*, "Harlem Runs Wild"

Hurston:	*Dust Tracks on a Road*
Larsen:	*Quicksand*
Toomer:	*Cane*
Fisher:	"The City of Refuge"
Bonner:	"On Being Young—a Woman—and Colored"
Bontemps:	"A Black Man Talks of Reaping," "A Summer Tragedy"
Hughes:	"Madam and the Rent Man," "Madam and the Phone Bill," "Letter to the Academy"
Cullen:	"Saturday's Child," "From the Dark Tower"

Realism, Naturalism, Modernism

Tolson:	"Dark Symphony"
West:	*The Living Is Easy*
Wright:	all selections
Petry:	all selections
Hayden:	"Homage to the Empress of the Blues," "Middle Passage," "Those Winter Sundays"
Walker:	"Poppa Chicken"
Brooks:	*Maud Martha*
Hansberry:	*A Raisin in the Sun*

Black Arts Era

Giovanni:	"Nikki-Rosa"

Literature since 1975

Angelou:	"Still I Rise"
Marshall:	"Reena," "The Making of a Writer"
Morrison:	*Song of Solomon*
Gaines:	"The Sky Is Gray"
Forrest:	*There Is a Tree More Ancient Than Eden*
Wideman:	*Brothers and Keepers*
Williams:	"The Peacock Poems: 1," "Tell Martha Not to Moan"
Walker:	"In Search of Our Mothers' Gardens"
Cliff:	"Columba"
Komunyakaa:	"Banking Potatoes"
Jones:	*Corregidora*
Dove:	"The Oriental Ballerina"
Mosley:	"Equal Opportunity"
Phillips:	*Crossing the River*
Whitehead:	*John Henry Days*

Education and Literacy Theories

The titles in this section refer to texts that explore ways and situations in which African Americans learn some crucial aspect of life in the United States—from what *not* to do upon migration to New York City (e.g., "Living for the City") to the rudiments of formal academic education (e.g., "How to Write a Letter") to the true essence of motherlove and motherwit (e.g., "Jesus Was Crucified").

The Vernacular Tradition

SECULAR RHYMES AND SONGS

"You May Go But This Will Bring You Back"

BALLADS

"Sinking of the *Titanic*"

RHYTHM AND BLUES

"Living for the City"

HIP HOP

"The Revolution Will Not Be Televised"
"The Message"
"Don't Believe the Hype"
"Things Done Changed"
"I Ain't No Joke"

SERMONS

"The Ballot or the Bullet"

FOLKTALES

"Big Talk"
"How to Write a Letter"
"'Ah'll Beatcher Makin' Money'"
"'De Reason Niggers Is Working So Hard'"
"You Talk Too Much, Anyhow"
"What the Rabbit Learned"

Slavery and Freedom

almost any selection	
Smith:	*Narrative of the Life and Adventures*
Wheatley:	all selections
Stewart:	*Religion and the Pure Principles of Morality*, "Lecture Delivered at the Franklin Hall"
Delany:	*The Condition*
Jacobs:	*Incidents in the Life of a Slave Girl*, Chaps. 1, 5, 21
Douglass:	all selections
Harper:	"Aunt Chloe's Politics," "Learning to Read," "Fancy Etchings," "Woman's Political Future"
Wilson:	*Our Nig*

Reconstruction to the New Negro Renaissance

Washington:	*Up From Slavery*
Hopkins:	"Famous Men of the Negro Race," "Letter from Cordelia A. Condict"
J. Johnson:	"O Black and Unknown Bards," *The Book of American Negro Poetry*

Harlem Renaissance

Spencer:	"At the Carnival"
Fauset:	*Plum Bun*
G. Johnson:	"Lost Illusions"
Toomer:	*Cane*
Fisher:	"The City of Refuge"
Bonner:	"On Being Young—a Woman—and Colored"
Brown:	"Old Lem"
Hughes:	"Letter to the Academy," "Theme for English B"

Realism, Naturalism, Modernism

Tolson:	"Dark Symphony," *Libretto for the Republic of Liberia*
Wright:	"The Ethics of Living Jim Crow," *Black Boy*
Petry:	*The Street*
Hayden:	"Those Winter Sundays," "El-Hajj Malik El-Shabazz,"
Ellison:	*Invisible Man*, Chap. 1, "The World and the Jug"
Brooks:	"Maxie Allen," "The Chicago *Defender* "
Baldwin:	"Stranger in the Village," "Sonny's Blues"

Black Arts Era

Fuller:	"Towards a Black Aesthetic"
Malcolm X:	*The Autobiography*
King:	"Letter from Birmingham Jail"
Gayle:	*The Black Aesthetic*
Lorde:	"Poetry Is Not a Luxury," *Zami*, Chaps. 3, 11
Jordan:	*Civil Wars*
Neal:	"The Black Arts Movement"
Karenga:	"Black Art: Mute Matter Given Force and Function"
Giovanni:	"Nikki-Rosa"
Rodgers:	"Jesus Was Crucified"

Literature since 1975

Murray:	*Train Whistle Guitar*
Marshall:	all selections
Morrison:	*Song of Solomon*, "Unspeakable Things Unspoken"
Gaines:	"The Sky Is Gray"
Delany:	*Atlantis: Model 1924*
Walker:	"Women," " 'Good Night, Willie Lee,' " "In Search of Our Mothers' Gardens," "Everyday Use," "Advancing Luna," *The Color Purple*
Wilson:	*Joe Turner's Come and Gone*
Butler:	"Bloodchild"
Johnson:	"The Education of Mingo"
Shange:	"Nappy Edges"
Kincaid:	*Annie John*
Bradley:	*The Chaneysville Incident*
Naylor:	*The Women of Brewster Place*
Dove:	"Parsley," "Demeter's Prayer to Hades"
Mosley:	"Equal Opportunity"
Mullen:	*Muse & Drudge*
Danticat:	*Breath, Eyes, Memory*

Family

The texts listed here engage some aspect of biological or social collectivity among blacks. The family as community may be represented in utopic or dystopic terms.

The Vernacular Tradition

SPIRITUALS

"City Called Heaven"

BALLADS

"John Henry"

SONGS OF SOCIAL CHANGE

"Four Women"

RHYTHM AND BLUES

"Respect"
"What's Goin' On?"
"Living for the City"

HIP HOP

"The Message"

FOLKTALES

"All God's Chillen Had Wings"
"Why the Sister in Black Works Hardest"
"The Awful Fate of Mr. Wolf"

Slavery and Freedom

Smith:	*Narrative of the Life and Adventures*
Equiano:	*The Interesting Narrative of the Life*
Wheatley:	"To the Right Honourable William"
Delany:	*The Condition*
Jacobs:	*Incidents in the Life of a Slave Girl*
Brown:	*Clotel*
Séjour:	"The Mulatto"
Keckley:	*Behind the Scenes*
Douglass:	*Narrative of the Life*
Harper:	"Eliza Harris," "The Slave Mother," "The Two Offers"
Wilson:	*Our Nig*

Reconstruction to the New Negro Renaissance

Washington:	*Up From Slavery*
Chesnutt:	"The Passing of Grandison," "The Wife of His Youth"
Cooper:	"Womanhood"
Hopkins:	"Talma Gordon"
Du Bois:	"The Damnation of Women"
J. Johnson:	"Brothers," *The Autobiography of an Ex-Colored Man*
Dunbar:	"Little Brown Baby"
F. Johnson:	"The Lonely Mother," "Tired," "The Scarlet Woman"

Harlem Renaissance

Fauset:	*Plum Bun*
McKay:	"My Mother"
Hurston:	"The Gilded Six-Bits"
Toomer:	*Cane*
Bontemps:	"A Black Man Talks of Reaping," "A Summer Tragedy"
Hughes:	"Mother to Son," "Mulatto," "Christ in Alabama"
Cullen:	"Saturday's Child"

Realism, Naturalism, Modernism

Tolson:	"The Birth of John Henry"
West:	*The Living Is Easy*
Wright:	"The Ethics of Living Jim Crow," *Black Boy*
Petry:	*The Street*
Hayden:	"Those Winter Sundays"
Ellison:	*Invisible Man* (prologue, epilogue), "Richard Wright's Blues"
Brooks:	"the mother," "a song in the front yard," "Maxie Allen," "A Lovely Love," "when you have forgotten Sunday," *Maud Martha*
Baldwin:	"Going to Meet the Man," "Notes of a Native Son," "Sonny's Blues"
Hansberry:	*A Raisin in the Sun*

Black Arts Era

Knight:	"The Idea of Ancestry"
Lorde:	"Equinox," "Now That I Am Forever with Child," "A Litany for Survival," *Zami*
Baraka:	"Preface to a Twenty Volume Suicide Note," "SOS"
Jordan:	"Poem about My Rights," *Soldier*

Clifton:	"the lost baby poem"
Harper:	"Deathwatch," "Grandfather"
Giovanni:	"Nikki-Rosa," "Knoxville, Tennessee"
Rodgers:	"Jesus Was Crucified," "It Is Deep"

Literature since 1975

Murray:	*Train Whistle Guitar*
Marshall:	all selections
Kennedy:	*A Movie Star Has to Star in Black and White*
Morrison:	*Song of Solomon,* "The Site of Memory," "Unspeakable Things Unspoken"
Gaines:	"The Sky Is Gray"
Major:	"Chicago Heat"
Wideman:	*Brothers and Keepers*
Williams:	all selections
Walker:	" 'Good Night, Willie Lee,' " "In Search of Our Mothers' Gardens," "Everyday Use"
Wilson:	*Joe Turner's Come and Gone*
Cliff:	"Columba"
Butler:	"Bloodchild"
Komunyakaa:	"Sunday Afternoons," "Banking Potatoes," "Birds on a Powerline"
Shange:	"Bocas: A Daughter's Geography"
Jones:	*Corregidora*
Kincaid:	*Annie John*
Bradley:	*The Chaneysville Incident*
Dove:	"Motherhood," "Daystar," "The Oriental Ballerina," "Pastoral"
Hemphill:	*Conditions* (xxi)
Phillips:	*Crossing the River*
Danticat:	*Breath, Eyes, Memory*

Gender Portraits, Differences, and/or Conflicts

The works included here are *NAFAM* texts that achieve one or more of the following: a depiction of the development of a gender identity (e.g., "Stackolee" or "I Am a Black Woman"), a characterization of maleness and/or femaleness—that is, what it means to be a "man" and/or a "woman" (e.g., "Four Women"), and discussion or depiction of relationships between a man and a woman (e.g., "The Gilded Six-Bits").

The Vernacular Tradition

THE BLUES

"Hellhound on My Trail"
"C. C. Rider"
"Prove It on Me Blues"
"How Long Blues"
"Rock Me, Baby"
"St. Louis Blues"
"The Hesitating Blues"
"Goin' to Chicago Blues"
"Fine and Mellow"
"Hoochie Coochie"
"Sunnyland"
"Handy Man"

BALLADS

"John Henry"
"Frankie and Johnny"
"Stackolee"
"Sinking of the *Titanic*"
"Shine and the *Titanic*"

SONGS OF SOCIAL CHANGE

"Four Women"

RHYTHM AND BLUES

"Respect"

HIP HOP

"The Evil That Men Do"

FOLKTALES

"Big Talk"
"How to Write a Letter"
" 'Member Youse a Nigger' "
"Why the Sister in Black Works Hardest"

Slavery and Freedom

Wheatley:	"To the University of Cambridge"
Walker:	*Appeal in Four Articles*

Truth:	"Ar'n't I a Woman?" (both versions)
Stewart:	"Lecture Delivered at the Franklin Hall"
Delany:	*The Condition*
Jacobs:	*Incidents in the Life of a Slave Girl*
Brown:	*Narrative, Clotel*
Keckley:	*Behind the Scenes*
Douglass:	*Narrative of the Life*, "What to the Slave Is the Fourth of July?" *Life and Times*
Harper:	"Eliza Harris," "The Slave Mother," "A Double Standard," "An Appeal to My Country Women," "The Two Offers," "Our Greatest Want," "Fancy Etchings"
Wilson:	*Our Nig*

Reconstruction to the New Negro Renaissance

Chesnutt:	"The Wife of His Youth"
Cooper:	"Womanhood"
Hopkins:	"Talma Gordon," "Famous Men of the Negro Race," "Famous Women of the Negro Race"
Wells-Barnett:	*A Red Record*
Du Bois:	"The Song of the Smoke," "The Damnation of Women"
J. Johnson:	"Fifty Years," "Brothers"
Dunbar:	"The Colored Soldiers," "Her Thought and His," "Dinah Kneading Dough"
Dunbar Nelson:	"I Sit and Sew"
F. Johnson:	"The Lonely Mother," "The Scarlet Woman"

Harlem Renaissance

Spencer:	"At the Carnival"
Fauset:	*Plum Bun*
G. Johnson:	"The Heart of a Woman"
McKay:	"Harlem Shadows," "If We Must Die," *Home to Harlem*, "Harlem Runs Wild"
Hurston:	"Sweat," "The Gilded Six-Bits"
Larsen:	*Quicksand*
Toomer:	*Cane*
Bonner:	"On Being Young—a Woman—and Colored"
Brown:	"Strong Men," "Old Lem"
Bennett:	"To a Dark Girl"
Bontemps:	"A Black Man Talks of Reaping," "A Summer Tragedy"
Hughes:	"Gal's Cry for a Dying Lover," "Trumpet Player,"

	"Madam and the Phone Bill," "Song for Billie Holiday"
Cullen:	"To John Keats"
H. Johnson:	"Poem," "Sonnet to a Negro in Harlem"

Realism, Naturalism, Modernism

Tolson:	"Dark Symphony," "The Birth of John Henry"
West:	*The Living Is Easy*
Wright:	"The Ethics of Living Jim Crow," "Long Black Song," *Black Boy*
Himes:	"To What Red Hell"
Petry:	all selections
Hayden:	"Homage to the Empress of the Blues," "Those Winter Sundays," "Runagate Runagate," "Frederick Douglass," "Mourning Poem for the Queen of Sunday," "El-Hajj Malik El-Shabazz," "A Letter from Phillis Wheatley"
Ellison:	"Change the Joke and Slip the Yoke"
Walker:	"Poppa Chicken," "For Malcolm X"
Brooks:	"the mother," "a song in the front yard," "Sadie and Maud," "The Vacant Lot," "The Sundays of Satin-Legs Smith," "Maxie Allen," "The Rites for Cousin Vit," "The Lovers of the Poor," "Malcolm X," "Young Heroes," *Maud Martha*
Baldwin:	"Going to Meet the Man," "Notes of a Native Son," "Sonny's Blues"

Black Arts Era

Evans:	"I Am a Black Woman"
Williams:	*The Man Who Cried I Am*
Gayle:	*The Black Aesthetic*
Lorde:	"Now That I Am Forever with Child," "Poetry Is Not a Luxury," *Zami*
Baraka:	*Dutchman*
Bullins:	*Goin'a Buffalo*
Cleaver:	*Soul on Ice*
Jordan:	"Poem about My Rights," *Soldier*, "Poem for Guatemala"
Clifton:	"the lost baby poem," "homage to my hips," "wishes for sons"
Neal:	"The Black Arts Movement"
Reed:	"I am a cowboy in the boat of Ra," "Chattanooga"

Harper:	"Deathwatch"
Bambara:	"Raymond's Run"
Giovanni:	"Beautiful Black Men"
McPherson:	"A Solo Song: For Doc"
Troupe:	"In Texas Grass"
Rodgers:	"Jesus Was Crucified," "For Sistuhs Wearin' Straight Hair"

Literature since 1975

Murray:	*Train Whistle Guitar*
Marshall:	all selections
Kennedy:	*A Movie Star Has to Star in Black and White*
Morrison:	*Song of Solomon*, "The Site of Memory"
Gaines:	"The Sky Is Gray"
Major:	"Chicago Heat"
Forrest:	*There Is a Tree More Ancient Than Eden*
Wideman:	*Brothers and Keepers*
Williams:	"I Want Aretha to Set This to Music," "Tell Martha Not to Moan"
Walker:	"Women," "On Stripping Bark from Myself," "In Search of Our Mothers' Gardens," "Everyday Use," "Advancing Luna"
Wilson:	*Joe Turner's Come and Gone*
Cliff:	"Columba"
Butler:	"Bloodchild"
Mackey:	"Song of the Andoumboulou: 8"
Johnson:	"The Education of Mingo"
Shange:	*for colored girls*
Jones:	*Corregidora*
Kincaid:	*Annie John*
Bradley:	*The Chaneysville Incident*
Naylor:	*The Women of Brewster Place*
Dove:	"David Walker (1785–1830)," "Parsley," "The Event," "Motherhood," "Daystar," "The Oriental Ballerina," "Pastoral," "Mother Love," "Demeter Mourning," "Demeter's Prayer to Hades"
Mosley:	"Equal Opportunity"
Mullen:	*Muse & Drudge*
Hemphill:	*Conditions* (xxi and xxii)
Phillips:	*Crossing the River*
Danticat:	*Breath, Eyes, Memory*
Whitehead:	*John Henry Days*

Ghosts and Gothicism

Black magic and supernatural or occult powers are investigated in the texts listed below.

The Vernacular Tradition

SPIRITUALS

"Swing Low, Sweet Chariot"

THE BLUES

"Hellhound on My Trail"
"Rock Me, Baby"
"St. Louis Blues"
"Hoochie Coochie"

SECULAR RHYMES AND SONGS

"You May Go But This Will Bring You Back"

BALLADS

"Stackolee"

FOLKTALES

" 'Ah'll Beatcher Makin' Money' "
"The Ventriloquist"
"You Talk Too Much, Anyhow"

Slavery and Freedom

Séjour: "The Mulatto"

Reconstruction to the New Negro Renaissance

Chesnutt: "The Goophered Grapevine"
Hopkins: "Talma Gordon"

Harlem Renaissance

Grimké: "When the Green Lies Over the Earth"
McKay: "Outcast"
Hurston: *Mules and Men*

Bontemps: "Southern Mansion"
Cullen: "Heritage," "To John Keats"

Realism, Naturalism, Modernism

Tolson: "Satchmo"
Wright: "The Man Who Lived Underground"
Hayden: "O Daedalus, Fly Away Home," "Runagate Runagate"

Literature since 1975

Wideman: *Damballah*
Wilson: *Joe Turner's Come and Gone*
Mackey: "Song of the Andoumboulou: 8"
Dove: "Mother Love"

Home and Heritage

"Home and Heritage" incorporates a range of "domestic" sites and issues—from traditional residence and hearthstone (e.g., *Incidents in the
Life of a Slave Girl*) even when dysfunctional (e.g., *Soldier*) or dystopic
(e.g., "Division of an Estate"), or back to the larger African continent
(*Narrative of the Life and Adventures of Venture*), or beyond to the Christian construction of an idealized afterlife (e.g., "City Called Heaven"), and
culminating farthest in idealized black nationalist ideologies (e.g., "Back
Again, Home").

The Vernacular Tradition

SPIRITUALS

"City Called Heaven"
"Swing Low, Sweet Chariot"
"Steal Away to Jesus"

THE BLUES

"Good Morning Blues"
"Backwater Blues"
"Rock Me, Baby"
"Handy Man"

	Country Women," "The Two Offers," "Our Greatest Want," "Woman's Political Future"
Wilson:	*Our Nig*

Reconstruction to the New Negro Renaissance

Washington:	*Up From Slavery*
Hopkins:	"Talma Gordon," "Famous Men of the Negro Race"
Du Bois:	"The Damnation of Women"
J. Johnson:	"Lift Ev'ry Voice and Sing," *The Autobiography of an Ex-Colored Man, The Book of American Negro Poetry*
Dunbar:	"We Wear the Mask," "Little Brown Baby," "The Fourth of July and Race Outrages"
Dunbar Nelson:	"I Sit and Sew"
Braithwaite:	"The House of Falling Leaves"

Harlem Renaissance

Schomburg:	"The Negro Digs Up His Past"
Grimké:	"Tenebris"
Fauset:	*Plum Bun*
Locke:	*The New Negro*
G. Johnson:	"The Heart of a Woman"
Garvey:	"Africa for the Africans"
McKay:	"America," *Home to Harlem*, "Harlem Runs Wild"
Hurston:	"Sweat," "How It Feels to Be Colored Me," *Their Eyes Were Watching God*
Larsen:	*Quicksand*
Toomer:	*Cane*
Schuyler:	"The Negro-Art Hokum"
Fisher:	"The Caucasian Storms Harlem"
Bonner:	"On Being Young—a Woman—and Colored"
Bennett:	"Heritage," "To a Dark Girl"
Thurman:	*Infants of the Spring*
Bontemps:	"Nocturne at Bethesda," "Southern Mansion," "A Summer Tragedy"
Hughes:	"Afro-American Fragment," "Ballad of the Landlord," "Madam and the Rent Man," "Theme for English B"
Cullen:	"Saturday's Child," "Heritage"

Realism, Naturalism, Modernism

Tolson:	"Dark Symphony," *Libretto for the Republic of Liberia*
West:	*The Living Is Easy*

Wright:	all selections
Petry:	*The Street*
Hayden:	"Those Winter Sundays," "O Daedalus, Fly Away Home," "Soledad"
Ellison:	"Richard Wright's Blues," *Invisible Man*, "Change the Joke and Slip the Yoke"
Walker:	"For My People"
Brooks:	"kitchenette building," "a song in the front yard," "Sadie and Maud," "The Vacant Lot," "The Sundays of Satin-Legs Smith," "Maxie Allen," "The Lovers of the Poor," "The Chicago *Defender*," "Two Dedications," *Maud Martha*
Baldwin:	"Stranger in the Village," "Notes of a Native Son," "Sonny's Blues"
Hansberry:	*A Raisin in the Sun*

Black Arts Era

Williams:	*The Man Who Cried I Am*
Lorde:	"A Litany for Survival," *Zami*, Chaps. 3, 11
Baraka:	"SOS"
Sanchez:	"poem at thirty"
Jordan:	*Soldier*, "Intifada," "Poem for Guatemala"
Clifton:	"move"
Reed:	"Chattanooga"
Harper:	"Grandfather"
Giovanni:	"Nikki-Rosa," "Knoxville, Tennessee"
Madhubuti:	"Back Again, Home," "The Long Reality," "Malcolm Spoke / who listened?"
Rodgers:	"Jesus Was Crucified," "It Is Deep"

Literature since 1975

Murray:	*Train Whistle Guitar*
Marshall:	"To Da-duh, in Memoriam," "The Making of a Writer"
Kennedy:	*A Movie Star Has to Star in Black and White*
Wideman:	*Brothers and Keepers*
Williams:	"I Want Aretha to Set This to Music," "Tell Martha Not to Moan"
Walker:	"In Search of Our Mothers' Gardens," "Everyday Use"
Wilson:	*Joe Turner's Come and Gone*
Cliff:	all selections

Butler:	"Bloodchild"
Komunyakaa:	"Sunday Afternoons," "Birds on a Powerline"
Shange:	"Nappy Edges," "Bocas: A Daughter's Geography"
Kincaid:	*Annie John*
Naylor:	*The Women of Brewster Place*
Dove:	"Parsley," "Motherhood," "Daystar," "The Oriental Ballerina," "Mother Love"
Hemphill:	*Conditions* (xxiv)
Phillips:	*Crossing the River*
Danticat:	*Breath, Eyes, Memory*

The Influence of Ancestry

Each of the texts listed below overtly or tacitly invokes some other text, usually by another African American writer, and also implies or asserts that its own inspiration, its very existence, results from at least one other literary text that represents the tradition(s) or genre to which it ascribes. Courses focusing on the trope of "signifying" might well draw chiefly from this list.

The Vernacular Tradition

"Maple Leaf Rag" (both versions)

SPIRITUALS

"Ezekiel Saw de Wheel"
"Go Down, Moses"
"Didn't My Lord Deliver Daniel?"
"God's a-Gonna Trouble the Water"

GOSPEL

"Peace Be Still"
"Stand by Me"

THE BLUES

"Trouble in Mind"
"Rock Me, Baby"
"Yellow Dog Blues"
"Handy Man"

Secular Rhymes and Songs

"Me and My Captain"

Ballads

"Sinking of the *Titanic*"
"Shine and the *Titanic*"

Work Songs

"Can't You Line It?"

Songs of Social Change

"Four Women"

Jazz

"It Don't Mean a Thing (If It Ain't Got That Swing)"
"(What Did I Do to Be So) Black and Blue"
"Parker's Mood"

Rhythm and Blues

"The Tracks of My Tears"
"Dancin' in the Street"
"What's Goin' On?"
"Living for the City"

Hip Hop

"The Revolution Will Not Be Televised"
"The Message"
"Don't Believe the Hype"
"The Evil That Men Do"

Sermons

"God"
"The Eagle Stirreth Her Nest"
"I Have a Dream"
"I've Been to the Mountaintop"
"The Ballot or the Bullet"
"O God of Love, Power and Justice"

Folktales

"All God's Chillen Had Wings"
"How to Write a Letter"
" 'De Reason Niggers Is Working So Hard' "
"You Talk Too Much, Anyhow"
"A Flying Fool"
"What the Rabbit Learned"

Slavery and Freedom

Hammon:	"An Address to Miss Phillis Wheatley"
Wheatley:	all selections
Walker:	*Appeal in Four Articles*
Jacobs:	*Incidents in the Life of a Slave Girl*
Brown:	*Clotel*
Séjour:	"The Mulatto"
Keckley:	*Behind the Scenes*
Douglass:	*Narrative of the Life*
Harper:	"Fancy Etchings"

Reconstruction to the New Negro Renaissance

Washington:	*Up From Slavery*
Chesnutt:	"The Goophered Grapevine"
Hopkins:	all selections
Wells-Barnett:	*A Red Record*
Du Bois:	*The Souls of Black Folk*, "The Damnation of Women"
Corrothers:	"Paul Laurence Dunbar"
J. Johnson:	"Sence You Went Away," "Lift Ev'ry Voice and Sing," "O Black and Unknown Bards," "Fifty Years," "The Creation," *The Autobiography of an Ex-Colored Man*, *The Book of American Negro Poetry*
Dunbar:	"An Ante-Bellum Sermon," "When Malindy Sings," "A Cabin Tale," "Dinah Kneading Dough," "Douglass," "Black Samson of Brandywine," "The Fourth of July and Race Outrages"
Braithwaite:	"Sic Vita," "Quiet Has a Hidden Sound"
F. Johnson:	"Singing Hallelujia," "Song of the Whirlwind," "My God in Heaven Said to Me"

Harlem Renaissance

Schomburg:	"The Negro Digs Up His Past"
Spencer:	"Dunbar"

Fauset:	*Plum Bun*
Locke:	*The New Negro*
G. Johnson:	"The Heart of a Woman," "Lost Illusions"
Larsen:	*Quicksand*
Toomer:	*Cane*
Schuyler:	"The Negro-Art Hokum"
Fisher:	"The City of Refuge," "The Caucasian Storms Harlem"
Bonner:	"On Being Young—a Woman—and Colored"
Brown:	"Old Lem"
Bennett:	"Sonnet—2"
Thurman:	*Infants of the Spring*
Bontemps:	"A Black Man Talks of Reaping," "Nocturne at Bethesda," "Miracles"
Hughes:	"Negro Servant," "Song for Billie Holiday," "The Blues I'm Playing"
Cullen:	"Yet Do I Marvel," "To John Keats," "The Shroud of Color," "Heritage," "From the Dark Tower"
H. Johnson:	"Poem," "Sonnet to a Negro in Harlem"

Realism, Naturalism, Modernism

Tolson:	"An Ex-Judge at the Bar," "Dark Symphony," *Libretto for the Republic of Liberia*, "The Birth of John Henry," "Satchmo"
Wright:	"Blueprint for Negro Writing," "The Man Who Lived Underground," *Black Boy*
Hayden:	"Homage to the Empress of the Blues," "Middle Passage," "O Daedalus, Fly Away Home," "Runagate Runagate," "Frederick Douglass," "Mourning Poem for the Queen of Sunday," "Soledad," "El-Hajj Malik El-Shabazz," "A Letter from Phillis Wheatley"
Ellison:	all selections
Walker:	all selections
Brooks:	"The Sundays of Satin-Legs Smith," "Maxie Allen," "The Rites for Cousin Vit," "The Children of the Poor," "The Lovers of the Poor," "We Real Cool," "The Chicago *Defender*," "The Third Sermon on the Warpland," "Young Heroes," *Maud Martha*
Baldwin:	"Everybody's Protest Novel," "Stranger in the Village," "Notes of a Native Son," "Sonny's Blues"

Black Arts Era

Knight:	"The Idea of Ancestry"
Gayle:	*The Black Aesthetic*
Lorde:	"Poetry Is Not a Luxury"
Baraka:	*Dutchman*
Sanchez:	"for our lady"
Spellman:	"Did John's Music Kill Him?"
Jordan:	*Civil Wars*
Cortez:	"How Long Has Trane Been Gone"
Neal:	"The Black Arts Movement"
Reed:	"I am a cowboy in the boat of Ra," "Dualism," "Chattanooga," "Neo-Hoodoo Manifesto," *Mumbo Jumbo*
Harper:	"Dear John, Dear Coltrane," "Deathwatch," "Br'er Sterling and the Rocker"
Madhubuti:	"Malcolm Spoke / who listened?"
Giovanni:	"Beautiful Black Men"
Troupe:	"Conversation Overheard," "Impressions / of Chicago"
Rodgers:	"Jesus Was Crucified," "It Is Deep"

Literature since 1975

Murray:	*Train Whistle Guitar*
Angelou:	"Still I Rise," "My Arkansas"
Marshall:	"To Da-duh, in Memoriam," "The Making of a Writer"
Kennedy:	*A Movie Star Has to Star in Black and White*
Morrison:	all selections
Major:	"Round Midnight"
Forrest:	*There Is a Tree More Ancient Than Eden*
Wideman:	*Brothers and Keepers*
Delany:	*Atlantis: Model 1924*
Williams:	"I Want Aretha to Set This to Music"
Walker:	"Women," "In Search of Our Mothers' Gardens," "Everyday Use," "Advancing Luna," *The Color Purple*
Wilson:	*Joe Turner's Come and Gone*
Cliff:	all selections
Butler:	"Bloodchild"
Komunyakaa:	"February in Sydney," "Birds on a Powerline"
Mackey:	all selections
Johnson:	"The Education of Mingo"
Shange:	*for colored girls,* "Nappy Edges"
Jones:	*Corregidora*

Bradley:	*The Chaneysville Incident*
Naylor:	*The Women of Brewster Place*
Dove:	"David Walker (1785–1830)," "Receiving the Stigmata," "Motherhood," "Statistic: The Witness," "Demeter Mourning," "History," "Demeter's Prayer to Hades"
Mosley:	"Equal Opportunity"
Mullen:	*Muse & Drudge*
Hemphill:	*Conditions* (xxi and xxiv)
Danticat:	*Breath, Eyes, Memory*
Whitehead:	*John Henry Days*

Labor

Because Africans were first brought into the New World as laborers, it is not surprising that labor forms a central theme of many African American literary texts.

The Vernacular Tradition

SECULAR RHYMES AND SONGS

"[We raise de wheat]"
"Me and My Captain"
"Promises of Freedom"
"No More Auction Block"

BALLADS

"John Henry"

WORK SONGS

"Pick a Bale of Cotton"
"Go Down, Old Hannah"
"Can't You Line It?"

SONGS OF SOCIAL CHANGE

"The Backlash Blues"
"Four Women"

HIP HOP

"The Message"

Sermons

"I've Been to the Mountaintop"

Folktales

"All God's Chillen Had Wings"
"Big Talk"
" 'Ah'll Beatcher Makin' Money' "
"Why the Sister in Black Works Hardest"
" 'De Reason Niggers Is Working So Hard' "
"The Ventriloquist"
"Brer Rabbit Tricks Brer Fox Again"

Slavery and Freedom

Smith:	*Narrative of the Life and Adventures*
Wheatley:	"On Imagination"
Truth:	"Ar'n't I a Woman?" (both versions)
Stewart:	"Lecture Delivered at the Franklin Hall"
Delany:	*The Condition*
Jacobs:	*Incidents in the Life of a Slave Girl*, Chaps. 1, 2, 5
Keckley:	*Behind the Scenes*
Douglass:	*Narrative of the Life, My Bondage and My Freedom, Life and Times*
Harper:	"The Two Offers," "Our Greatest Want," "Fancy Etchings," "Woman's Political Future"
Wilson:	*Our Nig*

Reconstruction to the New Negro Renaissance

Washington:	*Up From Slavery*
Chesnutt:	"The Goophered Grapevine," *The Journals*
Cooper:	"Womanhood"
Hopkins:	"Famous Men of the Negro Race," "Famous Women of the Negro Race"
Du Bois:	"The Song of the Smoke," "The Damnation of Women"
Corrothers:	"Me 'n' Dunbar"
J. Johnson:	"Fifty Years"
Dunbar:	"The Colored Soldiers," "Dinah Kneading Dough"
Dunbar Nelson:	"I Sit and Sew"
F. Johnson:	"Tired," "The Scarlet Woman"

Harlem Renaissance

McKay:	"Harlem Shadows"
Toomer:	*Cane*
Brown:	"Odyssey of Big Boy," "Old Lem"
Bontemps:	"A Black Man Talks of Reaping," "Southern Mansion," "A Summer Tragedy"
Hughes:	"Red Silk Stockings," "Negro Servant," "The Blues I'm Playing"

Realism, Naturalism, Modernism

West:	*The Living Is Easy*
Wright:	"Blueprint for Negro Writing," "The Ethics of Living Jim Crow," "Long Black Song," *Black Boy*
Petry:	"Like a Winding Sheet"
Hayden:	"Those Winter Sundays"

Black Arts Era

Evans:	"Status Symbol"
Williams:	*The Man Who Cried I Am*
King:	"Letter from Birmingham Jail"
Lorde:	"Poetry Is Not a Luxury," *Zami*, Chap. 11
Jordan:	*Civil Wars*
McPherson:	"A Solo Song: For Doc"
Troupe:	"In Texas Grass"
Rodgers:	"Jesus Was Crucified," "It Is Deep"

Literature since 1975

Murray:	*Train Whistle Guitar*
Marshall:	"Reena," "The Making of a Writer"
Williams:	"The Peacock Poems: 1"
Walker:	"Women," "In Search of Our Mothers' Gardens," "Everyday Use"
Wilson:	*Joe Turner's Come and Gone*
Cliff:	"Columba"
Komunyakaa:	"Banking Potatoes"
Dove:	"Motherhood," "Daystar"
Mosley:	"Equal Opportunity"
Phillips:	*Crossing the River*
Whitehead:	*John Henry Days*

Authority and Critical Theories

The texts here assert or debate theories of how to create or to critique (African American) literature.

The Vernacular Tradition
"Maple Leaf Rag" (both versions)

The Blues

"Rock Me, Baby"
"Handy Man"

Ballads

"The Signifying Monkey"
"Shine and the *Titanic*"

Jazz

"It Don't Mean a Thing (If It Ain't Got That Swing)"
"(What Did I Do to Be So) Black and Blue"
"Parker's Mood"

Rhythm and Blues

"Dancin' in the Street"
"What's Goin' On?"

Hip Hop

"Don't Believe the Hype"
"The Evil That Men Do"
"Things Done Changed"
"N.Y. State of Mind"
"I Ain't No Joke"

Sermons

"God"
"I Have a Dream"

Folktales

"Big Talk"
"How to Write a Letter"

" 'De Reason Niggers Is Working So Hard' "
"The Ventriloquist"
"You Talk Too Much, Anyhow"
"The Wonderful Tar-Baby Story"
"The Awful Fate of Mr. Wolf"

Slavery and Freedom

Smith:	*Narrative of the Life and Adventures*
Wheatley:	"To Maecenas," "To the University of Cambridge," "On Being Brought from Africa to America," "To the Right Honourable William, Earl of Dartmouth," "On Imagination"
Walker:	*Appeal in Four Articles*
Horton:	"George Moses Horton, Myself"
Truth:	*Narrative of Sojourner Truth*
Séjour:	"The Mulatto"
Douglass:	*My Bondage and My Freedom*, "What to the Slave Is the Fourth of July?" *Life and Times*
Harper:	"Songs for the People"

Reconstruction to the New Negro Renaissance

Washington:	*Up From Slavery*
Chesnutt:	"The Goophered Grapevine," *The Journals*
Hopkins:	"Talma Gordon," "Famous Women of the Negro Race," "Letter from Cordelia A. Condict"
Wells-Barnett:	*A Red Record*
Du Bois:	"Criteria of Negro Art," "Two Novels"
Corrothers:	"Paul Laurence Dunbar"
J. Johnson:	"O Black and Unknown Bards," *The Book of American Negro Poetry*
Dunbar:	"When Malindy Sings," "Sympathy," "Black Samson of Brandywine," "The Poet"

Harlem Renaissance

Schomburg:	"The Negro Digs Up His Past"
Spencer:	"Dunbar"
Locke:	*The New Negro*
McKay:	"Outcast," "Harlem Runs Wild"
Hurston:	"Characteristics of Negro Expression," *Mules and Men*
Schuyler:	"The Negro-Art Hokum"

Fisher: "The Caucasian Storms Harlem"
Bonner: "On Being Young—a Woman—and Colored"
Thurman: *Infants of the Spring*
Hughes: "Letter to the Academy," "Theme for English B," "Not What Was," "The Negro Artist and the Racial Mountain," "The Blues I'm Playing"
Cullen: "Yet Do I Marvel," "To John Keats," "Heritage"

Realism, Naturalism, Modernism

Tolson: "An Ex-Judge at the Bar," "Dark Symphony," *Libretto for the Republic of Liberia*
Wright: "Blueprint for Negro Writing," *Black Boy*
Hayden: "Middle Passage," "Runagate Runagate," "Mourning Poem for the Queen of Sunday," "El-Hajj Malik El-Shabazz," "A Letter from Phillis Wheatley"
Ellison: all selections
Walker: "Prophets for a New Day"
Brooks: "Young Heroes"
Baldwin: "Everybody's Protest Novel," "Stranger in the Village"

Black Arts Era

Fuller: "Towards a Black Aesthetic"
Malcolm X: *The Autobiography*
Williams: *The Man Who Cried I Am*
Gayle: *The Black Aesthetic*
Lorde: "Poetry Is Not a Luxury"
Baraka: "Black Art"
Jordan: *Civil Wars*
Neal: "The Black Arts Movement"
Reed: "Dualism," "Chattanooga," "Neo-Hoodoo Manifesto"
Harper: "Br'er Sterling and the Rocker"
Karenga: "Black Art"
Madhubuti: "Introduction"
Giovanni: "Nikki-Rosa"

Literature since 1975

Murray: *Train Whistle Guitar*
Angelou: "Still I Rise"
Marshall: "The Making of a Writer"
Morrison: "Rootedness," "The Site of Memory," "Unspeakable Things Unspoken"
Forrest: *There Is a Tree More Ancient Than Eden*

Wideman:	*Brothers and Keepers, Damballah*
Delany:	*Atlantis: Model 1924*
Walker:	"Outcast," "On Stripping Bark from Myself," " 'Good Night, Willie Lee,' " "In Search of Our Mothers' Gardens," "Everyday Use," "Advancing Luna," *The Color Purple*
Wilson:	*Joe Turner's Come and Gone*
Cliff:	"Within the Veil"
Mackey:	"Djbot Baghostus's Run"
Jones:	*Corregidora*
Bradley:	*The Chaneysville Incident*
Dove:	"David Walker (1785–1830)," "Pastoral," "Demeter Mourning," "History"
Mullen:	*Muse & Drudge*
Whitehead:	*John Henry Days*

Major Authors

Courses on major authors might begin with shared class reflections about (the various debates surrounding) literary worth and highbrow versus lowbrow literature. Or you might want to start with class discussions about how notions of aesthetic "greatness" and "value" shift and fluctuate, or about how technology and media (especially film) influence and shape an author's popularity. A less conventional approach to a major authors course could perhaps include arranged readings by authors like Phillis Wheatley or vernacular traditions like the blues, whose literary status has not consistently "endured" but has shifted with controversy over time. You might want to ask students to assess the degree of irony they find (or do not find) in judging the literary worth of authors who represent a people once considered biologically uneducable and unintelligible. (Of course, that particular debate rages on in the twenty-first century.)

Whatever focus you decide for a course under this rubric, you might want to ask students to identify a favorite (and "great"?) black author who is not represented. In other words, consider opening the course by asking students to establish criteria that constitute, control, or merit "major" literary status.

Slavery and Freedom

Wheatley
Brown
Douglass
Harper

Reconstruction to the New Negro Renaissance

Chesnutt
Hopkins
Du Bois
Dunbar

Harlem Renaissance

Hurston
Toomer
Brown
Hughes

Realism, Naturalism, Modernism

Hayden
Ellison
Brooks
Baldwin

Black Arts Era

Lorde
Baraka
Jordan
Reed

Literature since 1975

Morrison
Walker
Wilson
Dove

Marriage

The texts listed here explore one or more aspects of the institution of legal, civil marriage between heterosexual romantic partners. They overtly or indirectly confront the idea that African Americans (do not) possess the capacity for the kind of romantic love on which marriage is traditionally based. Instructors generating courses on this theme might want to also see the texts listed under the theme of romantic love.

The Vernacular Tradition

THE BLUES

"The Hesitating Blues"

Slavery and Freedom

Smith:	*Narrative of the Life and Adventures*
Jacobs:	*Incidents in the Life of a Slave Girl*
Brown:	*Clotel*, Chap. 1
Séjour:	"The Mulatto"
Keckley:	*Behind the Scenes*
Harper:	"The Two Offers"

Reconstruction to the New Negro Renaissance

Chesnutt:	"The Passing of Grandison," "The Wife of His Youth"
Cooper:	"Womanhood"
Hopkins:	"Talma Gordon," "Letter from Cordelia A. Condict"
Du Bois:	"The Damnation of Women"
J. Johnson:	*The Autobiography of an Ex-Colored Man*
Dunbar Nelson:	"Violets" (1895)
F. Johnson:	"Tired"

Harlem Renaissance

Fauset:	*Plum Bun*
Hurston:	"Sweat," "The Gilded Six-Bits"
Larsen:	*Quicksand*
Toomer:	*Cane*
Bontemps:	"A Summer Tragedy"
H. Johnson:	"Invocation"

Realism, Naturaism, Modernism

West:	*The Living Is Easy*
Wright:	"Long Black Song"
Petry:	"Like a Winding Sheet"
Brooks:	"The Vacant Lot," "when you have forgotten Sunday"
Baldwin:	"Going to Meet the Man," "Sonny's Blues"

Black Arts Era

Jordan:	*Soldier*

Literature since 1975

Marshall:	"Reena"
Walker:	" 'Good Night, Willie Lee,' " "In Search of Our Mothers' Gardens"
Jones:	*Corregidora*
Kincaid:	*Annie John*
Dove:	"Daystar," "The Oriental Ballerina"
Hemphill:	*Conditions* (xxiv)
Phillips:	*Crossing the River*

Migration, Exodus, Passages

Not exclusively about the Great Migrations of blacks from the Deep South to points north and west that began at Reconstruction, the texts below address African American movement, usually from one geographical locale to another.

The Vernacular Tradition

SPIRITUALS

"City Called Heaven"
"I Know Moon-Rise"
"I'm a-Rollin' "
"Go Down, Moses"
"Swing Low, Sweet Chariot"
"Steal Away to Jesus"
"Didn't My Lord Deliver Daniel?"
"God's a-Gonna Trouble the Water"
"Walk Together Children"
"Soon I Will Be Done"

GOSPEL

"Take My Hand, Precious Lord"
"Peace Be Still"

THE BLUES

"Hellhound on My Trail"
"Backwater Blues"
"Trouble in Mind"
"How Long Blues"
"Yellow Dog Blues"

"St. Louis Blues"
"Beale Street Blues"
"Goin' to Chicago Blues"
"Sunnyland"

Secular Rhymes and Songs

"No More Auction Block"
"Jack and Dinah Want Freedom"
"Run, Nigger, Run"
"Another Man Done Gone"
"You May Go But This Will Bring You Back"

Ballads

"John Henry"
"Stackolee"

Songs of Social Change

"Oh, Freedom"
"Ain't Gonna Let Nobody Turn Me 'Round"
"The Backlash Blues"

Jazz

"It Don't Mean a Thing (If It Ain't Got That Swing)"
"(What Did I Do to Be So) Black and Blue"
"Parker's Mood"

Rhythm and Blues

"Living for the City"

Sermons

"The Eagle Stirreth Her Nest"
"I Have a Dream"
"I've Been to the Mountaintop"

Folktales

"All God's Chillen Had Wings"
"'Member Youse a Nigger'"
"A Flying Fool"

Slavery and Freedom

Hammon:	all selections
Smith:	*Narrative of the Life and Adventures*
Equiano:	*The Interesting Narrative of the Life*
Wheatley:	all selections
Walker	*Appeal in Four Articles*
Horton:	"The Lover's Farewell," "Division of an Estate," "George Moses Horton, Myself"
Truth:	*Narrative of Sojourner Truth*
Delany:	*The Condition*
Jacobs:	*Incidents in the Life of a Slave Girl*
Brown:	*Clotel*
Garnet:	"An Address to the Slaves of the United States"
Keckley:	*Behind the Scenes*
Douglass:	*Narrative of the Life, My Bondage and My Freedom, Life and Times*
Harper:	"Eliza Harris"
Wilson:	*Our Nig*

Reconstruction to the New Negro Renaissance

Washington:	*Up From Slavery*
Chesnutt:	"The Passing of Grandison," "The Wife of His Youth"
Hopkins:	"Talma Gordon," "Famous Men of the Negro Race"
Wells-Barnett:	*A Red Record*
J. Johnson:	"Lift Ev'ry Voice and Sing," *The Autobiography of an Ex-Colored Man*
Dunbar:	"Not They Who Soar," "Sympathy"
Braithwaite:	"The Watchers," "The House of the Falling Leaves," "Quiet Has a Hidden Sound"
F. Johnson:	"Song of the Whirlwind," "My God in Heaven Said to Me"

Harlem Renaissance

Spencer:	"The Wife-Woman"
Fauset:	*Plum Bun*
Locke:	*The New Negro*
G. Johnson:	"The Heart of a Woman"
Garvey:	"Africa for the Africans," "The Future as I See It"
McKay:	all selections
Hurston:	*Their Eyes Were Watching God, Dust Tracks on a Road*

Larsen:	*Quicksand*
Toomer:	*Cane*
Fisher:	"The City of Refuge"
Brown:	"Odyssey of Big Boy," "Long Gone," "Tin Roof Blues"
Bontemps:	"Southern Mansion," "A Summer Tragedy"
Hughes:	"Po' Boy Blues," "Afro-American Fragment"
Cullen:	"Incident," "The Shroud of Color," "Heritage"
H. Johnson:	"Invocation"

Realism, Naturalism, Modernism

Tolson:	"Dark Symphony," *Libretto for the Republic of Liberia*
West:	*The Living Is Easy*
Wright:	all selections
Hayden:	"The Diver," "Middle Passage," "O Daedalus, Fly Away Home," "Runagate Runagate," "A Letter from Phillis Wheatley"
Ellison:	"Richard Wright's Blues," "Remembering Richard Wright"
Brooks:	"Sadie and Maud," "The Vacant Lot," "The Rites for Cousin Vit"
Baldwin:	"Stranger in the Village," "Sonny's Blues"
Hansberry:	*A Raisin in the Sun*

Black Arts Era

Malcolm X:	*The Autobiography*
Williams:	*The Man Who Cried I Am*
Lorde:	*Zami*
Sanchez:	"poem at thirty," *A Blues Book for Blue Black Magical Women*
Bullins:	*Goin'a Buffalo*
Clifton:	"move"
Reed:	"Chattanooga"
Madhubuti:	"Back Again, Home"
McPherson:	"A Solo Song: For Doc"

Literature since 1975

Marshall:	"To Da-duh, in Memoriam," "The Making of a Writer"
Morrison:	*Song of Solomon,* "Unspeakable Things Unspoken"
Major:	"Swallow the Lake"
Wideman:	*Damballah*

Delany:	*Atlantis: Model 1924*
Walker:	"Women," " 'Good Night, Willie Lee,' " "Advancing Luna"
Wilson:	*Joe Turner's Come and Gone*
Johnson:	"The Education of Mingo"
Shange:	"Nappy Edges," "Bocas: A Daughter's Geography"
Jones:	*Corregidora*
Bradley:	*The Chaneysville Incident*
Dove:	"The Event," "Daystar," "Demeter Mourning"
Mullen:	*Muse & Drudge*
Hemphill:	*Conditions* (xxii)
Phillips:	*Crossing the River*
Danticat:	*Breath, Eyes, Memory*
Whitehead:	*John Henry Days*

Natural Landscapes

The texts listed here draw on the natural world for imagery, analogy, and inspiration.

The Vernacular Tradition

SPIRITUALS

"I Know Moon-Rise"
"Steal Away to Jesus"
"Didn't My Lord Deliver Daniel?"

GOSPEL

"Peace Be Still"
"Stand by Me"

SONGS OF SOCIAL CHANGE

"Strange Fruit"

SERMONS

"God"
"The Eagle Stirreth Her Nest"

FOLKTALES

"How Mr. Rabbit Was Too Sharp for Mr. Fox"

Slavery and Freedom

Equiano:	*The Interesting Narrative of the Life*
Horton:	"Division of an Estate"
Whitfield:	"Yes! Strike Again That Sounding String"

Reconstruction to the New Negro Renaissance

Chesnutt:	"The Goophered Grapevine"
Du Bois:	"The Song of the Smoke"
Corrothers:	"Me 'n' Dunbar," "Paul Laurence Dunbar"
J. Johnson:	"The Creation," "My City"
Dunbar:	"When Malindy Sings," "Dinah Kneading Dough," "The Haunted Oak"
Dunbar Nelson:	"April Is on the Way," "Violets" (1917)
Braithwaite:	"The Watchers," "The House of the Falling Leaves," "Sic Vita," "Turn Me to My Yellow Leaves"

Harlem Renaissance

Grimké:	"A Winter Twilight," "When the Green Lies over the Earth," "Tenebris"
Spencer:	"The Wife-Woman"
G. Johnson:	"Youth"
McKay:	"My Mother"
Hurston:	*Their Eyes Were Watching God*
Toomer:	*Cane*
Brown:	"Ma Rainey"
Bennett:	"Heritage," "Sonnet—2," "Hatred"
Bontemps:	"A Black Man Talks of Reaping," "Nocturne at Bethesda," "Southern Mansion," "A Summer Tragedy"
Hughes:	"Mulatto"
Cullen:	"Heritage," "To John Keats," "From the Dark Tower"
H. Johnson:	"Sonnet to a Negro in Harlem," "Invocation"

Realism, Naturalism, Modernism

Wright:	"Long Black Song"
Hayden:	"The Diver"
Baldwin:	"Stranger in the Village"

Black Arts Era

Lorde:	"Now That I Am Forever with Child"
Baraka:	"The Invention of Comics"

Sanchez:	*A Blues Book for Blue Black Magical Women*
Giovanni:	"For Saundra," "Knoxville, Tennessee"
Troupe:	"In Texas Grass"

Literature since 1975

Murray:	*Train Whistle Guitar*
Marshall:	"To Da-duh, in Memoriam"
Gaines:	"The Sky Is Gray"
Major:	"Swallow the Lake," "On Watching a Caterpillar Become a Butterfly"
Williams:	"The Peacock Poems: 1"
Walker:	"In Search of Our Mothers' Gardens," *The Color Purple*
Komunyakaa:	"Sunday Afternoons," "Banking Potatoes"
Dove:	"Parsley," "Receiving the Stigmata," "Motherhood"

Periodical Literature

The texts listed here began as publications in the popular press or in limited-edition periodicals; others discuss some aspect of mass-marketed or print media.

Slavery and Freedom

Séjour:	"The Mulatto"
Harper:	"The Two Offers," "Fancy Etchings"

Reconstruction to the New Negro Renaissance

Chesnutt:	"The Goophered Grapevine," *The Journals*
Hopkins:	"Famous Men of the Negro Race," "Famous Women of the Negro Race," "Letter from Cordelia A. Condict"

Harlem Renaissance

Locke:	*The New Negro*
McKay:	"Harlem Runs Wild"
Schuyler:	"The Negro-Art Hokum"
Hughes:	"The Negro and the Racial Mountain"
H. Johnson:	"Poem"

Realism, Naturalism, Modernism

| Wright: | "Blueprint for Negro Writing," *Black Boy* |
| Ellison: | "Change the Joke and Slip the Yoke," "The World and the Jug," "Remembering Richard Wright" |

Black Arts Era

| Fuller: | "Towards a Black Aesthetic" |
| Gayle: | *The Black Aesthetic* |

Literature since 1975

Marshall:	"The Making of a Writer"
Dove:	"David Walker (1785–1830)"
Whitehead:	*John Henry Days*

Protest Literature

Virtually all African American literature falls into the category of protest literature. Nonetheless, the list below is not quite the full contents of *NAFAM* but instead consists of selections that in one or more ways protest against the political, economic, artistic, or social mistreatment of U.S. residents of African descent. While the tone and rhetoric of protest literature are legendarily impassioned and even vitriolic (e.g., David Walker's *Appeal in Four Articles*), this list consists of many texts that calmly, rationally, sometimes even tacitly denounce racism and racial discrimination (e.g., Braithwaite's "Turn Me to My Yellow Leaves").

The Vernacular Tradition

SPIRITUALS

"I'm a-Rollin'"
"Go Down, Moses"
"Been in the Storm So Long"
"Soon I Will Be Done"

GOSPEL

"This Little Light of Mine"

THE BLUES

"Good Morning Blues"
"Backwater Blues"

"St. Louis Blues"
"Fine and Mellow"

SECULAR RHYMES AND SONGS

"[We raise de wheat]"
"Promises of Freedom"
"No More Auction Block"
"Jack and Dinah Want Freedom"

BALLADS

"John Henry"
"Frankie and Johnny"
"The Signifying Monkey"
"Sinking of the *Titanic*"
"Shine and the *Titanic*"

WORK SONGS

"Can't You Line It?"

SONGS OF SOCIAL CHANGE

"Oh, Freedom"
"Ain't Gonna Let Nobody Turn Me 'Round"
"Strange Fruit"
"The Backlash Blues"
"Four Women"

RHYTHM AND BLUES

"A Change Is Gonna Come"
"Respect"
"We're a Winner"
"What's Goin' On?"

HIP HOP

"The Revolution Will Not Be Televised"
"The Message"
"Don't Believe the Hype"
"The Evil That Men Do"
"Things Done Changed"
"N.Y. State of Mind"
"I Ain't No Joke"

SERMONS

"Listen, Lord, a Prayer"
"The Eagle Stirreth Her Nest"
"I Have a Dream"
"I've Been to the Mountaintop"
"The Ballot or the Bullet"

FOLKTALES

"All God's Chillen Had Wings"
"Big Talk"
"Deer Hunting Story"
"'Member Youse a Nigger'"
"'Ah'll Beatcher Makin' Money'"
"Why the Sister in Black Works Hardest"
"'De Reason Niggers Is Working So Hard'"
"You Talk Too Much, Anyhow"
"A Flying Fool"
"The Wonderful Tar-Baby Story"
"How Mr. Rabbit Was Too Sharp for Mr. Fox"
"The Awful Fate of Mr. Wolf"
"What the Rabbit Learned"

Slavery and Freedom

Smith:	*Narrative of the Life and Adventures*
Equiano:	*The Interesting Narrative of the Life*
Wheatley:	"To Mæcenas," "On Being Brought from Africa to America," "To the Right Honourable William, Earl of Dartmouth," "On Imagination," "To Samson Occom"
Walker:	*Appeal in Four Articles*
Horton:	"On Hearing of the Intention of a Gentleman," "The Creditor to His Proud Debtor," "George Moses Horton, Myself"
Truth:	"Ar'n't I a Woman?" (both versions)
Stewart:	*Religion and the Pure Principles of Morality,* "Lecture Delivered at the Franklin Hall"
Delany:	*The Condition*
Jacobs:	*Incidents in the Life of a Slave Girl*
Brown:	*Narrative, Clotel*
Garnet:	"An Address to the Slaves of the United States"
Séjour:	"The Mulatto"
Keckley:	*Behind the Scenes*

Douglass:	*Narrative of the Life, My Bondage and My Freedom,* "What to the Slave Is the Fourth of July?"
Whitfield:	"America," "Yes! Strike Again That Sounding String"
Harper:	"Eliza Harris," "The Slave Mother," "Bury Me in a Free Land," "Songs for the People," "An Appeal to My Country Women," "Our Greatest Want," "Fancy Etchings," "Woman's Political Future"
Wilson:	*Our Nig*

Reconstruction to the New Negro Renaissance

Washington:	*Up From Slavery*
Chesnutt:	all selections
Cooper:	"Womanhood"
Hopkins:	"Talma Gordon," "Letter from Cordelia A. Condict"
Wells-Barnett:	*A Red Record*
Du Bois:	"A Litany of Atlanta," "The Song of the Smoke," *The Souls of Black Folk*, "The Damnation of Women"
Corrothers:	"The Snapping of the Bow," "At the Closed Gate of Justice," "An Indignation Dinner"
J. Johnson:	"Lift Ev'ry Voice and Sing," "O Black and Unknown Bards," "Fifty Years," "Brothers," *The Autobiography of an Ex-Colored Man*
Dunbar:	"Worn Out," "The Colored Soldiers," "An Ante-Bellum Sermon," "Ere Sleep Comes Down to Soothe the Weary Eyes," "We Wear the Mask," "Little Brown Baby," "A Cabin Tale," "Sympathy," "The Haunted Oak," "Douglass," "Philosophy," "Black Samson of Brandywine," "The Poet," "The Fourth of July and Race Outrages"
Dunbar Nelson:	"April Is on the Way"
Braithwaite:	"Sic Vita," "Turn Me to My Yellow Leaves"
F. Johnson:	"Song of the Whirlwind," "Tired," "The Scarlet Woman"

Harlem Renaissance

Schomburg:	"The Negro Digs Up His Past"
Grimké:	"The Black Finger," "Tenebris"
Fauset:	*Plum Bun*
G. Johnson:	"The Heart of a Woman"
Garvey:	"Africa for the Africans"
McKay:	"Harlem Shadows," "If We Must Die," "To the White

	Fiends," "America," "Enslaved," "Outcast," *Home to Harlem,* "Harlem Runs Wild"
Larsen:	*Quicksand*
Toomer:	*Cane*
Fisher:	"The Caucasian Storms Harlem"
Bonner:	"On Being Young—a Woman—and Colored"
Brown:	"Strong Men," "Old Lem"
Bennett:	"To a Dark Girl," "Sonnet—2," "Hatred"
Bontemps:	"A Black Man Talks of Reaping," "Nocturne at Bethesda," "Southern Mansion," "A Summer Tragedy"
Hughes:	"Mulatto," "Song for a Dark Girl," "Christ in Alabama," "Letter to the Academy," "Ballad of the Landlord," "Merry-Go-Round," "Madam and the Rent Man," "Madam and the Phone Bill"
Cullen:	"Yet Do I Marvel," "Tableau," "Incident," "Saturday's Child," "The Shroud of Color," "Heritage," "From the Dark Tower"
H. Johnson:	"Invocation"

Realism, Naturalism, Modernism

Tolson:	all selections
West:	*The Living Is Easy*
Wright:	all selections
Himes:	"To What Red Hell"
Petry:	all selections
Hayden:	"Middle Passage," "O Daedalus, Fly Away Home," "Runagate Runagate," "Frederick Douglass," "Mourning Poem for the Queen of Sunday," "El-Hajj Malik El-Shabazz," "A Letter from Phillis Wheatley"
Ellison:	*Invisible Man,* "Change the Joke and Slip the Yoke," "The World and the Jug," "Remembering Richard Wright," "Letter to Stanley Edgar Hyman"
Walker:	"For My People," "Prophets for a New Day"
Brooks:	"The Children of the Poor," "The Lovers of the Poor," "We Real Cool," "The Chicago *Defender,*" "Riot," "The Third Sermon on the Warpland," "Young Heroes"
Baldwin:	all selections

Black Arts Era

Evans:	"Status Symbol"
Fuller:	"Towards a Black Aesthetic"
Malcolm X:	*The Autobiography*
King:	"Letter from Birmingham Jail"
Gayle:	*The Black Aesthetic*
Lorde:	"Equinox," "A Litany for Survival," "Poetry Is Not a Luxury"
Baraka:	"A Poem for Black Hearts"
Jordan:	"In Memoriam: Martin Luther King, Jr.," "Poem about My Rights," "Intifada," *Civil Wars*, "Poem for Guatemala"
Clifton:	"move"
Neal:	"The Black Arts Movement"
Reed:	"I am a cowboy in the boat of Ra," "Chattanooga," "Neo-Hoodoo Manifesto," *Mumbo Jumbo*
Harper:	"Deathwatch"
Bambara:	"Raymond's Run"
Karenga:	"Black Art"
Madhubuti:	all selections
Giovanni:	"For Saundra," "Nikki-Rosa," "From a Logical Point of View"
Troupe:	"In Texas Grass," "Conversation Overheard," "Impressions / of Chicago"
Rodgers:	"Jesus Was Crucified"

Literature since 1975

Murray:	*Train Whistle Guitar*
Angelou:	"Still I Rise," "My Arkansas"
Marshall:	"Reena"
Morrison:	*Song of Solomon*, "Unspeakable Things Unspoken"
Major:	"Swallow the Lake," "Round Midnight"
Forrest:	*There Is a Tree More Ancient Than Eden*
Wideman:	*Brothers and Keepers*, *Damballah*
Williams:	"Tell Martha Not to Moan"
Walker:	"Outcast," "On Stripping Bark from Myself," "In Search of Our Mothers' Gardens," "Everyday Use," "Advancing Luna," *The Color Purple*
Wilson:	*Joe Turner's Come and Gone*
Cliff:	all selections
Butler:	"Bloodchild"
Komunyakaa:	"February in Sydney," "Facing It," "Banking Potatoes"
Johnson:	"The Education of Mingo"

Shange:	*for colored girls*, "Bocas: A Daughter's Geography"
Jones:	*Corregidora*
Naylor:	*The Women of Brewster Place*
Dove:	"David Walker (1785–1830)," "Parsley," "Receiving the Stigmata," "The Event," "Motherhood," "The Oriental Ballerina," "Statistic: The Witness," "Demeter Mourning," "History"
Mosley:	"Equal Opportunity"
Mullen:	*Muse & Drudge*
Hemphill:	*Conditions*
Phillips:	*Crossing the River*
Whitehead:	*John Henry Days*

Resisting Women

No pun intended: the characters, figures, and writers listed here are women who resist(ed) race and gender oppression—and not characters, figures, and/or writers who defy or oppose women.

The Vernacular Tradition

JAZZ

"(What Did I Do to Be So) Black and Blue"

RHYTHM AND BLUES

"Respect"

Reconstruction to the New Negro Renaissance

Chesnutt:	"The Wife of His Youth"
Cooper:	"Womanhood"
Hopkins:	"Talma Gordon," "Famous Women of the Negro Race," "Letter from Cordelia A. Condict"
Wells-Barnett:	*A Red Record*
Du Bois:	"The Damnation of Women," "Two Novels"
J. Johnson:	*The Book of American Negro Poetry*

Harlem Renaissance

| Spencer: | "Before the Feast of Shushan," "At the Carnival," "The Wife-Woman" |
| Fauset: | *Plum Bun* |

McKay: *Home to Harlem*
Larsen: *Quicksand*
Toomer: *Cane*
Bonner: "On Being Young—a Woman—and Colored"
Bennett: "To a Dark Girl"
Hughes: "Madam and the Rent Man," "Madam and the Phone
                    Bill," "Song for Billie Holiday"

Realism, Naturalism, Modernism

West: *The Living Is Easy*
Wright: "Long Black Song"
Petry: *The Street*
Hayden: "Homage to the Empress of the Blues," "Runagate
                    Runagate," "A Ballad of Remembrance," "Mourning
                    Poem for the Queen of Sunday," "A Letter from
                    Phillis Wheatley"

Black Arts Era

Evans: "I Am a Black Woman"
Sanchez: *A Blues Book for Blue Black Magical Women*
Rodgers: "It Is Deep"

Literature since 1975

Angelou: "Still I Rise"
Marshall: all selections
Morrison: "Unspeakable Things Unspoken"
Gaines: "The Sky Is Gray"
Forrest: *There Is a Tree More Ancient Than Eden*
Williams: "I Want Aretha to Set This to Music"
Walker: "Women," "Outcast," "On Stripping Bark from My-
                    self," "In Search of Our Mothers' Gardens," "Everyday
                    Use," "Advancing Luna," *The Color Purple*
Cliff: all selections
Shange: *for colored girls,* "Bocas: A Daughter's Geography"
Jones: *Corregidora*
Kincaid: *Annie John*
Naylor: *The Women of Brewster Place*
Dove: "Motherhood," "Daystar," "The Oriental Ballerina,"
                    "Pastoral," "Statistic: The Witness," "Mother Love,"
                    "Demeter Mourning," "Demeter's Prayer to Hades"
Mullen: *Muse & Drudge*

Phillips: *Crossing the River*
Danticat: *Breath, Eyes, Memory*

Romantic Love

One especially destructive yet abiding myth about people of African descent is that they cannot feel, experience, or express romantic love. As if tacitly to debunk stereotypes of Africans as brimming with base, lascivious passions and primitive, overwrought sexuality, many early African American writers carefully avoided any allusions to emotions associated with the heart—lest they be mistaken for titillation in the loins. Thus the list here identifies *NAFAM* selections that celebrate and embrace infatuation, admiration, excitement, fervor, and other manifestations of and including the giddy onset of romantic love.

The Vernacular Tradition

SPIRITUALS

"I Know Moon-Rise"

THE BLUES

"Hellhound on My Trail"
"C. C. Rider"
"Down-Hearted Blues"
"Prove It on Me Blues"
"How Long Blues"
"Rock Me, Baby"
"Yellow Dog Blues"
"St. Louis Blues"
"The Hesitating Blues"
"Fine and Mellow"
"Sunnyland"
"Handy Man"

SECULAR RHYMES AND SONGS

"You May Go But This Will Bring You Back"

BALLADS

"Frankie and Johnny"
"Railroad Bill"
"Stackolee"

Rhythm and Blues

"The Tracks of My Tears"
"Respect"

Slavery and Freedom

Horton:	"The Lover's Farewell"
Brown:	*Narrative, Clotel*
Whitfield:	"Self-Reliance"
Harper:	"Vashti," "A Double Standard," "The Two Offers"

Reconstruction to the New Negro Renaissance

Chesnutt:	"The Passing of Grandison," "The Wife of His Youth"
Hopkins:	"Talma Gordon"
J. Johnson:	"Sence You Went Away"
Dunbar:	"A Negro Love Song," "Her Thought and His," "Dinah Kneading Dough"
Dunbar Nelson:	"Violets" (1895), "Violets" (1917)
Braithwaite:	"Sic Vita"

Harlem Renaissance

Grimké:	"When the Green Lies over the Earth"
Spencer:	"Before the Feast of Shushan"
G. Johnson:	"I Want to Die While You Love Me"
McKay:	*Home to Harlem*
Hurston:	"The Gilded Six-Bits," *Their Eyes Were Watching God*
Larsen:	*Quicksand*
Toomer:	*Cane*
Bontemps:	"A Summer Tragedy"
Hughes:	"Juke Box Love Song"
Cullen:	"Tableau"
H. Johnson:	"Remember Not," "Invocation"

Realism, Naturalism, Modernism

Hayden:	"Homage to the Empress of the Blues," "A Letter from Phillis Wheatley"
Brooks:	"when you have forgotten Sunday"

Black Arts Era

Williams:	*The Man Who Cried I Am*
Lorde:	*Zami*, Chap. 31
Jordan:	*Soldier*
Harper:	"Dear John, Dear Coltrane"

Literature since 1975

Marshall:	"Reena"
Williams:	"Tell Martha Not to Moan"
Naylor:	*The Women of Brewster Place*
Hemphill:	*Conditions* (xxiv)
Phillips:	*Crossing the River*

Separation and Segregation

Most of the texts in this list describe and denounce U.S. institutions that uphold racial discrimination. Some, like "Incident," grieve the hatred that supports racial segregation; others, like "A Flying Fool," mock the absurdity of separate racial spheres. Still others, like "Nikki-Rosa," advocate racial divide by embracing life behind the veil as exclusive and privileged.

The Vernacular Tradition

THE BLUES

"Handy Man"

JAZZ

"It Don't Mean a Thing (If It Ain't Got That Swing)"
"(What Did I Do to Be So) Black and Blue"
"Parker's Mood"

RHYTHM AND BLUES

"A Change Is Gonna Come"
"What's Goin' On?"

HIP HOP

"The Evil That Men Do"

Sermons

"I Have a Dream"
"I've Been to the Mountaintop"
"The Ballot or the Bullet"

Folktales

"All God's Chillen Had Wings"
"A Flying Fool"

Slavery and Freedom

any/all authors and selections

Reconstruction to the New Negro Renaissance

Washington:	*Up From Slavery*
Chesnutt:	"The Wife of His Youth," *The Journals*
Cooper:	"Womanhood"
Hopkins:	"Letter from Cordelia A. Condict"
Wells-Barnett:	*A Red Record*
Du Bois:	"A Litany of Atlanta"
Corrothers:	"At the Closed Gate of Justice"
J. Johnson:	*The Autobiography of an Ex-Colored Man*
Dunbar:	"The Colored Soldiers," "We Wear the Mask," "Sympathy," "The Fourth of July and Race Outrages"
Dunbar Nelson:	"Violets" (1895)

Harlem Renaissance

Schomburg:	"The Negro Digs Up His Past"
Fauset:	*Plum Bun*
Locke:	*The New Negro*
Garvey:	"Africa for the Africans"
Larsen:	*Quicksand*
Toomer:	*Cane*
Bonner:	"On Being Young—a Woman—and Colored"
Brown:	"Old Lem"
Bontemps:	"Southern Mansion"
Hughes:	"I, Too," "Merry-Go-Round," "Theme for English B"
Cullen:	"Incident," "Saturday's Child," "The Shroud of Color," "Heritage," "From the Dark Tower"

Realism, Naturalism, Modernism

Tolson:	"Dark Symphony," *Libretto for the Republic of Liberia*, "Satchmo"
Wright:	all selections
Petry:	all selections
Hayden:	"Soledad," "A Letter from Phillis Wheatley"
Ellison:	*Invisible Man* (prologue), "Richard Wright's Blues," "Remembering Richard Wright"
Brooks:	"a song in the front yard," "the preacher," "The Lovers of the Poor," "The Chicago *Defender*"
Baldwin:	"Going to Meet the Man," "Stranger in the Village," "Notes of a Native Son"

Black Arts Era

Evans:	"Status Symbol"
Fuller:	"Towards a Black Aesthetic"
Malcolm X:	*The Autobiography*
King:	"Letter from Birmingham Jail"
Gayle:	*The Black Aesthetic*
Jordan:	"Intifada"
Neal:	"The Black Arts Movement"
Karenga:	"Black Art"
Madhubuti:	"Introduction"
Giovanni:	"Nikki-Rosa," "From a Logical Point of View"

Literature since 1975

Marshall:	"Reena," "The Making of a Writer"
Gaines:	"The Sky Is Gray"
Walker:	"Outcast," "On Stripping Bark from Myself," "In Search of Our Mothers' Gardens," "Everyday Use," "Advancing Luna"
Cliff:	all selections
Butler:	"Bloodchild"
Shange:	"Nappy Edges"
Naylor:	*The Women of Brewster Place*
Dove:	"Mother Love"
Mosley:	"Equal Opportunity"

Sexual Identities

The texts grouped here encompass a wide spectrum of human sexual identities. Some, like *Soul on Ice* and "The Black Aesthetic," notoriously express vicious homophobia and other forms of sexual anxiety. Conversely, others, like "Violets" and "Going to Meet the Man," interrogate or expose the intersection of race, sex acts, sexualities, violence, morality, and social stricture or social license. Also included here are such texts as "Hoochie Coochie" and *A Blues Book for Blue Black Magical Women* that luxuriate in the complex sensuality of an essential African American identity.

The Vernacular Tradition

The Blues

"Hellhound on My Trail"
"C. C. Rider"
"Prove It on Me Blues"
"Rock Me, Baby"
"St. Louis Blues"
"Hoochie Coochie"
"Handy Man"

Ballads

"Stackolee"
"Shine and the *Titanic*"

Songs of Social Change

"Four Women"

Rhythm and Blues

"Respect"

Slavery and Freedom

Jacobs: *Incidents in the Life of a Slave Girl*

Reconstruction to the New Negro Renaissance

Hopkins: "Talma Gordon," "Letter from Cordelia A. Condict"
Wells-Barnett: *A Red Record*
Du Bois: "The Damnation of Women"
J. Johnson: *The Autobiography of an Ex-Colored Man*

Dunbar Nelson: "Violets" (1895)
F. Johnson: "The Scarlet Woman"

Harlem Renaissance

Spencer: "Before the Feast of Shushan"
G. Johnson: "I Want to Die While You Love Me"
McKay: "Harlem Shadows," *Home to Harlem*
Larsen: *Quicksand*
Toomer: *Cane*
Cullen: "Tableau"

Realism, Naturalism, Modernism

West: *The Living Is Easy*
Wright: "The Ethics of Living Jim Crow," "Long Black Song"
Himes: "To What Red Hell"
Hayden: "A Letter from Phillis Wheatley"
Ellison: *Invisible Man*, Chap. 1
Walker: "Poppa Chicken"
Brooks: "a song in the front yard," "The Sundays of Satin-Legs Smith"
Baldwin: "Going to Meet the Man"

Black Arts Era

Williams: *The Man Who Cried I Am*
Gayle: *The Black Aesthetic*
Lorde: *Zami*, Chap. 31
Sanchez: *A Blues Book for Blue Black Magical Women*
Cleaver: *Soul on Ice*
Neal: "The Black Arts Movement"

Literature since 1975

Delany: *Atlantis: Model 1924*
Williams: "I Want Aretha to Set This to Music," "Tell Martha Not to Moan"
Walker: "Advancing Luna"
Butler: "Bloodchild"
Johnson: "The Education of Mingo"
Shange: *for colored girls*
Jones: *Corregidora*
Kincaid: *Annie John*

Bradley:	*The Chaneysville Incident*
Naylor:	*The Women of Brewster Place*
Dove:	"Daystar"
Mullen:	*Muse & Drudge*
Hemphill:	*Conditions* (xxi and xxiv)

Slave Narratives

A course on slave narratives might begin by defining the term and distinguishing the conventions of those slave narratives written and published before 1865 from those written and published later in the nineteenth century. It might explore various ways that slave narrative conventions differ among slave narratives written within the same period as well as across historical periods. You might investigate whether neo-slave narratives should be read and regarded in the same way as antebellum slave narratives. Or you might distinguish traditional antebellum and post-Emancipation slave narratives from other forms of African American autobiography and life writing. Finally, such a course might examine chattel slavery and blacks' struggles for freedom as reconstructed both in traditional autobiographies by fugitive or former slaves and in various other literary forms.

The Vernacular Tradition

SPIRITUALS

"I'm a-Rollin'"
"Go Down, Moses"
"Swing Low, Sweet Chariot"
"Steal Away to Jesus"
"Didn't My Lord Deliver Daniel?"
"God's a-Gonna Trouble the Water"
"Walk Together Children"

GOSPEL

"Take My Hand, Precious Lord"
"Peace Be Still"

SECULAR RHYMES AND SONGS

"Promises of Freedom"
"Jack and Dinah Want Freedom"
"Run, Nigger, Run"
"Another Man Done Gone"

BALLADS

"The Signifying Monkey"

SONGS OF SOCIAL CHANGE

"Oh, Freedom"

FOLKTALES

"Big Talk"
" 'Member Youse a Nigger"
" 'Ah'll Beatcher Makin' Money' "
"Why the Sister in Black Works Hardest"

Slavery and Freedom

Smith:	*Narrative of the Life and Adventures*
Equiano:	*The Interesting Narrative of the Life*
Horton:	"The Lover's Farewell," "On Hearing of the Intention of a Gentleman"
Jacobs:	*Incidents in the Life of a Slave Girl*
Brown:	*Narrative, Clotel*
Keckley:	*Behind the Scenes*
Douglass:	*Narrative of the Life, My Bondage and My Freedom*
Harper:	"Eliza Harris," "The Slave Mother"
Wilson:	*Our Nig*

Reconstruction to the New Negro Renaissance

Washington:	*Up From Slavery*
Chesnutt:	"The Goophered Grapevine," "The Passing of Grandison," "The Wife of His Youth"
J. Johnson:	"Fifty Years," *The Autobiography of an Ex-Colored Man*
Dunbar:	"An Ante-Bellum Sermon"
Braithwaite:	"Turn Me to My Yellow Leaves"

Harlem Renaissance

Toomer:	*Cane*
Bontemps:	"Southern Mansion"

Realism, Naturalism, Modernism

Tolson: "Dark Symphony"
Hayden: "Middle Passage," "Runagate Runagate," "A Letter
                   from Phillis Wheatley"

Black Arts Era

Malcolm X: *The Autobiography*
Baraka: *Dutchman*

Literature since 1975

Angelou: "My Arkansas"
Morrison: "The Site of Memory"
Wideman: *Damballah*
Butler: "Bloodchild"
Johnson: "The Education of Mingo"
Jones: *Corregidora*
Dove: "The Oriental Ballerina"
Phillips: *Crossing the River*

Southern Traditions

The works listed here are texts that specify sociopolitical institutions and
cultural ways—from antebellum spirituals to bus boycotts—that emerged
from the South and were generally practiced there.

The Vernacular Tradition

"Maple Leaf Rag" (on the Audio Companion only; both versions)

SPIRITUALS

"Go Down, Moses"

THE BLUES

"Backwater Blues"
"How Long Blues"
"Yellow Dog Blues"
"St. Louis Blues"
"Handy Man"

Secular Rhymes and Songs

"Promises of Freedom"
"Run, Nigger, Run"
"Another Man Done Gone"

Songs of Social Change

"Strange Fruit"
"We Shall Overcome"

Jazz

"(What Did I Do to Be So) Black and Blue"

Sermons

"I Have a Dream"
"I've Been to the Mountaintop"

Folktales

"All God's Chillen Had Wings"
" 'Ah'll Beatcher Makin' Money' "

Slavery and Freedom

Walker:	*Appeal in Four Articles*
Horton:	"The Creditor to His Proud Debtor"
Jacobs:	*Incidents in the Life of a Slave Girl*
Brown:	*Narrative, Clotel*
Keckley:	*Behind the Scenes*
Douglass:	*Narrative of the Life, My Bondage and My Freedom*
Harper:	"Learning to Read," "An Appeal to My Country Women"

Reconstruction to the New Negro Renaissance

Washington:	*Up From Slavery*
Chesnutt:	all selections
Hopkins:	"Famous Men of the Negro Race"
Wells-Barnett:	*A Red Record*
Du Bois:	"A Litany of Atlanta," *The Souls of Black Folk*, "The Damnation of Women"
J. Johnson:	"Brothers," *The Autobiography of an Ex-Colored Man*
Dunbar:	"The Colored Soldiers," "A Cabin Tale," "The

Haunted Oak," "The Fourth of July and Race Outrages"

Harlem Renaissance

Hurston:	"Characteristics of Negro Expression," *Mules and Men*
Brown:	"Southern Road," "Memphis Blues," "Ma Rainey," "Old Lem"
Larsen:	*Quicksand*
Toomer:	*Cane*
Bontemps:	"Southern Mansion," "A Summer Tragedy"
Hughes:	"Mulatto," "Song for a Dark Girl," "Christ in Alabama," "Merry-Go-Round"
Cullen:	"Incident"

Realism, Naturalism, Modernism

Tolson:	"Dark Symphony," "The Birth of John Henry," "Satchmo"
West:	*The Living Is Easy*
Wright:	"The Ethics of Living Jim Crow," "Long Black Song," *Black Boy*
Hayden:	"O Daedalus, Fly Away Home," "Runagate Runagate," "A Ballad of Remembrance"
Ellison:	"Richard Wright's Blues," *Invisible Man*, Chap. 1, epilogue, "Remembering Richard Wright"
Brooks:	"The Chicago *Defender*"
Baldwin:	"Going to Meet the Man"

Black Arts Era

King:	"Letter from Birmingham Jail"
Reed:	"Chattanooga," *Mumbo Jumbo*
Harper:	"Grandfather"
Giovanni:	"Knoxville, Tennessee"
Troupe:	"In Texas Grass"

Literature since 1975

Murray:	*Train Whistle Guitar*
Angelou:	"My Arkansas"
Morrison:	*Song of Solomon*
Gaines:	"The Sky Is Gray"

Williams:	"The Peacock Poems: 1"
Walker:	"In Search of Our Mothers' Gardens," "Everyday Use," "Advancing Luna"
Wilson:	*Joe Turner's Come and Gone*
Johnson:	"The Education of Mingo"
Shange:	"Nappy Edges"
Jones:	*Corregidora*
Dove:	"Receiving the Stigmata"
Whitehead:	*John Henry Days*

Spirits and Gods

The texts here address Judeo-Christianity or other sacred systems.

The Vernacular Tradition

SPIRITUALS

"City Called Heaven"
"Ezekiel Saw de Wheel"
"I'm a-Rollin' "
"Go Down, Moses"
"Steal Away to Jesus"
"Didn't My Lord Deliver Daniel?"
"God's a-Gonna Trouble the Water"
"Walk Together Children"
"Soon I Will Be Done"

GOSPEL

"This Little Light of Mine"
"Freedom in the Air"
"Take My Hand, Precious Lord"
"Peace Be Still"

THE BLUES

"Hoochie Coochie"

BALLADS

"Stackolee"
"Sinking of the *Titanic*"

Sermons

"God"
"Listen, Lord, a Prayer"
"The Eagle Stirreth Her Nest"
"O God, I Need Thee"
"I've Been to the Mountaintop"
"The Ballot or the Bullet"
"O God of Love, Power and Justice"
"Elder Eatmore's Sermon on Generosity"

Folktales

"A Flying Fool"

Slavery and Freedom

Hammon:	all selections
Equiano:	*The Interesting Narrative of the Life*
Wheatley:	"On Being Brought from Africa to America," "On the Death of the Rev. Mr. George Whitefield"
Walker:	*Appeal in Four Articles*
Horton:	any selection(s)
Stewart:	*Religion and the Pure Principles of Morality*, "Lecture Delivered at the Franklin Hall"
Garnet:	"An Address to the Slaves of the United States"
Douglass:	*Narrative of the Life*
Whitfield:	"America," "Self-Reliance"
Harper:	"Ethiopia," "An Appeal to My Country Women"

Reconstruction to the New Negro Renaissance

Cooper:	"Womanhood"
Du Bois:	"A Litany of Atlanta," *The Souls of Black Folk*, "The Damnation of Women"
Corrothers:	"The Snapping of the Bow"
J. Johnson:	"Lift Ev'ry Voice and Sing," "Fifty Years," "The Creation"
Dunbar:	"An Ante-Bellum Sermon," "When Malindy Sings"
Braithwaite:	"Sic Vita"
F. Johnson:	"Singing Hallelujia," "Song of the Whirlwind," "My God in Heaven Said to Me"

Harlem Renaissance

Spencer:	"At the Carnival," "The Wife-Woman"
McKay:	"To the White Friends," "St. Isaac's Church, Petrograd"
Toomer:	*Cane*
Bontemps:	"Nocturne at Bethesda," "Miracles"
Hughes:	"Dear Lovely Death," "Christ in Alabama"
Cullen:	"Yet Do I Marvel," "The Shroud of Color," "Heritage"

Realism, Naturalism, Modernism

Wright:	"Long Black Song," "The Man Who Lived Underground"
Himes:	"To What Red Hell"
Hayden:	"El-Hajj Malik El-Shabazz," "A Letter from Phillis Wheatley"
Walker:	"For Malcolm X," "Prophets for a New Day"
Brooks:	"the preacher," "A Lovely Love"
Baldwin:	"Going to Meet the Man," "Notes of a Native Son," "Sonny's Blues"

Black Arts Era

King:	"Letter from Birmingham Jail"
Baraka:	"In Memory of Radio"
Sanchez:	*A Blues Book for Blue Black Magical Women*
Jordan:	"Intifada"
Reed:	"Neo-Hoodoo Manifesto," *Mumbo Jumbo*
Rodgers:	"Jesus Was Crucified," "It Is Deep"

Literature since 1975

Murray:	*Train Whistle Guitar*
Wideman:	*Damballah*
Walker:	" 'Good night, Willie Lee,' " "In Search of Our Mothers' Gardens," *The Color Purple*
Wilson:	*Joe Turner's Come and Gone*
Komunyakaa:	"Birds on a Powerline"
Mackey:	"Falso Brilhante," "Song of the Andoumboulou: 8"
Dove:	"Receiving the Stigmata"

Trauma—and in Some Cases Recovery

Like protest literature, the theme of trauma might seem a catchall for
African American literature because so much of black history in the
United States has involved the corporal, psychological, or social devasta-
tion of black people.

The Vernacular Tradition

SPIRITUALS

"City Called Heaven"
"I Know Moon-Rise"
"I'm a-Rollin' "
"Didn't My Lord Deliver Daniel?"
"Soon I Will Be Done"
"Come Sunday"

GOSPEL

"Down by the Riverside"
"Take My Hand, Precious Lord"

THE BLUES

"Good Morning Blues"
"C. C. Rider"
"Backwater Blues"
"Down-Hearted Blues"
"Trouble in Mind"
"How Long Blues"
"St. Louis Blues"
"Fine and Mellow"
"Sunnyland"
"Handy Man"

SECULAR RHYMES

"Run, Nigger, Run"
"Another Man Done Gone"

BALLADS

"John Henry"
"Frankie and Johnny"
"The Signifying Monkey"

"Sinking of the *Titanic*"
"Shine and the *Titanic*"

Songs of Social Change

"Strange Fruit"
"Four Women"

Jazz

"It Don't Mean a Thing (If It Ain't Got That Swing)"
"(What Did I Do to Be So) Black and Blue"
"Parker's Mood"

Rhythm and Blues

"The Tracks of My Tears"
"We're a Winner"
"What's Goin' On?"

Hip Hop

"The Message"
"Don't Believe the Hype"
"The Evil That Men Do"
"Things Done Changed"
"N.Y. State of Mind"

Sermons

"I Have a Dream"
"I've Been to the Mountaintop"
"The Ballot or the Bullet"

Folktales

"All God's Chillen Had Wings"
"Big Talk"
" ''Member Youse a Nigger' "
" 'Ah'll Beatcher Makin' Money' "
"De Reason Niggers Is Working So Hard"
"The Wonderful Tar-Baby Story"
"How Mr. Rabbit Was Too Sharp for Mr. Fox"
"What the Rabbit Learned"

Slavery and Freedom

Hammon:	"An Address to Miss Phillis Wheatley"
Smith:	*Narrative of the Life and Adventures*
Terry:	"Bars Fight"
Equiano:	*The Interesting Narrative of the Life*
Wheatley:	"On Being Brought from Africa to America," "To the Right Honourable William, Earl of Dartmouth"
Walker:	*Appeal in Four Articles*
Horton:	"The Lover's Farewell," "Division of an Estate," "George Moses Horton, Myself"
Truth:	*Narrative of Sojourner Truth*
Stewart:	*Religion and the Pure Principles of Morality*, "Lecture Delivered at the Franklin Hall"
Delany:	*The Condition*
Jacobs:	*Incidents in the Life of a Slave Girl*
Séjour:	"The Mulatto"
Keckley:	*Behind the Scenes*
Douglass:	*Narrative of the Life of Frederick Douglass, My Bondage and My Freedom*, "What to the Slave Is the Fourth of July?"
Whitfield:	"America," "Yes! Strike Again That Sounding String"
Harper:	"Ethiopia," "Eliza Harris," "The Slave Mother," "Learning to Read," "A Double Standard," "An Appeal to My Country Women," "The Two Offers," "Fancy Etchings"
Wilson:	*Our Nig*

Reconstruction to the New Negro Renaissance

Washington:	*Up From Slavery*
Chesnutt:	"The Goophered Grapevine"
Hopkins:	"Talma Gordon," "Letter from Cordelia A. Condict"
Wells-Barnett:	*A Red Record*
Du Bois:	"A Litany of Atlanta," "The Damnation of Women"
J. Johnson:	"Sence You Went Away," "Lift Ev'ry Voice and Sing," "O Black and Unknown Bards," "Fifty Years," "Brothers," *The Autobiography of an Ex-Colored Man, The Book of American Negro Poetry*
Dunbar:	"Ode to Ethiopia," "Worn Out," "The Colored Soldiers," "Ere Sleep Comes Down to Soothe the Weary Eyes," "We Wear the Mask," "Sympathy," "The Haunted Oak," "Douglass," "Philosophy," "The Fourth of July and Race Outrages"

Dunbar Nelson: "Violets" (1895)
F. Johnson: "Song of the Whirlwind," "The Lonely Mother,"
    "Tired," "The Scarlet Woman"

Harlem Renaissance

Fauset: *Plum Bun*
G. Johnson: "The Heart of a Woman"
McKay: "If We Must Die," "Enslaved," "The White House,"
    Home to Harlem, "Harlem Runs Wild"
Larsen: *Quicksand*
Toomer: *Cane*
Brown: "Ma Rainey," "Sam Smiley," "Old Lem"
Bennett: "To a Dark Girl," "Hatred"
Bontemps: "A Black Man Talks of Reaping," "Nocturne at
    Bethesda," "Miracles," "A Summer Tragedy"
Hughes: "Po' Boy Blues," "Afro-American Fragment," "Song
    for Billie Holiday," "Harlem"
Cullen: "Incident," "Saturday's Child," "The Shroud of
    Color," "Heritage," "From the Dark Tower"
H. Johnson: "Invocation"

Realism, Naturalism, Modernism

Tolson: "Dark Symphony," *Libretto for the Republic of
    Liberia*, "The Birth of John Henry," "Satchmo"
Wright: all selections
Himes: "To What Red Hell"
Petry: all selections
Hayden: "Homage to the Empress of the Blues," "Middle Pas-
    sage," "Those Winter Sundays," "Runagate Runa-
    gate," "Mourning Poem for the Queen of Sunday,"
    "Soledad," "El-Hajj Malik El-Shabazz," "A Letter
    from Phillis Wheatley"
Ellison: all selections
Walker: "For My People," "For Malcolm X"
Brooks: "the mother," "Maxie Allen," "The Rites for Cousin
    Vit," "The Children of the Poor," "The Lovers of the
    Poor," "The Chicago *Defender*," "when you have for-
    gotten Sunday," *Maud Martha*
Baldwin: "Going to Meet the Man," "Stranger in the Village,"
    "Notes of a Native Son," "Sonny's Blues"
Kaufman: "Grandfather Was Queer, Too"

Black Arts Era

Evans:	"I Am a Black Woman"
Malcolm X:	*The Autobiography*
Williams:	*The Man Who Cried I Am*
King:	"Letter from Birmingham Jail"
Knight:	"Hard Rock"
Gayle:	*The Black Aesthetic*
Lorde:	"Equinox," "A Litany for Survival," *Zami,* Chaps. 3, 11
Sanchez:	"homecoming," "poem at thirty," "for our lady"
Jordan:	"In Memoriam: Martin Luther King, Jr.," "Poem about My Rights," *Soldier,* "Poem for Guatemala," "Intifada"
Clifton:	"the lost baby poem," "malcolm," "move"
Cortez:	"How Long Has Trane Been Gone"
Harper:	"Dear John, Dear Coltrane," "Deathwatch," "Grandfather"
Bambara:	*The Salt Eaters*
Madhubuti:	"The Long Reality," "a poem to complement other poems"
Troupe:	all selections

Literature since 1975

Angelou:	"Still I Rise," "My Arkansas"
Marshall:	"Reena," "The Making of a Writer"
Kennedy:	*A Movie Star Has to Star in Black and White*
Morrison:	*Song of Solomon,* "The Site of Memory," "Unspeakable Things Unspoken"
Gaines:	"The Sky Is Gray"
Forrest:	*There Is a Tree More Ancient Than Eden*
Wideman:	*Brothers and Keepers*
Delany:	*Atlantis: Model 1924*
Williams:	"I Want Aretha to Set This to Music," "Tell Martha Not to Moan"
Walker:	"On Stripping Bark from Myself," "In Search of Our Mothers' Gardens," "Advancing Luna"
Wilson:	*Joe Turner's Come and Gone*
Cliff:	all selections
Butler:	"Bloodchild"
Komunyakaa:	"February in Sydney," "Facing It"
Johnson:	"The Education of Mingo"
Shange:	*for colored girls,* "Bocas: A Daughter's Geography"

Jones:	*Corregidora*
Kincaid:	*Annie John*
Naylor:	*The Women of Brewster Place*
Dove:	"Parsley," "Receiving the Stigmata," "The Event," "Motherhood," "The Oriental Ballerina," "Statistic: The Witness," "Demeter Mourning," "Demeter's Prayer to Hades"
Mosley:	"Equal Opportunity"
Mullen:	*Muse & Drudge*
Hemphill:	*Conditions* (xxi and xxii)
Phillips:	*Crossing the River*
Danticat:	*Breath, Eyes, Memory*
Whitehead:	*John Henry Days*

Tricksters and Shape-Shifters

The trickster is a figure or character who usually acts dim-witted, docile, and ignorant but in actuality is just the opposite—sharp, shrewd, and quick-witted. Here, "shape-shifting" includes passing and masking in all their manifold forms.

The Vernacular Tradition

SPIRITUALS

"Swing Low, Sweet Chariot"
"Steal Away to Jesus"
"Didn't My Lord Deliver Daniel?"

THE BLUES

"Hellhound on My Trail"
"Prove It on Me Blues"
"Rock Me, Baby"
"Yellow Dog Blues"
"Fine and Mellow"
"Handy Man"

SECULAR RHYMES AND SONGS

"Me and My Captain"
"Promises of Freedom"
"You May Go But This Will Bring You Back"

BALLADS

"The Signifying Monkey"
"Stackolee"
"Sinking of the *Titanic*"
"Shine and the *Titanic*"

SONGS OF SOCIAL CHANGE

"Oh, Freedom"

JAZZ

"It Don't Mean a Thing (If It Ain't Got That Swing)"
"(What Did I Do to Be So) Black and Blue"
"Parker's Mood"

RHYTHM AND BLUES

"The Tracks of My Tears"

HIP HOP

"I Ain't No Joke"

SERMONS

"The Ballot or the Bullet"
"Elder Eatmore's Sermon on Generosity"

FOLKTALES

"All God's Chillen Had Wings"
" 'Ah'll Beatcher Makin' Money' "
"The Ventriloquist"
"A Flying Fool"
"Brer Rabbit Tricks Brer Fox Again"
"The Wonderful Tar-Baby Story"
"How Mr. Rabbit Was Too Sharp for Mr. Fox"
"The Awful Fate of Mr. Wolf"

Slavery and Freedom

Wheatley:	"On Being Brought from Africa to America"
Horton:	"The Lover's Farewell"
Truth:	"Ar'n't I a Woman?" (both versions)
Brown:	*Narrative*

Douglass: *Narrative of the Life, My Bondage and My Freedom*
Harper: "Learning to Read"
Wilson: *Our Nig*

Reconstruction to the New Negro Renaissance

Washington: *Up From Slavery*
Chesnutt: "The Goophered Grapevine," "The Passing of Grandi-
                     son"
Hopkins: "Talma Gordon," "Famous Men of the Negro Race"
Du Bois: "The Song of the Smoke"
J. Johnson: *The Autobiography of an Ex-Colored Man*
Dunbar: "We Wear the Mask," "Her Thought and His," "A
                     Cabin Tale"
Dunbar Nelson: "Violets" (1895)

Harlem Renaissance

Grimké: "Tenebris"
Spencer: "At the Carnival," "The Wife-Woman"
Fauset: *Plum Bun*
Locke: *The New Negro*
Hurston: "The Gilded Six-Bits," *Mules and Men, Dust Tracks
                     on a Road*
Toomer: *Cane*
Schuyler: "The Negro-Art Hokum"
Fisher: "The City of Refuge"
Brown: "Strong Men," "Slim Greer," "Cabaret," "Sporting
                     Beasley"
Bennett: "Heritage"
Thurman: *Infants of the Spring*
Bontemps: "Miracles"
Hughes: "Jazzonia," "When Sue Wears Red," "The Weary
                     Blues"
Cullen: "The Shroud of Color," "Heritage"

Realism, Naturalism, Modernism

Tolson: "An Ex-Judge at the Bar," "The Birth of John Henry,"
                     "Satchmo"
West: *The Living Is Easy*
Wright: "Long Black Song," "The Man Who Lived Under-
                     ground"
Hayden: "O Daedalus, Fly Away Home," "Runagate Runagate,"

	"A Ballad of Remembrance," "El-Hajj Malik El-Shabazz," "A Letter from Phillis Wheatley"
Ellison:	*Invisible Man*, "Change the Joke and Slip the Yoke," "Remembering Richard Wright"
Brooks:	"the mother," "The Vacant Lot," "The Rites for Cousin Vit," "The Chicago *Defender*," "Malcolm X"

Black Arts Era

Malcolm X:	*The Autobiography*
Knight:	"Hard Rock"
Lorde:	"Coal," "Now That I Am Forever with Child," *Zami*
Sanchez:	"homecoming," "Summer Words of a Sistuh Addict," *A Blues Book for Blue Black Magical Women*
Spellman:	"Did John's Music Kill Him?"
Reed:	"I am a cowboy in the boat of Ra," "Chattanooga," "Neo-Hoodoo Manifesto," *Mumbo Jumbo*
Harper:	"Br'er Sterling and the Rocker"
Madhubuti:	"Back Again, Home," "Malcolm Spoke / who listened?"

Literature since 1975

Angelou:	"Still I Rise"
Marshall:	"The Making of a Writer"
Kennedy:	*A Movie Star Has to Star in Black and White*
Morrison:	*Song of Solomon*
Major:	"On Watching a Caterpillar Become a Butterfly"
Wideman:	*Damballah*
Williams:	"Tell Martha Not to Moan"
Walker:	"Outcast," "In Search of Our Mothers' Gardens," "Advancing Luna," *The Color Purple*
Wilson:	*Joe Turner's Come and Gone*
Cliff:	"Columba"
Butler:	"Bloodchild"
Komunyakaa:	"Birds on a Powerline"
Mackey:	"Djbot Baghostus's Run"
Johnson:	"The Education of Mingo"
Shange:	*for colored girls*
Bradley:	*The Chaneysville Incident*
Dove:	"David Walker (1785–1830)," "Receiving the Stigmata," "The Event," "Motherhood," "Daystar," "The Oriental Ballerina," "Statistic: The Witness," "Mother Love," "History"

Mullen:	*Muse & Drudge*
Danticat:	*Breath, Eyes, Memory*

Urban Landscapes

The works listed here are set in or invoke U.S. urban settings and/as sites of (ersatz) social and economic advancement.

The Vernacular Tradition

"Maple Leaf Rag" (on Audio Companion only; both versions)

SPIRITUALS

"Come Sunday"

THE BLUES

"St. Louis Blues"
"Beale Street Blues"
"Goin' to Chicago Blues"

JAZZ

"It Don't Mean a Thing (If It Ain't Got That Swing)"
"(What Did I Do to Be So) Black and Blue"
"Handyman"
"Parker's Mood"

RHYTHM AND BLUES

"Dancin' in the Street"
"What's Goin' On?"
"Living for the City"

HIP HOP

"The Revolution Will Not Be Televised"
"The Message"
"Don't Believe the Hype"
"The Evil That Men Do"
"Things Done Changed"
"N.Y. State of Mind"

Reconstruction to the New Negro Renaissance

Chesnutt: "The Wife of His Youth"
J. Johnson: "My City," *The Autobiography of an Ex-Colored Man*
Dunbar Nelson: "April Is on the Way"
Braithwaite: "Quiet Has a Hidden Sound"

Harlem Renaissance

Fauset: *Plum Bun*
Locke: *The New Negro*
McKay: "Harlem Shadows," "The White House," *Home to Harlem*, "Harlem Runs Wild"
Larsen: *Quicksand*
Toomer: *Cane*
Fisher: "The City of Refuge," "The Caucasian Storms Harlem"
Brown: "Memphis Blues," "Tin Roof Blues," "Cabaret," "Sporting Beasley"
Thurman: *Infants of the Spring*
Hughes: "Jazzonia," "The Weary Blues," "Jazz Band in a Parisian Cabaret," "Homesick Blues," "Po' Boy Blues," "Negro Servant," "Juke Box Love Song," "Harlem," "Theme for English B"
Cullen: "Incident"
H. Johnson: "Poem," "Sonnet to a Negro in Harlem"

Realism, Naturalism, Modernism

West: *The Living Is Easy*
Wright: "The Ethics of Living Jim Crow," "The Man Who Lived Underground," *Black Boy*
Petry: *The Street*
Hayden: "A Ballad of Remembrance"
Ellison: *Invisible Man* (prologue, epilogue), "Remembering Richard Wright"
Brooks: "kitchenette building," "a song in the front yard," "The Vacant Lot," "The Sundays of Satin-Legs Smith," "Maxie Allen," "The Lovers of the Poor," "We Real Cool," "The Chicago *Defender*," "A Lovely Love," "Riot," "The Third Sermon on the Warpland," "when you have forgotten Sunday," *Maud Martha*
Baldwin: "Notes of a Native Son," "Sonny's Blues"
Hansberry: *A Raisin in the Sun*

Black Arts Era

Williams:	*The Man Who Cried I Am*
King:	"Letter from Birmingham Jail"
Lorde:	"Equinox"
Baraka:	*Dutchman*
Sanchez:	"homecoming"
Bullins:	*Goin'a Buffalo*
Jordan:	*Civil Wars*
Clifton:	"move"
Cortez:	"How Long Has Trane Been Gone"
Reed:	*Mumbo Jumbo*
Bambara:	"Raymond's Run"
Giovanni:	"For Saundra"

Literature since 1975

Marshall:	all selections
Major:	"Swallow the Lake," "Chicago Heat"
Wideman:	*Brothers and Keepers*
Wilson:	*Joe Turner's Come and Gone*
Delany:	*Atlantis: Model 1924*
Shange:	all selections
Naylor:	*The Women of Brewster Place*
Mosley:	"Equal Opportunity"

Violence against African Americans

Some of the texts listed here describe violence perpetrated by blacks on blacks—but generally not.

The Vernacular Tradition

SPIRITUALS

"I'm a-Rollin' "
"Soon I Will Be Done"

THE BLUES

"Good Morning, Blues"
"C. C. Rider"
"Backwater Blues"
"Prove It on Me Blues"
"Fine and Mellow"

SECULAR RHYMES AND SONGS

"[We raise de wheat]"
"Me and My Captain"
"Promises of Freedom"
"No More Auction Block"
"Jack and Dinah Want Freedom"
"Run, Nigger, Run"
"Another Man Done Gone"

BALLADS

"Frankie and Johnny"
"Railroad Bill"
"The Signifying Monkey"
"Stackolee"
"Sinking of the *Titanic*"
"Shine and the *Titanic*"

WORK SONGS

"Can't You Line It?"

SONGS OF SOCIAL CHANGE

"Strange Fruit"
"The Backlash Blues"
"Four Women"

RHYTHM AND BLUES

"What's Goin' On?"

HIP HOP

"The Revolution Will Not Be Televised"
"The Message"
"Don't Believe the Hype"
"The Evil That Men Do"
"Things Done Changed"
"N.Y. State of Mind"
"I Ain't No Joke"

SERMONS

"I Have a Dream"
"I've Been to the Mountaintop"
"The Ballot or the Bullet"

Folktales

"All God's Chillen Had Wings"
"Big Talk"
" 'Ah'll Beatcher Makin' Money' "
"Why the Sister in Black Works Hardest"
"A Flying Fool"
"The Wonderful Tar-Baby Story"
"What the Rabbit Learned"

Slavery and Freedom

any/all selections and authors

Reconstruction to the New Negro Renaissance

Chesnutt:	"The Goophered Grapevine"
Cooper:	"Womanhood"
Hopkins:	"Talma Gordon," "Letter from Cordelia A. Condict"
Wells-Barnett:	A Red Record
Du Bois:	"A Litany of Atlanta," "The Damnation of Women"
J. Johnson:	"Fifty Years," "Brothers," The Autobiography of an Ex-Colored Man
Dunbar:	"Ode to Ethiopia," "The Colored Soldiers," "The Haunted Oak," "The Fourth of July and Race Outrages"
Dunbar Nelson:	"Violets" (1895), "April Is on the Way"
F. Johnson:	"The Scarlet Woman"

Harlem Renaissance

McKay:	"If We Must Die," "To the White Fiends," "The White House," "Outcast"
Hurston:	"Sweat"
Larsen:	Quicksand
Toomer:	Cane
Bonner:	"On Being Young—a Woman—and Colored"
Brown:	"Sam Smiley," "Old Lem"
Hughes:	"Mulatto," "Song for a Dark Girl," "Christ in Alabama"
Cullen:	"Incident"

Realism, Naturalism, Modernism

Tolson:	"An Ex-Judge at the Bar," "Dark Symphony," *Libretto for the Republic of Liberia*, "Satchmo"
West:	*The Living Is Easy*
Wright:	"Long Black Song," "The Man Who Lived Underground," *Black Boy*
Himes:	"To What Red Hell"
Petry:	*The Street*
Hayden:	"The Diver," "Middle Passage," "Runagate Runagate," "Mourning Poem for the Queen of Sunday," "El-Hajj Malik El-Shabazz"
Ellison:	"Richard Wright's Blues," *Invisible Man*, Chap. 1
Walker:	"Prophets for a New Day"
Brooks:	"the mother," "The Children of the Poor," "The Lovers of the Poor," "The Chicago *Defender*," "A Lovely Love," "The Third Sermon on the Warpland"
Baldwin:	all selections

Black Arts Era

Evans:	all selections
Fuller:	"Towards a Black Aesthetic"
Malcolm X:	*The Autobiography*
King:	"Letter from Birmingham Jail"
Knight:	"Hard Rock"
Gayle:	*The Black Aesthetic*
Lorde:	"Equinox"
Baraka:	"Three Movements and a Coda"
Sanchez:	"homecoming," "for our lady"
Bullins:	*Goin' a Buffalo*
Spellman:	"Did John's Music Kill Him?"
Jordan:	"In Memoriam: Martin Luther King, Jr.," "Poem about My Rights," *Soldier*
Clifton:	"the lost baby poem," "malcolm," "move"
Reed:	"Dualism"
Harper:	"Dear John, Dear Coltrane," "Grandfather"
Troupe:	"In Texas Grass," "Conversation Overheard"

Literature since 1975

Murray:	*Train Whistle Guitar*
Angelou:	"My Arkansas"
Morrison:	*Song of Solomon*
Gaines:	"The Sky Is Gray"

Major:	"Chicago Heat"
Wideman:	all selections
Walker:	"In Search of Our Mothers' Gardens," "Advancing Luna"
Wilson:	*Joe Turner's Come and Gone*
Butler:	"Bloodchild"
Shange:	"Nappy Edges," "Bocas: A Daughter's Geography"
Jones:	*Corregidora*
Naylor:	*The Women of Brewster Place*
Dove:	"David Walker (1785–1830)," "Receiving the Stigmata," "Motherhood," "Statistic: The Witness," "Mother Love"
Phillips:	*Crossing the River*

"The Ways of White Folks":* Blacks Define Whiteness

Each of the texts listed here somehow enumerates—and bemoans—"white" ways and/or admits an obsession with trying to figure out what constitutes "whiteness," perhaps by juxtaposing "blackness." The texts may also confront the often frustrating reality of white people in the context of U.S. race or racialized relations.

The Vernacular Tradition

SECULAR RHYMES AND SONGS

"Me and My Captain"
"Promises of Freedom"

BALLADS

"John Henry" .
"The Signifying Monkey"
"Sinking of the *Titanic*"
"Shine and the *Titanic*"

WORK SONGS

"Can't You Line It?"

SONGS OF SOCIAL CHANGE

"Strange Fruit"
"The Backlash Blues"

*A collection of short stories by Langston Hughes.

Hip Hop

"The Revolution Will Not Be Televised"
"Don't Believe the Hype"
"The Evil That Men Do"

Sermons

"Listen, Lord, a Prayer"
"I Have a Dream"
"I've Been to the Mountaintop"
"The Ballot or the Bullet"

Folktales

"All God's Chillen Had Wings"
"Deer Hunting Story"
"How to Write a Letter"
" 'Member Youse a Nigger"
"'Ah'll Beatcher Makin' Money'"
"Why the Sister in Black Works Hardest"
"'De Reason Niggers Is Working So Hard'"
"The Ventriloquist"
"A Flying Fool"
"What the Rabbit Learned"

Slavery and Freedom

Smith:	*Narrative of the Life and Adventures*
Wheatley:	"On Being Brought from Africa to America," "On the Death of the Rev. Mr. George Whitefield," "To Samson Occom"
Walker:	*Appeal in Four Articles*
Delany:	*The Condition*
Jacobs:	*Incidents in the Life of a Slave Girl*
Brown:	*Narrative*
Séjour:	"The Mulatto"
Keckley:	*Behind the Scenes*
Douglass:	all selections
Harper:	"Aunt Chloe's Politics," "Learning to Read"
Wilson:	*Our Nig*

Reconstruction to the New Negro Renaissance

Washington:	*Up From Slavery*
Chesnutt:	all selections

Hopkins:	"Talma Gordon," "Letter from Cordelia A. Condict"
Wells-Barnett:	*A Red Record*
Du Bois:	"A Litany of Atlanta," "The Damnation of Women," "Criteria of Negro Art," "Two Novels"
J. Johnson:	*The Autobiography of an Ex-Colored Man*
Dunbar:	"An Ante-Bellum Sermon," "The Haunted Oak," "The Poet"

Harlem Renaissance

Schomburg:	"The Negro Digs Up His Past"
Garvey:	"Africa for the Africans"
McKay:	"To the White Fiends," "The White House"
Larsen:	*Quicksand*
Toomer:	*Cane*
Fisher:	"The Caucasian Storms Harlem"
Bonner:	"On Being Young—a Woman—and Colored"
Brown:	"Slim Greer," "Sam Smiley," "Old Lem"
Bontemps:	"A Black Man Talks of Reaping," "Nocturne at Bethesda"
Hughes:	"Mulatto," "Christ in Alabama," "Letter to the Academy," "Theme for English B," "The Blues I'm Playing"

Realism, Naturalism, Modernism

Tolson:	"An Ex-Judge at the Bar," "Dark Symphony," "A Legend of Versailles," *Libretto for the Republic of Liberia*
West:	*The Living Is Easy*
Wright:	"The Ethics of Living Jim Crow," "Long Black Song," "The Man Who Lived Underground," *Black Boy*
Petry:	"Like a Winding Sheet"
Hayden:	"Middle Passage," "Runagate Runagate," "A Letter from Phillis Wheatley"
Ellison:	all selections
Walker:	"Prophets for a New Day"
Brooks:	"the preacher," "The Children of the Poor," "The Lovers of the Poor," "The Chicago *Defender*," "Riot," "The Third Sermon on the Warpland"
Baldwin:	"Going to Meet the Man," "Stranger in the Village," "Notes of a Native Son"
Hansberry:	*A Raisin in the Sun*

Black Arts Era

Fuller:	"Towards a Black Aesthetic"
Malcolm X:	*The Autobiography*
Williams:	*The Man Who Cried I Am*
King:	"Letter from Birmingham Jail"
Gayle:	*The Black Aesthetic*
Baraka:	"I don't love you," "Three Movements and a Coda," *Dutchman*
Jordan:	"Poem about My Rights"
Neal:	"The Black Arts Movement"
Reed:	"Chattanooga," "Neo-Hoodoo Manifesto," *Mumbo Jumbo*
Harper:	"Grandfather"
Madhubuti:	"Introduction," "The Long Reality"
Giovanni:	"Nikki-Rosa," "From a Logical Point of View"
Troupe:	"Conversation Overheard"

Literature since 1975

Murray:	*Train Whistle Guitar*
Marshall:	"Reena," "The Making of a Writer"
Kennedy:	*A Movie Star Has to Star in Black and White*
Morrison:	*Song of Solomon*, "Unspeakable Things Unspoken"
Gaines:	"The Sky Is Gray"
Forrest:	*There Is a Tree More Ancient than Eden*
Wideman:	all selections
Delany:	*Atlantis: Model 1924*
Walker:	"In Search of Our Mothers' Gardens," "Advancing Luna," *The Color Purple*
Cliff:	"Within the Veil"
Wilson:	*Joe Turner's Come and Gone*
Johnson:	"The Education of Mingo"
Shange:	"Nappy Edges," "Bocas: A Daughter's Geography"
Jones:	*Corregidora*
Dove:	"Motherhood," "History," "Demeter's Prayer to Hades"
Mosley:	"Equal Opportunity"
Phillips:	*Crossing the River*
Whitehead:	*John Henry Days*

The Vernacular Tradition

Spirituals

Works in the Anthology

"City Called Heaven"
"I Know Moon-Rise"
"Ezekiel Saw de Wheel" • (Tuskegee Institute Choir)
"I'm a-Rollin'"
"Go Down, Moses" • (Audio Companion performance by Paul Robeson)
"Been in the Storm So Long" • (Audio Companion performance by Fisk
    Jubilee Singers)
"Swing Low, Sweet Chariot"
"Steal Away to Jesus" • (Audio Companion performance by Bernice
    Johnson Reagon)
"Didn't My Lord Deliver Daniel?"
"God's a-Gonna Trouble the Water"
"Walk Together Children"
"Soon I Will Be Done" • (Audio Companion performance by Mahalia
    Jackson)
"Come Sunday"

The spirituals form a literature of struggle and liberation. Their religious
lyrics primarily demonstrate trust in the biblical tradition and, conse-

quently, devotion to Judeo-Christian principles. Formed across centuries of slavery, spirituals attest to early African Americans' pain in bondage, hope of freedom, and faith in their own fortitude as well as in divine release from mortal suffering. In addition, they confirm African American awareness of the promises of American democratic ideals in the era of the American Revolution and after. As early African American literature, they forecast many of the themes and forms that subsequent traditions would embody and sustain. Without the idioms and rhythms of the spirituals, there could well be no rap or hip-hop literature in the twenty-first century; without the spirituals' transcendental elements, the literary legacy of protest literature could well be far more pessimistic, more myopic, less fervent or cogent.

Ancient heroes of Judeo-Christian religion loom large in spirituals as symbols of conquest over degradation: thus the spirituals narrate epic stories of leadership and triumph, as in "Go Down, Moses" and "Didn't My Lord Deliver Daniel?"

Teaching Strategies

- To begin a conversation about the transference of religious musical traditions to African American sermonic discourse, ask students to compare the common themes and formal features of the spirituals "Go Down, Moses" and "Oh, Freedom!" with Paul Laurence Dunbar's "An Ante-Bellum Sermon" and Martin Luther King Jr.'s "I've Been to the Mountaintop."
- Select from spirituals and gospels such as "No More Auction Block," "Go Down, Moses," "Oh, Freedom!" and "Freedom in the Air" to discuss ways that black vernacular traditions address and depict issues of physical, psychological, and spiritual bondage and corresponding freedoms.
- The sacred song "Swing Low" served as the basis both of several chants performed by late-twentieth-century popular musical artist Sun Ra and of the mass chants in which Sun Ra often led his audiences during many of his mid-1970s concerts (Reed 141). In this way, contemporary artists continue to emphasize the themes of flight and migration as well as those of spirituality and Christianity that have defined African American literature since its origins. Ask students to identify and share recordings of other contemporary music that attests to that influence today.

Bibliography

Brooks, Tim. "'Might Take One Disc of This Trash as a Novelty': Early Recordings by the Fisk Jubilee Singers and the Popularization of 'Negro Folk Music.'" *American Music* 19 (2001): 278–81.

Reed, Teresa L. *The Holy Profane: Religion in Black Popular Music.* Lexington: UP of Kentucky, 2003.

Gospel

Works in the Anthology

"This Little Light of Mine" • (Audio Companion performance by James Shorty, Viola James, and Congregation)
"Down by the Riverside"
"Freedom in the Air"
"Take My Hand, Precious Lord" • (Audio Companion performance by Clara Ward)
"Peace Be Still"
"Stand by Me"

Although only slight distinctions exist between gospel and the spirituals tradition from which it emerged, one difference is key: from the beginning (ca. 1930) gospel has consisted of a blend of sacred and material cultures. It often references a for-profit venture, as James Baldwin delineates in *Just Above My Head*, his 1978 novel about a gospel singer's efforts to commercialize his music. Baldwin's fictional protagonist, Arthur Montana, like the real Little Richard, exemplifies another defining trait of gospel: the distinctiveness of the lead (or individual) singer's personality. At the same time, however, gospel also has strong ties to the social-minded civil rights campaign of the 1960s.

Gospel traditions are further associated with the Great Migration of African Americans from the South to the Midwest, especially Chicago, where such gospel lyricists and singers as Mahalia Jackson (featured on the Audio Companion) and Muddy Waters developed successful careers. Thus gospel marks a key point along the continuum of black vernacular traditions between sacred spirituals and secular blues music, between rural and urban societies (think Sam Cooke), between regions emphasizing agrarianism/production and materialism/consumption.

A fuller discussion of the differences between spirituals and gospel songs is presented in the introduction to the gospel section in *NAFAM*.

Bibliography

Hardy, James Earl. "Hip Deep in Gospel." *American Visions* 10 (1995): 46–49.

Jackson, Joyce Marie. "The Changing Nature of Gospel Music: A Southern Case Study." *African American Review* 29 (1995): 185–200.

Williams, Dana. " 'Preachin' and Singin' Just to Make it Over': The Gospel Impulse as Survival Strategy in Leon Forrest's *Bloodworth* Trilogy." *African American Review* 36 (2002): 475–86.

Secular Rhymes and Songs, Ballads, Work Songs, and Songs of Social Change

Works in the Anthology

SECULAR RHYMES AND SONGS

["We raise de wheat"]
"Me and My Captain"
"Promises of Freedom"
"No More Auction Block"
"Jack and Dinah Want Freedom"
"Run, Nigger, Run"
"Another Man Done Gone"
"You May Go But This Will Bring You Back" • (Audio Companion performance by Zora Neale Hurston)

BALLADS

"John Henry"
"Frankie and Johnny"
"Railroad Bill"
"The Signifying Monkey"
"Stackolee"
"Sinking of the *Titanic*"
"Shine and the *Titanic*"

WORK SONGS

"Pick a Bale of Cotton"
"Go Down, Old Hannah"
"Can't You Line It?"

Songs of Social Change

"Oh, Freedom"
"Ain't Gonna Let Nobody Turn Me 'Round"
"Strange Fruit" • (Audio Companion performance by Billie Holiday)
"We Shall Overcome"
"Backlash Blues" • (Audio Companion performance by Nina Simone)
"Four Women"

The lyrics in this vernacular subgroup address a broad range of topics in various forms, but they share figures of recalcitrance or insurgence—either black folk who, to put it in vernacular terms, "get some get-back" every chance they can or black folk who applaud the "bad niggers" they themselves cannot muster up the courage to become.

The "bad man," "bad woman," and "bad nigger"—not quite interchangeable figures—all emerge from southern society after Reconstruction. Often based on actual persons, they are (anti-) heroes who resist the strictures of Jim Crow institutions. Their violent natures express their belief that, politically and economically subjugated and nearly subdued, they have nothing to lose and only self-esteem to gain through acts of hatred against white America. Thus they combine the tricksterism and conjure tools of slavery days for their own survival in the post-Emancipation United States. If they manage to escape the rampant lynching of their day, they live heroically among other blacks who celebrate their destructiveness, lawlessness, and sexual prowess. No wonder so many blues images—especially trains and tunnels—permeate the ballads, hollers, and rimes that have made John Henry an American icon.

Bibliography

Katz, Joel, filmmaker. *Strange Fruit*. Video [color & b/w; 57 min.] Oniera Films, distributed by California Newsreel, 2003.

Margolick, David. *Strange Fruit: Billie Holiday, Cafe Society, and an Early Cry for Civil Rights*. Philadelphia: Running P, 2000.

Margolick, David, and Hilton Als. *Strange Fruit: The Biography of a Song*. New York: Ecco, 2001.

Nikola-Lisa, W. "John Henry: Then and Now." *African American Review* 32 (1998): 51–57.

The Blues

Works in the Anthology

"Good Morning Blues" • (Audio Companion performance by Lead-Belly)

"Hellhound on My Trail"

"C. C. Rider" • (Audio Companion performance by Gertrude "Ma" Rainey)

"Backwater Blues" • (Audio Companion performance by Bessie Smith)

"Down-Hearted Blues"

"Prove It on Me Blues"

"Trouble in Mind"

"How Long Blues"

"Rock Me, Baby" • (Audio Companion performance by Sam "Lightnin' " Hopkins)

"Yellow Dog Blues"

"St. Louis Blues"

"Beale Street Blues" • (Audio Companion performance by Big Maybelle)

"The Hesitating Blues"

"Goin' to Chicago Blues"

"Fine and Mellow"

"Hoochie Coochie"

"Sunnyland" • (Audio Companion performance by Elmore James)

"My Handy Man" • (Audio Companion performance by Alberta Hunter)

Counterintuitively, the blues is primarily a literature—arguably, *the* literature—of transcendence. Full of despair and grit, blues lyrics nevertheless confirm resurrection rather than decline. The vernacular expression of the blues "coming down" on a person bespeaks blues lyrics' articulation of the messiness and crudeness life sometimes manifests. Rather than succumbing to the rawest elements of life, becoming mired in the dirtiness of human intricacies and disappointments, however, blues singers sing themselves into a more positive frame of mind. Thus the blues is a ritualistic literature of purgation, cleansing, release, sometimes ultimately even joy.

In terms of the temporal evolution of the blues, its appearance as such falls after the spirituals musical tradition. Saturday night blues brings the most fundamental features of Sunday morning sacred music to bear on the more secular form: improvisation, orality, and suffering. The improvisation of the blues *is* orality, in fact: virtually all blues bespeak the language patterns and rhythms of African American vernacular English discourses. In addition, it continues the spirituals' modes of essential rhythms, testifyin', call and response, and echo or repetition (the blues structure is usually *aab* with only slight variation in the *b* line). Like the spirituals before and the gospel tradition after, the blues musical tradition also emphasizes in lyric and structure emotionality, passion, and vitality.

The themes of the blues also follow from the surrounding black vernacular traditions: suffering, survival, and communal identity are foremost, the latter true even when a lone singer sings about being alone or lonely. The blues tradition has a broad repertoire of symbols; or rather, it is a symbol with a separate set of symbols to illustrate primarily love, lust, and sex as trains, tunnels, and fires. The venue of the blues also conforms to a symbolic setting in that the honky-tonk is to the blues as the sanctuary is to the spirituals. The blues' cruder site—literally and figuratively rougher—attests to the poor and working-class economic status generally ascribed to its models and artists, if not also its aficionados.

"Hellhound on My Trail" invokes a myth epitomized in blues man Robert Johnson. According to legend, Johnson's prowess and fame, like those of other blues artists, lie in part in the selling of his soul to the devil, in making a pact with Satan in exchange for virtuoso mastery of the blues guitar (Reed 92). This blues myth allows us to trace the impact of the blues on later black vernacular musical traditions like the rap group Run-DMC. This trio found fame in the early 1980s with "Walk This Way," a remake of a 1970s rock song of the same name by (the white group) Aerosmith. Their version propelled Run-DMC's album *Raising Hell* into million-dollar sales and at the same time propelled rap into a racial crossover limelight. The integrated, multiethnic following that Run-DMC garnered paved the way for the broad appeal of hip hop in the 1990s (Sylvan 191). It is important to underscore African American blues as one of the sources of the music produced by rock artists such as Eric Clapton and Jimi Hendrix, as well as by artists such as the heavy metal band Aerosmith. All borrowed specifically from the classic blues (or "twelve-bar") and rock artistry of Robert Johnson, Muddy Waters, and other masters (Sylvan 153).

Bibliography

Davis, Angela Y. *Blues Legacies and Black Feminism: Gertrude "Ma" Rainey, Bessie Smith, and Billie Holiday*. New York: Pantheon, 1998.

Fulmer, Douglas. "String Band Traditions: Black String Bands, Banjo, Fiddle, Mandolin and Guitar." *American Visions* 10 (1995): 46.

Reed, Teresa L. *The Holy Profane: Religion in Black Popular Music*. Lexington: UP of Kentucky, 2003.

Sylvan, Robin. *Traces of the Spirit: The Religious Dimensions of Popular Music*. New York: New York UP, 2002.

Titon, Jeff Todd. *Early Downhome Blues: A Musical and Cultural Analysis.* 2nd ed. Chapel Hill: U of North Carolina P, 1994.

Weisethaunet, Hans. "Is There Such a Thing as the 'Blue Note'?" *Popular Music* 20 (2001): 99–116.

Jazz

Works in the Anthology

"It Don't Mean a Thing (If It Ain't Got That Swing)" • (Audio Companion performance by Duke Ellington Orchestra)

"(What Did I Do to Be So) Black and Blue" • (Audio Companion performance by Louis Armstrong)

"Parker's Mood" • (Audio Companion performance by King Pleasure)

OTHER ARTISTS

Thelonious Monk (1917–1982)
John Birks "Dizzy" Gillespie (1917–1993)
Charlie Parker (1920–1955)
John Coltrane (1926–1967)

Jazz transformed (African) American vernacular cultures from the moment of its birth in the earliest years of the twentieth century. It grew initially in New Orleans, but like the folk with whom it originated soon migrated from the Deep South to major urban centers, including Chicago, Kansas City, St. Louis, New York, and Washington, D.C. Like the blues, its first cousin, the roots of jazz are unpredictability, irregularity, syncopation, spirituality, and repetition—roots intricately intertwined with a powerful sense of pathos: the music grieves the oppression from which it springs. And like the blues, too, its primary impetuses are signifyin' and sex—doing it, loving it, missing it, wanting it, begging for it, and calling it down from as many sources as will put out (i.e., *intertextuality*).

Paradoxically, the distinction of jazz may lie most in its mixture of influences. Back in New Orleans, it drew on all images and manifestations of blackness for its base. Shortly after it reached Harlem, ca. 1920, it evolved into swing, an urbane form of jazz in which different sections of a large (mostly brass and reed) band echo and explore signature jazz riffs in rhythmic play. The Audio Companion's version of "It Don't Mean a Thing (If It Ain't Got That Swing)," performed by the Duke Ellington Orchestra, plainly makes the point.

Perhaps the first and most famous of early jazz artists was Louis Armstrong, who, like John Coltrane in the latter half of the twentieth century, would prove truly inspirational to African American writers in diverse literary forms. For different reasons the two musicians offer literary artists access to the elegiac. Armstrong's "Black and Blue" strongly influenced both Ralph Ellison's 1952 novel *Invisible Man* and James Baldwin's 1957 story "Sonny's Blues," which vividly reconstructs the modern jazz club scene, the illicit drugs therein, and the transcendentalism of the music.

Gloria Randle describes Toni Morrison's "language" in *Jazz* as like the vernacular art form for which the novel is named: "The language is marked by blurred messages, interdictions, repetitions, syncopation, and a lack of punctuation. Like jazz, the narrative is distinctly nonlinear and is also at points circular and repetitive. Some passages are disjointed and fragmented; others are replayed—sometimes more than once—from a slightly different vantage point than a previous rendering, like variations on a theme or a chord . . . this carefully crafted, highly stylized narrative is, in fact, improvisation" (cited by Conyers 142).

Learthen Dorsey locates the African roots of jazz in its qualities from "rhythmic improvised music" to textured syncopation "and surging percussion," to call and response "that allows jazz musicians to establish a base for musical change and rhythmic tensions, to collective participation, antiphony, and polyrhythmic structures which allow for textual and melodic variations" (49).

Bibliography

African American Review 29 (1995). Special issue on jazz.

The Antioch Review 57 (1999). Special issue on jazz.

Boundary 2 22 (1995). Special issue on jazz.

Conyers, James L. Jr., ed. *African American Jazz and Rap: Social and Philosophical Examinations of Black Expressive Behavior*. Jefferson, NC: McFarland, 2001.

Dorsey, Learthen. "'And All That Jazz' Has African Roots!" In Conyers, *African American Jazz and Rap*. 35–54.

Early, Gerald. "Ode to John Coltrane: A Jazz Musician's Influence." *The Antioch Review* 57 (1999): 371–85.

Edwards, Brent H. "Louis Armstrong and the Syntax of Scat." *Critical Inquiry* 28 (2002): 618–49.

Frost, Richard. "Jazz and Poetry." *The Antioch Review* 57 (1999): 386–401.

Porter, Horace. "Jazz Beginnings: Ralph Ellison and Charlie Christian in Oklahoma City." *The Antioch Review* 57 (1999): 277–88.

Tucker, Mark. *Ellington: The Early Years.* Urbana: U of Illinois P, 1995.

Willard, Patricia. "Dance: The Unsung Element of Ellingtonia." *The Antioch Review* 57 (1999): 402–14.

Rhythm and Blues

Works in the Anthology

"A Change Is Gonna Come" • (Audio Companion performance by
Aretha Franklin)
"Tracks of My Tears"
"Dancin' in the Street" • (Audio Companion performance by Martha
and the Vandellas)
"Respect"
"We're a Winner"
"What's Goin' On?"
"Living for the City"

Rhythm and blues initially aroused suspicion among Afro-Protestants. Martin Luther King Jr., for example, was one among many black Baptist preachers who generally denounced secular music. However, committed to integrations of all kinds, he eventually confined his cautionary notes to an assertion that "the profound sacred and spiritual meaning of the great music of the church must never be mixed with the transitory quality of rock and roll music" (cited by Reed 105).

The intertextuality of rhythm and blues is evident in the figure of Sam Cooke, who "reclaimed gospel flavoring in 'A Change Is Gonna Come.' Recorded in 1964, the song bears a resemblance to 'Pilgrim of Sorrow' " (Reed 112). Moreover, Cooke evokes the earlier blues man type: he "died of a gunshot wound in 1964, and Otis Redding in a plane crash three years later in 1967 . . . and Marvin Gaye was shot to death by his father in 1984. The tragic ends of these artists, all of whom were once either amateur or professional gospel singers, tend to conjure up images of the Robert Johnson legend" (Reed 96)—that is, of the black musician's selling his soul to the devil in exchange for musical skill and fame.

Similarly, Marvin Gaye illustrates the intersection of rhythm and blues with the spirituals tradition. Gaye was the son of a Pentecostal preacher; his last music tended toward the sermonic, transcendental, visionary, plaintive, prophetic, evangelical, exhortatory. This quality may have annoyed the black church (which often—and vainly—continued to call for separation of sacred and secular musical traditions); however, by the time Gaye released "What's Goin' On?" the figure of the Black Preacher as social activist had been popularized and exalted in the now-dead figure of Martin Luther King Jr. (Reed 130). Similar themes emerge in the biography and music of Curtis Mayfield, whose grandmother served as pastor of the Traveling Soul spiritualist church in 1950s Chicago (Reed 122).

The twin themes of flight and migration, always central to black vernacular cultures and traditions, come together in Stevie Wonder's "Living for the City." The unusual narrative that ends the song forms a compelling prelude to the rap/hip hop recordings that followed it.

In essence, rhythm and blues constitutes a grown-up, modernized, and citified version of "down-home" blues. It is classic blues transported and transplanted from country jook joints and popularized in the urban settings that became centers of attention throughout the 1960s and 1970s. Rhythm and blues marks the lyrical shift from love's travails and train-whistle woes to zealous insistence on social and economic justice. That is, rhythm and blues is more didactic than traditional blues, retaining the somber tones and messages of the spirituals and gospel (compare, for example, "Living for the City" with "City Called Heaven"). For all that, however, much of the sound from the Motown era distills to fun, vivacious dance music.

Bibliography

Hornby, Nick. "Pain in My Heart: Analysis of Rhythm and Blues Music." *The New Yorker* 72 (August 26, 1996): 172–73.

Reed, Teresa L. *The Holy Profane: Religion in Black Popular Music*. Lexington: UP of Kentucky, 2003.

Stewart, Alexander. " 'Funky Drummer': New Orleans, James Brown and the Rhythmic Transformation of American Popular Music." *Popular Music* 19 (2000): 293–319.

Hip Hop

Works in the Anthology

"The Revolution Will Not Be Televised"
"The Message" • (Audio Companion performance by Grandmaster Flash & the Furious Five)
"Don't Believe the Hype"
"The Evil That Men Do"
"Things Done Changed"
"N.Y. State of Mind"
"I Ain't No Joke"

Key Terms

While in "Africana Cosmology, Ethos, and Rap," ethnomusicologist James L. Conyers Jr. explains that the origins of the term *hip hop* are hard to pinpoint, he suggests that it originated in the early 1990s and was probably culled from the recurring phrase "hip hop hippit de hop hop" in the Sugar Hill Gang's "Rapper's Delight" (1979). Conyers further writes: "Kool Herc notes that Afrika Bambatta coined the term hip-hop, while Herc himself used B-Boy. Because of Bambatta's cultural nationalist views, it could be interpreted that the term hip-hop was fusion of black traditional and popular culture, with emphasis on call and response to beats and rhythm of music" (189). Elsewhere, Conyers reports that Kool Herc (an early hip hop artist, once named Clive Campbell) had himself brought a "fusion of reggae party music and mixing" (182) from Jamaica to the Bronx as early as 1969.

Conyers also provides a very useful chronology of early hip hop development, highlighting dates from 1969, with the emergence in the Bronx of Jamaican reggae music and mixing, to a rapid succession of transformative breakthrough hits that included "Rappers Delight" (1979), Curtis Blow's "These Are the Breaks" (1980), and "The Message" of Grandmaster Flash & the Furious Five (1982). By the end of the 1980s another series of bona fide hip hop hits had espoused a more virulent and aggressive message, among them songs by Eric B. and Rakim (1987) and Public Enemy (1988). Among the first women hip hop artists was Roxanne Shante, with the 1984 hit "Roxanne's Revenge" (Conyers 182).

Hip hop as *edutainment*, a term coined by KRS One (born Krisna Laurence Parker) in 1997, explicitly announces the conceptualization of the art form as both education and entertainment (Walker 213–14). A transitional period between rap and hip hop witnessed the rise of the "teacher rap" among musical artists. Lessons of hip hop lyrics generally focus on human development, increased political awareness, and resistance to various forms of oppression.

Theresa Perry and James Fraser acknowledge the origins of hip hop as teacher rap in their description of "the broad, far-reaching, popular nature" of the 1990s national conversation about the impact of the multicultural literacy movement on U.S. higher education: "The video, 'You Must Learn,' by KRS One, is a case in point. The video opens with KRS One in the position of a teacher standing in front of a class of students. Behind him is a map of Africa. He is lecturing the class about Shim, one of the sons of Noah, who is a Black man. Enter the police, who promptly pull the map of Africa up and drag KRS One out of the school into the streets. In the next frame, we see KRS One outside the school standing on the corner. Instead of lecturing, he is now rapping. The refrain, 'I must learn,' brackets his exhortations to African American youth to learn about their African heritage" (Perry and Fraser 6).

Teaching Strategies

- Before engaging students in a discussion of individual hip hop selections, require them to read the *NAFAM* introduction to hip hop. Then in class, work with students to contextualize hip hop as an art form by reviewing connections made in the introduction between hip hop and other black vernacular traditions.

- Professors worried that they can't hang with their students' hip hop repertoire can bone up on their slang by browsing some of the dictionaries listed in the Bibliography to this section.

- If your course goals include increasing students' knowledge of different cultural positions, consider exercises that repackage unfamiliar terminology and concepts within a framework they might find more familiar. Nancy Dawson addresses this issue in "Can You Sing Jazz?" While Dawson's essay primarily documents the cultivation of (black) students' desire to learn more about jazz as an art form, it can be applied to the teaching of all other black vernacular cultural forms. Some students will (mis)judge the blues to be an art form inferior to rap and hip hop because the persona in the blues lyric "Trouble in Mind," for example, contemplates suicide whereas the persona in the more energetic rap "The Revolution Will Not Be Televised" preaches defiance. Discussing the temporal, stylistic, tonal, and thematic differences between blues, rhythm and blues, and the other vernacular music forms represented in *NAFAM* and on the Audio Companion can develop students' awareness of the multiple functions, various contexts, and historical antecedents of the literary and artistic genres.

- A viewing of the video "You Must Learn," by KRS One, could serve as the basis of a provocative discussion about the role of literature, music, and popular culture in formal education as well as about social responsibilities in educating American youth.

- Following from Perry and Fraser's observation that "Countless Rap songs [assert messages about] the obligation of African American youth to learn about their heritage, and the corresponding failure of America's schools to provide them with this knowledge" (6–7), lead students in a discussion of the function of rap, hip hop, and spoken-word traditions in diverse sites of learning or, alternatively, as African American art forms engaged in current debates about educational curricula in U.S. schools and universities.

- Assign Toni Bambara's 1971 short story "Raymond's Run" along with this section on hip hop. Explore ways that the story functions as a precursor to hip hop discourse, especially through emphasis on teaching, learning, epiphany, and transformation.

- Hip hop conventions derive from literary features of the Black Arts era a highly ritualistic, frank, and profane language that resents and resists (and also mimics) a white supremacist and capitalist status quo. Ask students to trace the confrontational and socially conscious origins of hip hop and R&B back to earlier black vernacular traditions, especially in the (anti)heroic figures of early secular works—such as Br'er Rabbit—and the (sexual) bravado of many blues lyrics.

- Work with students to contrast the shared emphasis on economic and social significance in blues like "The Backlash Blues" and "Backwater Blues" as compared with more recent lyrics like "The Message." Discuss with students how these same selections (or your own preferences) have been musically influenced by such pastiche techniques from (verbal and instrumental) jazz and blues as scatting, speech-singing, choral chanting, and other virtuoso voice- and/or verse-magic.

- Hip hop also shares with the Black Arts era some forms and themes of misogyny, violence, profanity, homophobia, anti-Semitism, and other types of racism. To teach this sensitive aspect of black vernacular art forms, turn to the hip hop introduction in the anthology and discuss the editor's commentary on the function of parody, satire, (self-)mocking, and derision in hip hop, especially as a counterattack on dominant forces invested in sociopolitical and economic injustices in the United States and elsewhere. Have students focus on the long echo in African American literature of such themes as violence and retribution, powerlessness and insolence, uplift and degradation: what Martin Delany preached in 1852, for example, Venture Smith had told in 1798, then Chesnutt's Julius signified the same thing in 1899; what Zora spelled out in 1928, Nikki and Malcolm broke down in 1968, and Biggie Smalls rapped it all up in ironic inverse in 1994 with "Things Done Changed."

- Address the discomfiture that hip hop's profanity and candor will arouse in some students by sharing concepts and conclusions from sociological studies, like Binder's (see Bibliography to this section), that found that media frames for rap music both affect and effect public perceptions of the music. (What Binder labels "rap" shares evident conventions and origins with hip hop.)

- Provide students who indicate discomfort with hip hop's mores and unexpurgated lexicon with an opportunity to speculate about ways that media and social conventions shape access and learning. Binder's particular study (see Bibliography to this section) analyzes race and class elements to demonstrate that sociopolitical forces are generally more significant than specific moral messages in determining a music form's acceptance by the public and its affirmation by the media.

- Address misogynistic aspects of hip hop by discussing with students studies of the psychological and sociological impact of these lyrics on interpersonal relationships. You might share findings from the study by Barongan and Hall (see Bibliography to this section) as well as ask your students to research and present additional studies.

- Address homophobic and misogynistic aspects of hip hop by discussing with students editorials condemning the psychological and sociological impact of these lyrics on disadvantaged and marginalized groups in the United States and other nations. You might share the essays by Brownworth and Tyler (see Bibliography to this section), both of which specifically criticize the hip hop lyrics of white rapper Eminem. Ask your students to research, disseminate, and discuss additional opinions about the social and economic effects of hip hop and, further, about the cross-over phenomenon and appeal of hip hop.

Hip hop as contemporary urban folk poetry with its nuances of blues, jazz, and rap appeared early in the twentieth century, artistically woven throughout poems by Langston Hughes and others of his day. Urban folk poets of the 1960s who advanced this art form include Sonia Sanchez, Amiri Baraka, Haki R. Madhubuti, Nikki Giovanni, Carolyn M. Rodgers, June Jordan, and Michael S. Harper.

Notes on Some Artists and Recordings

- Gil Scott-Heron (b. 1952). One of The Last Poets, a funk group most famous during the late 1960s and early 1970s. They were critical trailblazers for contemporary hip hop artists. Their music blended militant black nationalism and spoken word traditions with conga drums and African rhythms (Sylvan 185).
- Grandmaster Flash. The rap origins of hip hop emerged in the late 1970s and early 1980s, influenced by funk, blues, soul/R&B, and "The Message," by Grandmaster Flash & the Furious Five, "featured raps laid over what were essentially reworked disco grooves" (Sylvan 187). Grandmaster Flash was "one of the early creators and masters of both the scratch and the backspin. . . . Both these techniques produced cross-rhythms on one turntable while the other supplied the main groove, a clearly polyrhythmic approach to musical composition" (Sylvan 189).
- Chuck "D," or Carlton Douglas Ridenhour (b. 1960). Leader of Public Enemy, a hip hop group espousing black nationalist ideology.
- Queen Latifah (b. 1970 as Dana Owens).

Bibliography

Barongan, Christy, and Gordon C. N. Hall. "The Influence of Misogynous Rap Music on Sexual Aggression against Women." *Psychology of Women Quarterly* 19 (1995): 195–208.

Binder, Amy. "Constructing Racial Rhetoric: Media Depictions of Harm in Heavy Metal and Rap Music." *American Sociological Review* 58 (1993): 753–68.

Brownworth, Victoria A. "Less Than Lyrical: Hate Speech against Women in Rap Music." *Curve* 11 (2001): 48–50.

Chang, Jeff. "'Stakes Is High': Conscious Rap, Neo-soul and the Hip-Hop Generation." *The Nation* 276 (2003): 17–23.

Clay, Andreana. "Keepin' It Real: Black Youth, Hip-Hop Culture, and Black Identity." *American Behavioral Scientist* 46 (2003): 1346–59.

Conyers, James L. Jr. "Africana Cosmology, Ethos, and Rap: A Social Study of Black Popular Culture." In James L. Conyers Jr., ed., *African American Jazz and Rap: Social and Philosophical Examinations of Black Expressive Behavior.* Jefferson, NC: McFarland, 2001. 180–97.

Dawson, Nancy J. "Can You Sing Jazz? Perception and Appreciation of Jazz Music among African American Young Adults." In Conyers, *African American Jazz and Rap.* 201–10.

Fried, Carrie B. "Bad Rap for Rap: Bias Reaction to Music Lyrics." *Journal of Applied Social Psychology* 26 (1996): 135–47.

Jamilah, Evelyn. "To the Academy with Love, From a Hip-Hop Fan." *Black Issues in Higher Education* 17 (Dec. 7, 2000): 6–8.

Lusane, Clarence. "Rap, Race and Politics." *Race and Class* 35 (1993): 41–57.

Major, Clarence, ed. *Juba to Jive: A Dictionary of Afro-American Slang.* New York: Penguin, 1994.

Perry, Theresa, and James W. Fraser, eds. *Freedom's Plow: Teaching in the Multicultural Classroom.* New York: Routledge, 1993.

Roberts, Robin. "'Ladies First': Queen Latifah's Afrocentric Feminist Music Video." *African American Review* 28 (1994): 245–57.

Rosen, Ralph M., and Donald R. Marks. "Comedies of Transgression in Gangsta Rap and Ancient Classical Poetry." *New Literary History* 30 (1999): 897–929.

Salaam, Mtume ya. "The Aesthetics of Rap." *African American Review* 29 (1995): 303–15.

Smitherman, Geneva. *Black Talk: Words and Phrases from the Hood to the Amen Corner.* Boston: Houghton Mifflin, 1994.

Sylvan, Robin. *Traces of the Spirit: The Religious Dimensions of Popular Music.* New York: New York UP, 2002.

Tyler, Robin. "Eminem: Pied Piper of Hate." *The Gay and Lesbian Review Worldwide* 8 (2001): 12–16.

Walker, Tshombe. "Hip-Hop and the Rap Industry." In Conyers, *African American Jazz and Rap.* 211–23.

Walser, Robert. "Rhythm, Rhyme, and Rhetoric in the Music of Public Enemy." *Ethnomusicology* 39 (1995): 193–217.

Westbrook, Alonzo. *The Hip Hoptionary: The Dictionary of Hip Hop Terminology.* New York: Harlem Moon, 2002.

Sermons and Prayers

Works in the Anthology

"God"

"Listen, Lord, a Prayer"

"The Eagle Stirreth Her Nest"

"O God, I Need Thee"

"The Way Out Is to Pray Out" • (Audio Companion, sermon by G. I. Townsel)

"I Have a Dream" • (Audio Companion, speech by Martin Luther King Jr.)

"I've Been to the Mountaintop"

"The Ballot or the Bullet" • (Audio Companion, speech by Malcolm X)

"O God of Love, Power and Justice"

"Elder Eatmore's Sermon on Generosity" • (Audio Companion, sermon parody by Bert Williams)

Teaching Strategies

- Play for students all four of the sermons on the Audio Companion, which illustrate in part the expansive range of the black sermonic tradition. Ask them to identify both the traits the four recordings share and the distinctive characteristics of each text.

- Have students select one of the four sermons on the Audio Companion and contrast the recorded performance with the written script. Ask them to identify the particular performance elements that enrich the recorded version and to articulate the advantages of having the script available. What aspects of performativity do they hear in the recorded versions that correspond to other vernacular literary forms they have studied?

- The introduction to the sermons in *NAFAM* draws a repeated comparison between the black folk sermon and jazz. Listen with students to Duke Ellington's "It Don't Mean a Thing" (on the Audio Companion); then read in class Ellington's 1958 hymn "Come Sunday" (in *NAFAM*). Ask students to assess the validity of the editor's analogy by comparing and contrasting the two texts by Ellington with one another and with the script of a selected sermon.

- Assign King's "Letter from Birmingham Jail." After your students have read it, listen together to the recorded version of King's "I Have a Dream" speech as sermon. How do the contrasts between the two texts help students comprehend more fully those characteristics that distinguish sermons from related literary and oral forms?

- Like a hip hop lyric, a sermon can surprise with an unexpected but apt use of humor. Ask students to trace and comment on instances of humor and wit in selected assigned sermons. Do the humorous elements seem derived from other black vernacular sources? If so, from what specific traditions?

Bibliography

Hubbard, Dolan. *The Sermon and the African American Literary Imagination*. Columbia: U of Missouri P, 1994.

Lischer, Richard. *The Preacher King: Martin Luther King Jr. and the Word That Moved America*. New York: Oxford UP, 1995.

Reed, Teresa. "Elder Eatmore and Deacon Jones: Folk Religion as Humor in Black Secular Recordings, 1918–1961." *Popular Music and Society* 25 (2001): 25–44.

Folktales

Works in the Anthology

"All God's Chillen Had Wings"
"Big Talk"
"Deer Hunting Story"
"How to Write a Letter"
"'Member Youse a Nigger'"
"'Ah'll Beatcher Makin' Money'"
"Why the Sister in Black Works Hardest"
"'De Reason Niggers Is Working So Hard'"
"The Ventriloquist"
"You Talk Too Much, Anyhow"
"A Flying Fool"
"Brer Rabbit Tricks Brer Fox Again"

"The Wonderful Tar-Baby Story"
"How Mr. Rabbit Was Too Sharp for Mr. Fox"
"The Awful Fate of Mr. Wolf"
"What the Rabbit Learned"

Teaching Strategies

- Just as the lore of the Judeo-Christian Bible inspired the antebellum spirituals, it has also inspired many African American folktales from the beginning of black history in the United States. Ask students to trace the biblical origins of the tales that seem to revise Christian ideas. What moral codes do black folktales generally assert?
- Ask students to compare the depiction of creation and evolution in black folktales with other theories of human evolution they have encountered.
- Note the use of (comic) hyperbole in black tall tales, especially those that feature such larger-than-life figures as bad men and antiheroes —or smaller foes like Brer Rabbit. Discuss with students the relationship of black vernacular poetic exaggeration and the pathos of racial injustice throughout African American history.
- Ask students to research and present audio or video recordings of contemporary African American comedians whose work sustains the vernacular tradition of comic hyperbole.
- Black supernatural powers—black magic—permeate nearly all black vernacular texts as well as most literary texts by African American authors that deploy vernacular discourses and elements. Think through selected texts from David Walker's *Appeal* to the present to trace representations of the extraordinary gothic, psychological, and spiritual gifts of people of African descent. In what ways, if any, do such representations shift over time? For example, do students find conjure imagery and symbology in William Wells Brown's writings of the 1840s to be like, or unlike, that in Zora Neale Hurston's work one hundred years later?
- One extraordinary power of legendary Africans and their descendants is the power to fly. Trace iconic flying Africans throughout African American literature from *Clotel* to *Dutchman* to *The Salt Eaters* and *Song of Solomon*.
- Ask students to focus on two sets of folktales: the "Ol' Massa" variety and the adventures of Brer Rabbit. In what ways do these particular stories overlap? Is it fair to say they are in fact the *same* subgenre of black folklore? Why or why not?
- Written folk accounts of the black bandit/bad man Stackolee (also spelled Staggerlee, Stackalee, Stagolee, etc.) date back to the end of Reconstruction. From historical details cited in other literary sources

of that era—Charles Chesnutt's fiction, Ida Wells-Barnett's nonfiction, for example—what forces seem to have inspired the emergence of this figure?

- The figure of the (animal or black person as) trickster originates in African American folklore. The excerpts from William Wells Brown's *Narrative* provide an excellent opportunity to discuss this figure, generally a quick-witted thinker who devises ways to exercise control in an uncontrollable situation. More often than not, he outsmarts the master, overseer, any (white) person—or in the case of animals, any more powerful animal opponent—who is poised to exercise authority over him. Brown's *Narrative* presents the narrator as a trickster, a role that some slaves adopted to exercise some control over their lives and to survive. Sometimes, as is also true in Brown's *Narrative*, the trickster was a role forcibly imposed on slaves by others. Have students consider Brown's *Narrative* in relation to the two ballads of "Shine" ("Sinking of the *Titanic*" and "Shine and the *Titanic*") and/or the Brer Rabbit stories.

Bibliography

Bryant, Jerry H. *Born in a Mighty Bad Land: The Violent Man in African American Folklore and Fiction*. Bloomington: Indiana UP, 2003.

Teaching the Vernacular Tradition

> One's success or failure in teaching the poetry [of African Americans] has to do with attitude and learning to deal with semiotic features of literature that New Critical education did not address well. Success requires also what I would call a shattering of *innocence*, or the liberal vision of art as a privileged and universal object. . . . Preparing to teach African American poetry begins with reflection on speaking and singing (Ward 145).

Even if one is not especially interested in teaching African American poetry per se, Ward's pronouncement is an effective starting place for thinking about teaching African American vernacular traditions and/or their most prominent themes, for it reminds us of the musicality and auditory riches of African American literature. The selections within "The Vernacular Tradition" can be used to introduce students of all levels to African American poetics in diverse genres.

In teaching courses on African American poetry of any era, consider incorporating rap and hip hop to inform students of the extent of the poetic and musical traditions, to emphasize that the origins of rap and hip hop are not recent, developed, say, during the 1970s heyday of break-dancing, but rather are centuries old with literary representation dating back to the antebellum period. Your teaching might emphasize the longevity of the forms as well as the marvelous richness of all the vernacular traditions, enriched the more by ways they complement one another.

For example, for a course on African American poetry that begins with Jupiter Hammon's "Address to Miss Phillis Wheatley" and places Etheridge Knight's "The Idea of Ancestry" at its center, you might want to ask students to study the vernacular traditions section, some of the slave narratives, and selected Audio Companion pieces to perceive ways that Knight not only draws on vernacular and slave narrative conventions but embeds a number of them in his poem, including the figures of the fugitive and the bad man and the themes of familial estrangement and loss, deprivation, fear, and isolation as well as cultural identity, home, love, and community. In other words, the poem can be used to illustrate both themes and forms of earlier poetic traditions. In moving forward from "The Idea of Ancestry," students will perceive that many of the themes and forms found in Knight's poem and the slave narratives—especially migration, improvisation, hope and despair wrapped around each other— pervade black vernacular musical traditions from the blues and jazz to hip hop. Furthermore, the Audio Companion's spirituals and gospels can be positioned alongside the social change songs of the Black Arts era and both juxtaposed with the rhythms and themes of Knight's poem.

In addition, for interdisciplinary and multimedia instruction in this imaginary course, you can use Knight's poem to emphasize the importance of visual imagery and the power of the photograph and its significance for descendants of slaves. Here you might ask students to read Nell Painter's ground-breaking *Journal of American History* essay ("Representing Truth") on Sojourner Truth's manipulation of her own photographic image, Lorna Simpson's postmodern photography, Hilary Mac Austin and Kathleen Thompson's *The Face of Our Past*, and Deborah Willis's historical *Picturing Us*. Students are likely to be highly aware of international media coverage of the September 11 terrorist attacks, which has increased knowledge about the power and often the pathos of the photographic image. The focus on the photograph in Knight's poem can be used to trace photography as another, sometimes elusive, form of African American memory and self-representation.

Alternatively, for a slave narratives course, you could use vernacular traditions in several different ways. You might want to have students read the hip hop selections, for example, to emphasize the antebellum literature's recurring themes of familial loss and love—not necessarily apparent at first. Specifically, the collected hip hop lyrics, with their "teacher rap" qualities, correspond to the earlier tradition's didacticism. Slavery autobiographers make meta-textual a need to argue for abolition from a first-person perspective, on the basis of personal and lived experience; a complex and embittered example is *Life and Times of Frederick Douglass*. The bravado, signifying, and resistance to (illicit and immoral) authority of that postbellum slave narrative continue strong in hip hop and rap lyrics. Moreover, Douglass's commitment to depicting wasted African American human resources throughout his entire life encapsulates the essence of hip hop grief and fury with wasted black life in postmodern America, especially in such major urban sites as South Central Los Angeles, Manhattan, and Brooklyn.

If your course concentrates on slave narratives' rhetorical impact on the literary traditions that followed them, then it might be useful to emphasize hip hop, blues, and jazz in addition to the more familiar spirituals and gospels in terms of musical traditions. The slave narratives of the antebellum period themselves underscore the importance of music for early African Americans. However, as *NAFAM* indicates, antebellum spirituals were not the only music to become integral to slave narratives. Teaching slave narratives can be a more effective experience if you have students listen to spirituals and to the social change movement songs popular one hundred years after Emancipation—often the very same songs, of course. You might also incorporate other musical forms through hip hop to illustrate that the issues of antebellum slavery persist and that African Americans continue to develop and improvise musical traditions that rail against the injustices perpetrated against them.

Historical Perspectives

As with the oral literature of any tradition, the earliest literary expressions of the African diaspora are represented by folk songs and tales. African Americanists generally agree that spirituals arose from the eighteenth-century merging of African music and philosophies with other music and ideas encountered in the Americas. However, the versions of these vernacular texts that appear in the anthology and those recorded on the Audio Companion were written or collected long after their original compositions. Most scholars recognize Richard Allen's 1801 compilation titled *A Collection of Hymns and Spiritual Songs from Various Authors* as the earliest extant such text. (Significantly, while the lyrics compiled by the black minister and founder of Philadelphia's leading African Methodist Episcopal church were primarily religious songs written by whites, Allen's *Collection* also included many unsigned songs and folk hymns associated with religious camp meetings.)

Generally, the systematic collecting or recording of spirituals, work songs, and other early examples of African American vernacular traditions began after the Civil War. Lucy Terry's poem "Bars Fight," for example, though composed shortly after the 1746 confrontation between colonial Americans and Native Americans at Deerfield, Massachusetts, was sung as a ballad but not published in written form until 1855. Thus, while the oral forms and the vernacular literature predate works written for publication, there is little evidence on which to base priority of a particular song or story.

Moreover, African American vernacular traditions are always growing and changing—sometimes in direct response to changing social situations and sometimes in intertextual discourse. The 1950s and 1960s civil rights movement resurrected and revised songs such as "Oh, Freedom" and "This Little Light of Mine." The speeches of Martin Luther King Jr. echo and quote both in style and in substance sermons, songs, and stories common to the tradition of vernacular literature, even as they become in their own right additions to that tradition. King Pleasure's "Parker's Mood" builds on such songs as "Going to Kansas City" and "Goin' to Chicago Blues," even as it becomes a part of the jazz tradition. "The Message," as performed by Grandmaster Flash & the Furious Five in 1982, invokes and extends the traditions of sermons and spoken word, the tropes of signifying and rapping, and legendary figures like "Shine" (a character in "Sinking of the *Titanic*" and "Shine and the *Titanic*") and other tricksters as well as the "Bad Man" of poets like Langston Hughes. A historical approach to African American literature might explore such versions and revisions, the temporal moments in which they were more and less significant as literary models, and the historical or social situations that may have generated their significance.

Students should be made to understand that vernacular traditions pervade virtually all of African American literature and that the overwhelming majority of literary texts by black writers invoke or include representations of the speech, speech patterns, and/or other black discourses of African America and other sites of the African diaspora. The major mid-nineteenth-century slave narratives (by Frederick Douglass, William Wells Brown, Harriet Jacobs, and Elizabeth Keckley), for example, are highly dialogic and, moreover, represent direct discourse in a variety of regional dialects and in different degrees of "standardization." In addition, they often include fragments or whole texts of poems, songs, spirituals, sermons, and so on: literary texts by others that have been heard or read.

The Audio Companion

The Audio Companion is provided to maximize the teaching of orature, vernacular literature, spirituals, and the like. A wide variety of uses can be made of the selections on the two discs. The selections can be taught as texts in themselves, and they can be used to supplement the teaching of literary selections in the anthology proper. For example, while reading

Gayl Jones's *Corregidora*, students might be asked to listen to such classic 1940s and 1950s blues as "Rock Me, Baby" and "(What Did I Do to be So) Black and Blue" to understand more fully the kind of music the blueswoman protagonist Ursa produced or to listen to Aretha Franklin's or another artist's version of "Trouble in Mind" to speculate about the relationship of the musical qualities of the blues tradition to the themes and issues that Jones's novel addresses. Here are several other ways to use the Audio Companion:

- Use Stevie Wonder's "Living for the City" to illustrate its role as a late-twentieth-century precursor to hip hop music. Ask students to research (individually or in small groups) and share contemporary hip hop lyrics and performances that help trace the evolution of sociopolitical spoken word traditions from "Living for the City" or earlier musical texts.
- Assign group or individual comparative research projects that involve one or more Audio Companion selections and a corresponding text in any genre of the students' choice.
- For student research projects on the Black Arts era, assign group or individual comparative research projects that involve one or more Audio Companion selections and archival or historical materials about a black theater company (e.g., the Negro Ensemble Company or the Free Southern Theatre).
- Assign group or individual comparative research projects that involve one or more Audio Companion selections and a selection that appears in the anthology but not on the CDs. Ask students to present the issue of "lowbrow" or grass-roots poetry for action (orature) versus "highbrow" or elite poetry for distinction (literature).
- Assign individual or group projects that require students to find, analyze, and share visual images and/or film footage to supplement Audio Companion selections. Examples include a Marvin Gaye video, which would have been one of the earliest music videos, and footage of break-dancing to illustrate performance based on the "breaks" within song tracks.

Bibliography

Most of the articles and books listed here have been published since 1991. For a bibliography of earlier scholarship on black vernacular traditions, see the *Guide for Instructors* of the first edition of *NAFAM*. The items listed below discuss multiple forms of African American vernacular musical and verbal discourses. For texts that treat one specific genre, author, or text, see the bibliography in that section.

Allen, Richard. *A Collection of Hymns and Spiritual Songs: From Various Authors*. Philadelphia: Printed by T. L. Plowman, 1801.

Austin, Hilary Mac, and Kathleen Thompson, eds. *The Face of Our Past: Images of Black Women from Colonial America to the Present*. Bloomington: Indiana UP, 1999.

Carruth, Hayden. *Sitting In: Selected Writings on Jazz, Blues, and Related Topics*. Iowa City: U of Iowa P, 1993.

Cohn, Lawrence, ed. *Nothing but the Blues: The Music and the Musicians*. New York: Abbeville, 1993.

Conyers, James L. Jr., ed. *African American Jazz and Rap: Social and Philosophical Examinations of Black Expressive Behavior*. Jefferson, NC: McFarland, 2001.

———. "Africana Cosmology, Ethos, and Rap: A Social Study of Black Popular Culture." In Conyers, *African American Jazz and Rap*. 180–97.

Dawson, Nancy J. "Can You Sing Jazz? Perception and Appreciation of Jazz Music among African American Young Adults." In Conyers, *African American Jazz and Rap*. 201–10.

Dorsey, Learthen. " 'And All That Jazz' Has African Roots!" In Conyers, *African American Jazz and Rap*. 35–54.

Floyd, Samuel A. Jr. "Troping the Blues: From Spirituals to the Concert Hall." *Black Music Research Journal* 13 (1993): 31–51.

Fulmer, Douglas. "String Band Traditions: Black String Bands, Banjo, Fiddle, Mandolin and Guitar." *American Visions* 10 (1995): 46.

Jones, Kellie, Thelma Golden, and Chrissie Iles. *Lorna Simpson*. London; New York: Phaidon, 2002.

McMichael, Robert K. "We Insist—Freedom Now!: Black Moral Authority, Jazz, and the Changeable Shape of Whiteness." *American Music* 16 (1998): 375–427.

Olney, James. " 'I Ain't Gonna Be No Topsy' Because 'Paris Is My Old Kentucky Home': Stephen Foster's Cultural Role in American Music." *The Southern Review* 37 (2001): 155–66.

Ostendorf, Berndt. "Celebration or Pathology? Commodity or Art? The Dilemma of African-American Expressive Culture." *Black Music Research Journal* 20 (2000): 217–37.

Painter, Nell Irvin. "Representing Truth: Sojourner Truth's Ways of Knowing and Becoming Known." *Journal of American History* 81 (1994): 461–92.

Reed, Teresa L. *The Holy Profane: Religion in Black Popular Music*. Lexington: UP of Kentucky, 2003.

Shaw, Arnold. *Black Popular Music in America: From the Spirituals, Minstrels, and Ragtime to Soul, Disco, and Hip-Hop*. New York: Schirmer, 1986.

Southern, Eileen. *Music of Black Americans*. 3rd ed. New York: Norton, 1997.

Spencer, Jon Michael. *Re-Searching Black Music*. Knoxville: U of Tennessee P, 1996.

Sylvan, Robin. *Traces of the Spirit: The Religious Dimensions of Popular Music*. New York: New York UP, 2002.

Sundquist, Eric J. *The Hammers of Creation: Folk Culture in Modern African American Fiction*. Athens: U of Georgia P, 1992.

Ward, Jerry W. "To Shatter Innocence: Teaching African American Poetry." In Marianna W. Davis and Sharon Pineault-Burke, eds., *Teaching African American Literature: Theory and Practice*. New York: Routledge, 1998. 141–50.

Weheliye, Alexander. "In the Mix: Hearing the Souls of Black Folk." *Amerikastudien/American Studies* 45 (2000): 535–54.

Willis, Deborah. *Lorna Simpson*. San Francisco: Friends of Photography, 1992.

———, ed. *Picturing Us: African American Identity in Photography*. New York: New P, 1994.

Wright, Lee Alfred. *Identity, Family, and Folklore in African American Literature*. New York: Garland, 1995.

The Literature of Slavery and Freedom, 1746–1865

Jupiter Hammon

1711–1806?

Works in the Anthology

"An Evening Thought" (1760)
"An Address to Miss Phillis Wheatley" (1778)

Other Works

"Address to the Negroes in the State of New York" (speech, 1786)

Themes

- Blacks' capacity for Christian piety
- Virtues of Afro-Protestantism and evangelicalism
- Abolitionism
- Community of early-nineteenth-century Africans and African Americans writing in the United States
- Celebration of African intelligence and piety
- Implicit call for black intellectual development

Characteristics

- Poems apparently represent same tradition as early Christian hymns
- Antiphonal harmonies
- Subversion of conventional ideas about Christianity

Questions

- Why does Hammon address a poem to Phillis Wheatley? Do you sense any urgency in his lines to her? If so, how does he achieve that effect?
- Use the selections by Hammon to support or refute the oft-debated contention that his poetry is more reactionary than revolutionary in that it calls for black spiritual acquiescence to the status quo rather than vehement resistance to it.
- What do Hammon's poems suggest about the function of Christianity in sociopolitical as well as religious contexts in New England? What do they suggest about the process of Christianization among African people in colonial New England?

Bibliography

Richards, Phillip M. "Nationalist Themes in the Preaching of Jupiter Hammon." *Early American Literature* 25 (1990): 123–39.

Seeman, Erik R. "'Justise must take phase': Three African Americans Speak of Religion in Eighteenth-Century New England." *William and Mary Quarterly* 56 (1999): 393–95.

Venture Smith

1729?–1805

Works in the Anthology

A Narrative of the Life and Adventures of Venture, A Native of Africa (1798)

Themes

- Free but tragic childhood in Africa versus bound and tragic adulthood in colonial America
- Devastation of the Middle Passage
- Cruelties of slavery in the African diaspora

- Argument for abolition
- Personal, political, and social costs of not educating slaves
- Black economic motivations, slavery notwithstanding
- Existential crises
- African devotion to family

Characteristics

- Narrative was dictated to and transcribed by a white amanuensis
- Emphasis on pathos of slavery through sentimental conventions
- Dispassionate, detached tone—perhaps because dictated

Teaching Strategies

- *A Narrative of the Life and Adventures of Venture* is one of very few texts in the anthology not written by a person of African descent. Engage students in a discussion of its rhetorical differences from the overwhelming number of self-authored *NAFAM* texts, *if* they find that differences do exist. Ask them to speculate about the editors' decision to include it.
- As a dictated slave narrative *A Narrative of the Life and Adventures of Venture* differs from other slave narratives included in the anthology. Review the conventions of the more familiar genre with students; then ask them to list ways that dictated antebellum narratives differ from their self-authored counterparts. You might use this discussion as a springboard for considering larger questions central to the study of autobiography and, further under that rubric, the study of slave narratives: self-representation, truth value, doublespeak, memory, mediation, and so on.

Questions

- Review the headnote to Smith in the anthology, and expand on the comparison there of Smith to Equiano. How do the narratives of these two African-born slaves differ? To what degree do you think their geographical locations outside Africa determine the kinds of details each reports in his story?
- Compare Smith's accounts of his experiences in the Middle Passage with reconstructions of the Middle Passage by twentieth-century writers Clarence Major and Robert Hayden, who obviously did not live through it. What historical experiences seem to inform the modern-day writers' imaginative revisions of the transport into bondage?
- Like the narrator of Frederick Douglass's *Narrative*, Smith's narrator falls into conflict with a white man and ends up in a one-on-one fight

with him. Review Douglass's fight with Covey, and contrast it with the experience that left Smith's narrator hanging on the gallows. In what ways are the two men's experiences differently represented? The "truth" of what happened aside, what seems to drive the differences in these accounts?

- Compare and contrast Smith's account of purchasing first himself and then his immediate family with Elizabeth Keckley's account of her self-purchase and subsequent manumission. How do the temporal situations of these two slave autobiographers seem to influence the tone each uses? What role does the author's gender seem to play in the respective narrators' efforts to buy themselves?
- Support or refute the contention that the dispassionate, straightforward tone of Smith's *Narrative* is specifically a result of its mediation as a dictated text rather than any desire of Smith's to represent himself as detached or unmoved by the tragedies he suffered.

Bibliography

Desrochers, Robert E. Jr. " 'Not Fade Away': The Narrative of Venture Smith, an African American in the Early Republic." *Journal of American History* 84 (1997): 40–67.

Lucy Terry

c. 1730–1821

Works in the Anthology

"Bars Fight"

Themes

- Intercultural and interracial conflicts
- Racialized disputes over land and territory
- Violent resistance to colonial rule
- Violent assault on women

Characteristics

- Native-born African who entered colonial America as a child through the Middle Passage
- Counternarration, subversion, signifying discourse
- Revision of the (Indian) captivity narrative genre

- Vernacular tradition of oral storytelling
- Traditional *belles lettres* rhyming tetrameter couplets

Teaching Strategies

- Terry's poem survived in the vernacular for over a century before being published in a volume; this ballad was composed to record for posterity a significant event in the life of her community: a fight between Native Americans and New England settlers.
- Historical records of her prominence in the community at Deerfield, Massachusetts, and of legal and judicial experiences she had there indicate that Terry fulfilled a number of social roles: Christian, orator, historian, storyteller, mother, wife, and activist.

Questions

- Given that (contrary to Western ideals of "art for art's sake") African aesthetics proverbially posit that nothing artful not also be useful or functional, speculate about purposes Terry might have intended her poem to serve in colonial New England.
- List and discuss reasons scholars might think it important to celebrate the recovery of the fragment of Terry's poem.
- Terry's legal battles reputedly included a racial discrimination case filed against Williams College for rejecting her son's application for admission. Are there rhetorical tropes or features (e.g., tone, theme, or image) in "Bars Fight" that you think lend validity to this legend?

Bibliography

Langley, April. "Lucy Terry Prince: The Cultural and Literary Legacy of Africana Womanism." *The Western Journal of Black Studies* 25 (2001): 153–63.

Smith, Barbara. "Teaching about Black Women Writers." *Women's Studies Quarterly* 25 (1997): 100–3.

Olaudah Equiano

c. 1745–1797

Works in the Anthology

The Interesting Narrative of the Life of Olaudah Equiano, or Gustavas Vassa, the African, Written by Himself, Vol. 1, Chaps. 1–4 (1789)

Themes

- African humanity, intelligence, and self-actualization
- Savagery of the Middle Passage
- Moral outrage at the atrocities of chattel slavery
- Argument for immediate and categorical abolition of slavery
- Physical and psychological transition from self as property to proper-tied self
- Conversion to Christianity
- Blacks' capacity for assimilation into white society and culture
- Blacks' capacity for successful economic development
- Idyllic portrait of Ibo life and culture

Characteristics

- First-hand account of Africa, African slavery, and the Middle Passage
- *Narrative* is neither ghostwritten nor white-endorsed.
- Hybrid text as slave narrative, abolitionist treatise, sea adventure, rags-to-riches story
- Commitment to storytelling; inaugurates some elements of African American vernacular storytelling tradition
- Engagement with white readers through sentimentalization of slaves' plight

Questions

- Unlike Frederick Douglass and other formerly enslaved autobiographers, Equiano does not locate the origins of his freedom or selfhood in an acquisition of literary skills. To what does he attribute his sense of self? How does this difference from the American-born authors affect your understanding of the formation of identity among enslaved blacks?
- Given that he spent so little time in the United States, why do you suppose the editors decided to include Equiano in *NAFAM*?
- Compare and contrast Equiano's *Narrative* with selections from other non-U.S.-born authors in the anthology (e.g., Caryl Phillips and Jamaica Kincaid). In what ways do their texts overlap differently than they do with texts by U.S.-born blacks?
- Why does Equiano include his manumission papers in his *Narrative*? What difference from U.S.-born slaves like Frederick Douglass does Equiano imply about himself with the inclusion of these papers?

Bibliography

Hinds, Elizabeth Jane Wall. "The Spirit of Trade: Olaudah Equiano's Conversion, Legalism, and the Merchant's *Life*." *African American Review* 32 (1998): 635–36.

Ito, Akiyo. "Olaudah Equiano and the New York Artisans: The First American Edition of *The Interesting Narrative of the Life of Olaudah Equiano, or Gustavus Vassa, the African*." *Early American Literature* 32 (1997): 82–102.

Potkay, Adam, Srinivas Aravamudan, and Roxann Wheeler. "Teaching Equiano's *Interesting Narrative*." *Eighteenth-Century Studies* 34 (2001): 601–25.

Sabino, Robin, and Jennifer Hall. "The Path Not Taken: Cultural Identity in the *Interesting Life* of Olaudah Equiano." *MELUS* 24 (1999): 5–19.

Phillis Wheatley

1753?–1784

Works in the Anthology

"Preface" (1773)
["Letter Sent by the Author's Master to the Publisher"] (1772)
["To the Publick"] (1773)
"To Mæcenas" (1773)
"To the University of Cambridge, in New-England" (1773)
"On Being Brought from Africa to America" (1773)
"On the Death of the Rev. Mr. George Whitefield" (1773)
"To the Right Honourable William, Earl of Dartmouth" (1773)
"On Imagination" (1773)
"To S. M., a Young *African* Painter, on Seeing His Works" (1773)
"To Samson Occom" (1774)
"To His Excellency General Washington" (1776)

Other Works

Poems on Various Subjects, Religious and Moral (1773)
Liberty and Peace (1784)

Themes

- Power of literacy and literature to soothe human suffering
- Leadership in the struggle for human and civil rights
- Duties of a sovereign, democratic society to protect human and civil rights
- Oppression of Native Americans
- Natural rights for Africans
- Human desire for independence
- Literary authority
- New England society and American revolutionary zeal
- Methodism, Christianity, African spirituality

Characteristics

- Puritan
- First African to publish poems
- First African to publish a book in English
- Often begins with invocations to the Muses
- Allusions to figures of Greek and Roman mythologies

Teaching Strategies

- Wheatley's milestones include an infamous "trial" (i.e., examination) by prominent white men; a marriage to a free black man; an early death (December 5, 1784). Remind students that before Wheatley faced these hardships, her ambition or audacity and her poetic accomplishments had led her to secure an education that few people in eighteenth-century Europe, England, or the American colonies had. Engage them in a discussion about shifting—and persistent—ideas about the intelligibility and educability of people of African descent, in place even before Wheatley was brought to the New World, throughout the nineteenth century, through *Brown v. Board of Education*, through *The Bell Curve*.
- Remind students of sociopolitical issues operative during the era of the American Revolution, emphasizing that context as an added impetus for Wheatley's passionate arguments for human freedom. Ask students to enumerate parallels they find between the debates America presented to Britain regarding its liberty and the debates both free and enslaved Americans presented to colonial white America regarding their right to the same.

Questions

- What themes and conventions articulate Wheatley's position as precursor to black poets after her? How do her poems anticipate later poets like Langston Hughes, Gwendolyn Brooks, and Rita Dove? Speculate on the reasons for Wheatley's circumvention of the personal voice and first-person singular pronoun in her poems.
- Identify in Wheatley's poetry covert responses to charges that, as an African, she was naturally unintelligent and unintelligible.
- Read Jupiter Hammon's poem dedicated to Wheatley in the context of Wheatley's own poetry. What qualities of Wheatley's poetry seem most to have influenced Hammon's poetic style and sensibility?
- Like Lucy Terry's poem "Bars Fight," the poetry of Wheatley reflects multiple cultural traditions. Compare and contrast the selections by the two poets to outline some of the cultural contexts in which early black women writers were immersed.
- Research the allusions to Western mythology in Wheatley's poems. Do they seem to hold particular significance in poems by an African American woman? What do these rich allusions suggest about Wheatley's unique position as an educated, African-born slave woman?
- What aesthetic philosophy emerges in "On Imagination," "To Mæcenas," and "To S. M., a Young *African* Painter"? According to Wheatley in these poems, what spiritual elements of human imagination compel the production of art?
- Based on the evidence of her poetry, what can one infer about the extent of Wheatley's education? How do her educational accomplishments affect the European and colonial view of the period that blacks are incapable of learning?
- Examine Wheatley's development of Protestant ideals in "On the Death of the Rev. Mr. George Whitefield." How do the sermonic elements in this poem compare with those used by C. L. Franklin and Martin Luther King Jr. (on the Audio Companion)?
- Review the anthology's headnote to Wheatley. What details of her personal life can readers discern in "To the University of Cambridge," "On Being Brought from Africa to America," and "To the Right Honourable William, Earl of Dartmouth"?
- Based on your knowledge of late-eighteenth-century New England's cultural norms, what risks do you think Wheatley took in having the speaker of "To the University of Cambridge" identify herself as "An Ethiop"? What does the slave poet stand to gain by reminding Harvard students of their freedoms and their privileges?
- Do you read race pride in Wheatley's poetry? If so, pinpoint specific passages that reveal it.

Bibliography

Bassard, Katherine Clay. *Spiritual Interrogations: Culture, Gender, and Community in Early African American Women's Writings*. Princeton, NJ: Princeton UP, 1999.

Gates, Henry Louis Jr. *The Trials of Phillis Wheatley: America's First Black Poet and Encounters with the Founding Fathers*. New York: Basic/Civitas, 2003.

Herrnstein, Richard J., and Charles Murray. *The Bell Curve: Intelligence and Class Structure in American Life*. New York: Simon & Schuster, 1996.

Jordan, June. "The Difficult Miracle of Black Poetry in America, or Something Like a Sonnet for Phillis Wheatley." In Joanne M. Braxton and Andrée Nicola Mclaughlin, eds., *Wild Women in the Whirlwind*. New Brunswick, NJ: Rutgers UP, 1990. 22–34.

Shields, John C. "Phillis Wheatley's Struggle for Freedom in Her Poetry and Prose." In John C. Shields, ed., *The Collected Works of Phillis Wheatley*. New York: Oxford UP, 1988. 229–70.

Willard, Carla. "Wheatley's Turns of Praise: Heroic Entrapment and the Paradox of Revolution." *American Literature* 67 (1995): 233–56.

David Walker

1785–1830

Works in the Anthology

David Walker's Appeal in Four Articles, Together with a Preamble, to the Coloured Citizens of the World, Preamble, Chap. 1 (1829)

Other Works

David Walker's Appeal to the Coloured Citizens of the World, ed. Peter Hinks (2000)

Themes

- Social, political, and economic inequalities based on racial differences
- Christian theology
- Call for armed resistance to oppression

- U.S. slavery versus African and ancient slavery
- Abolition of chattel slavery
- Program for international black spiritual, political, and economic growth
- Exposé and denunciation of international white supremacy across time
- Interracial marriage

Characteristics

- Jeremiadic, unexpurgated, excoriating rhetoric
- Militant black nationalist position
- Parodies the structure and arguments of the Constitution to condemn tyranny
- Chronicles history of slavery from ancient times
- Invocation of the Founding Fathers

Teaching Strategies

- Require students to research and summarize the position on Africans made by Thomas Jefferson in *Notes on the State of Virginia*. Then in class discuss Walker's interpretation of Jefferson's writing. How persuasive do they find Walker's contentions about Jefferson as "one of the great characters as ever lived among the whites"? Do they read this judgment as contradictory to other conclusions Walker reaches about Jefferson? Why or why not?

Questions

- How does Walker's 1829 *Appeal* contrast with the extant versions of Sojourner Truth's 1851 speech calling for women's rights?
- Trace the impact of Walker's *Appeal* on the rhetorical tradition of black (male) resistance to oppression, from Martin Delany's *Condition* through Eldridge Cleaver's *Soul on Ice*. What other texts in *NAFAM* seem to you to descend from the *Appeal*?
- Summarize Walker's chronicle of slavery from ancient Western history. How apt or persuasive do you find the analogies he draws between that history and early-nineteenth-century U.S. slavery?
- Summarize the portrait of God that Walker draws in the *Appeal* and compare and contrast it with the vision of God that Maria Stewart draws in her Franklin Hall lecture and *Religion and the Pure Principles*. How do their Afro-Protestant deities differ from the image of God drawn in Anglo-American texts of the same period?
- Can Walker's *Appeal* rightly be said to argue for what we currently

identify as affirmative action? If so, specify the points in the text where it does so. How do these points compare or contrast with a case made for affirmative action in Martin Delany's *Condition*?

- Review the slave narratives by Venture Smith and Olaudah Equiano, and debate whether or not they support Walker's claims about African slavery.
- Support or refute the contention that Walker's stance on interracial marriage contradicts the overall argument of the *Appeal*.

Bibliography

Asukile, Thabiti. "The All-Embracing Black Nationalist Theories of David Walker's *Appeal*." *The Black Scholar* 29 (1999): 16–25.

Hinks, Peter. *To Awaken My Afflicted Brethren: David Walker and the Problem of Antebellum Slave Resistance*. University Park: Pennsylvania State UP, 1997.

Jefferson, Thomas. *Notes on the State of Virginia*. 1801. Ed. William Peden. Chapel Hill: U of North Carolina P, 1995.

George Moses Horton

1797?–1883?

Works in the Anthology

"The Lover's Farewell" (1829)
"On Hearing of the Intention of a Gentleman to Purchase the Poet's Freedom" (1829)
"Division of an Estate" (1845)
"The Creditor to His Proud Debtor" (1845)
"George Moses Horton, Myself" (1865)

Other Works

The Hope of Liberty (poems, 1829)
The Poetical Works of George M. Horton (1854)
Naked Genius (poems, 1865)

Themes

- Romantic love
- Christianity

- Pathos of death and loss
- Horrors and injustices of chattel slavery
- Value of poetry in elevating and redeeming the human spirit

Characteristics

- Wrote (mostly love) lyrics for hire, bought by University of North Carolina students
- Wrote in bondage until freed by the Thirteenth Amendment
- Doublespeak, subversion, and irony: the writer as trickster

Questions

- Very few of Horton's poems explicitly address slavery. Read "The Lover's Farewell," "On Hearing of the Intention of a Gentleman to Purchase the Poet's Freedom," and "Division of an Estate" and comment on the tacit and understated critique of slavery in these poems as well as on their more overt condemnation of the peculiar institution.
- Some scholars have suggested that most of Horton's poetry is indistinguishable from that of the white poets of his day and place. Do you take such a comment to be a compliment or an insult? On what criteria do you base your response? Locate one or two poems by antebellum southern white poets, and compare and contrast their poems with Horton's. Does reading specific poems by white (male) poets of Horton's day alter your opinion? If so, how? Why?

Bibliography

Pitts, Reginald. " 'Let us desert this friendless place': George Moses Horton in Philadelphia." *Journal of Negro History* 80 (1995): 145–57.

Sherman, Joan R., ed. *The Black Bard of North Carolina: George Moses Horton*. Chapel Hill: U of North Carolina P, 1997.

Sojourner Truth

1797–1883

Works in the Anthology

"Ar'n't I a Woman?" Speech to the Women's Rights Convention in Akron, Ohio, 1851 (two versions): From *The Anti-Slavery Bugle*, June 21, 1851; from *Narrative of Sojourner Truth*, 1878

Other Works

> *The Narrative of Sojourner Truth* (1850, 1878)
> *The Book of Life* (autobiography, 1875)

Themes

- Women's rights versus the Cult of True Womanhood
- Abolition of slavery
- Civil and human rights
- Enslaved motherhood
- Religions, spirituality, Christianity
- Race relations among abolitionists

Characteristics

- *Narrative* is dictated, rather than self-authored
- Vernacular traditions of community leadership, storytelling, testimonial, signifying
- Freedom fighter, extemporaneous orator, itinerant preacher, protofeminist, labor organizer

Teaching Strategies

- To broaden students' introduction to Truth, provide them with Harriet Beecher Stowe's "Sojourner Truth, the Libyan Sibyl" (included in Truth's 1878 *Narrative*) and require them to read the Frances Gage version of the text of Truth's speech—both of which have significantly contributed to the legends and myths about this author. (For more on these legends, see texts listed in the bibliography for Truth.) Then ask students to locate and bring in some of the extant photographs made of Truth. Discuss with students the differences in these various texts, with efforts to generate a fuller, more "composite" portrait of Truth.

Questions

- Compare and contrast *The Narrative of Sojourner Truth* with *A Narrative of the Life and Adventures of Venture,* another dictated slave narrative included in *NAFAM.* Examine these two narratives alongside the self-authored *Narrative of the Life of Frederick Douglass* and *Incidents in the Life of a Slave Girl.* Discuss differences among these texts that fall along the lines of literacy, gender, class, and temporal and geographical settings. What do such differences signify about the slave narrative tradition?

Bibliography

Accomando, Christina. *"The Regulations of Robbers": Legal Fictions of Slavery and Resistance*. Columbus: Ohio State UP, 2002.

Douglass-Chin, Richard. *Preacher Woman Sings the Blues: The Autobiographies of Nineteenth-Century African American Evangelists*. Columbia: U of Missouri P, 2001.

Mandziuk, Roseann M., and Suzanne Pullon Fitch. "The Rhetorical Construction of Sojourner Truth." *The Southern Communication Journal* 66 (2001): 120–38.

McCarthy, Nick. "Authority, Orality, and Specificity: Resisting Inscription in Sojourner Truth's 'Ar'n't I a Woman?'" *SAGE: A Scholarly Journal on Black Women* 9 (1995): 30–36.

Painter, Nell I. *Sojourner Truth: A Life, A Symbol*. New York: Norton, 1996.

Truth, Sojourner. *Narrative of Sojourner Truth; A Bondswoman of Olden Time*. 1878. Ed. Jeffrey C. Stewart. New York: Oxford, 1991.

Wortham, Anne. "Sojourner Truth: Itinerant Truth-Teller." *World and I* 15 (2000): 291–93.

Maria W. Stewart

1803–1879

Works in the Anthology

Religion and the Pure Principles of Morality, the Sure Foundation on Which We Must Build, Introduction (1831)
"Lecture Delivered at the Franklin Hall" (1835)

Other Works

The Productions of Mrs. Maria W. Stewart (1835)
Meditations from the Pen of Mrs. Maria W. Stewart (1879)

Themes

- African American racial uplift and self-determination
- Cult of True Womanhood versus women's rights
- Right of women to preach and exhort Christianity

- Application of revolutionary values to African American freedom
- National, collective, and individual moral reform
- Economic reform through educational reform
- Egalitarianism of the Gospel
- Abolition of slavery
- Prophesy of millennialism
- Critique of American betrayal of revolutionary promises to citizens

Characteristics

- First woman to address audiences composed of both men and women
- Protégé of David Walker
- Jeremiadic, eschatological, fiery, impassioned rhetoric
- Cites scriptural support for all contentions
- Debates virtues of the Cult of True Womanhood as a widow (of a military officer) without children
- *The Productions* consist of political and religious speeches, prayers, and meditations
- Autobiographical confession and religious confession
- Hybrid of sacred and secular issues
- Vernacular usages of confrontational direct address, signifying, and conversational rhythms

Teaching Strategies

- Play one or more of the sermonic texts included on the Audio Companion and ask students to enumerate aspects of Stewart's Franklin Hall lecture that participate in the African American vernacular tradition of sermon making.
- Play one or more of the songs for social change included on the Audio Companion and discuss with students aspects of Stewart's Franklin Hall lecture that draw on African American vernacular conventions to inspire social activism.
- Play one or more of the hip hop selections included on the Audio Companion and ask students to enumerate elements of Stewart's Franklin Hall lecture that position it as foreshadowing the "teacher rap" conventions that have recently developed in African American vernacular rap and hip hop traditions.

Questions

- As a literary precursor to later black women writers like Frances E. W. Harper and Harriet E. Wilson, what themes and tropes does

Stewart establish for African American women writing after her? How does her Franklin Hall address compare with the speech by Sojourner Truth included in *NAFAM*?

- It is often noted that Stewart was highly influenced by David Walker. In what ways does the rhetorical style of his *Appeal* compare with her Franklin Hall lecture? What gendered differences, if any, do you find between their respective texts? What aspects of Stewart's writings, if any, suggest that she was aware that her audience might object to her stepping out of "woman's place" onto the lecture platform?

- Walker's *Appeal* is thought to have incited slave revolts by Nat Turner and Denmark Vesey. Are there characteristics of Stewart's writings that might have inspired slave revolts as well? Are there characteristics of Stewart's writings that might rather have mollified slaves not into complacency but perhaps into something more like King's notion of civil disobedience?

- Contrast Stewart's deployment of Christian scripture to substantiate claims in her fervent texts with Martin Luther King Jr.'s in his "Letter from Birmingham Jail" over one hundred years later.

- Research cultural and historical differences between the Boston in which Phillis Wheatley wrote and the city a generation later, in which Stewart wrote. What sociohistorical factors seem to have influenced the theology as well as the form and tone of these women's religious writings?

Bibliography

Hankins, Gail A. "In the Beginning . . . Maria W. Stewart: Forerunner of American Women Orators." *Women and Language* 15 (1992): 20–25.

Moody, Joycelyn. *Sentimental Confessions: Spiritual Narratives of Nineteenth-Century African American Women*. Athens: U of Georgia P, 2000.

Martin R. Delany

1812–1885

Works in the Anthology

The Condition, Elevation, Emigration and Destiny of the Colored People of the United States (1852), Chaps. 1–2, 5, 23–24

Other Works

> "Declaration of the Principles of the National Emigration Convention"
>   (1854)
> *Blake, or the Huts of America* (novel, 1861)
> *The Origin of the Races and Color* (1879)

Themes

- African American education and/or self-determination
- Struggle for black independence
- Constructions of gender and motherhood
- Migration, emigration, and (anti)colonization
- Resistance to racialized oppression and disenfranchisement of blacks
- Brutalities of chattel slavery
- Failure of U.S. antebellum abolitionist movement

Characteristics

- Delany worked in more than a dozen different areas of professional expertise: dentist, writer, editor, medical doctor (professionally trained, including a short stint at Harvard Medical School before being asking to leave), political theorist, abolitionist, geographical explorer, scientist, philosopher, diplomat, civil rights activist, ethnologist, and politician.
- During the Civil War, he further served as army major, surgeon, and recruiter.
- Passionate, often acerbic tone
- Philosophical, dialogic, contemplative style

Teaching Strategies

- Delany has been called the "Father of Black Nationalism." Also, his 1859 use of the phrase "Africa for Africans" is the first recorded use of it (see Ogunleye). You might guide students through *NAFAM* to later uses of the same phrase, especially by Marcus Garvey, or related phrases invoked by black nationalist leaders during the Harlem Renaissance and the Black Arts era. Have students debate the pros and cons of the various "return to Africa" movements.

Questions

- On what textual evidence might Delany's *Condition* be said to argue for affirmative action?
- Compare Delany's use of the word *sympathy* with other antebellum

writers' use of it and with Paul Dunbar's in the post-Emancipation poem of the same name.

- Contrast Delany's position on the impact of black motherhood on African American self-actualization with Sojourner Truth's, Harriet Jacobs's, and Frances Harper's.
- Review the selections by Frederick Douglass and speculate about the assertions in *The Condition* that might have led to the split between these two men as leaders, journalists, activists, and abolitionists.
- Summarize the tenets of Delany's *Condition* that render its analysis of African Americans' condition in the antebellum era more class based than race based.
- Clarify Delany's distinction between policy and nature in Chapter 2 of *The Condition*. In that same chapter, he contends that Africans were not enslaved because of their race but because of their personality. How might other antebellum writers—black and not—respond to these claims?

Bibliography

Crane, Gregg D. "The Lexicon of Rights, Power, and Community in *Blake*: Martin R. Delany's Dissent from *Dred Scott*." *American Literature* 68 (1996): 527–54.

Ogunleye, Tolagbe. "Dr. Martin Robison Delany, 19th-Century Africana Womanist: Reflections on His Avant-Garde Politics Concerning Gender, Colorism, and Nation Building." *Journal of Black Studies* 28 (1998): 628–40.

Harriet Jacobs

c. 1813–1897

Works in the Anthology

Incidents in the Life of a Slave Girl, Preface, Chaps. 1–2, 5, 10, 14, 17, 21, 29, 39, 40, 41 (1861)

Themes

- Peculiar horrors of slavery for female slaves of all ages, for women in different stages of life, especially enslaved mothers
- Sexual and physical violence perpetrated on enslaved women and men

- Slavery's psychological and emotional rupture of black families
- Abolition
- Relationships between antebellum white women and enslaved women
- Fugitive Slave Law
- Slaves' diverse forms of resistance to bondage
- Dispute with Harriet Beecher Stowe
- Enslaved women's exploitation of sex acts and other endeavors to gain freedom for themselves and their family members
- Revision of tragic mulatto/a stereotype
- African American networking
- Slavery's corruption of the ideals of the Cult of True Womanhood: Christian chastity, devotion, domesticity, and submissiveness

Characteristics

- Only extant self-authored antebellum enslaved woman's narrative
- Often sentimental and emotional, sometimes ironic and acerbic tone
- Hybrid of conventions of the (male) slave narrative, the seduction tale/fallen woman narrative, the domestic novel
- Subverts prevailing antebellum feminine model of the "true woman": a domestic, self-sacrificing, pious woman of the white middle class

Teaching Strategies

- Guide students through a discussion of the implications of Jacobs's self-authored Preface by having them contemplate the complexities of writing to readers who were not used to accepting the authority or authenticity of African Americans' perspectives. Have them compare Jacobs's Preface with those by other writers who argued for the truthfulness of their renditions, including Phillis Wheatley and Frederick Douglass.
- "Students from the Southeast of the United States might take an excursion to Edenton, North Carolina, to observe how the town is only now beginning to make visitors aware of the historical circumstances that surrounded Harriet Jacobs" (Herzog 141).
- Like Olaudah Equiano, Frederick Douglass, William Wells Brown, and other male slave autobiographers, Jacobs employs many slave narrative conventions. Thus a review of these conventions would be helpful to (re-)orient students to the genre. However, unlike the abovementioned authors, Jacobs focuses on sexual oppression within slavery as she exposes the precariousness and vulnerability of women within that institution. To situate *Incidents* among other antebellum slave narratives, ask students to summarize how Jacobs's account of

her escape differs from those of the male autobiographers'. They might also begin by distinguishing the various ways that slavery affects white society, men of diverse races, and women of diverse races.

Questions

- What are the unique contributions of Jacobs's singular narrative to slaves' accounts of bondage across the literature of slavery? What does *Incidents* articulate that is unavailable in all other related texts?
- How does the representation of slavery in *Incidents* differ from that in other slaves' stories?
- How does the representation of freedom in *Incidents* differ from that in other slaves' stories?
- Discuss the implications and nuances of Jacobs's metaphor of the "loophole" of retreat.
- How does Jacobs illustrate and insinuate the disparity between white women's access to virtues mandated by the Cult of True Womanhood and enslaved women's? In what ways does she argue *against* the cultivation of such values?
- How does *Incidents* compare with literary texts by other early African American women writers, including Maria W. Stewart, Frances E. W. Harper, and Harriet E. Wilson. How do these writers' depictions of antebellum African American women's lives differ? What themes and stylistic features do they share?
- Identify the various genre conventions to which *Incidents* subscribes. What genre conventions seem to work in Jacobs's favor as an author? How do particular genre conventions seem to inhibit her writing, to restrict what she can write? In what ways do these limitations seem more integral to Jacobs's gender than to her choice of genre?
- Discuss Jacobs's choice of *war* as a metaphor to describe her struggle with Flint. How does she define *war*? How does she define *violence*?
- Discuss Jacobs's choice of *loophole* and *tomb* as contradictory metaphors to describe the garret in which she spent seven years.
- Discuss Jacobs's choice of Isaiah 32.9 as an epigraph for her autobiography. How does this passage anticipate religious attitudes she develops or reveals in *Incidents*? What does it reveal about the audience(s) Jacobs targets? About her rhetorical purposes?
- Examine Jacobs's Preface and discuss the implications of her insistence that *Incidents* "is no fiction" but that her descriptions do "fall far short of the facts."
- What rhetorical features and narrative details of *Incidents* reveal that Jacobs was restricted by the protocol of women's writing and literary propriety, by prohibitions against women's speaking of incidents that

violate "literary propriety"? For your answer, consider particularly Jacobs's bold representation of slaveholders in the chapter "The New Master and Mistress."

Bibliography

Accomando, Christina. "*The Regulations of Robbers*": *Legal Fictions of Slavery and Resistance*. Columbus: Ohio State UP, 2002.

Andrews, William L. "The Changing Moral Discourse of Nineteenth-Century African American Women's Autobiography: Harriet Jacobs and Elizabeth Keckley." In Sidonie Smith and Julia Watson, eds., *De/ Colonizing the Subject: The Politics of Gender in Women's Autobiography*. Minneapolis: U of Minnesota P, 1992. 225–41.

Barbeito, Felisa. "'Making Generations' in Jacobs, Larsen, and Hurston: A Genealogy of Black Women's Writing." *American Literature* 70 (1998): 365–96.

Blackford, Holly. "Figures of Orality: The Master, The Mistress, The Slave Mother in Harriet Jacobs's *Incidents in the Life of a Slave Girl: Written by Herself*." *Papers on Language & Literature* 37 (2001): 314–36.

Castronovo, Russ. "Incidents in the Life of a White Woman: Economies of Race and Gender in the Antebellum Nation." *American Literary History* 10 (1998): 239–66.

Greeson, Jennifer Rae. "The 'Mysteries and Miseries' of North Carolina: New York City, Urban Gothic Fiction, and *Incidents in the Life of a Slave Girl*." *American Literature* 73 (2001): 277–310.

Herzog, Kristin. "*Uncle Tom's Cabin* and *Incidents in the Life of a Slave Girl*: The Issue of Violence." Elizabeth Ammons and Susan Belasco, eds., *Approaches to Teaching Stowe's Uncle Tom's Cabin*. New York: MLA, 2000. 132–41.

Wesley, Marilyn C. "A Woman's Place: The Politics of Space in Harriet Jacobs's *Incidents in the Life of a Slave Girl*." *Women's Studies* 26 (1997): 59–73.

Yellin, Jean Fagan. "Harriet Jacobs's Family History." *American Literature* 66 (1994): 765–67.

Zafar, Rafia, and Deborah M. Garfield, eds. *Harriet Jacobs and* Incidents in the Life of a Slave Girl: *New Critical Essays*. Cambridge, UK: Cambridge UP, 1996.

William Wells Brown

1814?–1884

Works in the Anthology

Narrative of William Wells Brown, a Fugitive Slave, Chaps. 5–6 (1846)
Clotel; or, The President's Daughter, Chaps. 1–2, 4, 15, 19 (1850)

Other Works

Three Years in Europe (travelogue, 1852)
The Escape; or, A Leap to Freedom (drama, 1858)
The Black Man: His Antecedents, His Genius, and His Achievements
  (history chronicle, 1863)

Themes

- Struggle for freedom
- Slave intelligence and resistance to bondage
- Brutality of chattel slavery
- Harmful effects of slavery on American families, black and white
- Slavery's corruption of Christian values
- Tragic mulattas, fancy girls
- Miscegenation, adultery
- Dissipation and temperance
- Intraracial conflicts and classism among African Americans
- Hypocrisy of "free northern states"

Characteristics

- Brown was a prolific writer and thinker; prominent dramatist, editor, historian, social reform activist.
- Modest, plain, often sentimental style
- Self-effacing narrator
- Use of understatement as irony
- Humor, satire, pathos
- Dialogs that blend standard American English with African American vernacular English

Teaching Strategies

- Review with students the concepts of miscegenation and the figure of the "tragic mulatta."

- Consider sharing with students selected excerpts from Lydia Maria Child's *The Quadroon* to illustrate one white woman writer's treat-'ment of literature protesting miscegenation and the formation of the "mulatto" class. Ask students to identify ways that Brown's *Clotel* functions as a very close adaptation of Child's novel.

Questions

- How closely does Brown follow slave narrative conventions deployed by other fugitive slave authors of his day?
- How, and how much, does he shape the genre according to his particular rhetorical interests?
- How do autobiographical details in Brown's *Narrative* compare with the incidents and self-characterizations in *Narrative of the Life of Frederick Douglass* and Harriet Jacobs's *Incidents in the Life of a Slave Girl,* particularly in regard to honesty, racial solidarity, and explicit opposition to slavery?
- In what ways might Delany and his precursor David Walker be read as "counter-voices" to abolitionist texts by white authors like Harriet Beecher Stowe? (Carson 166)
- Identify some of the elements of the literary tradition of illustrating miscegenation that *Clotel* represents. In what ways does Brown's novel subvert that tradition?
- Support or refute the contention that while Clotel meets a tragic end as a result of discovering her African heritage, she does not suffer it passively.
- Genetics testing and DNA evidence in recent years have brought renewed fervor to the debate about Thomas Jefferson's relationship to Sally Hemings and her descendants. Ask students to research the current state of the debate and its implications for revisions of U.S. history.
- In what ways does the narrator of Brown's autobiography function as a trickster figure? Does the autobiographer depict any other characters in this role as well? Do Brown's tricksters perform the role to subvert domination by slaveholders or to practice domination over others? Are there other reasons the narrator (and other characters) performs as trickster?

Bibliography

Adeeko, Adeleke. "Signatures of Blood in William Wells Brown's 'Clotel.'" *Nineteenth-Century Contexts* 21 (1999): 115–35.

Berthold, Michael. "Cross-Dressing and Forgetfulness of Self in William Wells Brown's 'Clotel.' *College Literature* 20 (1993): 19–30.

Blair, Sara. "Feeling, Evidence, and the Work of Literary History: Response to DuCille." *American Literary History* 12 (2000): 463–67.

Carson, Sharon. "Africana Constellations: African American Studies and *Uncle Tom's Cabin*." Elizabeth Ammons and Susan Belasco, eds. *Approaches to Teaching Uncle Tom's Cabin*. New York: MLA, 2000. 162–71.

DuCille, Ann. "Where in the World Is William Wells Brown? Thomas Jefferson, Sally Hemings, and the DNA of African-American Literary History." *American Literary History* 12 (2000): 443–63.

Simmons, Ryan. "Naming Names: *Clotel* and *Behind the Scenes*." *CLA Journal* 43 (1999): 19–20.

Henry Highland Garnet

1815–1882

Works in the Anthology

"An Address to the Slaves of the United States of America" (delivered 1843)

Themes

- Exemplary black manhood
- African and African American leadership styles
- Abolition and the atrocities of slavery
- African American Christianity
- Armed resistance to involuntary servitude and bondage
- Advocacy of black emigration
- Slavery's corrupting properties

Characteristics

- Unabashed, impassioned revolutionary rhetoric
- Exaltation of leaders of early-nineteenth-century slave revolts
- Comparison of antebellum slaves with leaders of the American Revolution
- Call to resistance, "Call to Rebellion"

Questions

- Compare and contrast Garnet's speech with speeches of the same era made by Maria W. Stewart and Sojourner Truth. How are the respective addresses different according to gender? What themes and features do they share as antislavery texts?
- How does Garnet, a Presbyterian minister, use Christian ideas and traditions to his advantage?
- Speculate about the rhetorical effects of Garnet's inflammatory assertion that "Slaves' intellect has been destroyed as much as possible." How might such a statement arouse slaves' furor and resistance?
- Like many slave narrators, Garnet posits that in holding slaves, "The oppressors themselves have become involved in the ruin." What evidence does the "Address" offer to argue that slavery ruins slaveholders as well as slaves?

Bibliography

Butler Jones, Katherine. "Garnets, Diamonds and Other Black Jewels." *American Visions* 12 (1997): 42–44.

Victor Séjour

1817–1874

Works in the Anthology

"The Mulatto" (1837)

Other Works

"Le Retour de Napoléon" (poem, 1841)
Richard III (drama, 1852)

Themes

- Impact of miscegenation on mixed-race people
- Sexual violation of enslaved people
- Physical and psychological brutalities of slavery
- Slavery's devastation of families and family life
- Abolition of slavery

Characteristics

- Sentimental, melodramatic style
- Embedded narrative by a former slave told to first-person narrator

Questions

- Séjour introduces the theme of the tragic mulatto in "The Mulatto" before William Wells Brown develops it in *Clotel*. His short story also depicts miscegenation as psychological trauma. What role do time and place play in the differences among Brown's *Clotel*, Séjour's "The Mulatto," and Harriet E. Wilson's *Our Nig*? How do the authors' representations of gender identity affect each story?
- Compare Séjour's use of sentimental conventions with that of other early-nineteenth-century African Americans writing about slavery. For example, how does the melodrama of "The Mulatto" contrast with the sentimentalism of Harriet Jacobs's *Incidents in the Life of a Slave Girl*?
- The opening paragraph of "The Mulatto" situates the story outside the United States. What do the details of the embedded narrative reveal about slavery in other parts of the African diaspora?
- Compare Séjour's use of an elderly black man recounting a specific episode from slavery to a man removed from slavery with the use of very similar constructs fifty years later by Charles W. Chesnutt in "The Goophered Grapevine." How do the narrators differ from one another? How do you think the stories' different publication dates affect the representation of the embedded storytellers? To what do you attribute other significant differences in these two stories?

Bibliography

Haddox, Thomas F. "The 'Nous' of Southern Catholic Quadroons: Racial, Ethnic, and Religious Identity in *Les Cenelles*." *American Literature* 73 (2001): 757–78.

Perret, J. John. "Victor Séjour, Black Playwright from Louisiana." *The French Review* 57 (1983): 187–93.

Elizabeth Keckley

1818–1907

Works in the Anthology

Behind the Scenes; or, Thirty Years a Slave and Four Years in the White House, Preface, Chaps. 1–4 (1868)

Themes

- Blacks' self-determination and self-actualization
- Slaves' education in the "school of slavery"
- Peculiar plight of enslaved women, especially sexual violation
- Enslaved motherhood
- Slaves' resistance to bondage and brutality
- Christian hypocrisy
- Relationships between slaveholders and enslaved people
- Relationship between President Lincoln and enslaved people, partic- ularly the author
- Relationship between Mrs. Lincoln and Keckley
- Relationships between white women and black women
- Promise of the future for blacks as franchised U.S. citizens

Characteristics

- Doublespeak and subversion
- Marks shift from antebellum slave narrative issues to postbellum concerns
- Concentrates on relative benefits of slavery to slaves rather than on injurious effects
- Optimism about future eminence of the race
- Self-purchase and manumission as indicators of black self-reliance

Questions

- Keckley is one of the first former slaves to refer to slavery as a "school" wherein she and other slaves learned a range of survival skills and developed self-reliance. Compare and contrast the excerpt from her autobiography with *Up From Slavery*, in which Booker T. Washington also refers to slavery as a "school" to specify the source of his self-reliance.
- Compare and contrast slavewomen's experiences in bondage as rep-

resented before the Civil War by Harriet Jacobs and after the war by Keckley.

• Like Olaudah Equiano, Keckley uses her autobiography to chronicle the transition of her personal circumstances from capital to capitalist. Although the selections by the two authors do not include chapters that focus on their later lives as entrepreneurs, what details do you find in the selections that arguably foreshadow each respective author's change in fortunes?

Bibliography

Berthold, Michael. "Not 'Altogether' the 'History of Myself': Autobiographical Impersonality in Elizabeth Keckley's *Behind the Scenes. Or, Thirty Years a Slave and Four Years in the White House.*" *American Transcendental Quarterly* 13 (1999): 105–19.

Hoffert, Sylvia. "Jane Grey Swisshelm, Elizabeth Keckley, and the Significance of Race Consciousness in American Women's History." *Journal of Women's History* 13 (2001): 8–35.

Simmons, Ryan. "Naming Names: *Clotel* and *Behind the Scenes.*" *CLA Journal* 43 (1999): 19–20.

Sorisio, Carolyn. "Unmasking the Genteel Performer: Elizabeth Keckley's *Behind the Scenes* and the Politics of Public Wrath." *African American Review* 34 (2000): 19–38.

Frederick Douglass

1818–1895

Works in the Anthology

Narrative of the Life of Frederick Douglass, an American Slave, Written by Himself (1845)
"What to the Slave Is the Fourth of July?" (1853)
My Bondage and My Freedom, Chaps. 23–24 (1855)
Life and Times of Frederick Douglass, Part 2, Chap. 15; Part 3, Chap. 1 (1881)

Other Works

The Heroic Slave (novel, 1853)

Themes

- Horrors of slavery detailed with personal experience
- Mental, psychological, physical, and emotional ardor of living in bondage as property
- Fugitive slave status
- Slaves' faith in redemptive value of Christian principles
- Slaves' cultures, especially for physical and spiritual survival of bondage
- Race relations in antebellum and post-Emancipation United States
- Emancipatory quality of literacy
- Subversion of status quo of the slaveocracy

Characteristics

- Prolific writer and editor in multiple genres: autobiography, fiction, essay, political treatise
- Leading statesman: abolitionist, writer, orator, journalist, civil rights activist, diplomat, politician
- Extraordinary command of nineteenth-century rhetorical strategies and literary craft
- Specific personal details used to argue for abolition of chattel slavery
- Sometimes sentimental, emotional style with emphasis on pathos— but other times, tone is dispassionate, without affect, detached
- Subversion of status quo of the slaveocracy

Teaching Strategies

- To engage students in an appreciation of Douglass's consummate rhetorical skill, you might have them select a passage for close reading in any of his anthologized texts and then analyze the significance of the rhetorical selections and omissions. Discussion might begin with a contrast of the extended episode of the apostrophe to the ships on Chesapeake Bay with the abridged account of his childhood witnessing of the brutal beating of his aunt Hester.
- In almost any teaching context, students will benefit from having Douglass's *Narrative* situated within the slave narrative genre by comparing it to other slave narratives, including those by Olaudah Equiano, William Wells Brown, and Harriet Jacobs. Ask students to describe and analyze the divergent temporal, geographical, national, gendered, and sociopolitical circumstances of each former slave's account.
- Douglass's second autobiography was published ten years after his first autobiography and fourteen years after he joined William Lloyd

Garrison and other northern abolitionists in their fight against slavery. *My Bondage and My Freedom* (1855) provides greater insight into Douglass's thoughts about the institution of slavery and the experiences that drew him to his conclusions. It also details Douglass's introduction to the Massachusetts Anti-Slavery Society and more of the circumstances that led him to write his *Narrative*. You might want to ask half the class to read the excerpts from *My Bondage and My Freedom* and half to read the *Narrative* and then exchange information and determine how their interpretations of the texts are influenced by this new information. You might begin the discussion by asking students how Douglass's *Narrative* informed, clarified, or mystified any prior knowledge they had about the conditions of slavery.

Questions

- In what ways is Douglass's representation of the physical violence of his conflict with Covey gendered? Would you describe that representation (or that violence) as *emotional* or *dispassionate*?
- How does the emotional quality of Douglass's 1845 *Narrative* compare or contrast with related slave narratives like William Wells Brown's or Harriet Jacobs's?
- Arguably, Sandy Jenkins in Frederick Douglass's 1845 *Narrative* can be read as a "father figure." In what ways, if any, do you see Douglass's portrait of Jenkins subverting the paternalism central to the proslavery project?
- In his Preface to Douglass's 1845 *Narrative* William Lloyd Garrison attacked antebellum U.S. chattel slavery as an institution in which "Nothing has been left undone to cripple [slaves'] intellects, darken their minds, debase their moral nature, obliterate all traces of their relationship to mankind." Locate passages in Douglass's and others' slave narratives that substantiate as truth Garrison's accusations.
- *Life and Times of Frederick Douglass* insists that the author's numerous personal writings emanate from a moral obligation encumbent on him as witness and advocate for an oppressed people who were prevented from speaking for themselves. By what strategies does Douglass's third autobiography set out to fulfill this obligation?
- Turn to these three milestones: Chapter 10 in the *Narrative*, detailing the fight with Covey; Chapter 23 of *My Bondage and My Freedom*, in which the narrator is "introduced to the Abolitionist"; and Chapter 1 of the Third Part of *Life and Times*, wherein the narrator contrasts his authorial accomplishments with those of Charles Dickens, Alexandre Dumas, Thomas Carlyle, and Sir Walter Scott. What conclusions can you draw about Douglass's skill from this chronological narrative of his existential and rhetorical development?

- Analyze Douglass's "What to the Slave Is the Fourth of July?" speech, delivered on July 5, 1852, in Rochester, New York, for its deployment of tropes standard in antebellum abolitionist rhetoric.
- Compare and contrast some of the antebellum abolitionist rhetoric tropes of Douglass's "What to the Slave Is the Fourth of July?" with those in David Walker's *Appeal* and speeches by Maria Stewart and Sojourner Truth.

Bibliography

Andrews, William L., ed. *The Oxford Frederick Douglass Reader*. New York: Oxford UP, 1996.

Chaney, Michael A. "Picturing the Mother, Claiming Egypt: *My Bondage and My Freedom* as Auto(bio)ethnography." *African American Review* 35 (2001): 391–408.

DeLombard, Jeannine. " 'Eye-Witness to the Cruelty': Southern Violence and Northern Testimony in Frederick Douglass's 1845 *Narrative*." *American Literature* 73 (2001): 245–76.

Dorsey, Peter A. "Becoming the Other: The Mimesis of Metaphor in Douglass's *My Bondage and My Freedom*." *PMLA* 111 (1996): 435–51.

Fanuzzi, Robert. "The Trouble with Douglass's Body." *American Transcendental Quarterly* 13 (1999): 27–49.

Gilmore, Paul. "Aesthetic Power: Electric Words and the Example of Frederick Douglass." *American Transcendental Quarterly* 16 (2002): 291–313.

McClure, Kevin R. "Frederick Douglass' Use of Comparison in His Fourth of July Oration: A Textual Criticism." *Western Journal of Communication* 64 (2000): 425–28.

McFeely, William S. *Frederick Douglass*. New York: Norton, 1991.

Sundquist, Eric J., ed. *Frederick Douglass: New Literary and Historical Essays*. Cambridge, UK: Cambridge UP, 1990.

Wardrop, Daneen. " 'While I Am Writing': Webster's 1825 'Spelling Book,' the Ell, and Frederick Douglass's Positioning of Language." *African American Review* 32 (1998): 649–60.

James M. Whitfield

1822–1871

Works in the Anthology

"America" (1853)
"Yes! Strike Again That Sounding String" (1853)
"Self-Reliance" (1853)

Other Works

America and Other Poems (1853)

Themes

- National hypocrisies
- Injustices against oppressed (and) people of color
- Natural, national, and civil rights
- Black spiritual resistance to white supremacy and domination

Characteristics

- Classical imagery
- Invective rhetoric
- Parody of Anglo-American sacred and secular forms
- Critique of slavery, argument for abolition

Questions

- What portrait of colonial Americans emerges in "America"? How does that portrait compare with the images of colonial Americans in Lucy Terry's "Bars Fight"? With images of colonial Americans in Wheatley's poems?
- Discuss ways that "America" seems to have been influenced by David Walker's *Appeal in Four Articles*.

Bibliography

Hill, James L. "James Monroe Whitfield." In Emmanuel S. Nelson, ed., *African American Authors, 1745–1945: A Bio-Bibliographical Critical Sourcebook*. Westport, CT: Greenwood, 2000. 474–78.

Sherman, Joan R. "James Monroe Whitfield, Poet and Emigrationist: A Voice of Protest and Despair." *Journal of Negro History* 57 (1972): 169–76.

Frances E. W. Harper

1825–1911

Works in the Anthology

"Ethiopia" (1853)
"Eliza Harris" (1853)
"The Slave Mother" (1854)
"Vashti" (1857)
"Bury Me in a Free Land" (1864)
"Aunt Chloe's Politics" (1872)
"Learning to Read" (1872)
"A Double Standard" (1895)
"Songs for the People" (1895)
"An Appeal to My Country Women" (1900)
"The Two Offers" (1859)
"Our Greatest Want" (1859)
"Fancy Etchings": "Enthusiasm and Lofty Aspirations" and "Dangerous Economies" (1873)
"Woman's Political Future" (1893)

Other Works

Forest Leaves (poems, 1845)
Poems on Miscellaneous Subjects (1854)
Moses: A Story of the Nile (poem, 1869)
Poems (1871)
Sketches of Southern Life (poems, 1872)
Sowing and Reaping (novel, 1876)
Trial and Triumph (novel, 1888–89)
Iola Leroy (novel, 1892)

Themes

- African American moral, economic, sociopolitical, and intellectual advancement
- Abolition of chattel slavery
- Power of African American motherwit
- Women's rights within marriage and outside of it
- Images of women
- Advancement for blacks
- African American suffrage and political enfranchisement
- Economic and political freedom

- African American racial and cultural pride
- Faith in the power of the word to motivate right action
- Temperance
- Celebration of black women's lives and social contributions
- Moral obligations encumbent on privileged persons

Characteristics

- Generally regarded as the most outstanding African American woman writer before the twentieth century
- Multigeneric professional writer across six decades: poet, novelist, essayist, journalist
- Elocutionist and speaker on a range of subjects, including abolition, education, suffrage, temperance, economics, art, and morality
- Strong orality in all works, especially texts cast in African American vernacular English
- Passion for freedom
- Revisions of negative stereotypes of women, enslaved and free

Teaching Strategies

- While it is commonplace to suggest that students should read poetry aloud, with Harper's poems, reading aloud is essential. Read aloud, the rhymes and rhythms that appear to the eye as quite basic, even repetitious, show her strong talent for evoking the spoken word and inviting dramatic recitations. Have students note the importance of orality in Harper's prose.
- Encourage appreciation of Harper's diverse uses of the vernacular by asking students to practice reciting selected texts. You might spend some class time in which students present interpretations of their individual favorites. If you're interested in having this activity also form a springboard to broader discussions of language and of intersections of poetry and prose, consider assigning several ballads and folktales in "The Vernacular Tradition" section and also listening to some of the early selections on the Audio Companion.

Questions

- Compare and contrast Harper's "Eliza Harris" or "Vashti" with other vernacular-based poems by Langston Hughes, Paul Laurence Dunbar, and Sterling Brown. What attributes do these works share? How do vernacular elements enrich these poems?
- What ideas, tropes, or other characteristics do Harper's antebellum poems share with the following twentieth-century poems: Robert

Hayden's "Runagate Runagate," Sherley Anne Williams's "I Want Aretha to Set This to Music," and Quincy Troupe's "In Texas Grass"?

- Read "Ethiopia"; then identify and analyze one or more additional poems by Harper that express her deep faith in the power of the word to motivate right action. Compare and contrast those poems with much later poems by Audre Lorde that address the same theme.
- The poems and essays by W. E. B. Du Bois and the sermons of Martin Luther King Jr. may seem an unlikely comparison with Harper's works, but begin such a comparison by exploring the effect of these authors' life experiences on their various texts and their use of sound and sense to enrich their writings.
- Review "Woman's Political Future." What relevance is there today in the following comment from that text:

> To-day women hold in their hands influence and opportunity, and with these they have already opened doors which have been closed to others. . . . To her is apparently coming the added responsibility of political power; and what she now possesses should only be the means of preparing her to use the coming power for the glory of God and the good of mankind.

- "The Two Offers," the earliest known short story by an African American woman, was first published in *The Anglo African*, a periodical by, for, and about black people. Given that the main characters are not racially defined, should one read this story as an example of the "tragic mulatto" tradition? Why or why not?

Bibliography

Boyd, Melba Joyce. *Discarded Legacy: Politics and Poetics in the Life of Frances E. W. Harper, 1825–1911*. Detroit: Wayne State UP, 1994.

Ernest, John. "From Mysteries to Histories: Cultural Pedagogy in Frances E. W. Harper's *Iola Leroy.*" *American Literature: A Journal of Literary History, Criticism, and Bibliography* 64 (1992): 497–518.

Harper, Frances E. W. *A Brighter Coming Day: A Frances Ellen Watkins Harper Reader*. Ed. Frances Smith Foster. New York: Feminist P, 1990.

Scheick, William J. "Strategic Ellipsis in Harper's 'The Two Offers.'" *The Southern Literary Journal* 23 (1991): 14–19.

Harriet E. Wilson

1828?–1863?

Works in the Anthology

Our Nig; or, Sketches from the Life of a Free Black, Preface, Chaps. 1–3,
   8, 10, 12

Themes

- Hypocrisy of antebellum northern Anglo-America regarding slavery
- Injustices against oppressed peoples, especially children, women,
  and poor people
- Intersection of racism, classism, elitism, and misogyny
- Race relations in antebellum U.S. society
- Economic inequities in antebellum U.S. society
- Gender conflicts in romantic relationships in antebellum U.S. soci-
  ety
- Subjugated position of the figure of the orphan in antebellum U.S.
  society
- Economic, physical, and emotional abuses in indentured servitude in
  antebellum U.S. society
- Tricksterly resistance to oppression
- Miscegenation, interracial marriage, mixed-race children
- Education and literacy deprivation of oppressed people, especially
  children, women, and poor people
- Familial relationships

Characteristics

- Conventions of domestic and sentimental fiction, satirized and sub-
  verted
- Hybrid text of autobiography, fiction, and exposé
- *Kunstlerroman:* story of coming of age of a (woman) literary artist
- Exposé of sadistic labor conditions within antebellum indentured
  servitude

Questions

- How does Frado's "L-chamber" in *Our Nig* compare with Linda's garret in *Incidents in the Life of a Slave Girl*? What analysis of antebellum black women's sociopolitical positions do Wilson and Harriet

Jacobs seem to make by situating their respective characters in these out of the way spaces?

- Although Frado is not literally enslaved, she is figuratively so. Compare and contrast Wilson's depiction of northern bondage with several slave autobiographers' accounts of slavery in the South. Why do you suppose that slave narratives were so much more popular in their day than was Wilson's novel?

- In the same year that *Our Nig* became (as far as we now know) the first novel published by an African American woman, "The Two Offers" by Frances E. W. Harper became the first short story published by an African American woman. Review Harper's story to determine what rhetorical features and thematic concerns the two women's texts share as well as the tropes and issues that divide them.

- Trace Wilson's critique of white northern hypocrisy about race relations as it plays out in black writers who came after her. What do more modern writers, such as Amiri Baraka and Toni Morrison, argue about the North's attitudes toward African Americans' civil and human rights?

- Support or refute the contention that the African American bad girl figure extends from Frado to the present. Consider such texts as Toni Cade Bambara's "Raymond's Run" and Paule Marshall's "Reena" to make your case.

Bibliography

Leveen, Lois. "Dwelling in the House of Oppression: The Spatial, Racial, and Textual Dynamics of Harriet Wilson's *Our Nig*." *African American Review* 35 (2001): 561–81.

Pratofiorito, Ellen. "'To demand your sympathy and aid': *Our Nig* and the Problem of No Audience." *Journal of American & Comparative Cultures* 24 (2001): 31–49.

Teaching the Literature of Slavery and Freedom

Contextualizing the earliest extant works by African Americans who wrote during either the Great Awakening in the United States or the Revolutionary War illuminates similarities between these works and other U.S. literatures produced during the same time. Such contextualization can also illuminate a range of differences, especially between Anglo Americans and African Americans, who lived dramatically divergent lives in a nation tolerating the "peculiar" legal enslavement of blacks. The trials and tribulations of African Americans, the manifestations of sin and, for some, of Satan, and black people's faith in salvation and deliverance were determined by their particular social locations. A course organized historically to examine African American literature written between 1746 and 1865 can initiate exciting analyses of the diverse texts that blacks produced both in bondage and out, the sociopolitical conditions under which they wrote, and the fact that so many publications survived.

- Discuss with students the "black and unknown bards" unearthed and honored in James Weldon Johnson's poem of that title. Grant Johnson's premise that many texts by African Americans were lost and remain so; then generate a list of speculations as to the historical reasons that African American literary traditions since the Revolutionary War have developed in the particular ways that they have.
- Assign several early African American literary works, perhaps representatives of different genres, and ask students to draw a profile of intended readers based on explicit and implicit assertions about the society or societies the texts depict. Then read for more subtle, even tacit comments in these texts to discern traces of double-speak and signifying. What evidence can students find of an author's use of a single literary text to convey disparate messages to black audiences and white?

Beginning with Jupiter Hammon's early lyrics, this section chronicles the conflation of oral and written works as well as the problem of establishing a reliable chronology of production. A fragment of Lucy Terry's poem "Bars Fight," for example, survived in the vernacular for over a century before finally being published. Moreover, this ballad evidently records for posterity a significant event in the life of Terry's multiethnic community: a fight between Native Americans and New England settlers.

Other writers whose works were closely connected to oral and vernacular sources, including hymns, sermons, and speeches, are Phillis Wheatley, George Moses Horton, Henry Highland Garnet, David Walker, and Maria W. Stewart. These and others in *NAFAM* emphasize Christianity, use classical and neoclassical poetic and rhetorical forms, and manifest concern for human rights within or based on Protestant theology—all of which represent eighteenth- and early-nineteenth-century America.

Historically, African American literature has been more inclusive and varied than Anglo-American literature. This literature is concerned with the literal and spiritual freedoms of African Americans as well as other Americans and with the disparity between what liberatory national documents like the Constitution proclaim and what they effect. Meditations on freedom and bondage, like David Walker's *Appeal*, pervade virtually all of African American literature through the twentieth century. In this period especially, however, one might examine Walker's *Appeal* alongside the two versions of Sojourner Truth's "Ar'n't I a Woman?" speech, and/or James Whitfield's "America," and/or Frances Harper's "Appeal to My Country Women," and/or Frederick Douglass's "What to the Slave Is the Fourth of July?"

Developing a course on the genre of slave narratives could address many compelling and overlapping issues. For example, Douglass writes of the "songs of the slave [that] represent the sorrows of the heart" and often adopts the voice of the storyteller. Olaudah Equiano's *Narrative* reconstructs images of Africa, the Middle Passage, and corporal confinement. The slave account of Venture Smith, who like Equiano passed through the Middle Passage and eventually reconstructed his story in freedom, narrates an altogether more besieged experience of abduction and bondage. The intricacies of slavery as the defining legal institution of the antebellum United States and its influence on all of humankind form the distilled focus of slave narratives by Douglass, Harriet Jacobs, and Elizabeth Keckley. Vernacular traditions and slave narrative conventions intertwine in early black novels; William Wells Brown begins *Clotel*, for example, with an autobiographical sketch in which the author identifies himself as "a Fugitive Slave" on the title page. This self-representation validates his authority to chronicle slavery, albeit as fiction. He parallels in that fiction his own poignant autobiographical depiction of a mother's piteous cries when separated from her child. Brown's recall of the songs of slaves "about to be carried to the far south" echoes throughout antebellum vernacular spirituals. Both Brown's *Clotel* and Harriet E. Wilson's *Our Nig* introduce themes that permeate other African American literature as well: the mulatto in crisis and "the North is no better than the South."

Since the first section in *NAFAM* covers almost a century, it invites historical comparisons within its chronological divisions that lead to questions that should make for provocative class discussion:

- What factors changed between the Boston experiences of Phillis Wheatley and those of Maria W. Stewart? How might those factors have influenced not merely the theology but the form and tone of these women's religious writings?
- What versions of slavery did Olaudah Equiano and Frederick Douglass experience, and how did their different slaveries affect these authors' narratives?
- The theme of the tragic mulatto emerges in William Wells Brown's *Clotel* and also in Victor Séjour's short story "The Mulatto." Séjour, however, depicts the mulatto figure as psychologically traumatized. Delineate the differences between Brown's and Séjour's respective assessments of the social, individual, and national effects of miscegenation.

Genres

Poetry

Hammon
Terry
Wheatley
Horton
Whitfield
Harper

Oration

Truth
Stewart
Garnet
Douglass
Harper

Periodical Literature/Journalism

A focus on the development and distribution of mid-nineteenth-century U.S. periodical literature can instruct students about literature as a market-driven phenomenon, one affected as much by (the cultivation of) popular tastes as by publishers' decisions. Describing a course she teaches on *Uncle Tom's Cabin* and periodical literature, Susan Belasco writes:

> In the 1830s a variety of technological developments in papermaking and the development and use of the cylinder press had altered the course of publication. Cheaper postal routes further contributed to wider distribution and a larger potential audience for printed materials. In addition, railroads were connecting various parts of the country very quickly. By 1840, there were nine thousand miles of track; by the beginning of the Civil War, the figure reached over thirty thousand. . . . Periodical publication soared as demand increased. According to the census of 1840, there were over six hundred on-going periodicals of various kinds in the country; by 1869, there were four thousand. (22)

NAFAM writers of the slavery and freedom period who published their own papers and/or whose literary work was serialized are the following:

Horton
Truth
Stewart
Delany

Jacobs
Brown
Douglass
Harper

Religious/Political Treatise

Walker
Stewart
Delany
Harper

Prose Narrative/Slave Narrative/Autobiography

Smith
Equiano
Jacobs
Brown
Keckley
Douglass

Short Fiction

Sejóur
Harper

Novel

Brown
Wilson

Bibliography

Ammons, Elizabeth, and Susan Belasco, eds. *Approaches to Teaching Stowe's* Uncle Tom's Cabin. New York: MLA, 2000.

Belasco, Susan. "The Writing, Reception, and Reputation of *Uncle Tom's Cabin.*" In Ammons and Belasco, eds., *Approaches to Teaching Stowe's* Uncle Tom's Cabin. 21–36.

Berlin, Ira. *Generations of Captivity: A History of African American Slaves.* Cambridge, MA: Belknap, 2003.

Bland, Lecater Jr. *African American Slave Narratives: An Anthology.* Westport, CT: Greenwood, 2001.

Carson, Sharon. "Africana Constellations: African American Studies and *Uncle Tom's Cabin*." In Ammons and Belasco, eds., *Approaches to Teaching Stowe's* Uncle Tom's Cabin. 162–71.

Ernest, John. *Resistance and Reformation in Nineteenth-Century African American Literature: Brown, Wilson, Jacobs, Delany, Douglass, and Harper*. Jackson: UP of Mississippi, 1995.

Fabi, M. Giulia. "The 'Unguarded Expressions of the Feelings of the Negroes': Gender, Slave Resistance, and William Wells Brown's Revisions of *Clotel*." *African American Review* 27 (1993): 639–54.

Hall, James C., ed. *Approaches to Teaching* Narrative of the Life of Frederick Douglass. New York: MLA, 1999.

Herzog, Kristin. "*Uncle Tom's Cabin* and *Incidents in the Life of a Slave Girl*: The Issue of Violence." In Ammons and Belasco, eds., *Approaches to Teaching Stowe's* Uncle Tom's Cabin. 132–41.

Ogunleye, Tolagbe. "Dr. Martin Robison Delany, 19th-Century Africana Womanist: Reflections on His Avant-Garde Politics Concerning Gender, Colorism, and Nation Building." *Journal of Black Studies* 28 (1998): 628–40.

Peterson, Mary Jane. "Raising a Passionate Voice: Teaching *Uncle Tom's Cabin* to Less Experienced Readers." In Ammons and Belasco, eds., *Approaches to Teaching* Uncle Tom's Cabin. 142–49.

Sharpe, Jenny. *Ghosts of Slavery: A Literary Archaeology of Black Women's Lives*. Minneapolis: U of Minnesota P, 2003.

Stanesa, Jamie. "Slaves, Slavery, and the Politics of 'Home': An Interdisciplinary Approach to Teaching *Uncle Tom's Cabin*." In Ammons and Belasco, eds., *Approaches to Teaching Stowe's* Uncle Tom's Cabin. 199–208.

Sundquist, Eric, ed. *New Essays on* Uncle Tom's Cabin. Cambridgeshire [UK]: Cambridge UP, 1986.

Yarborough, Richard. "Strategies of Black Characterization in *Uncle Tom's Cabin* and the Early Afro-American Novel." In Sundquist, ed., *New Essays on* Uncle Tom's Cabin. 45–84.

Literature of the Reconstruction to the New Negro Renaissance, 1865–1919

Charlotte Forten Grimké

1837–1914

Works in the Anthology

"A Parting Hymn" (1856)
From *Journals* 1 and 3 (1854–62)

Themes

- Daily life and work
- Restrictions on women's lives, gender subjugation
- Abolitionism
- African American intelligence, intellectualism, and academic education
- Literary and artistic pursuits of the antebellum black middle class
- Social activities of the antebellum black middle class
- Fallacies and hypocrisies of (white) liberal pretensions in antebellum Massachusetts
- Horrific effects of the Fugitive Slave Law
- Christian piety; exposé of the Cult of True Womanhood
- Power of the imagination

- Intraracial relationships, conflicts, harmonies
- Natural beauty of the South Carolina islands

Characteristics

- Chronological, autobiographical account of subject's daily life
- *Bildungsroman, Kunstlerroman*
- Sensitive, passionate, "feminine," sometimes sarcastic, youthful voice
- Incorporates contemporary literary texts into her journal
- Chronicles social and political activities of Boston abolitionists at midcentury

Questions

- At one point the young Grimké writes (in Journal 1), "It is impossible to be happy now." To what extent does this assertion seem melodramatic? Are you convinced by the details of her diary entries that she was reasonably depressed—or unhealthily so? Do you interpret the frequency of her expression of dejection as evidence of a depressed personality—or of a maudlin tendency?
- How does Grimké's private, not-for-publication assessment of early black vernacular music compare and contrast with the representation of African American folk singing in the 1845 *Narrative of the Life of Frederick Douglass* before it and W. E. B. Du Bois's 1903 *The Souls of Black Folk* after it?
- Compare Grimké's account of her first teaching experiences in the South with Booker T. Washington's in *Up From Slavery*.

Bibliography

Cobb-Moore, Geneva. "When Meanings Meet: The Journals of Charlotte Forten Grimké." In Suzanne L. Bunkers and Cynthia Huff, eds., *Inscribing the Daily: Critical Essays on Women's Diaries*. Amherst: U of Massachusetts P, 1996. 139–55.

Koch, Lisa M. "Bodies as Stage Props: Enacting Hysteria in the Diaries of Charlotte Forten Grimké and Alice James." *Legacy* 15 (1998): 59–64.

Booker T. Washington

1856–1932

Works in the Anthology

Up From Slavery, Chaps. 1–3, 14 (1901)

Other Works

The Story of My Life and Work (autobiography, 1900)
The Man Farthest Down (1910)

Themes

- African American education and intelligence
- Poverty and economic disability
- Migration for self-advancement
- Labor in bondage, labor in despair
- Black economic ambition
- Black citizenship
- Racial cooperation and coalition

Characteristics

- Author, educator, editor, and orator
- Reportorial, straightforward voice
- Trickster narrator, African American rhetorical masking

Teaching Strategies

- Require students to read Washington's Atlanta Exposition address on their own; afterward, in class, ask a few volunteers to read the text interpretively. Then listen with students to the Audio Companion recording of Washington reciting his speech and solicit their reactions to the emotional quality of his voice as compared with what students have heard in their own heads as well as from their classmates.
- Discuss with your students the form, diction, thesis, and rhetorical techniques of Washington's 1895 Atlanta Exposition address.
- Share with students the section of *The Autobiography of Benjamin Franklin* that recounts Franklin's journey to Philadelphia and his first few days in the city. Have students compare and contrast Washington's account with Franklin's. Then speculate together about Wash-

ington's motivations for invoking Franklin's legend and what the later author stood to gain by representing his own experience in the rhetoric and conventions of the earlier.

- Share with students an episode from Horatio Alger's Ragged Dick tales for comparison with Washington's own rags to riches story. Do they find the characterization of Washington's narrator as a Ragged Dick apt? If so, on what grounds? If not, why not?
- When paired with slave narratives published before Emancipation, *Up From Slavery* and Elizabeth Keckley's *Behind the Scenes* can help students understand significant differences between antebellum and postbellum narratives as well as postbellum African American attitudes toward class, industry, education, and self-respect. If the goals of your course include illustrating the expansiveness of the slave narrative genre (or African American autobiography more generally) and/or highlighting literary and sociopolitical shifts across the nineteenth-century, you might want to consider *Up From Slavery* and *Behind the Scenes* with a selection of earlier texts by black writers.

Questions

- Review conventions of the slave narrative, and situate *Up From Slavery* within this tradition. How does Washington's narrative compare to the antebellum *Narrative of the Life of Frederick Douglass*? How does it compare to Douglass's later narratives? What impact does the date of publication seem to have on the representation of slavery in these texts?
- Review the opening paragraph of *Narrative of the Life of Frederick Douglass*; then review the opening paragraph of *Up From Slavery*. In what ways does Washington rewrite Douglass's account of his life? What expectations do you have of *Up From Slavery* based on how it reiterates Douglass's opening?
- *Up From Slavery* is often compared to Elizabeth Keckley's postbellum slave narrative *Behind the Scenes*, in part because both texts describe the institution of slavery as a "school" wherein they and other slaves learned many survival skills and developed traits that rendered them ideal citizens. Review the two texts together and comment on the persuasiveness of this metaphor based on the evidence the authors provide.
- Discuss the effect of slavery on children as Washington, Olaudah Equiano, Harriet Jacobs, Elizabeth Keckley, William Wells Brown, and Frederick Douglass argue it. What variations in the depiction of a childhood in bondage do you find among these narratives? To what extent do those variations seem to result from the gender of the author? From the period in which he or she was writing?

- Select an episode from the first three chapters of *Up From Slavery* for close reading, and pay careful attention to the rhetorical strategies Washington deploys in developing his narrator. How do you characterize this narrative voice and persona? What advantages and disadvantages does Washington face with this particular narrative perspective?
- Given what you know about the period in which Washington lived and wrote—a period known among literary scholars and historians of African American culture as "the Nadir," the bottom or lowest point—how accurate do you find the historical perspective offered in *Up From Slavery*?
- Support or refute the contention that Washington refuses to verify slavery as a brutal and evil institution.
- In what ways, if any, do you read *Up From Slavery* as a contribution to the idealized racial uplift so prominent among blacks at the turn into the twentieth century?
- Discuss the rhetorical form and shape of the speech in Chapter 14 of *Up From Slavery*. Then reread it, focusing this time on its situatedness within the context of the larger chapter. How are your two readings different? What, if anything, is gained by reading the speech *apart from* the chapter in which Washington placed it in his autobiography as well as by reading it as *a part of* Chapter 14?

Bibliography

Andrews, William L., ed. *Up From Slavery.* New York: Norton, 1996.

Bly, Antonio T. "'We can be as separate as' the Pages of the Book: Booker T. Washington and the Work of Autobiography." *Prospects* 26 (2001): 163–82.

Jones, Evora W. "Booker T. Washington as Pastoralist: Authenticating the Man at Century's End." *CLA Journal* 43 (1999): 38–39.

Charles W. Chesnutt

1858–1932

Works in the Anthology

"The Goophered Grapevine" (1899)
"The Passing of Grandison" (1899)
"The Wife of His Youth" (1899)
From *The Journals of Charles W. Chesnutt* (1880)

Other Works

> *The Conjure Woman* (stories, 1899)
> *The Wife of His Youth and Other Tales of the Color Line* (1899)
> *The House behind the Cedars* (novel, 1900)
> *The Marrow of Tradition* (novel, 1901)
> "Post-Bellum—Pre-Harlem" (essay, 1931)

Themes

- The persistence of slavery's cruelties in the postbellum South
- Relations between whites and blacks
- Social and economic injustices
- The evils of white supremacy
- Conjure, hoodoo, voodoo, black magic, tricksterism
- Black and white family dynamics in the Reconstruction South
- Black family love and devotion
- Black romantic love and commitment
- Intraracial conflicts among blacks, African American elitism
- (Obstacles to) black survival and self-determination
- The beauty and complexities of black folk speech

Characteristics

- Mined the rural South for language, superstitions, and peculiar social rituals
- Cultivation of literary realism
- African American vernacular English and other regional dialects
- Subversion of primitivist literary conventions and expectations of black naïveté

Teaching Strategies

- Besides posing to students the question about Joel Chandler Harris (see below), you might consider sharing with them one or two pages from Thomas Nelson Page's *In Ole Virginia*. Then view with students a segment—any will suffice—of the Walt Disney film *The Song of the South*. Ask students to articulate and discuss ways that Chesnutt's portrayal of the ostensibly emancipated South differs from the white authors' depictions. Ask students to theorize as well ways those portraits have shaped national, regional, and racial attitudes about the South and about African Americans.
- Situate for students Chesnutt's fiction and nonfiction amid politico-historical events of his day—including *Plessy* v. *Fergusson*, rampant

lynching, *The Leopard's Spots*, and increasing U.S. imperialism—and ask students to debate whether or not Chesnutt's apparent reflections on the Old South engage these issues or evade them. What reasons do students suppose Chesnutt had for his focus on rural folk life?

Questions

- Compare Chesnutt's use of the trope of black conjure with Zora Neale Hurston's later use of it during the Harlem Renaissance. In what ways, if any, does Hurston borrow from her literary precursor? Would you describe either author's version of "hoodoo" as exotic or quaint, or does it strike you as dangerous or heretical? On what do you base your conclusions?
- Compare Chesnutt's representation of Julius with Joel Chandler Harris's Uncle Remus figure in the Br'er Rabbit stories. Support or refute the contention that the authors' respective racial identities are apparent in their stories.
- Grant that Chesnutt defies rather than glorifies the "plantation tradition" of Joel Chandler Harris and Thomas Nelson Page. How, then, do you see the Chestnutt stories in the anthology as parodies of romanticized southern literature?
- Compare Chesnutt's treatment of black folk culture with that of writers such as Paul Laurence Dunbar and James Weldon Johnson.
- In African American literary traditions, the trickster is a figure who usually acts dim-witted, docile, and ignorant but in actuality is just the opposite—sharp, shrewd, and quick-witted. How do Chesnutt's characters Julius and Grandison fit into this tradition?
- Compare Julius and Grandison with other African American tricksters you find in *NAFAM*, including the narrator of the *Narrative of William Wells Brown* and Zora Heale Hurston's John in the excerpt from *Mules and Men*. How are these tricksters' actions similar? How similar are their motivations? Does Ishmael Reed's "Railroad Bill, a Conjure Man" seem to fit into this tradition? Why or why not?

Bibliography

Brodhead, Richard H., ed. *The Journals of Charles W. Chesnutt*. Durham, NC: Duke UP, 1993.

Bryant, Earle V. "Scriptural Allusion and Metaphorical Marriage in Charles Chesnutt's 'The Wife of His Youth.'" *American Literary Realism* 33 (2000): 57–64.

Crisler, Jesse S., Robert C. Leitz III, and Joseph R. McElrath Jr., eds. *An Exemplary Citizen: Letters of Charles W. Chesnutt, 1906–1932*. Stanford, CA: Stanford UP, 2002.

Fossett, Judith Jackson. "The Civil War Imaginations of Thomas Dixon and Charles Chesnutt: Or, North Carolina, 'This Strange World of Poisoned Air.'" *North Carolina Literary Review* 8 (1999): 107–20.

McElrath, Joseph R. Jr. "Why Charles W. Chesnutt Is Not a Realist." *American Literary Realism* 32 (1999): 91–108.

McElrath, Joseph R. Jr., and Robert C. Leitz. *"To Be an Author": Letters of Charles W. Chesnutt.* Princeton, NJ: Princeton UP, 1996.

Pickens, Ernestine Williams. *Charles W. Chesnutt and the Progressive Movement.* New York: Pace UP, 1994.

Anna Julia Cooper

1858?–1964

Works in the Anthology

"Womanhood a Vital Element in the Regeneration and Progress of a Race" (1892)

Other Works

A Voice from the South by a Black Woman of the South (essays, 1892)

Themes

- African American education
- Black self-actualization and racial uplift
- African American women's self-determination and social activism
- The intersection of male dominance with white supremacy
- Black feminist ideology
- Transformation of norms and significance of the Cult of True Womanhood
- Black women's club movement

Characteristics

- Espouses African American women's privileged subject position to analyze social, political, economic, and gender inequities in the United States
- Sharply critiques local, national, and international (mis)treatment of women

- Excoriates stereotyping of black women
- Literary strategies include humor, allegory, satire, oratory, and auto-biography

Questions

- Compare Cooper's stance on the "admixture of African and Anglo blood" with that of earlier nineteenth-century writer Martin Delany (*The Condition*).
- Fifty years after Cooper delivered "Womanhood a Vital Element," Lorraine Hansberry produced on Broadway another African American woman's "live performance," her play *A Raisin in the Sun*. Review Hansberry's play and determine the degree to which her Christian women characters conform to the images of black womanhood that Cooper describes in her lecture. Then select another black woman writer's representation of African American womanhood from a different literary period and make a similar assessment about her depiction of black women. To what extent do these two writers seem to agree with Cooper's contention that black women (must) bear the responsibility of the reputation of the whole black race?
- Trace and discuss Cooper's use of humor and satire in the development of otherwise serious ideas. Are you surprised by these literary devices in her lecture, given the stereotypes of black women and feminists as essentially humorless creatures?
- How does Cooper's call for *men's* as well as women's deep commitment to the advancement of black women compare to Frances Harper's earlier call for True Men and True Women in "Our Greatest Want"?

Bibliography

Alexander, Elizabeth. " 'We must be about our father's business': Anna Julia Cooper and the Incorporation of the Nineteenth-Century African-American Woman Intellectual." *Signs* 20 (1995): 336–57.

Keller, Frances R. "An Educational Controversy: Anna Julia Cooper's Vision of Resolution." *NWSA Journal* 11 (1999): n.p.

Lemert, Charles, and Esme Bahn, eds. *The Voice of Anna Julia Cooper Including: A Voice from the South and Other Important Essays, Papers, and Letters.* Lanham, MD: Rowman & Littlefield, 1998.

Maguire, Roberta S. "Kate Chopin and Anna Julia Cooper: Critiquing Kentucky and the South." *Southern Literary Journal* 35 (2002): 123–38.

Wallinger, Hanna. "The Five Million Women of My Race: Negotiations of Gender in W. E. B. Du Bois and Anna Julia Cooper." In Karen Kilcup, ed., *Soft Canons: American Women Writers and Masculine Tradition*. Iowa City: U of Iowa P, 1999. 262–80.

Pauline E. Hopkins

1859–1930

Works in the Anthology

"Talma Gordon" (1900)

Famous Men of the Negro Race, "Booker T. Washington" (1901)

Famous Women of the Negro Race, "Literary Workers: Frances E. W. Harper" (1902)

"Letter from Cordelia A. Condict and Pauline Hopkins's Reply" (March 1903)

Other Works

Contending Forces: A Romance of Negro Life North and South (novel, 1900)

Hagar's Daughter: A Story of Southern Caste Prejudice (pseud. Sarah A. Allen, novel, 1901–02)

Winona: A Tale of Negro Life in the South and Southwest (pseud. Sarah A. Allen, novel, 1902)

Of One Blood; Or, the Hidden Self (pseud. Sarah A. Allen, novel, 1902–03)

Themes

- Contrasts of national regions after the Civil War
- Economic and social exploitations of U.S. women of color
- African American motherhood after slavery
- African American post-Emancipation (dis)enfranchisement
- African American racial uplift and civil rights movements
- Explorations of postbellum African American life and culture
- Popular early theories of Christian Scientists and French parapsychologists
- Miscegenation and racial identity formation
- Racial passing
- Figure of the tragic mulatto/a
- Interracial marriage

- Social Darwinism, (quasi-)scientific racism, eugenics
- U.S. imperialism

Characteristics

- Hybrid fictions: combinations of captivity narrative, slave narrative, historical romance, realism, allegory, fantasy, science fiction, adventure, mystery novel, sentimental fiction, and psychological realism
- Gothic elements
- Revisions of the stereotype of the tragic mulatto/a
- Rhetoric of U.S. temperance and African American racial uplift movements
- Racial assimilationist agenda
- Promotion of eugenics for racial uplift

Questions

- Compare and contrast Hopkins's treatment of women, whiteness, and class in "Talma Gordon" with Charles Chesnutt's treatment of men, whiteness, and class in "The Wife of His Youth." How do the authors' respective gender identities seem to influence the perspectives in their short stories? How does character development seem affected by each author's gender identity?
- Compare and contrast Hopkins's tragic mulatta figure in "Talma Gordon" with Harriet Wilson's in *Our Nig* and Harriet Jacobs's in *Incidents in the Life of a Slave Girl*. Do the two authors writing at midcentury seem to make similar claims about the plight of women of Anglo and African descent as Hopkins at the end of the century? If so, what are those claims? If not, how are the primary arguments of the antebellum texts different from Hopkins's in 1900?
- Read Hopkins's portrait of Booker T. Washington; then review Washington's self-portrait as it appears in *Up From Slavery*. Comment on the rhetorical differences between the narrators of these two texts. What common traits, if any, do the two texts examine in the figure of Washington? Which narrator do you find more persuasive?
- To what extent do you think Hopkins's portrait of Frances Harper is flawed by hyperbole? To what extent can Hopkins's narrator be trusted to offer an unbiased account of Harper's achievements and the sources of her fame?
- Describe the tone of Hopkins's response to Cordelia Condict. What is your response to Hopkins's letter? Do you think she has understood Condict's complaint and answered it responsibly? On what do you base your conclusions?
- Support or refute the contention that Hopkins's short story "Talma

Gordon" and her reply to Cordelia Condict are but slight variations of one another. In what ways would such a claim be valid?

Bibliography

Carby, Hazel V. " 'On the Threshold of Woman's Era': Lynching, Empire, and Sexuality in Black Feminist Theory." In Anne McClintock, Aamir Muftia, and Ella Shohab, eds., *Dangerous Liaisons: Gender, Nation, and Postcolonial Perspectives*. Minneapolis: U of Minnesota P, 1997.

Gruesser, John Cullen, ed. *The Unruly Voice: Rediscovering Pauline Elizabeth Hopkins*. Urbana: U of Illinois P, 1996.

Japtok, Martin. "Pauline Hopkins's *Of One Blood*, Africa, and the " 'Darwinist Trap.' " *African American Review* 36 (2002): 403–16.

Nickel, John. "Eugenics and the Fiction of Pauline Hopkins." *American Transcendental Quarterly* 14 (2000): 47–60.

Randle, Gloria T. "Mates, Marriage and Motherhood: Feminist Visions in Pauline Hopkins's *Contending Forces*." *Tulsa Studies in Women's Literature* 18 (1999): 193–215.

Ida B. Wells-Barnett

1862–1931

Works in the Anthology

A Red Record, Chaps. 1, 10 (1895)

Other Works

The Reason Why the Colored American Is Not Represented in the World's Columbian Exposition (essay, 1893)
On Lynchings (1969)
Crusade for Justice: The Autobiography of Ida B. Wells-Barnett (ed. Alfreda Duster, 1970)
The Memphis Diary of Ida B. Wells (ed. Miriam DeCosta-Willis, 1995)

Themes

- Lynching, violence, corporeal crimes against African Americans
- African American racial uplift through economic enfranchisement
- Black civil and human rights

- Black resistance to sociopolitical and economic inequities
- Black educability and postbellum education
- Women's suffrage
- Black women's club movement
- Preservation and enforcement of the Fourteenth Amendment

Characteristics

- Erudite yet impassioned, jeremiadic tone
- Reportorial, journalistic prose style
- Critique of "Lynch law" and mob rule
- Critique of white economic supremacy
- Exposé of racial bigotry and discrimination
- Exposé of the fallacies of the Cult of True Womanhood

Teaching Strategies

- Listen with your students to the Audio Companion recording of "Strange Fruit." Ask them to discuss how the song might be read and heard as a gloss on Wells-Barnett's anti-lynching writing.
- Engage your students in a discussion of the phenomenon of "teacher rap" as represented in *NAFAM* and on the Audio Companion by rap and hip hop artists from Gil Scott-Heron through Nas. Considering the themes and rhetorical style that Wells-Barnett deployed at the end of the nineteenth century, to what extent do students think she might have opted for a hip hop vernacular style were she writing *A Red Record* today? Now play one or more of the Songs for Social Change included on the Audio Companion. Do students think, rather, that Wells-Barnett would have opted for the vernacular approach of the 1960s?

Questions

- Review *David Walker's Appeal*, and discuss ways that the endorsement of armed resistance to racial violence and discrimination at the beginning of the nineteenth century contrasts with Wells-Barnett's particular methods of resisting racialized violence at the century's end.
- Compare and contrast the use of the rhetoric of the jeremiad in Wells-Barnett's *A Red Record* and Maria Stewart's lecture. What sociopolitical advancements for blacks, if any, since Stewart's day does *A Red Record* tacitly document?
- What attitude toward the figure of the white woman does *A Red*

Record generally assert? Contrast Wells-Barnett's discussion of this figure with Eldridge Cleaver's in *Soul on Ice*.

- What literary text by a black feminist author included in *NAFAM* do you think most resonates with *A Red Record*? Explain your choice.
- Comment on Wells-Barnett's rhetorical decision to include James Russell Lowell's "Freedom" in *A Red Record*. What are the rhetorical effects of this decision? What does she gain (and/or lose) by the poem's inclusion?

Bibliography

Athey, Stephanie. "Eugenic Feminisms in Late-Nineteenth-Century America: Reading Race in Victoria Woodhull, Frances Willard, Anna Julia Cooper and Ida B. Wells." *Genders* 31 (2000).

Domina, Lynn. "Ida B. Wells-Barnett (1862–1931)." In Emmanuel S. Nelson, ed., *African American Autobiographers: A Sourcebook*. Westport, CT: Greenwood, 2002. 373–78.

Giddings, Paula. "Missing in Action: Ida B. Wells, the NAACP, and the Historical Record." *Meridians* 1 (2001): 1–17.

W. E. B. Du Bois

1868–1963

Works in the Anthology

"A Litany of Atlanta" (1906)
"The Song of the Smoke" (1907)
The Souls of Black Folk, complete except for Chaps. 2, 7–9 (1903)
"The Damnation of Women" (1920)
"Criteria of Negro Art" (1926)
"Two Novels" (1928)

Other Works

The Philadelphia Negro (1899)
Dusk of Dawn (autobiography, 1940)
The Complete Published Works of W. E. B. Du Bois (ed. Herbert Aptheker, 1973–86)
Correspondence of W. E. B. Du Bois (ed. Herbert Aptheker, 1986)
W. E. B. Du Bois: Writings (ed. Nathan Huggins, 1986)

W. E. B. Du Bois: A Reader (ed. David L. Lewis, 1995)
The Oxford W. E. B. Du Bois Reader (ed. Eric J. Sundquist, 1996)

Themes

- Power, beauty, and significance of black history, culture, art forms, and folk ways
- International movements of black resistance to oppression
- Eradication of bigotry, racial subjugation, all forms of inequality
- African spirituality and soul(fullness)
- Communal experience of "life within the Veil"
- African American self-perception as "double consciousness"
- African America's "Talented Tenth"

Characteristics

- African American vernacular English
- Formal, contemplative, controlled nonfiction prose
- Poetry and fiction are passionate
- Unflinching critique of white (economic) supremacy

Teaching Strategies

- You will want to demonstrate for students that Du Bois was the most refined, esteemed, versatile, prolific, and thus influential writer of the twentieth century. As an essayist, short-story writer, journalist, autobiographer, poet, critic, editor, philosopher, historian, sociologist, and educator, Du Bois made literary contributions that were largely unparalleled. Students generally become aware of Du Bois's significance as they read *The Souls of Black Folk,* an essay collection that explores African American life and culture via history, sociology, religion, economics, politics, and music.
- To drive home to students the versatility of Du Bois's credentials, have them research *The Souls of Black Folk* as the intersection of literary elements with characteristics of another academic discipline.

Questions

- Consider Du Bois's development of iconoclastic images in "A Litany of Atlanta." Do you think it fair to say that, as a poet, Du Bois is a traditionalist in form but a maverick in subject matter?
- In what ways does Du Bois advocate the rights and respect of African American women?
- Compare Du Bois's use of African American heritage as a source of

artistic inspiration with that of other black writers you've studied, in-
cluding, perhaps, Charles W. Chesnutt, Paul Laurence Dunbar,
James Weldon Johnson, Langston Hughes, Zora Neale Hurston, and
Toni Morrison.

• Read Du Bois's essays "Criteria of Negro Art" and "Two Novels"
alongside James Weldon Johnson's Preface to *The Book of American
Negro Poetry*. How do these theories of African American literature
differ from that expressed in Langston Hughes's "The Negro Artist
and the Racial Mountain" and also from diverse writers' theories developed during the Black Arts era? Do Du Bois's essays seem to have
more in common with Richard Wright's "Blueprint for Negro Writing" or Larry Neal's "The Black Arts Movement" than with Hughes's
essay? Why or why not?

Bibliography

English, Daylanne. "W. E. B. Du Bois's Family *Crisis*." *American Literature* 72 (2000): 291–319.

Lemert, Charles. "The Race of Time: Du Bois and Reconstruction."
Boundary 2 27 (2000): 215–59.

Lemons, Gary L. "Womanism in the Name of the 'Father': W. E. B. Du
Bois and the Problematics of Race, Patriarchy, and Art." *Phylon* 49
(2001): 185–202.

Lewis, David Levering. "W. E. B. Du Bois: Biography of a Race,
1868–1919." *Journal of Negro Education* 63 (1994): 649–50.

Lorini, Alessandra. " 'The Spell of Africa Is Upon Me': W. E. B. Du Bois's
Notion of Art as Propaganda." In Genevieve Fabre and Michel Feith,
eds., *Temples for Tomorrow: Looking Back at the Harlem Renaissance*.
Bloomington: Indiana UP, 2001. 159–76.

Miles, Kevin. "Haunting Music in *The Souls of Black Folk*." *Boundary* 2
27 (2000): 199–214.

Reed, Adolph L. *W. E. B. Du Bois and American Political Thought*. New
York: Oxford UP, 1996.

Schneider, Ryan. "How to Be a (Sentimental) Race Man: Mourning and
Passing in W. E. B. Du Bois's *The Souls of Black Folk*." In Milette
Shamir and Jennifer Travis, eds., *Boys Don't Cry? Rethinking Narratives
of Masculinity and Emotion in the United States*. New York: Columbia
UP, 2002. 106–23.

Watts, Eric K. "Cultivating a Black Public Voice: W. E. B. DuBois and the
'Criteria of Negro Art.' " *Rhetoric and Public Affairs* 4 (2001): 181–201.

James D. Corrothers

1869–1917

Works in the Anthology

"The Snapping of the Bow" (1901)
"Me 'n' Dunbar" (1901)
"Paul Laurence Dunbar" (1912)
"At the Closed Gate of Justice" (1913)
"An Indignation Dinner" (1915)

Other Works

The Black Cat Club (essays, 1902)
In Spite of the Handicap (autobiography, 1916)

Themes

- Subversion of stereotypes of African Americans, especially in minstrel tradition
- Intertextuality and signifying on earlier African American texts
- The injustices of slavery and white supremacy
- Ridiculousness of black racial uplift movement
- Christianity

Characteristics

- Parody, satire, humor, sarcasm, critique
- Parody of African American vernacular English forms and discourses
- Vernacular traditions, including folktales and ballads
- (Mock) assimilation of (white) romanticized plantation tradition literature
- Condemnation of racism and white supremacy

Questions

- What attitude toward Paul Laurence Dunbar does the speaker of the poem by that title assert?

Bibliography

Bruce, Dickson D. Jr. "James Corrothers Reads a Book; Or, The Lives of Sandy Jenkins." *African American Review* 26 (1992): 665–75.

Gaines, Kevin. "Assimilationist Minstrelsy as Racial Uplift Ideology: James D. Corrothers's Literary Quest for Black Leadership." *American Quarterly* 45 (1993): 341–70.

James Weldon Johnson

1871–1938

Works in the Anthology

"Sence You Went Away" (1900)
"Lift Ev'ry Voice and Sing" (1921)
"O Black and Unknown Bards" (1908)
"Fifty Years" (1913)
"Brothers" (1916)
"The Creation" (1920)
"My City" (1923)
The Autobiography of an Ex-Colored Man (1912)
The Book of American Negro Poetry, Preface (1922)

Other Works

Fifty Years and Other Poems (1917)
God's Trombones: Seven Negro Sermons in Verse (1927)
Along This Way (autobiography, 1933)
Saint Peter Relates an Incident (poems, 1935)
The Selected Writings of James Weldon Johnson (ed. Sondra Kathryn Wilson, 1995)

Themes

- Beauty and power of African American vernacular English and folk traditions
- Black "voice," expression, and self-representation
- African American survival of race persecutions
- African Americans' triumph over racism, classism, cultural degradation, and so on
- Violence against African Americans
- Miscegenation, race hatred, and racial identity formation
- Tragic mulatto and mixed-race identities in the United States
- Passing as racial "cross-dressing"
- Great Migration
- Interracial marriage

Characteristics

- Celebration of African American vernacular English
- Commitment to preservation of black vernacular cultures
- Revision of the stereotype of the tragic mulatto
- Modernist psychological realism

Teaching Strategies

- Listen with students to the recording of "The Creation" on the Audio Companion.
- Listen with students to the recordings of "Strange Fruit" and "The Message" on the Audio Companion. Then discuss these recordings as variations on the theme of Johnson's "Brothers." Do your students think Johnson would situate his poem in the same tradition as more recent lyrics about violence against blacks, including Biggie Smalls's "Things Done Changed" and Eric B. & Rakim's "I Ain't No Joke"?

Questions

- Use other *NAFAM* selections in this section—including texts by Charles W. Chesnutt and Paul Laurence Dunbar—to analyze the literary contributions Johnson made to his era as well as the political implications of his rhetorical choices.
- Compare and contrast Johnson's vernacular diction and folk subjects to those of other African American poets. You might begin with Frances E. W. Harper's "Aunt Chloe's Politics," Paul Laurence Dunbar's "When Malindy Sings," Sonia Sanchez's "Summer Words of a Sistuh Addict," and Quincy Troupe's "Conversation Overheard." Based on your readings, do the rhetorical features and conventions of the black vernacular tradition change over time or do black poets seem to sustain the tradition by holding fast to original rhetorical characteristics?
- Johnson's poem "Lift Ev'ry Voice and Sing," written to commemorate Abraham Lincoln's birthday and set to music by Johnson's brother Rosemond, is now known as the "Black National Anthem." It has been sung by many and recorded by professional musicians since the first performance in 1900. Discuss the qualities of this lyric that you think have contributed to its longevity and prominence. Then discuss the implications of a *black* national anthem.
- Written on the fiftieth anniversary of the signing of the Emancipation Proclamation, "Fifty Years" evaluates the black historical past and its potential impact on African Americans' future in the United States. What themes emerge in this poem? How would you charac-

terize the poem's tone? Identify any points in the poem where you hear shifts in tone.

- Compare and contrast Johnson's representation of lynching as a theme in "Brothers" with Paul Laurence Dunbar's treatment of the same theme in "The Haunted Oak."
- Assess the validity of Johnson's argument for the production of African American literature and art as articulated in the Preface to *The Book of American Negro Poetry* by reading it alongside Phillis Wheatley's "To Mæcenas."
- Johnson developed his Preface to *The Book of American Negro Poetry* around the same time that Du Bois penned his "Criteria of Negro Art," Arthur A. Schomburg wrote "The Negro Digs Up His Past," and Langston Hughes authored "The Negro Artist and the Racial Mountain." Examine these four essays together and comment on the similarity of the ideas as well as on each author's rhetorical distinctiveness.
- In what ways, if any, do you think Johnson's Preface to *The Book of American Negro Poetry* influenced the later black literary criticism articulated in Hoyt Fuller's "Towards a Black Aesthetic" and Addison Gayle Jr.'s "The Black Aesthetic"?
- Compare and contrast Johnson's deployment of the figure of the tragic mulatto in *The Autobiography of an Ex-Colored Man* with treatments of miscegenation and passing in William Wells Brown's *Clotel*, Charles W. Chesnutt's "The Wife of His Youth," and Nella Larsen's *Quicksand*.
- Analyze *The Autobiography of an Ex-Colored Man* for its adherence to slave narrative conventions. Can one rightly argue that Johnson's novel is a neo-slave narrative?
- Situate *The Autobiography of an Ex-Colored Man* among other African American writings of its era that treat migration as a theme. After Emancipation what comments on the mass movement from the South to the North do black authors generally assert?

Bibliography

Carroll, Anne. "Art, Literature, and the Harlem Renaissance: The Messages of *God's Trombones*." *College Literature* 29 (2002): 57–81.

Marren, Susan, and Robert Cochran. "Johnson's *The Autobiography of an Ex-Coloured Man*." *The Explicator* 60 (2002): 147–150.

McCarthy, Timothy P. "Legalizing Cultural Anxieties: Plessy, Race and Literary Representation of 'Passing' in James Weldon Johnson's *Autobiography of an Ex-Colored Man*." *Griot* 16 (1997): 1–10.

Portelli, Alessandro. "The Tragedy and the Joke: James Weldon Johnson's *The Autobiography of an Ex-Colored Man*." In Genevieve Fabre and Michel Feith, eds., *Temples for Tomorrow: Looking Back at the Harlem Renaissance*. Bloomington: Indiana UP, 2001.

Ruotolo, Cristina. "James Weldon Johnson and the Autobiography of an Ex-Colored Musician." *American Literature* 72 (2000): 249–51.

Sheehy, John. "The Mirror and the Veil: The Passing Novel and the Quest for American Racial Identity." *African American Review* 33 (1999): 401–15.

Warren, Kenneth W. "Troubled Black Humanity in *The Souls of Black Folk* and *The Autobiography of an Ex-Colored Man*." In Donald Pizer, ed., *The Cambridge Companion to American Realism and Naturalism: Howells to London*. Cambridge: Cambridge UP, 1995. 263–77.

Washington, Salim. "Of Black Bards, Known and Unknown: Music as Racial Metaphor in James Weldon Johnson's *The Autobiography of an Ex-Colored Man*." *Callaloo* 25 (2002): 233–56.

Paul Laurence Dunbar

1872–1906

Works in the Anthology

"Ode to Ethiopia" (1893)
"Worn Out" (1893)
"A Negro Love Song" (1895)
"The Colored Soldiers" (1895)
"An Ante-Bellum Sermon" (1895)
"Ere Sleep Comes Down to Soothe the Weary Eyes" (1895)
"Not They Who Soar" (1895)
"When Malindy Sings" (1895)
"We Wear the Mask" (1895)
"Little Brown Baby" (1897)
"Her Thought and His" (1899)
"A Cabin Tale" (1899)
"Sympathy" (1899)
"Dinah Kneading Dough" (1899)
"The Haunted Oak" (1903)
"Douglass" (1903)
"Philosophy" (1903)

"Black Samson of Brandywine" (1903)
"The Poet" (1903)
"The Fourth of July and Race Outrages" (1903)

Other Works

Oak and Ivy (poems, 1893)
Lyrics of Lowly Life (poems, 1896)
Poems of Cabin and Field
The Sport of the Gods (novel, 1903)
The Paul Laurence Dunbar Reader (ed. Jay Martin and Gossie Hudson, 1975)
The Collected Poetry of Paul Laurence Dunbar (ed. Joanne M. Braxton, 1993)

Themes

- African American race pride
- Double consciousness
- Revisions of (white) plantation literature and minstrelsy traditions
- Denunciation of lynching and other violent assaults on blacks
- Devotion and trustworthiness, pledges of faith and romantic love
- African American patriotism
- African American cultural and political achievements after slavery

Characteristics

- African American vernacular English, especially as rhythmic dialect cadences
- Humor and/or pathos
- Classical lyric forms, including sonnets, ballads, folksongs

Teaching Strategies

- Listen with your students to the literary sermons included on the Audio Companion. Then engage them in a discussion of vernacular characteristics of those selections and Dunbar's "An Ante-Bellum Sermon." Which features seem particularly designed to engage a *listening* audience? How do the students distinguish between these performances and more popular cultural/stereotypical versions of black folk sermons?

Questions

- Compare Dunbar's "The Fourth of July and Race Outrages" with Frederick Douglass's "What to the Slave Is the Fourth of July." What common political attitudes and perspectives do the two essays share? What does the Civil War seem to mean to each author?

- What common features as a political rhetorician (in "The Fourth of July and Race Outrages") does Dunbar share with Frances Harper, James Baldwin, and Martin Luther King Jr.?

- Do you find sufficient overlap in the themes and ideas of Dunbar's poems written in "Negro dialect" and his poems written in "standard English" to dismiss the conventional division of his work into these two separate categories? Explain your conclusion and identify the poems that led you to it.

- For all the grace, style, dignity, and "soul" that distinguish Dunbar's portrayal of ordinary folk in his dialect verse, critics have also read ambivalence in those poems. Select a representative dialect poem and read it closely for evidence of the poet's hesitation.

- Compare and contrast Dunbar's articulation of respect for common people and black vernacular folkways with that of some of his literary contemporaries and descendants: Charles W. Chesnutt, James Weldon Johnson, Langston Hughes, and Zora Neale Hurston. What particular characteristics of Dunbar's folk representations do you find in their literary works?

- Read Dunbar's poems, paying close attention to depictions of scenes, emotions, and issues that cross racial, economic, and cultural lines. What common attitudes does Dunbar isolate, modify, or revise using elements that render his poetry distinctive?

- Explain the double entendre at work in Dunbar's "An Ante-Bellum Sermon." How does this poem compare to other sermons included in *NAFAM*? What message seems to be at the heart of Dunbar's homily? How does Dunbar's preacher define *freedom*? According to the poem, how will enslaved people know when freedom has been achieved?

- Contrast Dunbar's "An Ante-Bellum Sermon" with James Weldon Johnson's "The Creation." What characteristics of the subgenre of folk sermons can you infer, based on these two texts? How do they differ from other sermons of other literary historical periods included in *NAFAM*?

- If you are familiar with Maya Angelou's autobiography *I Know Why the Caged Bird Sings*, read Dunbar's "Sympathy" to speculate about Angelou's reasons for borrowing from Dunbar's poem for her title. What kinds of intertextuality do you read in these two works?

Bibliography

Cavaioli, Frank. "Phillis Wheatley and Paul Laurence Dunbar Discover Christopher Columbus." *VIA: Voices in Italian-Americana* 10 (1999): 47–55.

Martin, Herbert W., and Ronald Primeau, eds. *In His Own Voice: The Dramatic and Other Uncollected Works of Paul Laurence Dunbar.* Columbus: Ohio UP, 2002.

Pitcher, Geoffrey. "The Readerly Ruse: Paul Laurence Dunbar's Dialect Poetry and the Aesthetics of Authenticity." In Marc Maufort and Jean-Pierre Noppen, eds., *Voices of Power: Co-Operation and Conflict in English Language and Literatures.* Liege, Belgium: L3–Liege Language and Literature, 1997. 183–90.

Ramsey, William. "Dunbar's Dixie." *Southern Literary Journal* 32 (1999): 30–45.

Sutton E. Griggs

1872–1933

Works in the Anthology

The Hindered Hand; or, The Reign of the Repressionist, Chaps. 19–20 (1905)

Other Works

Imperium in Imperio (novel, 1899)
Overshadowed (novel, 1901)
Unfettered (novel, 1902)
Pointing the Way (novel, 1908)
Wisdom's Call (1911)
The Story of My Struggles (1914)

Themes

- Lynching and other violence upon African Americans
- Rape of black women
- Forced migration to escape violence
- Economic and political inequities
- Social and racial uplift

- Critique of white racism and white supremacy
- Racial coalition and cooperation

Characteristics

- Straightforward language and reportorial style
- Fiction directed toward a readership diverse in race, class, and literacy
- Explicit political agenda for racial uplift

Questions

- Compare and contrast the representation of violent assault on African American men and African American women in Griggs's novel and the representation of sexual and physical violence in Harriet Jacobs's *Incidents in the Life of a Slave Girl* and in one of the accounts by Frederick Douglass. Besides genre, in what ways does Griggs's novel differ from the ex-slaves' autobiographical narratives?
- Compare and contrast the description of the lynching in *The Hindered Hand* with that of the lynching in James Weldon Johnson's *The Autobiography of an Ex-Colored Man*. What rhetorical features do the two contemporaneous texts share?

Bibliography

Chander, Harish. "Sutton Elbert Griggs (1872–1933)." In Emmanuel S. Nelson, ed., *African American Autobiographers: A Sourcebook*. Westport, CT: Greenwood, 2002. 166–70.

Kay, Roy. "Sutton E. Griggs (1872–1933)." In Emmanuel S. Nelson, ed., *African American Authors, 1745–1945: A Bio-Bibliographical Critical Sourcebook*. Westport, CT: Greenwood, 2000. 188–93.

Nowatzki, Robert. " 'Sublime Patriots': Black Masculinity in Three African-American Novels." *Journal of Men's Studies: A Scholarly Journal about Men and Masculinities* 8 (1999): 59–72.

Wallinger, Hanna. "Secret Societies and Dark Empires: Sutton E. Griggs's *Imperium in Imperio* and W. E. B. Du Bois's *Dark Princess*." In John G. Blair, et al., eds., *Selected Papers from the Bi-National Conference of the Swiss and Austrian Associations for American Studies at the Salzburg Seminar, Nov. 1996*. Tübingen, Germany: Narr, 1997. 197–210.

Alice Moore Dunbar Nelson

1875–1935

Works in the Anthology

"Violets" (1917)
"I Sit and Sew" (1920)
"April Is on the Way" (1927)
"Violets" (1895)

Other Works

Violets and Other Tales (1895)
The Goodness of St. Rocque (stories, 1899)
Give Us This Day: The Diary of Alice Dunbar-Nelson (ed. Gloria T. Hull, 1984)
The Works of Alice Dunbar-Nelson (ed. Gloria T. Hull, 1988)

Themes

- Race, racialization, and regionalisms
- Gender conflicts, especially among African Americans
- Proto-feminist issues
- Social and economic justice
- Creole life and culture in the U.S. South
- Breadth and variety of African American identities
- Revisions of the figure of the tragic mulatta
- Lesbian identity, lesbian relationships
- Homophobia

Characteristics

- Dunbar Nelson achieved distinction as an author of poems, reviews, sketches, and short fiction as well as for her musicianship, editorial work, journalism, teaching, and literary criticism and scholarship.
- Local color attention to characteristics and distinctions of New Orleans life and culture

Questions

- Compare Dunbar Nelson's use of the short story form in "Violets" (1895) with that of her contemporary Charles W. Chesnutt.

- Compare and contrast the depiction of lesbian romantic relationships by Dunbar Nelson and Audre Lorde, separated by nearly a century. What progress in women's (sexual) rights, if any, appears to have been made by the time Lorde wrote *Zami: A New Spelling of My Name?*

Bibliography

Brooks, Kristina. "Alice Dunbar-Nelson's Local Colors of Ethnicity, Class, and Place." *MELUS* 23 (1998): 3–4.

Gowdy, Anne R. "Alice Dunbar-Nelson." In Carolyn Perry and Mary-Louise Weaks, eds., *The History of Southern Women's Literature*. Baton Rouge: Louisiana State UP, 2002. 225–30.

Grandt, Jurgen. "Rewriting the Final Adjustment of Affairs: Culture, Race, and Politics in Alice Dunbar-Nelson's New Orleans." *Short Story* 9 (2001): 46–57.

Menke, Pamela. "Behind the 'White Veil': Alice Dunbar-Nelson, Creole Color, and *The Goodness of St. Rocque*." In Suzanne Disheroon-Green and Lisa Abney, eds., *Songs of Reconstructing South: Building Literary Louisiana, 1865–1945*. Westport, CT: Greenwood, 2002. 77–88.

William Stanley Braithwaite

1878–1962

Works in the Anthology

"The Watchers" (1904)
"The House of the Falling Leaves" (1908)
"Sic Vita" (1908)
"Turn Me to My Yellow Leaves" (1948)
"Quiet Has a Hidden Sound" (1948)

Other Works

Lyrics of Life and Love (1904)
The House of Falling Leaves, with Other Poems (1908)
The House under Arcturus (autobiography, 1940)
The William Stanley Braithwaite Reader (1972)

Themes

- Universality of (African) American life and culture
- Black flight and migration

Characteristics

- Traditional forms and conventions of nineteenth-century Anglo-American lyric
- Hauntingly poetic lines with images of pathos

Questions

- Braithwaite's poems obliquely address issues and aspects of African American life that other poets of his era and beyond depict more overtly. Read "The House of the Falling Leaves" and "Sic Vita" and locate in them some of the subtly invoked themes that mark Braithwaite as a *black* man of his day.
- Trace the theme of migration in Braithwaite's poems. How does Braithwaite's development of it compare with Phillis Wheatley's in the eighteenth century? With Claude McKay's in the generation after Braithwaite?
- Compare "Sic Vita" with the antebellum spiritual "I Know Moon-Rise." With what conventions and tools has Braithwaite adapted this vernacular text into a much more formal literary tradition? Decide whether the overall attitude of "Sic Vita" is more secular than sacred or vice versa.
- At the center of "Turn Me to My Yellow Leaves," Braithwaite makes an assertion that resonates with virtually every antebellum slave narrative and many after Emancipation: "I, who never had a name." Review the conventions of the slave narrative by examining at least one such text included in *NAFAM* and explore ways that this poem, which cites no other references to bondage, can be read as representative of the slave narrative tradition.
- How is your reading of "Quiet Has a Hidden Sound" affected by a reminder that Boston's Beacon Hill was renowned for Underground Railroad activity during the slavery era, particularly during the years of fervor around the Fugitive Slave Law?

Bibliography

Szefel, Lisa. "Encouraging Verse: William S. Braithwaite and the Poetics of Race." *New England Quarterly* 74 (2001): 32–61.

Thomas, Lorenzo. "W. S. Braithwaite vs. Harriet Monroe: The Heavyweight Poetry Championship, 1917." In Aldon Nielsen, ed., *Reading*

Race in American Poetry: "An Area of Act." Urbana: U of Illinois P, 2000. 84–106.

Fenton Johnson

1888–1958

Works in the Anthology

"Singing Hallelujia" (1915)
"Song of the Whirlwind" (1915)
"My God in Heaven Said to Me" (1915)
"The Lonely Mother" (1916)
"Tired" (1919)
"The Scarlet Woman" (1922)

Other Works

A Little Dreaming (poems, 1913)
Visions of the Dusk (poems, 1915)
Songs of the Soil (poems, 1916)
Tales of Darkest America (essays, 1920)
For the Highest Good (stories, 1920)

Themes

- Distinction of African American literary voice
- Beauty of black vernacular cultural elements
- Traditional elements of antebellum spirituals
- Christian hope and religious piety
- Despair, dejection, sorrow—without the cathartic uplift of the blues
- Economic deprivations and injustices
- Sexual and economic exploitation of women

Characteristics

- African American vernacular English and other vernacular traditional elements
- Black vernacular traditional musical forms
- Somber tone, pessimistic voice, pathos

Questions

- Compare and contrast the antebellum spirituals by Johnson with one or two spirituals from the vernacular section of *NAFAM*. What features and tropes, if any, do you find in Johnson's lyrics that render them more texts for reading than texts for hearing? Why do you suppose Johnson's lyrics have been less popular over the years than the earlier songs?
- Contrast Johnson's "The Scarlet Woman" with similar poems by Langston Hughes that depict women sex workers just a few years later, at the height of the Harlem Renaissance. How do the portraits of economically disadvantaged women differ? What poems by African American women have you encountered that treat such women in similar ways?

Bibliography

Harrington, Joseph. "A Response to Linda Woolley [re: Fenton Johnson]." *Langston Hughes Review* 14 (1996): 49–51.

Russell-Robinson, Joyce. "Renaissance Manque: Black WPA Artists in Chicago." *The Western Journal of Black Studies* 18 (1994): 36–44.

Teaching the Literature of the Reconstruction to the New Negro Renaissance

From the beginning of Reconstruction well into the beginning of the twentieth century, from 1865 to 1919, African American authors continued to address the issues of slavery and freedom, color and racial discrimination. Moreover, they expanded the already broad range of uses to which their literary predecessors had vigorously put literature and a black aesthetic. Postbellum black writers retold the story of slavery by challenging myths of black passivity with stories of their ancestors' heroism. Revising earlier narratives of black women's roles and mores, Charlotte Forten Grimké's *Journal* offers students an opportunity to examine a committed writer's account of the effects of the Civil War on her life and letters. At the end of the century, Booker T. Washington's *Up From Slavery*, when juxtaposed with post-Reconstruction and Gilded Age texts, tells one story about African American strife and heroism but tells a strikingly different one when juxtaposed with antebellum narratives by other former or fugitive slaves.

Washington's name graces a phrase commonly used in discussing the end of the nineteenth century in the United States: "the Age of Washington and Du Bois." By that time, Frederick Douglass had died, and citizens filled in the spaces he left with two indisputable leaders from among many prominent and skillful African American figures. The ostensibly contrary philosophies espoused by Booker T. Washington and W. E. B. Du Bois compounded national interest in these two leaders.

Booker T. Washington and W. E. B. Du Bois and their historical context at the end of the nineteenth century are better comprehended when the period is reconstituted in the terms of the time: "the Woman's Era." Ida B. Wells-Barnett, Anna Julia Cooper, Pauline E. Hopkins, and Alice Moore Dunbar Nelson worked alongside Washington and Du Bois as well as with many other African American women—particularly within the Black Women's Club movement—to create a literature that influenced lives and attitudes deep into the twentieth century. Wells-Barnett's *Red Record,* then, stands with Washington's Atlanta Exposition address and Du Bois's "Song of the Smoke" for breadth and depth. Hopkins's literary career becomes immediately clearer in the knowledge that Washington purchased the *Colored American Magazine* in which Hopkins frequently opposed his pronouncements during her tenure as the magazine's editor.

Students' research into some of the personal histories of the authors of this period can also enrich knowledge. In addition to the more familiar study in opposites presented by Charles W. Chesnutt and Paul Laurence Dunbar, for example, professors might introduce a less familiar analysis by assigning *NAFAM* selections by Dunbar Nelson.

Some students are likely at first to misapprehend uses of African American vernacular English and vernacular dialect or the development of blue-vein characters as authorial pandering to racial stereotypes. If so, you might want to use the following questions to engage students in a discussion of historical contexts:

- According to the literature, what effective rhetorical strategies did post-Reconstruction African American writers devise to protest demeaning and dismissive racial attitudes?
- What were black authors' literary responses to the rampant lynching and legalized racial discrimination so pervasive during the sociopolitical "nadir" of African American history?
- Where were most of the publishing houses; who owned them; and who determined what was published, where, and how it was marketed? That is, what was the impact of the publishing industry on the development and dissemination of African American literature circa 1900?
- What were the dominant literary forms, plots, and character types deployed by late-nineteenth-century African American writers? Granted that these choices were not coincidental but deliberate, on what factors and phenomena do these literary choices seem based?

- If the most dominant rhetorical forms in African American literature are signifying and masking, find examples of them and examine how they are deployed in African American writings of the Reconstruction and afterward.
- Return to the vernacular section of *NAFAM* and ask students to trace the development of key figures from the vernacular traditions in Reconstruction literature. For example, where is the figure of the Signifying Monkey in Charles W. Chesnutt's short fiction? Can they locate folk sermons in Paul Laurence Dunbar's poetry? In James Weldon Johnson's? In other poets'?

Genres

Poetry

Grimké
Du Bois
Corrothers
J. W. Johnson
Dunbar
Dunbar Nelson
Braithwaite
F. Johnson

Oration

Washington
Cooper

Periodical Literature

Chesnutt
Hopkins
Du Bois
J. W. Johnson
Dunbar

Religious/Political Treatise

Cooper
Wells-Barnett
Du Bois

J. W. Johnson
Dunbar

Prose Narrative/Autobiography/Slave Narrative

Grimké
Washington
Chesnutt
Cooper
Du Bois

Short Fiction

Chesnutt
Hopkins
Dunbar Nelson

Novel

J. W. Johnson
Griggs

Bibliography

Brandwein, Pamela. "Slavery as an Interpretative Issue in the Reconstruction Congresses." *Law and Society Review* 34 (2000): 315–66.

Cardyn, Lisa. "Sexualized Racism/Gendered Violence: Outraging the Body Politic in the Reconstruction South." *Michigan Law Review* 100 (2002): 675–868.

Edwards, Laura F. "The Disappearance of Susan Daniel and Henderson Cooper: Gender and Narratives in the Reconstruction-Era U.S. South." *Feminist Studies* 22 (1996): 363–87.

Hardwig, Bill. "Who Owns the Whip?: Chesnutt, Tourgee, and Reconstruction Justice." *African American Review* 36 (2002): 5–21.

Harrison, John. "The Lawfulness of the Reconstruction Amendments." *University of Chicago Law Review* 68 (2001): 375–462.

Keely, Karen A. "Marriage Plots and National Reunion: The Trope of Romantic Reconciliation in Postbellum Literature." *Mississippi Quarterly* 51 (1998): 621–48.

McGee, Brian R. "Thomas Dixon's *The Clansman*: Radicals, Reactionaries, and the Anticipated Utopia." *Southern Communication Journal* 65 (2000): 300–318.

Schweninger, Loren. "Slavery and Southern Violence: County Court Petitions and the South's Peculiar Institution." *Journal of Negro History* 85 (2000): 33–36.

Silver, Andrew. "Making Minstrelsy of Murder: George Washington Harris, the Ku Klux Klan, and the Reconstruction Aesthetic of Black Fright." *Prospects* 25 (2000): 339–53.

Walker, Clarence E. "The A.M.E. Church and Reconstruction." *Negro History Bulletin* 48 (1985): 10–13.

Harlem Renaissance, 1919–1940

Arthur A. Schomburg

1874–1938

Works in the Anthology

"The Negro Digs Up His Past" (1925)

Other Works

The Arthur Schomburg Papers (1991)

Themes

- Importance of blacks' contribution to their own independence
- Black self-determination and racial uplift around the world
- Importance of accurate and authentic accounts of African American history
- Distinction between objectification of blacks and African subjectivity
- African contributions to international history
- Black historical archives and exhibitions
- African American education
- Fallacy of scientific racism

Characteristics

- Formal, erudite, sociological tone
- Critique of white "well-wishers" who inadvertently thwart black self-advancement
- Documentation of "facts" of black history
- Catalogue of African literary and historical achievements in the New World/America
- Call for re-examination of black historical documents
- Call for renewed appreciation of African contributions to international history

Questions

- "The Negro Digs Up His Past" cites an 1808 study and collection of black literature. What is Schomburg's assessment of this French-authored book? How do you think Schomburg would evaluate W. E. B. Du Bois's *The Souls of Black Folk*?
- Summarize the three conclusions about black history Schomburg claims are apparent in 1925. Based on your knowledge of the historical and literary developments in African American history from the end of the nineteenth century through the Harlem Renaissance, do you agree with Schomburg's conclusions? Why or why not? What significance do you think Schomburg's report of the state of black affairs held in 1925? On what do you base your answer?
- What evidence does Schomburg provide for his argument that "the mind of the Negro has leapt forward faster than the slow clearings of scholarship will yet safely permit"? Do you think this pronouncement holds true today? Why or why not?

Bibliography

Clarke, John Henrik. "The Influence of Arthur A. Schomburg on My Concept of Africana Studies." *Phylon* 49 (1992): 4–10.

Sinnette, Elinor Des Verney. *Arthur Alfonso Schomburg, Black Bibliophile and Collector: A Biography*. Detroit: Wayne State UP, 1989.

Angelina Weld Grimké

1880–1958

Works in the Anthology

"A Winter Twilight" (1923)
"The Black Finger" (1925)
"When the Green Lies over the Earth" (1927)
"Tenebris" (1927)

Other Works

Selected Works of Angelina Weld Grimké (ed. Carolivia Herron, 1991)

Themes

- Isolation, loneliness, alienation
- Suppressed racial conflicts
- Beauty as blackness
- Disappointed romantic love

Characteristics

- Traditional lyric forms
- Experimental lyric forms
- Natural imagery
- Irony
- Rhetorical questions

Questions

- Listen to the Audio Companion recording of "Strange Fruit" and compare and contrast the use of the figure of the tree in the recording and in Grimké's poem "Tenebris."
- The quality of blackness is sometimes sinister and other times endearing in Grimké's work. Analyze the attitude toward blackness as a construct in the selections printed in *NAFAM*.

Bibliography

Gourdine, Angeletta. "The Drama of Lynching in Two Blackwomen's Drama, or Relating Grimke's *Rachel* to Hansberry's *A Raisin in the Sun*." *Modern Drama* 41 (1998): 533–65.

Anne Spencer

1882–1975

Works in the Anthology

"Before the Feast of Shushan" (1920)
"Dunbar" (1920)
"At the Carnival" (1923)
"The Wife-Woman" (1931)

Themes

- Natural world
- Race, gender, and culture

Characteristics

- High modernist conventions
- Enigmatic, elusive, and allusive style
- Ironic perspectives on race and gender

Questions

- Compare and contrast the portrait of Queen Vashti in Spencer's "Before the Feast of Shushan" with Frances Harper's mid-nineteenth-century lyric on the same Old Testament figure. What do these two poems suggest about African American women's preoccupation with Vashti?
- What does Spencer gain with the use of first-person male royalty perspective in "Before the Feast of Shushan"? How do you suppose the poem's tone and timbre would differ if the speaker and perspective were different?
- Compare the attitude of the speaker of Spencer's "Dunbar" with that of Countee Cullen's "To John Keats, Poet, at Spring Time" to get a better sense of Spencer's irony. How are the two lyrics different? Do you think this difference is gendered? Why or why not?

Bibliography

Greene, J. Lee. *Time's Unfolding Garden: Anne Spencer's Life and Poetry*. Baton Rouge: Louisiana State UP, 1977.

Johnston, Sara Andrews. "Anne Spencer (1882–1975)." In Laurie Champion, ed., *American Women Writers, 1900–1945: A Bio-Bibliographical Critical Sourcebook*. Westport, CT: Greenwood, 2000. 312–17.

Stetson, Erlene. "Anne Spencer." *College Language Association Journal* 21 (1978): 400–409.

Jessie Redmon Fauset

c. 1884–1961

Works in the Anthology

Plum Bun: A Novel without a Moral, "Home," Chaps. 1–2 (1928)

Other Works

"The Negro in Art: How Shall He Be Portrayed" (1926)
There Is Confusion (novel, 1924)
The Chinaberry Tree and Selected Writings (novel and other forms, 1931)
Comedy: American Style (mixed prose form, 1933)

Themes

- International questions of race, class, and gender
- Political issues facing modern African American women
- Middle class (black) American life and values
- Du Boisian "Talented Tenth"
- The color line in the black family
- African American pride, resilience, survival
- Miscegenation, amalgamation, and racial passing
- African American generational families
- Black women's relationships and friendships
- Romantic love and marriage
- African American labor, wages, class locations, and economic situations

Characteristics

- Sentimental novel conventions masking realistic treatment of urgent political questions
- Traditional prose forms
- Avant-garde attitudes and themes
- (Apparent) promotion of black bourgeoisie and bourgeois values

Questions

- Compare and contrast the representation of relationships between sisters as well as between mothers and daughters in Fauset's *Plum Bun* and Dorothy West's *The Living Is Easy*. What do these two women writers, both known for their "bourgeois aesthetic," assert about black womanhood within family contexts?

Bibliography

Kuenz, Jane. "The Face of America: Performing Race and Nation in Jessie Fauset's *There Is Confusion*." *Yale Journal of Criticism* 12 (1999): 89–112.

Lutes, Jean-Marie. "Making Up Race: Jessie Fauset, Nella Larsen, and the African American Cosmetics Industry." *Arizona Quarterly* 58 (2002): 77–108.

Miller, Nina. "Femininity, Publicity, and the Class Division of Cultural Labor: Jessie Redmon Fauset's *There Is Confusion*." *African American Review* 30 (1996): 205–21.

Pfeiffer, Kathleen. "The Limits of Identity in Jessie Fauset's *Plum Bun*." *Legacy* 18 (2001): 79–93.

Stetz, Margaret D. "Jessie Fauset's Fiction: Reconsidering Race and Revisiting Aestheticism." In Teresa Hubel and Neil Brooks, eds., *Literature and Racial Ambiguity*. Amsterdam: Rodopi, 2002. 253–70.

Tomlinson, Susan. "Vision to Visionary: The New Negro Woman as Cultural Worker in Jessie Redmon Fauset's *Plum Bun*." *Legacy* 19 (2002): 90–98.

Zackodnik, Teresa. "Passing Transgressions and Authentic Identity in Jessie Fauset's *Plum Bun* and Nella Larsen's *Passing*." In Teresa Hubel and Neil Brooks, eds., *Literature and Racial Ambiguity*. Amsterdam: Rodopi, 2002. 45–69.

Alain Locke

1886–1954

Works in the Anthology

"The New Negro" (1925)

Other Works

> *Plays of Negro Life* (co-editor, 1927)
> *Four Negro Poets* (editor, 1927)
> *The Negro in Art: A Pictorial Record of the Negro Artist and of the Negro Theme in Art* (editor, 1940)
> *When Peoples Meet: A Study in Race and Culture Contacts* (co-editor, 1942)

Themes

- Shifts in African American values, identities, and ideologies
- Definition of the New Negro as sociopolitical construct
- Great Migration of the early twentieth century
- Impact of industrialization on the (African American) arts and humanities
- Harlem as (atypical) microcosm of national transformations
- Race radicalism

Characteristics

- Formal, erudite, scholarly tone
- Sociological scrutiny and objectification of "the New Negro"
- Infusion of poignant literary lines from New Negro poets

Questions

- Locke opens his famous essay with a contrast of the "Old Negro" and the "New Negro," categories apparently more rooted in ideology than in chronology. Based on your studies of African American literature, are there figures or personalities you associate with each of these two groups? Who are they and why?
- Based on your knowledge of Harlem Renaissance literature and its sociohistorical contexts, how accurate is Locke's contention that "by shedding the old chrysalis of the Negro problem we are achieving something like a spiritual emancipation"?
- Compare and contrast Locke's theory of African American literature with that espoused by James Weldon Johnson just a few years before "The New Negro," in 1921, and with that articulated by Langston Hughes in 1926.

Bibliography

Charras, Francoise. "The West Indian Presence in Alain Locke's *The New Negro*." In Genevieve Fabre and Michel Feith, eds., *Temples for Tomor-*

row: *Looking Back at the Harlem Renaissance.* Bloomington: Indiana UP, 2001. 270–87.

Fitchue, M. Anthony. "Locke and Du Bois: Two Major Voices Muzzled by Philanthropic Organizations." *Journal of Blacks in Higher Education* 14 (1996–97): 111–16.

Kelley, James. "Blossoming in Strange New Forms: Male Homosexuality and the Harlem Renaissance." *Soundings* 80 (1997): 499–517.

Lott, Tommy. "Du Bois and Locke on the Scientific Study of the Negro." *Boundary 2* 27 (2002): 135–52.

Napier, Winston. "Affirming Critical Conceptualism: Harlem Renaissance Aesthetics and the Formation of Alain Locke's Social Philosophy." *Massachusetts Review* 39 (1998): 93–112.

Stewart, Jeffrey C. "Alain Leroy Locke at Oxford: The First African-American Rhodes Scholar." *Journal of Blacks in Higher Education* 31 (2001): 112–17.

Watts, Eric King. "African American Ethos and Hermeneutical Rhetoric: An Exploration of Alain Locke's *The New Negro*." *Quarterly Journal of Speech* 88 (2002): 19–32.

Georgia Douglas Johnson

1886–1966

Works in the Anthology

"The Heart of a Woman" (1918)
"Youth" (1918)
"Lost Illusions" (1922)
"I Want to Die While You Love Me" (1927)

Other Works

The Heart of a Woman (poems, 1918)
Bronze: A Book of Verse (1922)
An Autumn Love Cycle (poems, 1928)
Share My World (poems, 1962)

Themes

- Romantic love and human sexuality
- African American womanhood

- Double consciousness
- Flight and migration

Characteristics

- Sentimental lyrics
- Natural imagery

Questions

- In what ways do Johnson's poems borrow from those of her predecessor Alice Dunbar Nelson? What common constructs do you find in the two poets' texts?
- Illusion is a recurring theme in the poems of Countee Cullen. Choose one of his lyrics and decide whether different gender identities make for different rhetorical effects in the treatment of the theme in Cullen's poem and Johnson's "Lost Illusions."
- Johnson's "I Want to Die While You Love Me" borrows from the British Renaissance conceit of sexual orgasm as human death, but critics do not condemn the beautiful lyric as reinscribing harmful myths about black women's sexuality. What rhetorical tropes does Johnson deploy to circumvent negative stereotypes of African Americans?

Bibliography

McHenry, Elizabeth. *Forgotten Readers: Recovering the Lost History of African-American Literary Societies*. Durham, NC: Duke UP, 2002.

Marcus Garvey

1887–1940

Works in the Anthology

"Africa for the Africans" (1923)
"The Future as I See It" (1923)

Other Works

The Philosophy and Opinions of Marcus Garvey (ed. Amy Jacques-Garvey, 1923–25)
The Poetical Works of Marcus Garvey (ed. Tony Martin, 1983)

Message to the People: The Course of African Philosophy (ed. Tony Martin, 1986)

The Marcus Garvey and the Universal Negro Improvement Association Papers (ed. Robert Hill, 1983–87)

Themes

- African American and West Indian ethnic and cultural pride
- Racial solidarity and separatism
- African liberation through decolonization and relocation to Africa
- White economic supremacy
- Human and civil rights for laborers
- Africa as "Motherland" for Africans
- Intraracial conflict about the future of "the race"

Characteristics

- Unexpurgated critique of political opponents and adversaries
- Inclusive language, collective voice, first-person plural perspective
- Jeremiadic tone, invocation of Christian righteousness and divine protection
- Inspirational, motivational rhetoric

Questions

- During the early years of the Universal Negro Improvement Association (UNIA), W. E. B. Du Bois was one of Garvey's severest critics. Read an early selection by Du Bois alongside the Garvey essays, and identify points at which the two leaders' political ideas intersect and points at which they diverge.
- What conflicts, if any, do you find in (1) Garvey's contention in "Africa for the Africans" that "when the time has come for [people of African descent] to get back together, we shall do so in the spirit of brotherly love" and (2) his persistent allusion to "bombastic Negroes" "who believe themselves so much above their fellows"? In other words, given his critique of racial discord in the United States, what seems to be the basis for Garvey's optimism about racial harmony in Africa?

Bibliography

Harrison, Paul Carter. " 'The Black Star Line': The De-Mystification of Marcus Garvey." *African American Review* 31 (1997): 713–17.

Juneja, Renu. "The Caribbean-American Connection: A Paradox of Success and Subversion." *Journal of American Culture* 21 (1998): 63–67.

Lewis, Rupert. "Marcus Garvey and the Early Rastafarians: Continuity and Discontinuity." In Nathaniel Murrell, William David Spencer, and Adrian A. McFarlane, eds., *Chanting Down Babylon: The Rastafari Reader*. Philadelphia: Temple UP, 1998. 145–58.

Satter, Beryl. "Marcus Garvey, Father Divine, and the Gender Politics of Race Difference and Race Neutrality." *American Quarterly* 48 (1996): 43–77.

Stephens, Michelle. "Black Transnationalism and the Politics of National Identity: West Indian Intellectuals in Harlem in the Age of War and Revolution." *American Quarterly* 50 (1998): 592–608.

Watson, Hilbourne. "Theorizing the Racialization of Global Politics and the Caribbean Experience." *Alternatives: Global, Local, Political* 26 (2001): 449–84.

Claude McKay

1889–1948

Works in the Anthology

"Harlem Shadows" (1918)
"If We Must Die" (1919)
"To the White Fiends" (1919)
"Africa" (1921)
"America" (1921)
"My Mother" (1921)
"Enslaved" (1921)
"The White House" (1922)
"Outcast" (1922)
"St. Isaac's Church, Petrograd" (1925)
Home to Harlem, Chap. 17 (1928)
"Harlem Runs Wild" (1935)

Other Works

Songs of Jamaica (poems, 1912)
Constab Ballads (poems, 1912)
Spring in New Hampshire and Other Poems (1920)
Harlem Shadows (poems, 1922)

Banjo: A Story without a Plot (novel, 1929)
Gingertown (stories, 1932)
Banana Bottom (novel, 1933)
A Long Way from Home (autobiography, 1937)
Harlem: Negro Metropolis (essays, 1940)
Selected Poems of Claude McKay (1953)
The Dialect Poetry of Claude McKay (ed. Wayne Cooper, 1972)
The Passion of Claude McKay: Selected Poetry and Prose, 1912–1948
   (ed. Wayne Cooper, 1973)
Trial by Lynching (stories, 1977)
My Green Hills of Jamaica (stories, 1979)
The Negroes in America (essays, 1979)

Themes

- Racial prejudice and discrimination
- Devotion to international black folk community
- Transnational migration
- African diasporas
- Impact of hatred and bigotry on individuals and societies
- Sexual and economic exploitation of black women
- Moral, spiritual, and emotional degradation and decay
- African American sexual identities

Characteristics

- Traditional lyric forms, especially the sonnet
- African American vernacular English for fictional dialogues
- Passionate, furious tone and rhetoric

Teaching Strategies

- Listen with students to the Audio Companion recordings of the readings by McKay and Langston Hughes. Discuss differences in presentation, tone, theme, and perspective.

Questions

- Choose a few poems from among the selections by McKay that you think form a representative sample of his style and content. Then compare and contrast these texts with poems by Paul Laurence Dunbar, Jean Toomer, and Langston Hughes.
- What does McKay's work imply about artistic freedom? About artistic responsibility? About authors' sociopolitical duties to their readers?

- Why do you suppose McKay's *Home to Harlem* drew sharp censure from critics of his day?
- Among leaders whom McKay most admired was Booker T. Washington. Review the excerpt from *Up From Slavery* to discern Washington's influence on the younger writer.
- By 1925, when McKay published "St. Isaac's Church, Petrograd," his close association with Marcus Garvey had been severed. Are there rhetorical aspects of this sonnet that suggest the ideological break between the two West Indians?
- Literature of the Harlem Renaissance generally explores folk and genteel art forms and subjects. Into which of these two categories would you place McKay's work?
- Assess the validity of James Weldon Johnson's judgment of McKay's poetry, asserted in the Preface to *The Book of American Negro Poetry*: "Mr. McKay gives evidence that he has passed beyond the danger which threatens many of the new Negro poets–the danger of allowing the purely polemical phases of the race problem to choke their sense of artistry." Who among McKay's contemporaries do you suppose are these other "new Negro poets" that Johnson references?
- To what extent does McKay seem influenced or in sync with Langston Hughes's "The Negro Artist and the Racial Mountain" and Zora Neale Hurston's "How It Feels to Be Colored Me"?
- Articulate any resonance you perceive between McKay's poetry and such earlier poetic statements as Phillis Wheatley's "To S. M., a Young *African* Painter" and Frances E. W. Harper's "Fancy Etchings." In the generation following McKay, what influence seems to continue in such polemical works as Richard Wright's "Blueprint for Negro Writing" and Maulana Karenga's "Black Art"?
- What distinction between art and propaganda does McKay assert in "Harlem Runs Wild"?

Bibliography

Callahan, John F. " 'A Long Way from Home': The Art and Protest of Claude McKay and James Baldwin." *Contemporary Literature* 34 (1993): 767–76.

Keller, James R. " 'A Chafing Savage, Down the Street': The Politics of Compromise in Claude McKay's Protest Sonnets." *African American Review* 28 (1994): 447–56.

Lowney, John. "Haiti and Black Transnationalism: Remapping the Migrant Geography of *Home to Harlem*." *African American Review* 34 (2000): 413–29.

Characteristics

- Challenge to various myths about women of African descent
- Exposé of economic proscriptions of black women's work
- Exposé of harmful effects of primitivist aesthetic
- Valorization of Africa-affirming primitivist aesthetic
- Exploration of healing powers of black vernacular traditions
- Psychological realism
- Critique of restrictive and oppressive sociopolitical forces

Questions

- Compare *Quicksand* with selections from other African America women's novels; what do you take to be Larsen's greatest skills an achievements as a novelist? How does her novel compare with re lated novels?
- Read W. E. B. Du Bois's acrid review of *Quicksand* and Claud McKay's *Home to Harlem*. Do you agree with Du Bois's assessmer of Larsen's accomplishments? Why or why not?
- How does Larsen's revision of the figure of the tragic mulatta com pare with Harriet Jacobs's and Harriet E. Wilson's representations f this figure in the middle of the nineteenth century? In what wa s does Helga differ from Victor Séjour's hero in "The Mulatto"?
- In her own generation, how does Larsen's revision of the figure the tragic mulatta compare with James Weldon Johnson's in *The A tobiography of an Ex-Colored Man*? With Jessie Redmon Fauset's i *Plum Bun*?
- In *Quicksand*, Larsen uses Helga's experience in Copenhagen to ex amine racism outside the United States. Analyze carefully Larsen's characterization of such domestic details as home and personal fur nishings, clothing, and colors for ways that the novel exposes and ex coriates international race and gender oppression.
- What rhetorical features does Larsen deploy to dispel racial and gen dered stereotypes of black women? In what ways does she debunk and revise prevailing myths about African American women?

Bibliography

Barbeito, Patricia Felisa. " 'Making Generations' in Jacobs, Larsen, and Hurston: A Genealogy of Black Women's Writing." *American Literature* 70 (1998): 365–96.

Barnett, Pamela E. " 'My Picture of You Is, After All, the True Helga Crane': Portraiture and Identity in Nella Larsen's *Quicksand*." *Signs* 20 (1995): 575–600.

Brickhouse, Anna. "Nella Larsen and the Intertextual Geography of *Quicksand*." *African American Review* 35 (2001): 533–61.

Davis, Thadious M. *Nella Larsen, Novelist of the Harlem Renaissance*: A *Woman's Life Unveiled*. Baton Rouge: Louisiana State UP, 1994.

English, Daylanne. "W. E. B. Du Bois's Family Crisis." *American Literature* 72 (2000): 291–319.

Lackey, Michael. "Larsen's *Quicksand*." *The Explicator* 59 (2001): 103–6.

Larson, Charles R. *Invisible Darkness: Jean Toomer and Nella Larsen*. Iowa City: U of Iowa P, 1993.

McDowell, Deborah E. "Introduction." In Deborah E. McDowell, ed., *Quicksand and Passing*. Boston: Beacon, 1986. ix–xxxi.

Monda, Kimberly. "Self-Delusion and Self-Sacrifice in Nella Larsen's *Quicksand*." *African American Review* 31 (1997): 23–40.

Jean Toomer

1894–1967

Works in the Anthology

Cane (complete except for last section) (1923)

Other Works

Balo (1922)
Blue Meridian (poem, 1936)
An Interpretation of Friends Worship (theology, 1947)
The Flavor of Man (theology, 1949)

Themes

- Beauty and complexity of black agrarian society in the rural South
- Women's racialized experiences in a misogynist and negrophobic society
- Anxiety about miscegenation and racial mixing
- African American sexual identities
- Economic exploitation of U.S. blacks
- Cultural and spiritual contributions of African Americans to U.S. national identities
- Great Migration of the early twentieth century
- Cultural differences among U.S. geographical regions

Characteristics

- Experimental literary forms; polygeneric methodology
- Critique of stereotypes of African Americans
- Critique of cross-racial and cross-cultural prejudices
- Humor, satire, irony
- Pathos
- Iconoclastic perspectives on race and gender in the Harlem Renaissance

Teaching Strategies

- To introduce Toomer as a literary bridge between the predominantly white Greenwich Village "Jazz Age" scene downtown and the New Negro cultural revolution uptown in Harlem, discuss with students the variety of literary genres as well as the graphics Toomer uses to construct *Cane*.
- Provide students with the following excerpt from a 1922 letter Toomer penned to Waldo Frank. After they have read *Cane* (note that only the last section of the work has been omitted from *NAFAM*), discuss with students the accuracy of Toomer's description of the text's design:

  From three angles, *Cane's* design is a circle. Aesthetically, from simple forms to complex ones, and back to simple ones. Regionally, from the South up to the North, and back into the South again. Or, from the North down into the South, and a return North. From the point of view of the spiritual entity behind the work, the curve really starts with Bona and Paul (awakening), plunges into Kabnis, emerges in Karintha, etc., swings upward into Theater and Box Seat, and ends (pauses) in Harvest Song.

- Scholar Nellie McKay has argued very differently about the design of *Cane*: that Part 1 forms an antithesis of Part 2 and that Part 3 synthesizes the first two parts. Ask students to juxtapose and debate these two theories. How valid do they find each theory to be? Are the two theories complementary or exclusionary?

Questions

- In what ways is the poem "Song of the Son" representative of all other parts of *Cane*?
- How do Toomer's notions of African American heritage and its origins in *Cane* correspond to other Harlem Renaissance writers on this topic? You might want to start with such poets as Gwendolyn B. Bennett and Countee Cullen, who explicitly designate "heritage" as a subject in their work.

- What echoes of poems like Countee Cullen's "Saturday's Child," Gwendolyn B. Bennett's "To a Dark Girl," and Arna Bontemps's "A Black Man Talks of Reaping" do you find in *Cane*? In what ways does *Cane* differ from these later, shorter texts?
- What is the role of African American history in the development of *Cane*? How does Toomer reconstruct slavery in his work?
- Trace Toomer's recurring allusion to sugar cane throughout *Cane*. According to the text, what are its ultimate origins? What ultimately does the plant symbolize?
- Six of the prose titles in Part 1 bear the names of women (five black and one white). These pieces present women as stereotyped and objectified by the men in their respective societies. What generalizations, if any, does *Cane* suggest about male behavioral norms? About women's roles in patriarchal societies? About racialized gender dynamics?
- Analyze Toomer's use of environment, nature, and black vernacular cultures in *Cane*. To what extent does he suggest that these three are *not* disparate or exclusive categories?
- Analyze the three main divisions of *Cane*. How does Toomer use geographic settings to establish and sustain these divisions? What kinds of differences does he explore among regions? What oppositions does he locate within a single geographical area? How do individual black identities develop in these regions, according to *Cane*? In what ways does each area thwart, nurture, or complicate the development of an African American identity?
- What is the rhetorical role of the "genius of the South" that Toomer situates in various sections of *Cane*?
- Compare one or two of the South-based poems in Toomer's *Cane* with poems by later African American southerners, including Margaret Walker's "For My People," Nikki Giovanni's "Knoxville, Tennessee," and Ishmael Reed's "Chattanooga."
- How different from *Cane*'s portrayal do you find Arna Bontemps's portrayal of southern black agrarian experience in "A Summer Tragedy"? On what do you think any differences between *Cane* and "A Summer Tragedy" are based?
- Describe the graphics that appear before each part of *Cane*. Write a verbal caption that encapsulates the idea of each graphic. Discuss the advantages Toomer gained by deploying visual art in place of verbal text in these places.
- Analyze the poems that preface and/or frame individual prose texts in *Cane*. How do they work to enhance the prose pieces?
- What is the rhetorical function of antebellum spirituals, work songs, jazz, and other black vernacular forms within *Cane*? Focus on one or two vernacular elements to form your answer.

Bibliography

Guterl, Matthew. *The Color of Race in America, 1900–1940.* Cambridge, MA: Harvard UP, 2001.

Jones, Robert B., ed. *Jean Toomer: Selected Essays and Literary Criticism.* Knoxville: U of Tennessee P, 1996.

Kodat, Catherine Gunther. "To 'Flash White Light from Ebony': The Problem of Modernism in Jean Toomer's *Cane.*" *Twentieth Century Literature* 46 (2000): 1–19.

Larson, Charles R. *Invisible Darkness: Jean Toomer and Nella Larsen.* Iowa City: U of Iowa P, 1993.

McKay, Nellie. *Jean Toomer, Artist: A Study of His Literary Life and Work, 1894–1936.* Chapel Hill: U of North Carolina P, 1984.

George Samuel Schuyler

1895–1977

Works in the Anthology

"The Negro-Art Hokum" (1926)

Other Works

Black No More; Being an Account of the Strange and Wonderful Workings of Science in the Land of the Free (novel, 1931)
Slaves Today (novel, 1931)
Black and Conservative (autobiography, 1966)

Themes

- U.S. race relations in the early twentieth century
- African American assimilationism
- Fraudulence of New Negro interventions in art, culture, humanities
- African American caste differentials
- Pervasiveness of stereotypes of African Americans

Characteristics

- Satire, lampoon, derision
- Iconoclastic call for denunciation of "Negro art"

- Critique of Harlem Renaissance claims for black artistic development
- Catalog of black leaders and writers whose "color is incidental"

Questions

- Read "The Negro-Art Hokum" alongside Langston Hughes's "The Negro Artist and the Racial Mountain," which Schuyler's work inspired. Summarize the divergent attitudes in these two essays, which were published in the same issue of *The Nation* in June 1926. With which side of the debate do you most agree? Why?
- To what extent does Schuyler's contention that black vernacular musical traditions emerge from a "peasant class [that] happens to be of a darker hue than the other inhabitants of the land" correspond with ideas expressed by Zora Neale Hurston at the same time? To what extent do they resonate with ideas asserted by Booker T. Washington at the turn into the twentieth century?
- Do you find Schuyler's contention that "your American Negro is just plain American" to be at odds with W. E. B. Du Bois's theory of double consciousness? Why or why not?

Bibliography

Tucker, Jeffrey A. " 'Can Science Succeed Where the Civil War Failed?' George S. Schuyler and Race." In Judith Jackson Fossett, ed., *Race Consciousness, African-American Studies for the New Century*. New York: New York UP, 1997. 136–53.

Rudolph Fisher

1897–1934

Works in the Anthology

"The City of Refuge" (1925)
"The Caucasian Storms Harlem" (1927)

Other Works

The Walls of Jericho (novel, 1928)
The Conjure Man Dies: A Mystery Tale of Dark Harlem (novel, 1932)
The City of Refuge: The Collected Stories of Rudolph Fisher (ed. John A. McCluskey, 1987)

Themes

- Drug trafficking
- Complexity and diversity of modern African American labor forces
- Miscegenation, racial passing
- Great Migration of the twentieth century
- Black southern folkways
- Black urban experiences
- Intraracial oppression and exploitation

Characteristics

- Traditional conventions of mystery and detective fiction, subverted
- Satire, irony, humor, wit
- Pathos of injustice
- African American urban slang
- African American vernacular English and other regional and racial-ized dialects
- Black vernacular conventions, especially from jazz and blues traditions

Questions

- Fisher's "The City of Refuge" vividly describes black life in Harlem from the perspective of a black southern emigrant. Compare and contrast this story with Charles W. Chesnutt's "The Goophered Grape-vine," narrated by two men, one of whom is a (white) northerner who has migrated to the South.
- Compare and contrast the arrival of King Solomon Gillis in Harlem with that of the central subject in Stevie Wonder's "Living for the City."
- Explore the implications and ironies of the narrator's contention in "The City of Refuge" that "in Harlem, black was white."
- Discuss with your classmates Fisher's lament in "The Caucasian Storms Harlem" that "Negro stock is going up, and everybody's buy-ing." What historical validity did Fisher's pronouncement have? To what extent is the contention true today, in your estimation? If you think it true of either Fisher's era or your own, do you find the situa-tion as grievous as does Fisher? Why or why not?

Bibliography

Gosselin, Adrienne. "The Psychology of Uncertainty: (Re)Inscribing Inde-terminacy in Rudolph Fisher's *The Conjure-Man Dies*." *Other Voices* 1 (1999): n.p.

Heglar, Charles. "Rudolph Fisher and the African American Detective." *Armchair Detective* 30 (1997): 300–305.

Thompson, Clifford. "The Mystery Man of the Harlem Renaissance: Novelist Rudolph Fisher Was a Forerunner of Walter Mosley." *Black Issues Book Review* 5 (2003): 63–65.

Marita Bonner

1899–1971

Works in the Anthology

"On Being Young—a Woman—and Colored" (1925)

Other Works

The Pot Maker (drama, 1927)
Ebony and Topaz (ed. Charles S. Johnson, stories and essays, 1927)
The Purple Flower (drama, 1928)
Exit, an Illusion (drama, 1929)
Frye Street and Environs: The Collected Works of Marita Bonner (ed. Joyce Flynn and Joyce O. Stricklin, 1987)

Themes

- African American ethnic identity
- African American women's race and gender identity formation
- White supremacy
- White ignorance
- The subjugation of women everywhere
- Intersections of race, class, gender, sexuality, and economic inequity
- Race relations in the modern United States

Characteristics

- Wit, humor, irony, sarcasm, pathos
- Powerful literary allusions to a broad range of literary texts
- Feminist analysis of racialized gender mandates

Questions

- Compare Bonner's "On Being Young—a Woman—and Colored" to articulations of black feminist theory published later in the twentieth century. To what extent do such writers as Gwendolyn Brooks, Audre Lorde, and Alice Walker seem influenced by Bonner's groundbreaking essay? In what ways do these three particular writers diverge from Bonner's perspective and attitudes?

- Near the beginning of "On Being Young—a Woman—and Colored," Bonner irresolutely asserts, "unless color is, after all, the real bond." To what degree does her essay argue for an essential African American identity?
- Summarize the portrait of "everything white; friendly; unfriendly" that emerges in "On Being Young—a Woman—and Colored." What attitudes toward whiteness does Bonner advance?

Bibliography

Berg, Allison, and Merideth Taylor. "Enacting Difference: Marita Bonner's *Purple Flower* and the Ambiguities of Race." *African American Review* 32 (1998): 469–80.

Berg, Allison. "Marita Odette Bonner (1898–1971)." In Laurie Champion, ed., *American Women Writers, 1900–1945: A Bio-Bibliographical Critical Sourcebook*. Westport, CT: Greenwood, 2000. 39–44.

Musser, Judith. "African American Women and Education: Marita Bonner's Response to the 'Talented Tenth.'" *Studies in Short Fiction* 34 (1997): 73–85.

Spahr, Heather E. "Marita Bonner (1898–1971)." In Emmanuel S. Nelson, ed., *African American Authors, 1745–1945: A Bio-Bibliographical Critical Sourcebook*. Westport, CT: Greenwood, 2000. 30–35.

Sterling A. Brown

1901–1989

Works in the Anthology

"Odyssey of Big Boy" (1927)
"Long Gone" (1931)
"Southern Road" (1931)
"Strong Men" (1931)
"Memphis Blues" (1931)
"Slim Greer" (1931)
"Tin Roof Blues" (1931)
"Ma Rainey" (1932)

"Cabaret" (1932)
"Sporting Beasley" (1932)
"Sam Smiley" (1975)
"Old Lem" (1980)

Other Works

Southern Road (poems, 1932)
The Negro in American Fiction (editor, 1937)
Negro Poetry and Drama (editor, 1937)
The Negro Caravan (editor, 1941)
The Last Ride of Wild Bill and Eleven Narratives (poems, 1975)
The Collected Poems of Sterling Brown (ed. Michael Harper, 1980)
"Unhistoric History" (essay, 1998)

Themes

- Beauty of black vernacular forms, especially musical traditions of jazz and blues
- African American triumph over strife and humiliation
- Black negotiation of risk and other survival strategies
- African American fear and perseverance in the face of oppression
- Racial discrimination and oppression
- Racist victimization of blacks in Jim Crow nation
- Southern black folkways, mores, and values
- African American intellectualism and intellectual traditions

Characteristics

- Folk expressions; vernacular discourses; dialogues in African American vernacular English
- Highly intertextual engagement with vernacular and literary predecessors
- Committed to perpetuating and developing African American literary tradition, especially with folk origins
- Humor
- Pathos
- Passionate love of black vernacular forms, especially musical traditions of jazz and blues

Teaching Strategies

- Listen with your students to Brown's reading of "Strong Men" on the Audio Companion.

- Special issues of the journals *African American Review* and *Callaloo* were published in 1997 and 1998, respectively. Consider assigning selected essays and articles from these texts, asking your students either to compare and contrast several different critical approaches to Brown's texts or to apply particular critical approaches to the *NAFAM* selections not covered in the cited journals.

Questions

- Brown's father was a professor at Howard University, and Brown himself was very well educated at some of the nation's most elite schools. To what extent, if at all, is this background apparent in Brown's folk poetry?
- Analyze Brown's juxtaposition of African American urban life with black rural life in the poems that develop a migration theme.
- In what ways does Brown's "Ma Rainey" transform the blues singer into a spiritual, or "soul," healer? Situate this poem among others across African American literary periods that exalt the figure of the musician and/or other artist.
- Locate and read a copy of the poem by Carl Sandburg that Brown takes as the *leit-motif* of "Strong Men." Examine carefully the ways that Brown revises Sandburg's poem.
- Critic Joanne Gabbin has asserted that Brown's "Slim Greer" figure "is based on a virtuoso tall-tale teller whom Brown met waiting tables at the Hotel Jefferson in Jefferson City, Missouri. In the Slim Greer tales, we find the hero in humorous situations that obliquely comment on the absurdity of Southern racism." Support or refute this claim with respect to your reading of "Slim Greer."
- Compare and contrast the "bad man" figures in selections by Brown with the "bad man" figures in the secular folk ballads in the vernacular section. In what ways does Brown extend the tradition he so loved? In what ways do his poems revise that tradition?
- Review Brown's "Old Lem" alongside "We raise de wheat" in the vernacular section. What does Brown gain—or lose—by embedding Lem's narrative within that of another first-person speaker? What can you infer about the *I* of the frame? Compare both works with Arna Bontemps's "A Black Man Talks of Reaping."

Bibliography

African American Review 31 (Fall 1997): 389–453. Special section on Sterling Brown.

Brown, Fahamisha Patricia. "And I Owe It All to Sterling Brown: The Theory and Practice of Black Literary Studies." *African American Review* 31 (1997): 449–53.

Gabbin, Joanne V. "Sterling Brown's Poetic Voice: A Living Legacy." *African American Review* 31 (1997): 423–32.

Rowell, Charles, and Kendra Hamilton, eds. *Sterling A. Brown: A Special Issue. Callaloo* 21 (1998).

Sanders, Mark A. *Afro-Modernist Aesthetics and the Poetry of Sterling A. Brown.* Athens: U of Georgia P, 1999.

———. "Sterling Brown and the Afro-Modern Moment." *African American Review* 31 (1997): 393–98.

Skinner, Beverly L. "Sterling Brown: An Ethnographic Perspective." *African American Review* 31 (1997): 417–23.

Thomas, Lorenzo. "Authenticity and Elevation: Sterling Brown's Theory of the Blues." *African American Review* 31 (1997): 409–17.

Tidwell, John Edgar. "Two Writers Sharing: Sterling A. Brown, Robert Frost, and 'In Dives' Dive.' " *African American Review* 31 (1997): 399–408.

Traylor, Eleanor W., R. Victoria Arana, and John M. Reilly. " 'Runnin' Space': The Continuing Legacy of Sterling Allen Brown." *African American Review* 31 (1997): 389–93.

Gwendolyn B. Bennett

1902–1981

Works in the Anthology

"Heritage" (1923)
"To a Dark Girl" (1927)
"Sonnet—2" (1927)
"Hatred" (1927)

Other Works

"The Ebony Flute" (magazine columns, 1924–26)

Themes

- Complex intrinsic beauty of people of African descent
- African American women's natural grace
- African American resilience

Characteristics

- Experimental lyrical forms
- Revision of stereotypes of African American women
- Revision of stereotypes of African American primitivism
- Comparison of blackness with natural world

Questions

- Compare the speaker's bitterness in Arna Bontemps's "A Black Man Talks of Reaping" with the speaker's tone in Bennett's "Hatred." Do you think Bennett's tone is also embittered? Why or why not?
- Bennett was as accomplished and acclaimed a visual artist as she was a poet. Identify aspects of her poetry that reveal her artist's eye.

Bibliography

Govan, Sandra Y. "Kindred Spirits and Sympathetic Souls: Langston Hughes and Gwendolyn Bennett in the Harlem Renaissance." In C. James Trotman, ed., *Langston Hughes: The Man, His Art, and His Continuing Influence*. New York: Garland, 1995. 75–85.

Jones, Gwendolyn S. "Gwendolyn Bennett (1902–1981)." In Emmanuel S. Nelson, ed., *A Bio-Bibliographical Critical Sourcebook*. Westport, CT: Greenwood, 2000. 18–23.

Wallace Thurman

1902–1934

Works in the Anthology

Infants of the Spring, Chap. 21 (1932)

Other Works

Negro Life in New York's Harlem (1928)
The Blacker the Berry (novel, 1929)
Harlem (co-dramatist, 1929)
The Interne (novel, 1932)
Tomorrow's Children (screenplay, 1934)
High School Girl (screenplay, 1935)
For the Inward Journey: The Writings of Howard Thurman (ed. Anne Spencer Thurman, 1984)

Themes

- Color-caste system among African Americans
- Skin color prejudices
- Intraracial oppression
- Literary self-consciousness and self-reflection
- Classism and social elitism among blacks

Characteristics

- Satire, humor
- *Roman á clef* form for fiction
- Critique of African American elitism
- Exposé of Harlem Renaissance writers' alleged pretentiousness

Questions

- Note that while W. E. B. Du Bois is not among the real-life personalities satirized in *Infants of the Spring*, Thurman renders him present at the salon in Chapter 21 through allusion to the writer and his work. Why do you suppose Thurman chose not to lampoon Du Bois or *The Souls of Black Folk* along with the Harlem Renaissance writers and their best-known productions? Or did he?
- The protagonist of Thurman's send-up of Harlem Renaissance society pointedly asks, "Is there really any reason why *all* Negro artists should consciously and deliberately dig into African soil for inspiration and material unless they actually wish to do so?" Formulate an answer to this question that engages Arthur Schomburg and Alain Locke, two distinguished Harlem Renaissance writers who wrote earnestly in support of the idea of black scholarly and artistic commitment to notions of African American heritage.
- Select a representative sampling of literature from the Harlem Renaissance to decide whether Raymond's insistence that "individuality is what we should strive for" is at odds with a diametrically opposed perspective collectively articulated by other writers.

Bibliography

Kelley, James. "Blossoming in Strange New Forms: Male Homosexuality and the Harlem Renaissance." *Soundings* 80 (1997): 499–517.

Arna Bontemps

1902–1973

Works in the Anthology

"A Black Man Talks of Reaping" (1926)
"Nocturne at Bethesda" (1926)
"Southern Mansion" (1931)
"Miracles" (1941)
"A Summer Tragedy" (1933)

Other Works

God Sends Sunday (novel, 1931)
Black Thunder (novel, 1936)
Drums at Dusk (novel, 1939)
Personals (poems, 1963)
"Negro Poets, Then and Now" (essay, 1996)
Arna Bontemps–Langston Hughes: Letters 1925–1967 (1980)

Themes

- Economic and sociopolitical injustices of sharecropping
- Heterosexual romantic love and marriage
- African American familial loss
- Suicide as strength and agency
- Celebration of African American grace, dignity, and agency

Characteristics

- Mournful, somber, melancholic tone
- African American vernacular English and southern dialects

Questions

- Compare the speaker's bitterness in Bontemps's "A Black Man Talks of Reaping" with the speaker's tone in Gwendolyn B. Bennett's "Hatred." Do you think Bennett's tone is also embittered? Why or why not?
- To what extent does Bontemps's preoccupation with the peonage of the Old South tell a modern story?
- What role do the "frizzly chickens" play in "A Summer Tragedy"? Do the guinea fowls that appear later in the story merely repeat this

function or do they add something different to the story? Link the rhetorical function both sets of birds serve to other tropes of conjure and migration you have encountered in African American literature.

Bibliography

Abney, Lisa. "Cakewalks, Cauls, and Conjure: Folk Practice in Arna Bontemps's *God Sends Sunday* and 'A Summer Tragedy.' " In Suzanne Disheroon-Green and Lisa Abney, eds., *Songs of Reconstructing South: Building Literary Louisiana, 1865–1945*. Westport, CT: Greenwood, 2002. 137–48.

Alvarez, Joseph A. "The Lonesome Boy Theme as Emblem for Arna Bontemps's Children's Literature." *African American Review* 32 (1998): 23–32.

Bishop, Rudine, and Jonda McNair. "A Centennial Salute to Arna Bontemps, Langston Hughes, and Lorenz Graham." *New Advocate* 15 (2002): 109–19.

Wixson, Jackson. " 'Black Writers and White!': Jack Conroy, Arna Bontemps, and Interracial Collaboration in the 1930s." *Prospects* 23 (1998): 401–4.

Langston Hughes

1902–1967

Works in the Anthology

"The Negro Speaks of Rivers" (1921)
"Mother to Son" (1922)
"Danse Africaine" (1922)
"Jazzonia" (1923)
"When Sue Wears Red" (1923)
"Dream Variations" (1924)
"The Weary Blues" (1925)
"I, Too" (1925)
"Jazz Band in a Parisian Cabaret" (1925)
"Homesick Blues" (1926)
"Po' Boy Blues" (1926)
"Mulatto" (1927)
"Red Silk Stockings" (1927)
"Song for a Dark Girl" (1927)

"Gal's Cry for a Dying Love" (1927)
"Dear Lovely Death" (1928)
"Afro-American Fragment" (1930)
"Negro Servant" (1930)
"Christ in Alabama" (1931)
"Letter to the Academy" (1933)
"Ballad of the Landlord" (1940, 1955)
"Merry-Go-Round" (1942)
"Madam and the Rent Man" (1943)
"Trumpet Player" (1947)
"Madam and the Phone Bill" (1949)
"Song for Billie Holiday" (1949)
"Juke Box Love Song" (1950)
"Dream Boogie" (1951)
"Harlem" (1951)
"Motto" (1951)
"Theme for English B" (1951)
"Not What Was" (1965)
"The Negro Artist and the Racial Mountain" (1926)
"The Blues I'm Playing" (1934)
The Big Sea: "When the Negro Was In Vogue," "Harlem Literati," "Downtown" (1940)

Other Works

The Weary Blues (poems, 1926)
Fine Clothes to the Jew (poems, 1927)
Not without Laughter (novel, 1930)
The Ways of White Folks (stories, 1934)
Montage of a Dream Deferred (poems, 1951)
I Wonder as I Wander (autobiography, 1956)
Selected Poems (1959)
Ask Your Mama: Twelve Moods for Jazz (1961)
The Best of Simple (stories, 1961)
Five Plays by Langston Hughes (ed. Webster Smalley, 1963)
Good Morning, Revolution: Uncollected Social Protest Writings by Langston Hughes (ed. Faith Berry, 1973)
The Collected Poems of Langston Hughes (ed. Arnold Rampersad and David Roessel, 1994)

Themes

• Poems emblematic of diverse African American experiences
• The role of art in everyday life and experience

- Artistic expression as African American salvation
- The mission of the black artist at the beginning of the twentieth century
- Chronicle of the spirit, fervor, and creativity of the Harlem Renaissance
- Characters and personae who represent the range of character among urban and working-class blacks during the early decades of the twentieth century
- Racism, racial discrimination, segregation, racial hatred
- African American strategies for enduring race and class oppression
- Black urban folk wisdom

Characteristics

- Wide range of creative literary forms including mastery as a poet, novelist, essayist, dramatist, editor, short-story writer, autobiographer, translator, lyricist, critic, historian, anthologist, and writer of children's books
- Committed to introducing both new subject matter and new creative technique into the American literary canon
- Black urban vernacular English

Teaching Strategies

- Play for students the poetry readings by Hughes included on the Audio Companion. Contrast these readings with other Audio Companion selections by poets who were similarly influenced by vernacular traditions, especially jazz and the blues. What differences do students find in these various applications and significations of black musical traditions?

Questions

- Survey the selections of Hughes's poetry and choose six or seven that represent the various themes that illustrate Hughes's major concerns.
- Compare selected texts by Hughes with writings by W. E. B. Du Bois and James Weldon Johnson. In what ways does each writer invoke, develop, and enrich African American vernacular traditions?
- Read Hughes's literary theories as developed in "The Negro Artist and the Racial Mountain"; then analyze a selection of his poems across several decades for ways they correspond to this artistic philosophy. How does "The Negro Speaks of Rivers," which predates the essay, anticipate ideas Hughes would espouse in "The Negro Artist and the Racial Mountain"?

- Discuss Hughes's advocacy for a black artist "to be himself." How does this advice compare to his contemporaries'—as well as later African American writers'—admonitions about the role of ethnic identity in black literature? Inspiring artists with which to start this discussion could include James Weldon Johnson's Preface to *The Book of American Negro Poetry*, W. E. B. Du Bois's "Criteria of Negro Art," George Samuel Schuyler's "The Negro-Art Hokum," Hoyt Fuller's "Towards a Black Aesthetic," and Larry Neal's "The Black Arts Movement."
- Compare and/or contrast the excerpt from *The Big Sea* with the excerpt from Hurston's autobiography, *Dust Tracks on the Road*.
- Compare and contrast the excerpt from *The Big Sea* with sections of Frederick Douglass's autobiographies. What aspects and themes of Douglass's personal narratives does Hughes borrow for his own autobiography? In what ways are the two writers' texts divergent?

Bibliography

Barrett, Lindon. "The Gaze of Langston Hughes: Subjectivity, Homoeroticism, and the Feminine in *The Big Sea*." *Yale Journal of Criticism* 12 (1999): 383–97.

Brooker, Peter. "Modernism Deferred: Langston Hughes, Harlem and Jazz Montage." In Alex Davis and Lee Jenkins, eds., *Locations of Literary Modernism: Region and Nation in British and American Modernist Poetry*. Cambridge, UK: Cambridge UP, 2000. 231–47.

Davidas, Lionel. " 'I, Too, Sing America': Jazz and Blues Techniques and Effects in Some of Langston Hughes's Selected Poems." *Dialectical Anthropology* 26 (2001): 267–72.

Davis, Arthur P. "The Tragic Mulatto Theme in Six Works of Langston Hughes." In Werner Sollors, ed., *Interracialism: Black-White Intermarriage in American History, Literature, and Law*. Oxford, UK: Oxford UP, 2000. 317–25.

Dawahare, Anthony. "Langston Hughes's Radical Poetry and the 'End of Race.' " *MELUS* 23 (1998): 21–41.

Gates, Henry Louis Jr., and K. A. Appiah, eds. *Langston Hughes: Critical Perspectives Past and Present*. New York: Amistad, 1993.

Hokanson, Robert O. "Jazzing It Up: The Be-Bop Modernism of Langston Hughes." *Mosaic* 31 (1998): 61–63.

The Langston Hughes Review 12 (1993) [special issue on Langston Hughes].

Loftus, Brian. "In/Verse Autobiography: Sexual (In)Difference and the Textual Backside of Langston Hughes's *The Big Sea*." *a/b: Auto/Biography* 15 (2000): 141–61.

Michlin, Monica. "Langston Hughes's Blues." In Genevieve Fabre and Michel Feith, eds., *Temples for Tomorrow: Looking Back at the Harlem Renaissance*. Bloomington: Indiana UP, 2001. 236–53.

Moglen, Seth. "Modernism in the Black Diaspora: Langston Hughes and the Broken Cubes of Picasso." *Callaloo* 25 (2002): 1188–2006.

Salaam, Kalamu. "Langston Hughes: A Poet Supreme." In Joanne Gabbin, eds., *The Furious Flowering of African American Poetry*. Charlottesville: U of Virginia P, 1999. 17–24.

Scanlon, Larry. "News from Heaven: Vernacular Time in Langston Hughes's *Ask Your Mama*." *Callaloo* 25 (2002): 45–65.

Countee Cullen

1903–1946

Works in the Anthology

"Yet Do I Marvel" (1925)
"Tableau" (1925)
"Incident" (1925)
"Saturday's Child" (1925)
"The Shroud of Color" (1925)
"Heritage" (1925)
"To John Keats, Poet, at Spring Time" (1925)
"From the Dark Tower" (1927)

Other Works

Color (poems, 1925)
The Ballad of the Brown Girl (poems, 1927)
The Black Christ and Other Poems (1929)
One Way to Heaven (poems, 1932)
The Medea and Some Poems (poems, 1935)
The Lost Zoo (stories, 1940)
My Lives and How I Lost Them (stories, 1942)
On These I Stand: An Anthology of the Best Poems of Countee Cullen (1947)

My Soul's High Song: The Collected Writings of Countee Cullen, Voice of the Harlem Renaissance (ed. Gerald Early, 1991)

Themes

- Racial ambivalence: African American identity—or the denial of it
- Racism
- Intersection of race and gender with economic inequity and poverty
- Aspirations and experiences of African American poets
- Natural beauty as poetic inspiration
- Illusion, deception, denial, fantasy, whimsy, derangement
- Pain, suffering, death, loss
- Homosexuality and homophobia

Characteristics

- Lyric poetry, generally in Spenserian sonnets and other classical forms
- Irony, pathos, contradiction, paradox
- Allusions to classical literature, including the Judeo-Christian Bible and Greek mythology
- Humor, wit

Teaching Strategies

- Listen with students to the Audio Companion recordings of readings by Cullen and Langston Hughes. Engage students in a discussion of the rhetorical contrasts in the two frequently paired poets' styles and attitudes, based on their different presentations of their work.

Questions

- Do you understand the final word *sing* of "Yet Do I Marvel" to reference black vernacular tradition? Why or why not?
- Contrast the speaker's attitude in Arna Bontemps's "A Black Man Talks of Reaping" with that in Cullen's "From the Dark Tower," published one year later. What do the two poems reveal about the disparate aspirations and aims of Harlem Renaissance poets?
- Identify the formal characteristics of Cullen's elegy for John Keats. Research a lyric by Keats, who died approximately one hundred years before Cullen wrote "To John Keats, Poet, at Spring Time," and trace common constructs in the two poems.
- Critic David E. Goldweber argues that "to Cullen and [John] Keats,

illusions are crucial antidotes to a pain that threatens to overwhelm us. Illusions are an ironic solution to life's problems; they are, after all, unreal." Trace the theme of illusion in the selections by Cullen to assess the validity of Goldweber's contention.

- "Tableau" is arguably a poem about interracial romantic love that thrives in spite of homophobic threats to defeat it. Contrast the ideas compactly expressed in this lyric of romance and resistance with the ideas expressed in Alice Moore Dunbar Nelson's efficient short story "Violets," published a generation before Cullen's own.
- Analyze the use of bird and flight imagery in "The Shroud of Color." In what ways does Cullen draw on conventional African American constructs to develop the themes and images in this poem?
- Compare and contrast Cullen's "Heritage" with Gwendolyn Bennett's contemporaneous poem of the same name.

Bibliography

Braddock, Jeremy. "The Poetics of Conjecture: Countee Cullen's Subversive Exemplarity." *Callaloo* 25 (2002): 1250–72.

Fetrow, Fred M. "Cullen's 'Yet Do I Marvel.' " *The Explicator* 56 (1998): 103–6.

Goldweber, David E. "Cullen, Keats, and the Privileged Liar." *Papers on Language and Literature* 38 (2002): 29–42.

Kelley, James. "Blossoming in Strange New Forms: Male Homosexuality and the Harlem Renaissance." *Soundings* 80 (1997): 499–517.

Ostrom, Hans. "Countee Cullen: How Teaching Rewrites the Genre of 'Writer.' " In Wendy Bishop and Hans Ostrom, eds., *Genre and Writing: Issues, Arguments, Alternatives*. Portsmouth, NH: Boynton/Cook, 1997. 93–104.

Powers, Peter. " 'The Singing Man Who Must Be Reckoned With': Private Desire and Public Responsibility in the Poetry of Countee Cullen." *African American Review* 34 (2000): 661–83.

Helene Johnson

1907–1995

Works in the Anthology

"Poem" (1927)
"Sonnet to a Negro in Harlem" (1927)

"Remember Not" (1931)
"Invocation" (1931)

Themes

- Beauty of African American people
- Transcendent nature of black vernacular forms
- African American racial and ethnic pride
- Beauty of black insouciance

Characteristics

- African American vernacular English
- Experimental poetic forms blended with traditional lyric forms
- Sonnet form

Questions

- Compare and contrast Johnson's celebration of essentialized African qualities in "Poem" with Countee Cullen's speaker's attitudes in "Heritage."
- Compare Johnson's "Sonnet to a Negro in Harlem" with any one of the traditional sonnets by Claude McKay. To what extent does Johnson's lyric seem influenced by McKay's?

Bibliography

Mitchell, Verner, ed. *This Waiting for Love: Helene Johnson, Poet of the Harlem Renaissance.* Amherst: U of Massachusetts P, 2000.

Teaching the Harlem Renaissance

At the beginning of the twentieth century, James Weldon Johnson observed in his Preface to *The Book of American Negro Poetry* that "little of the poetry by Negro poets . . . is being written in Negro dialect" and that poets are "trying to break away from . . . the limitations of Negro dialect." Critical essays and literary theory published during the Harlem Renaissance just twenty years into the century would assert and espouse a very different state of affairs. Alain Locke's "The New Negro," for example, notes a dramatic change "in the life-attitudes and self-expression of the Young Negro, in his poetry, his art . . . his new outlook." Even more radical transitions are theorized and promulgated in Marcus Garvey's "Africa for the Africans" and Langston Hughes's "The Negro Artist and the Racial

Mountain." However, other culture critics and writers of the Harlem Renaissance—as well as critics and writers since its decline—have suggested that the changes described by Locke, Garvey, Hughes, and numerous others constituted a phenomenon that took place on a very limited scale, if at all. Some opponents, perhaps most passionate or acerbic among them George Samuel Schuyler and Wallace Thurman, derided and satirized these social changes. A historical approach to black literature of the Harlem Renaissance, then, can retrospectively ask what in the 1920s and 1930s elicited such a range of critical opinion and perception and how accurate was each of these diverse assessments.

By the time of the Harlem Renaissance, there was an African American readership of considerable size and a corresponding increase in the number of declared writers. Writers had greater choice in audience and publication venues and greater freedom to experiment with subject matter, form, and literary techniques. Some, such as Anne Spencer and Jean Toomer, ultimately eschewed the vernacular and "racial" subjects. Available to all was a palate of extraordinarily different hues of African American life and culture, as a glance at works by Zora Neale Hurston and Jessie Redmon Fauset, for example, makes readily apparent. Even a cursory glance emphasizes the superficiality of the suggestion that Fauset's work is less grounded in "authentic" African American culture than Hurston's.

The Great Migration within the first decades of the twentieth century inspired many African American writers of the era to draw characters who experienced, often for the first time, the color, movement, sounds, and influences of the city. A question to consider with students is whether those characters on the whole found life significantly better in the northern cities to which they flocked than in the rural and/or southern locales from which many had come. Harlem Renaissance writers concerned with the effects of migration and of travel in general—Jean Toomer, Rudolph Fisher, Claude McKay, and Langston Hughes especially—vary in their ultimate attitudes toward the benefits of "home" in relation to frontier, of urban to rural, of North to South, of America to Europe or Africa or the Caribbean. Their texts offer important opportunities to explore the possibilities and actualities of life between two world wars.

Travel and travail emerge also in Harlem Renaissance writers' evaluation of the legacy and worth of a black historical past and in their revisions and reconstructions of African American history and an African heritage. Claude McKay's "Africa" and "America," Marcus Garvey's "Africa for the Africans," Jean Toomer's "Kabnis" and "Song of the Son," Langston Hughes's "The Negro Speaks of Rivers," and Arthur A. Schomburg's "The Negro Digs Up His Past" provide compelling examples of this theme. Not only were African Americans moving from rural South to urban North, but they were traveling from Los Angeles to Chicago and from

Cleveland to Mexico. Others were moving to and from the Caribbean, Europe, and Africa as merchant seamen, soldiers, nurses, teachers, students, tourists, and artists. The transitions of Africans and African Americans were paralleled and intersected by the changes resulting from continued territorial expansions, immigration and emigration, technological developments, and economic fluctuations that affected all the inhabitants of the United States.

The Depression and World War II had a major effect on African American literature. Among the changes was a new emphasis on literature as social protest. Writers presented a complex, affecting picture of the plight of African Americans, often emphasizing pain, anger, suffering, futility, and hopelessness. They offered "objective" and realistic depictions of life to explore unflinchingly critical sociological concepts. Responding to a decline in employment and income, an increase in acts of racial discrimination and prejudice, and Americans' growing disenchantment, many Harlem Renaissance writers detailed the despair of individuals whose condition seemed to have been created by environmental and/or hereditary determinism. Their work raised a range of questions from whether life is a trap with no escape to whether individuals can change or rather *must* perforce be shaped by the societies in which they live. What possibilities for viable and genuine social reform are offered by protest organizations associated with political parties and/or labor unions? Arna Bontemps's "A Summer Tragedy," detailing an elderly couple's final action, explores the sociopolitical determinism of a tenant farming system and the biological determinism of human aging and death. Bontemps's lack of editorializing allows readers to share the couple's emotional contemplation of their plight and the depth of their capacity for choice. Read alongside Bontemps's poem "Nocturne at Bethesda," the story illuminates many of the period's major themes and constructs.

The vernacular elements of gospel, blues, and jazz offer a captivating historical entry into the study of poetry by writers such as Sterling A. Brown and Langston Hughes. You might want to have students consider ways in which the structure and lexicon of written work captures and resonates with the structure and diction of the oral literature popular throughout African American literary production. Langston Hughes's "Ballad of the Landlord," "The Weary Blues," "Jazzonia," and "Dream Boogie" have obvious, indissoluble ties to the music of the Jazz Age. The vernacular musicality of poems such as Sterling A. Brown's "Slim Greer," "Southern Road," and "Strong Men" also emanates from the Harlem Renaissance period. Retention of the folk life and attention to the realism of place and time would suggest considerations of Zora Neale Hurston and her representation of black communal relationships and African American cultures in Florida. Hurston's essay "Characteristics of Negro Expression" and the excerpt from *Mules and Men* further underscore her commitment to the preservation and authentication of black folk life. The Audio Companion recordings of selections by Hughes, Brown, Hurston, and other writers effectively demonstrate key concepts of the Harlem Renaissance and can be insightfully paired with the musical recordings of the same era.

As a historical period, the decades of 1920 to 1940 present important and engaging questions. After all, the post–World War I period was not simply the vogue of the "New Negro" but was also the period of Prohibition, Al Capone, Dan Jackson, and the flappers. At this historical moment, did African American writers become more assertive, more aware of their cultural heritage, and consciously artistic or modern? If so, why? Can the argument be made that they were not "more" assertive but assertive in ways different from their artistic foreparents?

Genres

Poetry

Grimké
Spencer
G. Johnson
McKay
Toomer
Brown
G. Bennett
Bontemps
Hughes
Cullen
H. Johnson

Drama

Toomer

Political Essay/Periodical Literature/Critical Theory

Schomburg
Locke
Garvey
McKay
Hurston
Schuyler
Fisher

Bonner
Hughes

Short Fiction

Hurston
Toomer
Fisher
Bontemps
Hughes

Prose Narrative/Autobiography/Slave Narrative

Hurston
Toomer
Bonner
Hughes

Novel

Fauset
McKay
Hurston
Larsen
Toomer
Thurman

Bibliography

Allen, Carol. *Black Women Intellectuals: Strategies of Nation, Family, and Neighborhood in the Works of Pauline Hopkins, Jessie Fauset, and Marita Bonner*. New York: Garland, 1998.

Bontemps, Arna. "Negro Poets, Then and Now." In Cary D. Wintz, ed., *Remembering the Harlem Renaissance*. New York: Garland, 1996. 147–52.

Champion, Laurie, ed. *American Women Writers, 1900–1945: A Bio-Bibliographical Critical Sourcebook*. Westport, CT: Greenwood, 2000.

Dinerstein, Joel. *Swinging the Machine: Modernity, Technology, and African American Culture between the World Wars*. Amherst: U of Massachusetts P, 2003.

Guterl, Matthew. *The Color of Race in America, 1900–1940*. Cambridge, MA: Harvard UP, 2001.

Harper, Phillip Brian. "Passing for What? Racial Masquerade and the Demands of Upward Mobility." *Callaloo* 21 (1998): 381–97.

Honey, Maureen, ed. *Shadowed Dreams: Women's Poetry of the Harlem Renaissance*. New Brunswick: Rutgers UP, 1989.

Hull, Gloria. *Color, Sex, and Poetry: Three Women Writers of the Harlem Renaissance*. Bloomington: Indiana UP, 1988.

Lewis, David Levering, ed. *The Portable Harlem Renaissance Reader*. New York: Viking, 1994.

Lucky, Crystal J. "Black Women Writers of the Harlem Renaissance." In Joyce W. Warren and Margaret Dickie, eds., *Challenging Boundaries: Gender and Periodization*. Athens: U of Georgia P, 2000. 91–106.

McCaskill, Barbara. "The Folklore of the Coasts in Black Women's Fiction of the Harlem Renaissance." *CLA Journal* 39 (1996): 273–302.

McHenry, Elizabeth. *Forgotten Readers: Recovering the Lost History of African-American Literary Societies*. Durham, NC: Duke UP, 2002.

Simon, Zoltan. "From Lenox Avenue to the Charlotteborg Palace: The Construction of the Image of Europe by Harlem Renaissance Authors." *British and American Studies* 4 (1999): 105–12.

Sisney, Mary F. "The View from the Outside: Black Novels of Manners." In Sharon Felton and Michelle Loris, eds., *The Critical Response to Gloria Naylor*. Westport, CT: Greenwood, 1997. 63–75.

Stephens, Michelle A. "Black Transnationalism and the Politics of National Identity: West Indian Intellectuals in Harlem in the Age of War and Revolution." *American Quarterly* 50 (1998): 592–608.

Walker, Margaret. "New Poets." In Cary D. Wintz, ed., *Remembering the Harlem Renaissance*. New York: Garland, 1996. 177–86.

Wall, Cheryl A. "Histories and Heresies: Engendering the Harlem Renaissance." *Meridians* 2 (2001): 59–76.

———. *Women of the Harlem Renaissance*. Bloomington: Indiana UP, 1995.

Realism, Naturalism, Modernism, 1940–1960

Melvin B. Tolson

1900?–1966

Works in the Anthology

"An Ex-Judge at the Bar" (1944)
"Dark Symphony" (1944)
"A Legend of Versailles" (1944)
From *Libretto for the Republic of Liberia* (1953)
"The Birth of John Henry" (1965)
"Satchmo" (1965)

Other Works

Rendezvous with America (poems, 1944)
Harlem Gallery (poems, 1965)
"Harlem Gallery" and Other Poems (ed. Raymond Nelson, 1999)

Themes

- Defining an African American aesthetic
- African (American) influences on high Modernism

- Pretensions of the black bourgeoisie
- Importance of independence for modern African nations
- Intersection of African history with African American history
- White hypocrisy and racialized bigotry

Characteristics

- Weaves together several different literary and poetic traditions
- Traditional conventions of literary modernism
- African American vernacular English and traditions
- Revisions of black folk heroes
- Understated and oblique treatment of controversial subjects

Teaching Strategies

- A research project that investigates multiple versions of the legend of John Henry should expose your students to various accounts of this folk figure. Class presentations of student research would enable students to share findings and to draw conclusions together about the sociopolitical and historical contexts in which the figure is revised and reconstituted.
- Consider sharing with students high Modernist poetry from the Anglo American tradition, to expose them to texts by T. S. Eliot, Ezra Pound, William Carlos Williams, and others against whom Tolson wrote. You might find it useful to provide students with an excerpt from Eliot's *The Waste Land*, complete with explanatory footnotes, for comparison with Tolson's footnotes in *Libretto for the Republic of Liberia*.
- Listen with students to selections on the Audio Companion by the vernacular artists whom Tolson cites in "Satchmo." Engage students in discussion of the ways in which they perceive Tolson to be influenced by the musicians and singers he references. Trace for them the Modernist implications of this poem.

Questions

- What overlapping qualities and constructs do you find in Tolson's *Libretto for the Republic of Liberia* and the jazz recordings on the Audio Companion? What tropes indicate the artistic period from which these literary and musical texts emerge?
- Tolson and Gwendolyn Brooks have been regarded as the most Modernist of African American poets. Examine their poems and enumerate the conventions they share. In what ways are their styles different? What difference does each poet's gender identity seem to

make to his or her poetry? You might want to begin by comparing the two poets' divergent uses of the sonnet form.

- Compare and contrast the folk hero John Henry as developed in Tolson's "The Birth of John Henry," in the version of the ballad in *NAFAM*, and in Colson Whitehead's *John Henry Days*. Are there historical or political contexts for Tolson's poem that seem to influence his portrait of the folk hero and to differentiate it from Whitehead's?

- One key aspect of Tolson's poetic project was to demonstrate that Africa and its diaspora had greatly influenced literary and cultural constructs in the United States and throughout Europe. Identify aspects of each selection by Tolson that work toward powerful fulfillment of this goal.

- To what extent do you think the questions in the second stanza of "Satchmo" are rhetorical questions? Analyze the use of irony in this poem.

Bibliography

Mootry, Maria K. " 'The Step of Iron Feet': Creative Practice in the War Sonnets of Melvin B. Tolson and Gwendolyn Brooks." In Aldon L. Nielsen, ed., *Reading Race in American Poetry: "An Area of Act."* Urbana: U of Illinois P, 2000. 133–47.

Nielsen, Aldon L. "Melvin B. Tolson and the Deterritorialization of Modernism." *African American Review* 26 (1992): 241–56.

Russell, Mariann. "Langston Hughes and Melvin Tolson: Blues People." In Joanne Gabbin, ed., *The Furious Flowering of African American Poetry*. Charlottesville: U of Virginia P, 1999. 38–46.

Dorothy West

1907–1998

Works in the Anthology

The Living Is Easy (1948), Part 1, Chaps. 1–3

Other Works

"The Type-writer" (story, 1926)
"An Unimportant Man" (story, 1928)
"Jackpot" (story, rpt. 1970)

The Richer, the Poorer (stories, 1995)
The Wedding (novel, 1995)

Themes

- Great Migration of the twentieth century
- African Americans' economic suffering versus economic elitism
- African American domesticity, family commitments, sisterhood
- Marriage and motherhood for African American women
- Sexual violence against black women
- Myths of black female sexuality
- African American female independence
- Social differences between black northern bourgeoisie and black southern folk community

Characteristics

- Celebration of black women's communal love
- Satire of northern African American bourgeois pretensions
- Flashback technique to reconstruct characters' past
- Autobiographical details
- Critique of patriarchy, sexism, and misogyny
- Interior monologues
- Exploration of characters' psychological processes

Questions

- Compare and contrast the representation of myths of black female sexuality in West's *The Living Is Easy* and Ann Petry's *The Street*. How does each author shape her protagonist's perspective? How does this perspective affect readers' comprehension of the respective danger each protagonist faces?
- Compare the representation of woman's "wildness" in *The Living Is Easy* and Toni Morrison's *Song of Solomon*. Paraphrase the "wildness" in women characters developed by West and Morrison, respectively. Do you think the authors intend this characteristic to convey immorality or impurity? Why or why not?
- Why do you suppose West portrays her character as sexually obstinate with her husband? What other plot details reinforce a view of Cleo as a woman who does not experience sexual pleasure?
- What elements does West provide for her character to complicate Cleo beyond such stereotypes of black women as Jezebel, Mammy, or Sapphire? How does Cleo compare to other black female characters you have encountered in African American literature written before 1975?

Chester B. Himes

1909–1984

Works in the Anthology

"To What Red Hell?" (1934)

Other Works

If He Hollers Let Him Go (novel, 1945)
Lonely Crusade (novel, 1947)
Third Generation (novel, 1954)
The Primitive (novel, 1955)
Cast the First Stone (novel, 1955)
For Love of Imabelle (novel, 1957)
Cotton Comes to Harlem (novel, 1965)
The Quality of Hurt (autobiography, 1972)
My Life of Absurdity (autobiography, 1976)

Themes

- Nausea and fire as existential metaphors
- Bondage, incarceration, imprisonment
- Intersection of race, violence, maleness, and "manhood"

Characteristics

- Traditional conventions of literary naturalism
- Repeated use of similes
- Verbal repetition
- Slang, profanity, unexpurgated language and imagery

Questions

- Compare Himes's story of prison life with the selections by three other African American men who drew on personal experiences with the penal system in the generation after Himes: Malcolm X, Etheridge Knight, and Eldridge Cleaver. What do these authors collectively assert about the intersection of race, incarceration, and literary reconstruction?
- Himes's story bears the homophobia and sexual anxiety that would come to characterize literature by African American authors in the next literary period, the Black Arts era. What sociopolitical and his-

torical factors seem to contribute to their anxiety-ridden portraits of same-sex romantic and sexual encounters?

- The title "To What Red Hell?" appears again in the story as a speech by a musician. Analyze Himes's representation of music in this story. What function does it seem to serve? In what ways does Himes connect allusions to music with allusions to Judeo-Christianity?
- In African American studies, the modern prison is often read as a symbol of antebellum slavery. What conventions and tropes of chattel slavery, if any, do you find in Himes's story?

Bibliography

Glasrud, Bruce, and Laurie Champion. "Chester B. Himes (1909–1984)." In Emmanuel S. Nelson, ed., *Contemporary African American Novelists: A Bio-Bibliographical Critical Sourcebook*. Westport, CT: Greenwood, 1999. 203–10.

Glasrud, Bruce, and Laurie Champion. " 'No Land of the Free': Chester Himes Confronts California (1940–1946)." *CLA Journal* 44 (2001): 391–416.

Ikard, David. "Love Jones: A Black Male Feminist Critique of Chester Himes's *If He Hollers Let Him Go*." *African American Review* 36 (2002): 299–310.

Rand, William E. "Chester Himes as a Naturalistic Writer in the Tradition of Richard Wright and Theodore Dreiser." *CLA Journal* 44 (2001): 442–50.

Rosen, Steven J. "African American Anti-Semitism and Himes' *Lonely Crusade*." *MELUS* 20 (1995): 47–68.

Ann Petry

1911–1997

Works in the Anthology

"Like a Winding Sheet" (1945)
The Street, Chap. 1 (1946)

Other Works

Country Place (novel, 1947)
The Narrows (novel, 1953)
Miss Muriel and Other Stories (1971)

Themes

- Impoverished inner city/ghetto life, decaying urban landscapes
- Slumlords and segregated housing
- Impact of poverty and economic deprivation on African American women
- Single black motherhood
- Sexual politics, sexism, sexual and gendered domination of women
- Economic inequities
- Spiritual and intellectual poverty

Characteristics

- Documentary, journalistic style
- Traditional conventions of literary naturalism
- Urban and psychological realism
- Feminist critique of intersections of race, class, gender, violence, and sexuality
- Feminist critique of racialized power imbalances

Questions

- Analyze the juxtaposition of white sheets and black face in Petry's "Like a Winding Sheet." What cultural connotations give the two symbols their power in this story?
- Compare and contrast the scene in which Johnson asks for coffee in Petry's "Like a Winding Sheet" with a comparable scene in which James Baldwin's narrator asks for coffee in "Notes of Native Son." What difference does genre make in the respective representations of power and commodity? What difference does the author's gender make in these respective accounts of racial discrimination and economic power play?
- Like Petry's "Like a Winding Sheet," Richard Wright's "Long Black Song" depicts domestic physical assault of a woman by a black man. Compare and contrast these two stories to assess how each author's gender identity affects the structure, plot, and trope of the stories.
- Like Petry's "Like a Winding Sheet," Richard Wright's "Long Black Song" depicts domestic physical assault of a woman by a black man. To what extent does each author suggest that the violence originates in social forces outside the attacker? To what extent do these texts hold the assailants responsible for the violence they perpetrate?
- Analyze Petry's naturalistic description of the sexualized gaze in Chapter 1 of *The Street*. Why do you suppose the author has her protagonist read malice and danger in the eyes of both the woman and

the man she encounters in the apartment building? What related images of scrutiny, spectacle, objectification, watching, and being watched does the chapter develop?

• Chapter 1 of *The Street* invokes the black vernacular music tradition of antebellum spirituals and links it to Lutie's grandmother. What attitudes about the African American past does Petry give to Lutie with these cultural allusions? What attitude does Petry herself seem to hold toward antebellum spirituals and African American elders?

• What do Lutie's ironic interior monologues reveal about her character?

• Chapter 1 of *The Street* ends with references to a dog and a canary as abused pets. Have you encountered these figures elsewhere in your study of African American literature? How does Petry raise them to the level of symbol at the outset of her novel? What do the figures portend about the plot that will unfold in the novel?

Bibliography

Brody, Jennifer DeVere. "Effaced into Flesh: Black Women's Subjectivity." *Genders* 24 (1996): 184–206.

Bryant, Jacqueline. "Postures of Resistance in Ann Petry's *The Street*." *CLA Journal* 45 (2002): 444–59.

Fitzsimmons, Lorna. "The Socially 'Forsaken Race': Dantean Turns in Ann Petry's *The Street*." *Notes on Contemporary Literature* 30 (2000): 6–8.

Garvey, Johanna. "That Old Black Magic? Gender and Music in Ann Petry's Fiction." In Saadi A. Simawe, ed., *Black Orpheus: Music in African American Fiction from the Harlem Renaissance to Toni Morrison*. New York: Garland, 2000. 119–51.

Henderson, Carol. "The 'Walking Wounded': Rethinking Black Women's Identity in Ann Petry's *The Street*." *Modern Fiction Studies* 46 (2000): 849–67.

Hicks, Heather. " 'This Strange Communion': Surveillance and Spectatorship in Ann Petry's *The Street*." *African American Review* 37 (2003): 21–38.

———. "Rethinking Realism in Ann Petry's *The Street*." *MELUS* 27 (2002): 89–107.

Winter, Kari. "Narrative Desire in Ann Petry's *The Street*." *Journal x* 4 (2000): 101–12.

Robert Hayden

1913–1982

Works in the Anthology

"The Diver" (1962)
"Homage to the Empress of the Blues" (1962)
"Middle Passage" (1962)
"Those Winter Sundays" (1966)
"O Daedalus, Fly Away Home" (1962)
"Runagate Runagate" (1962)
"Frederick Douglass" (1962)
"A Ballad of Remembrance" (1962)
"Mourning Poem for the Queen of Sunday" (1962)
"Soledad" (1970)
"El-Hajj Malik El-Shabazz" (1970)
"A Letter from Phillis Wheatley" (1978)

Other Works

Heart-Shape in the Dust: Poems (1940)
The Lion and the Archer: Poems (1948)
Figure of Time (poems, 1955)
A Ballad of Remembrance (poems, 1962)
Selected Poems (1966)
Kaleidoscope: Poems by American Negro Poets (editor, 1967)
Words in the Mourning Time: Poems (1970)
Afro-American Literature: An Introduction (co-editor, 1971)
The Night-Blooming Cereus (poems, 1972)
American Models: A Collection of Modern Stories (co-editor, 1973)
Angle of Ascent: New and Selected Poems (1975)
American Journal (poems, 1978, 1982)
Collected Poems (ed. Frederick Glaysher, 1985)

Themes

- Black emotional power and self-determination
- Abduction, slavery, bondage, white supremacy
- Black religious, spiritual, and supernatural forces
- African American (gilded) romantic love and loss
- African American cultural mythologies and vernacular traditions
- Autobiographical/personal history and other African American histories

Characteristics

- Juxtaposition of the ideal with the real
- Indirect, intellectual, formal style
- Obscure, sometimes arcane diction
- Irony and signifying
- Classical and religious allusions and symbols
- Musical traditions, especially black vernacular music
- Multivalence and intertextuality, incorporation of diverse other texts

Teaching Strategies

- When working with your students to comprehend Hayden's "Middle Passage," ask them to research particular events, biographies, or terms with which they may be unfamiliar. For example, not all students will know that the opening line of "Middle Passage" references names of slave ships or that *Estrella* and *Esperanza* are Spanish words for "star" and "hope," respectively. The assignment might also ask students to analyze the irony Hayden deploys with these historical names.
- Listen with students to the Audio Companion recording of "Backwater Blues" when teaching "Homage to the Empress of the Blues." Ask students to research aspects of the life of Bessie Smith as well as her status as a cultural icon. Bring to class a reproduction of Smith in her signature pearls.
- To enrich students' appreciation for "Mourning Poem for the Queen of Sunday," listen with them to the recordings by Billie Holiday, Mahalia Jackson, and other women artists included on the Audio Companion. While Hayden's poem does not explicitly commemorate these artists, the Audio Companion recordings can perhaps help students understand historical and cultural figures who parallel "Queen(s) of Sunday."

Questions

- Compare Hayden with the poets Melvin B. Tolson, Michael S. Harper, and Nathaniel Mackey.
- Carefully consider Hayden's vocabulary and diction. Isolate phrases and lines that resonate with multiple meanings.
- Why does Hayden use both Spanish and English diction in "Middle Passage"?
- Hayden regarded his Baha'i religious faith as an important component of his poetic vision, for it espoused a fundamental unity of people and religions and emphasized art not only as service to humanity

but also as sacred worship. In an interview with John O'Brien, Hayden reflects on being a poet: "You respond in a particular way to yourself, to the basic questions that concern all human beings—the nature of the universe, love, death, God, and so forth. And that way of responding, of coming to grips with life, determines the kind of poetry you write." Trace the development of this philosophy in one or two of Hayden's poems.

- The richness of Hayden's "Middle Passage" lies largely in its ironic allusions to New England hymns, William Shakespeare's *The Tempest*, slave ships' log entries, the *Amistad* mutiny, court depositions, trial testimony, and numerous other historical documents. Discuss Hayden's use of irony in this poem and examine the juxtapositions that render it effective.

- Specify the multiple meanings implied by the title "Middle Passage." Which seem to pertain most to Hayden's poem?

- Given the way that Hayden uses the term "Middle Passage," can the character Clay in Amiri Baraka's *Dutchman* rightly be said to be situated within the Middle Passage? Does Hayden suggest that African Americans have not yet emerged from the Middle Passage?

- How does Hayden's representation of the Middle Passage compare with Olaudah Equiano's in his account of his journey from Africa to slavery?

- Review the conventions of antebellum slave narratives and determine how many Hayden deploys in "Runagate Runagate." Why do you suppose Hayden decided to revisit slavery in the middle of the twentieth century?

- Hayden underscores Malcolm X's premature death by restricting "El-Haij Malik El-Shabazz" to fifty-five short lines. What other elements and tropes of this elegy express grief and appreciation?

- Contrast Hayden's "A Letter from Phillis Wheatley" with Wheatley's own "To S. M., A Young *African* Painter." How aptly do you think Hayden represents Wheatley's image and interests?

Bibliography

Conniff, Brian. "Answering 'The Waste Land': Robert Hayden and the Rise of the African American Poetic Sequence." *African American Review* 33 (1999): 487–506.

Fetrow, Fred M. "Reading the Man: Robert Hayden and the Legacy of Frederick Douglass." *CLA Journal* 44 (2000): 189–203.

Friedlander, Benjamin. "Robert Hayden's Epic of Community." *MELUS* 23 (1998): 129–43.

Genge, Susan. "Hayden's 'Homage to the Empress of the Blues.' " *The Explicator* 57 (1999): 112–14.

Mullen, Harryette, and Stephen Yenser. "Theme and Variations on Robert Hayden's Poetry." *The Antioch Review* 55 (1997): 160–75.

Murphy, Jim. " 'Here Only the Sea Is Real': Robert Hayden's Postmodern Passages." *MELUS* 27 (2002): 107–29.

Nicholas, Xavier, ed. "Robert Hayden and Michael S. Harper: A Literary Friendship." *Callaloo* 17 (1994): 976–1016.

Pavlic, Edward M. " 'Something Patterned, Wild, and Free': Robert Hayden's Angles of Descent and the Democratic Unconscious." *African American Review* 36 (2002): 533–56.

Rashid, Frank. "Robert Hayden's Detroit Blues Elegies." *Callaloo* 24 (2001): 200–202.

Richards, Phillip. "Robert Hayden (1913–1980): An Appreciation." *Massachusetts Review* 40 (1999): 599–600.

Zabel, Darcy. "Hayden's 'Runagate Runagate.' " *The Explicator* 60 (2002): 100–103.

Ralph Ellison

1914–1994

Works in the Anthology

"Richard Wright's Blues" (1972)
Invisible Man, Prologue, Chap.1, Epilogue (1952)
"Change the Joke and Slip the Yoke" (1958)
"The World and the Jug" (1963, 1964)
"Remembering Richard Wright" (1986)
"Letter to Stanley Edgar Hyman" (May 1970)

Other Works

Shadow and Act (essays, 1964)
Going to the Territory (essays, 1986)
Juneteenth (novel, 2000)

Themes

- Racial discrimination, racism, and negrophobia
- The cyclical nature of (African) American history
- Racial identity formation, racial disillusionment
- Psychic landscapes and landmines of U.S. race relations
- The American Dream/Nightmare
- American promises of achievement manifest as wealth, education, competition, and (heteronormative) sexual prowess
- Tragicomedy of African American daily life

Characteristics

- An accomplished essayist and major cultural critic
- Between 1938 and 1944 wrote almost sixty articles and eight stories
- Style marked by irony, disingenuity, subversion, humor, signifying
- Imbues his fiction with rich and significant symbols: color, music, sermons, (in)sight and blindness, underground spaces, light, names, titles
- Extensive use of African American vernacular traditions, both verbal and musical
- Combines "high" and "low" cultural constructs in his fiction and essays

Teaching Strategies

- Ask students to research etymologies, denotations, and connotations of selected terms relevant to *Invisible Man*, including *invisibility*, *boomerang*, *spiral*, *cycles*, and *hibernation*.
- Ask students to research and share information about the battle royal as a traditional pastime in the antebellum United States wherein slavemasters pitted slaves against one another in much the same manner (and sometimes the same arenas) as they did dogs and roosters.
- After students have read the "Prologue" to *Invisible Man*, listen with them to "Black and Blue" on the Audio Companion. Discuss together the narrator's choice of that recording with his dessert of vanilla ice cream and sloe gin and his oblique characterization of it as "poetry [made] out of being invisible."
- Listen to a few of the blues selections on the Audio Companion with students and engage them in a discussion of the various definitions of the genre that Ellison offers in "Richard Wright's Blues." Ask them to assess the validity of Ellison's definition based on the selections they hear.

Questions

- Compare and contrast Ellison's debates about African American writing with white intellectuals Stanley Edgar Hyman and Irving Howe with the exchange between Pauline Hopkins and Cordelia A. Condict. How are the debates similar to one another? In what ways does the gender of the participants effect differences in the debate?
- At different points in time, Richard Wright served as mentor to both Ellison and James Baldwin. Select a text by each of the three authors that espouses a literary theory and trace Wright's influence on the two younger writers.
- Read both the excerpts from *Invisible Man* and Richard Wright's "The Man Who Lived Underground." What conventions and ideas do the two texts share? What in Ellison's novel reveals his biographical connection to the author of "The Man Who Lived Underground"?
- Compare Ellison's literary theories as set forth in his letter to Stanley Edgar Hyman, "The World and the Jug," and "Change the Joke and Slip the Yoke" to earlier essays of/on literary theory: "The Negro Artist and the Racial Mountain," by Langston Hughes, and "The New Negro," by Alain Locke. How do Ellison's ideas compare with those of his literary precursors? In what ways do they extend the older authors' critical tradition?
- Compare Ellison's literary theories as set forth in his letter to Stanley Edgar Hyman, "The World and the Jug," and "Change the Joke and Slip the Yoke" to texts of or on literary theory developed during the Black Arts era: "For Saundra," by Nikki Giovanni, and "Introduction" to *Think Black*, by Haki R. Madhubuti.
- Read the excerpts from *Invisible Man* as well as Ellison's literary theory as expressed in "The World and the Jug." Does the essay help illuminate the ideas and arguments that Ellison makes in the novel? Does Ellison's novel conform to his own literary theory?
- How might *Invisible Man* be read as an argument about American history and the American Dream, or Nightmare?
- Is *Invisible Man* a reconstruction of the Middle Passage?
- According to *Invisible Man*, what role does history play in the formation of identity?
- Compare and contrast the blindfolded boxing protagonist of *Invisible Man* with the narrator of the novel's Prologue. What views of black male identity do they express?
- Analyze the deathbed instructions of the protagonist's grandfather in *Invisible Man*. How do his words compare with the ideas expressed in Richard Wright's "The Ethics of Living Jim Crow"?

Bibliography

Moreland, Richard. *Learning from Difference: Teaching Morrison, Twain, Ellison, and Eliot.* Columbus: Ohio State UP, 1999.

Schor, Edith. *Visible Ellison: A Study of Ralph Ellison's Fiction.* Westport, CT: Greenwood, 1993.

Singh, Arnritjit, and Maryemma Graham, eds. *Conversations with Ralph Ellison.* Jackson: UP of Mississippi, 1995.

Sundquist, Eric J. *Cultural Contexts for Ralph Ellison's* Invisible Man. Boston: Bedford Books, 1995.

Margaret Walker

1915–1998

Works in the Anthology

"For My People" (1937, 1942)
"Poppa Chicken" (1942)
"For Malcolm X" (1970)
"Prophets for a New Day" (1970)

Other Works

For My People (poems, 1942)
Jubilee (novel, 1966)
Prophets for a New Day (poems, 1970)
October Journey (poems, 1973)
How I Wrote Jubilee and Other Essays on Life and Literature (ed. Maryemma Graham, 1990)
On Being Female, Black, and Free: Essays by Margaret Walker, 1932–1992 (ed. Maryemma Graham, 1997)

Themes

- Black freedom
- Freedom and civil rights movements
- Impact of Christian theology and spirituality on black life and culture
- Power of black vernacular traditions to sustain black life and culture

Characteristics

- Black sermonic tradition
- Black vernacular tradition
- Autobiographical details; personal experience

Questions

- Review the antiheroes (e.g., Stackolee) and heroes (e.g., John Henry) featured in the vernacular section of *NAFAM*. Then compare and contrast these folk figures with Walker's "Poppa Chicken." In what ways does Walker celebrate both the heroes and the antiheroes of the earlier tradition? How does she achieve this complex celebration of what would seem contrary figures?
- Compare and contrast Walker's sonnet for Malcolm X with other poems of appreciation for the assassinated leader. How does Walker's individual elegy seem representative of the form? How is her dirge distinctive?
- Comment on the narrative structure of "For My People." What does Walker gain with her use of the prose-poetry structure of this particular lyric?
- Walker, the daughter of a southern black minister, draws often on Judeo-Christian imagery in her writing. Isolate some of these allusions in "Prophets for a New Day" and discuss their significance in Walker's otherwise secular poem.

Bibliography

Baraka, Amiri. "Margaret Walker Alexander." *The Nation* 268 (1999): 32–33.

Gabbin, Joanne. "In Memoriam: Margaret Walker Alexander (1915–1998)." *Callaloo* 22 (1999): v–vii.

Gwendolyn Brooks

1917–2000

Works in the Anthology

"kitchenette building" (1945)
"the mother" (1945)
"a song in the front yard" (1945)
"Sadie and Maud" (1945)

"the vacant lot" (1945)
"the preacher: ruminates behind the sermon" (1945)
"The Sundays of Satin-Legs Smith" (1945)
"Maxie Allen" (1949)
"The Rites for Cousin Vit" (1949)
"The Children of the Poor" (1949)
"The Lovers of the Poor" (1960)
"We Real Cool" (1960)
"The Chicago *Defender* Sends a Man to Little Rock" (1960)
"A Lovely Love" (1960)
"Malcolm X" (1968)
"Two Dedications" (1968)
"Riot" (1969)
"The Third Sermon on the Warpland" (1969)
"Young Heroes" (1970)
"when you have forgotten Sunday: the love story" (1981)
Maud Martha (1953)

Other Works

A Street in Bronzeville (poems, 1945)
Annie Allen (poems, 1949)
Bronzeville Boys and Girls (poems, 1956)
Selected Poems (1963)
The Bean Eaters (poems, 1968)
In the Mecca (poems, 1968)
Family Pictures (poems, 1970)
Riot (poems, 1970)
Aloneness (poems, 1971)
A Broadside Treasury (editor, 1971)
Jump Bad: A New Chicago Anthology (editor, 1971)
Report from Part One (autobiography, 1972)
A Capsule Course in Black Poetry Writing (editor, 1975)
Beckonings (poems, 1975)
Primer for Blacks (poems, 1981)
To Disembark (poems, 1981)
Blacks (poems, 1987, 1991)

Themes

- Social commitment to African Americans
- African American interpersonal relationships
- African American communal and collective relationships
- The heroism of an individual life

- Heroism on a national scale
- Dreams of evolution beyond grim socio-economic realities
- Complexities and manifestations of mother love
- Complex interstices and courageousness of (black) urban life
- Poverty, racism, and other betrayals of the American Dream
- Special concern for children and women
- The beauty in common and everyday African American life
- Growing up in urban America within the context of race, class, sexuality, family, and community disenfranchisement
- Female socialization
- Interracial prejudice
- Repressed creativity, isolation, alienation, silence, and expression

Characteristics

- Defined African American experiences
- Excelled in standard literary forms
- Adept at showing the rare and heroic in the seemingly mundane
- Addresses an extensive and diverse readership

Teaching Strategies

- Brooks's poems may be taught on their own to good effect but when taught in tandem with her poetic and autobiographical novel *Maud Martha* their mutual themes and overlapping but distinct technical characteristics become abundantly clear.
- *Maud Martha* fits well into a thematic unit on African American depictions of family. Ask students to analyze family structures and relationships and the values, dreams, aspirations, creativity, and family commitment of the main characters.

Questions

- Both Brooks and Amiri Baraka were respected writers when encounters with other poet-activists of their day led them into the Black Arts era. Select one or two poems you think "representative" of each poet's work and discuss the formalistic and thematic aspects that reveal that each was already established in some way when the Black Arts era evolved.
- Compare and contrast Brooks's early poetry with the selections by Langston Hughes. Why do you suppose these two poets are frequently paired?
- Select one or two of Brooks's poems that strike you as her interpretation of the Black Arts era's call for a "black aesthetic." In what ways

are these poems overtly political and nationalistic, in accord with the black aesthetic? With which vernacular traditions do they experiment?

- Some of the selections by another Pulitzer Prize–winning poet, Rita Dove, have subjects and themes similar to Brooks's. Begin a comparison there. Then consider Brooks's and Dove's poetry in relation to poems by Robert Hayden and Yusef Komunyakaa, two male prize-winning poets of their eras.

- Compare *Maud Martha* with the excerpts from Maya Angelou's *I Know Why the Caged Bird Sings* and Jamaica Kincaid's *Annie John*, and one other coming-of-age story, perhaps Paule Marshall's "To Da-duh, in Memorium." What generalizations can you make about African American women's report of their life experiences, based on each *Bildungsroman*?

- Consider the significance of setting in *Maud Martha*. What is life like in northern cities? What relation does daily life there have to the American Dream? Are Maud Martha's hopes and aspirations realistic or valid?

- Enumerate the survival techniques Brooks attributes to Maud Martha. How does the protagonist defend herself? Consider her silences, her internal monologue, the points at which she seems more free, and when and how she speaks out. What thesis (or theses) about (black) women's self-expression does Brooks use her novel to articulate?

- What does *Maud Martha* argue about blacks who migrated to the urban North during the early twentieth century?

- Why do you suppose critics shunned *Maud Martha* but praised virtually everything else that Brooks published? To what extent do you think their neglect of the novel was affected by other African American literature published around the same time, including Ann Petry's *The Street*, Richard Wright's *Black Boy*, and Lorraine Hansberry's *A Raisin in the Sun*?

- In what ways is *Maud Martha* a novel about bondage and freedom? Do you think the novel can effectively be paired with antebellum slave narratives? Why or why not?

Bibliography

Kent, George E. A *Life of Gwendolyn Brooks*. Lexington: UP of Kentucky, 1990.

Wright, Stephen Caldwell. *On Gwendolyn Brooks: Reliant Contemplation*. Ann Arbor: U of Michigan P, 1996.

James Baldwin

1924–1987

Works in the Anthology

"Everybody's Protest Novel" (1949)
"Stranger in the Village" (1953)
"Notes of a Native Son" (1955)
"Sonny's Blues" (1957)
"Going to Meet the Man" (1965)

Other Works

Go Tell It on the Mountain (novel, 1953)
Giovanni's Room (novel, 1956)
Another Country (novel, 1962)
The Fire Next Time (essays, 1963)
Blues for Mr. Charlie (drama, 1964)
Going to Meet the Man (stories, 1965)
The Amen Corner (drama, 1968)
Tell Me How Long the Train's Been Gone (novel, 1968)
If Beale Street Could Talk (novel, 1974)
Just Above My Head (novel, 1979)
Notes of a Native Son (essays, 1955)
Nobody Knows My Name (essays, 1961)
The Price of the Ticket (essays, 1985)

Themes

- "The Negro problem"
- Race relations between blacks and others around the world
- Poverty and economic injustices
- Police brutality
- Religious oppression and domination
- African American intraracial and familial discord
- Sin, transgression, repentance, redemption, and salvation
- African American migrations
- The role of blackness in the white imagination
- Intersection of race and sexuality
- Homophobia, sexual intolerance, and U.S. Puritanism

Characteristics

- Confessional, often evangelical tone
- Jeremiadic, sermonic, exhortatory, didactic rhetoric
- Vernacular traditions, with emphasis on black musical (lyrical and instrumental) traditions and African American vernacular English
- Judeo-Christian biblical allusions and imagery
- Unflinching explorations into U.S. race relations and social injustices

Teaching Strategies

- Play for students the Audio Companion's blues and jazz selections and have them discuss the railroad imagery in the syncopations and lyrics. Then ask them to trace corresponding images in "Sonny's Blues," noting that Baldwin borrows from both vernacular musical traditions for his story but keeps them distinct from one another.

Questions

- To what extent do you agree with Baldwin's contention in "Everybody's Protest Novel" (1949) that *Uncle Tom's Cabin* (1852) collaborates with racialized violence against blacks rather than posits a redemptive message for both whites and blacks as Stowe claimed?
- Is it possible to reconcile Baldwin's argument in "Everybody's Protest Novel" that *Uncle Tom's Cabin* espouses "theological terror" with a personal faith in Christian doctrine? What does Baldwin's essay on *Uncle Tom's Cabin* demand of its Christian readers?
- Compare and contrast the lynching scenes in "Going to Meet the Man" and James Weldon Johnson's *Autobiography of an Ex-Colored Man*. How do the racial identities of the protagonists affect the authors' respective arguments of the two stories? In what ways does Baldwin's story echo and respond to Johnson's novel?
- In what ways does Baldwin insinuate that "Sonny's Blues" is a story about storytelling?
- Support or refute Baldwin's contention in "Stranger in the Village" that the white residents in the Swiss village about which he writes "cannot be, from the point of view of power, strangers anywhere in the world." What do you understand the claim to mean? What are the effects of Baldwin's juxtaposing the authenticity of the relationship of his Swiss neighbors to Dante, Shakespeare, and other European institutions?

Bibliography

Lopate, Phillip. "Teaching James Baldwin." *Teachers and Writers* 29 (1998): 1–3.

Savery, Pancho. "Baldwin, Bebop, and 'Sonny's Blues.' " In Joseph Trimmer and Tilly Warnock, eds., *Understanding Others: Cultural and Cross-Cultural Studies and the Teaching of Literature.* Urbana, IL: National Council of Teachers of English, 1992.

Sherard, Tracey. "Sonny's Bebop: Baldwin's 'Blues Text' as Intracultural Critique." *AAR* 32 (1998): 691–705.

Wilner, Arlene. "Confronting Resistance: Sonny's Blues—and Mine." *Pedagogy: Critical Approaches to Teaching Literature, Language, Composition, and Culture* 2 (2002): 173–96.

Bob Kaufman

1925–1986

Works in the Anthology

"Walking Parker Home" (1965)
"Grandfather was Queer, Too" (1965)
"Jail Poems" (1965)

Other Works

Abomunisto Manifesto (prose poems, 1959)
Solitudes Crowded with Loneliness (prose poems, 1965)
Golden Sardine (poems, 1967)
The Ancient Rain: Poems 1956–78 (1981)

Themes

- Same avant-garde themes that are associated with the American Beat poets of the 1950s and 1960s, inflected with African American cultural values
- Peculiar identity as black Beat poet
- Revision of W. E. B. Du Bois's concept of double consciousness from a culturally complex (African American mother and Jewish American father) perspective
- Paradoxes in mid-twentieth-century African American life
- Dialectic of existential joy and anger

- Disparagement of white appropriation of African American music, culture, and identity
- Condemnation of capitalism, Jim Crow segregation, and racism in the United States
- Impact of black music traditions on African American political defiance and resistance

Characteristics

- Vernacular: various forms of traditional African American music
- Borrows from jazz the techniques of improvisation; irregular, aggressive rhythm; reversals and regeneration
- Counter to jazz poets like Langston Hughes, who see jazz as an African American response to tough life in the United States, Kaufman sees jazz as a response to those who do not appreciate the toughness of African American life in the United States (Kohli 167).

Questions

- How do Kaufman's jazz rhythms differ from those of his jazz poet predecessor Langston Hughes?
- Research, then compare and contrast the three different versions of Kaufman's "War Memoir." (*NAFAM* contains the final version.) What changes did Kaufman make across time? How does knowing he spent five years in the U.S. Army affect your understanding of the poem's significance?
- Unlike contemporaries such as Etheridge Knight (who labored over the written forms of his poems but recited them from memory during public performances), "Kaufman was known for not writing his poetry down" (Kohli 181). In what ways do the Kaufman selections suggest this implied improvisational style?

Bibliography

Kohli, Amor. "Saxophones and Smothered Rage: Bob Kaufman, Jazz and the Quest for Redemption." *Callaloo* 25 (2002): 165–82.

Lorraine Hansberry

1930–1965

Works in the Anthology

  A Raisin in the Sun (1959)

Other Works

  The Movement: Documentary of a Struggle for Equality (editor, 1964)
  The Sign in Sidney Brustein's Window (drama, 1965)
  To Be Young, Gifted, and Black (autobiography, 1969)
  Lorraine Hansberry: The Collected Plays (ed. Robert Nemiroff, 1983)

Themes

  • Family issues and generational conflicts
  • Great Migration
  • Impact of urban socialization on African Americans
  • Christianity and Afro-Protestantism
  • Relationships between African Americans and continental Africans
  • American dreams as experienced by African Americans
  • Black maternity, black female sexuality, black female corporeality
  • Abortion

Characteristics

  • Classic dramatic structure
  • Realistic detail and setting
  • Sharp social analysis combined with realism and melodrama
  • Influential for social dramas of the 1960s and afterward
  • Unflinching look into racialized sociopolitical injustices

Teaching Strategies

  • To stimulate, inspire, or expand discussion of generic conventions
    and differences, schedule a viewing with your students of one of the
    film versions of *A Raisin in the Sun*.
  • Share with students parodies of Lena Younger as the stereotyped fig-
    ure of the Strong Black Woman such as that in George C. Wolfe's
    The Colored Museum. (You might find a copy of the 1991 PBS "Great
    Performances" production of this play, which Wolfe co-directed.) Or
    share with them Trudier Harris's sharp critique of Hansberry's Lena

in *Saints, Sinners, Saviors*. Discuss with them the degree to which Hansberry's figure conforms to (or inaugurates?) the stereotype.

- Ask students to research various historical events of the civil rights era in which *A Raisin* is situated. Have them make class presentations that report on Hansberry's political and intellectual contributions, explaining the play's relevance to such landmark developments as *Brown v. Board of Education* and the Montgomery bus boycotts.
- Ask students to research Hansberry's own family's Supreme Court case (*Hansberry v. Lee*), which ultimately upheld their right to live in an all-white neighborhood. Have them articulate in class presentations the differences they see between Hansberry's biographical experience and the experiences she develops for her characters in *A Raisin in the Sun*.
- Situate *A Raisin* amid black literature that documents and depicts Great Migration experiences. Ask students to identify ways that Hansberry contributes to this tradition and expands it.
- Define *dramatic realism* for your students, and have them assess ways that Hansberry deploys it in *A Raisin*.

Questions

- Winner of the New York Drama Critics Award as Best Play of the Year, *A Raisin in the Sun* ran for 538 performances and thus became the longest-running Broadway play by an African American; Hansberry was the first African American woman to write a Broadway hit play. Based on your knowledge of African American literature that predates the play, what themes, tropes, and conventions do you think critics and audiences celebrated about Hansberry's work?
- Analyze in turn each of the major characters and the transformations he or she undergoes. Then discuss how interpretations of the play shift depending on which character one sees as the protagonist.
- What elements of the play seem related to the establishment of independent governments across the African continent?
- What commonalities and what differences do you find between *A Raisin in the Sun* and two plays that followed it by only a few years: Amiri Baraka's *Dutchman* and Ed Bullins's *Goin'a Buffalo*?
- Read "Harlem," the poem by Langston Hughes from which Hansberry took the title of her play. Then discuss ways that Hansberry's play answers the questions Hughes's poem asks. Are there (other) specific elements from the Harlem Renaissance that you read in *A Raisin in the Sun*?
- Compare and contrast Hansberry's play with the excerpts from Ntozake Shange's *for colored girls* and with August Wilson's *Joe Turner's Come and Gone*. What have these later dramatists retained

of Hansberry's style, and which conventions have they transformed or transcended?

- Compare and contrast gender—the socialization of men and of women—as a theme in *A Raisin in the Sun*, Ntozake Shange's *for colored girls*, and August Wilson's *Joe Turner's Come and Gone*. How does the gender of the playwright seem to influence the particular representations of maleness and femaleness each offers?

- Compare and contrast gender—the socialization of men and of women—as a theme in *A Raisin in the Sun*, Ntozake Shange's *for colored girls*, and Adrienne Kennedy's *A Movie Star Has to Star in Black and White*. How does the female gender of all three playwrights seem to influence the particular representations of maleness and femaleness each offers? Can one safely generalize about black women playwrights' representation of gender based on these three plays? Do you think its production date—falling after the 1960s civil rights movement—renders *for colored girls* too different from the other two plays in theme, design, allusion, setting, and so forth, for effective or useful comparison?

- What does Hansberry's play argue about familial roles and responsibilities? Do the characters in *A Raisin in the Sun* seem to regard responsibility to self as less important than to the family unit? What economic responsibility does each character seem to espouse for the clan?

Bibliography

Bates, Randolph. "Teaching Film and *A Raisin in the Sun*." *Louisiana English Journal* 4 (1997): 62–67.

Harris, Trudier. *Saints, Sinners, Saviors: Strong Black Women in African American Literature*. New York: Palgrave, 2001.

Keppel, Ben. *The Work of Democracy: Ralph Bunche, Kenneth B. Clark, Lorraine Hansberry, and the Cultural Politics of Race*. Cambridge, MA: Harvard UP, 1995.

Kodat, Catherine G. "Confusion in a Dream Deferred: Context and Culture in Teaching *A Raisin in the Sun*." *Studies in the Literary Imagination* 31 (1998): 149–64.

Miller, Jeanne M. " 'Measure Him Right': An Analysis of Lorraine Hansberry's *Raisin in the Sun*." In David R. Peck, ed., *Teaching American Ethnic Literature: Nineteen Essays*. Albuquerque: U of New Mexico P, 1996. 133–45.

Wolfe, George C. *The Colored Museum*. 1986. In Branch, William, ed., *Black Thunder: An Anthology of Contemporary African American Drama*. New York: Mentor, 1992.

Teaching Realism, Naturalism, Modernism

The period from 1940 to 1960 combines philosophical inquiries and aesthetic experimentation with what we often call propaganda, protest, and politics with an emphasis on urban working-class life. Richard Wright, Ann Petry, and Chester B. Himes are among those writers who emphasize the harshness of African American life on a larger and more intense scale than did writers in the Harlem Renaissance. Many scholars argue that Richard Wright reigns supreme in the use of naturalism; they label other writers as members of, if not also pupils in, the "Wright School." Chapter 16 of Wright's *Black Boy*, on Chicago, and Wright's "The Man Who Lived Underground" are excellent examples of ways that the Wright School presents both environmental and social conditions as determinants of individuals' fates. Gwendolyn Brooks's *Maud Martha* offers a very different perspective from Wright's "The Man Who Lived Underground," not simply because of the authors' and their characters' different genders but also because of each author's distinct personality and philosophy. In addition, Ann Petry's use of naturalism may require a revision of our concept of the "Wright School."

Though Richard Wright helped both Ralph Ellison and James Baldwin personally and artistically, a study of the two is enriched by considerations of an expansive cultural context that includes the Korean conflict, McCarthyism, and other hostile geopolitical situations. Both Ellison and Baldwin experimented with various literary forms and techniques, seeking the best means to examine the conundrums of (African American) art, culture, and life. Both protégés were particularly interested in the potential of black vernacular expressions, especially jazz, blues, and sermons. A useful entry into the "Prologue" to Ralph Ellison's *Invisible Man* is the Audio Companion's recording of "(What Did I Do to Be So) Black and Blue." A discussion of James Baldwin's "Sonny's Blues" may be informed by listening to the blues and jazz selections from the 1950s and early 1960s on the Audio Companion. Moreover, the title of Baldwin's story and scenes such as the conversation between the narrator-teacher and his younger brother about the kind of musician Sonny wanted to become may lead to a discussion both of social caste and class and of musical metaphor and rhythmic imitations in fiction.

Two poets of the African American realism period who experimented with history and folk material as well as Modernist strategies are Melvin B. Tolson and Robert Hayden. They, like Margaret Walker and Gwendolyn Brooks, present history in unprecedented and provocative ways. While Hayden's "Middle Passage" and "Runagate Runagate" hark back to the slave narrative tradition, they clearly draw influence from Modernist traditions and the aesthetic forms of this movement. You might want to ask students to research the effect of the G.I. Bill, McCarthyism, and the increasing international agitation for civil rights on the substance and style of mid-twentieth-century black writers. What significant differences, if any, do students find in the literature produced by those who matriculated at colleges and universities during this time, those who worked with the WPA and various writers' groups, and those who spent time in Europe as part of the expatriate artist community?

Another important illustration of the influence on black literature of African American history and culture is the award-winning drama by Lorraine Hansberry, *A Raisin in the Sun*. Instructors can broaden students' appreciation for the social and temporal setting of the play by reviewing with them the legislation and public discourse concerning U.S. civil rights in the 1950s (e.g., *Brown v. Board of Education*) as well as the kinds of theater being produced on Broadway and being written by or about African Americans. You might also mention that Hansberry loosely based her drama on her own family's experience of redlining in Chicago and further that she responds in part to Richard Wright's *Native Son*, also set in Chicago. Hansberry takes her title from Langston Hughes's poem "Harlem." In *A Raisin*, Hansberry's ghettoized family demonstrates a less frequently portrayed but quite valid reason for African American integration of all-white suburbs: The Youngers seek the freedom to realize their dreams and their version of the American Dream, which is significantly *not* synonymous with a pursuit of friendship with whites or admiration of them. Moreover, Hansberry's play also presages the African heritage arguments of the 1960s with its introduction of Asagi and his dramatic interactions with Beneatha, Walter Lee, and Mama. Communication problems and misconceptions are apparent, but so too are the common interests and the possibilities of positive personal and familial alliances between Africans and African Americans. This aspect of the play is enhanced by considering the political and social implications of the African independence movements and the not-so-coincidental increase in the numbers of African students who entered U.S. universities during this time.

Genres

Poetry

Tolson
Hayden
Brooks
Kaufman
Walker

Drama

Hansberry

Periodical Literature

Ellison
Baldwin
Wright

Prose Narrative/Autobiography/Slave Narrative

Ellison
Baldwin
Wright

Short Fiction

Himes
Petry
Baldwin
Wright

Novel

West
Petry
Ellison
Brooks

Bibliography

Gikandi, Simon. "Race and the Idea of the Aesthetic." *Michigan Quarterly Review* 40 (2001): 318–41.

Griffiths, Frederick. "Ralph Ellison, Richard Wright, and the Case of Angelo Herndon." *African American Review* 35 (2001): 615–37.

Irons, Peter. *Jim Crow's Children: The Broken Promise of the Brown Decision.* New York: Viking. 2002.

Jimoh, A. Yesmisi. "Double Consciousness, Modernism, and Womanist Themes in Gwendolyn Brooks's 'The Anniad.' " *MELUS* 23 (1998): 167–86.

Johnson-Roullier, Cyraina. "(An)other Modernism: James Baldwin, *Giovanni's Room*, and the Rhetoric of Flight." *Modern Fiction Studies* 45 (1999): 932–34.

Kornweibel, Theodore Jr. *Seeing Red: Federal Campaigns against Black Militancy, 1919–1925*. Bloomington: Indiana UP, 1998.

Maxwell, William J. *New Negro, Old Left: African-American Writing and Communism between the Wars*. New York: Columbia UP, 1999.

Nielsen, Aldon Lynn. *Black Chant: Languages of African-American Postmodernism*. Cambridge, UK: Cambridge UP, 1997.

———, ed. *Reading Race in American Poetry: "An Area of Act."* Urbana: U of Illinois P, 2000.

Schueller, Malini Johar. "Performing Whiteness, Performing Blackness: Dorr's Cultural Capital and the Critique of Slavery." *Criticism* 41 (1999): 233–56.

Thomas, Lorenzo. *Extraordinary Measures: Afrocentric Modernism and Twentieth-Century American Poetry*. Tuscaloosa: U of Alabama P, 2000.

The Black Arts Era, 1960–1975

Mari Evans

b. 1923

Works in the Anthology

"Status Symbol" (1964)
"I Am a Black Woman" (1969)

Other Works

I Am a Black Woman (poems, 1970)
Nightstar, 1973–1978 (poems, 1981)
A Dark and Splendid Mass (poems, 1992)
Black Women Writers, 1950–1980: A Critical Evaluation (1984)

Themes

- Triumph
- Failed romantic love between African American heterosexual couples
- African American identity and history
- Feminist issues for black women
- African American struggle for self-actualization and self-reliance

Characteristics

- Blues aesthetic
- Historical figures from African and African American past

Questions

- Compare and contrast Evans's poems with poems by Gwendolyn Brooks and Margaret Walker writing before her and by Sonia Sanchez and Lucille Clifton writing after her. What do Evans's poems assert about the "middle" space she occupies among these poets?
- Evans's poetry challenges the male dominance of the Black Arts era. Which aspects of black womanhood do her poems highlight? Which do they celebrate?

Hoyt Fuller

1923–1981

Works in the Anthology

"Towards a Black Aesthetic" (1968)

Other Works

Journey to Africa (autobiography, 1971)
"An Aperitive in the Plaza" (1961)
"Notes from an African in Exile: A Personal Odyssey" (poem, 1970–71)
"Identity, Reality, and Responsibility: Elusive Poles of the World of Black Literature" (essay, 1972)
"The Question of Aesthetics" (1974)
"A Plundered World" (short story, 1975)
"Africa: Homeland to My Heart" (1975)
"Racism in Literary Anthologies" (essay, 1987)

Themes

- Critique of white supremacy as law of the land
- Celebration and affirmation of African cultural, literary, and vernacular values
- Denunciation of suppression of African expressions and values in U.S. society

- Critique of black bourgeoisie
- Call for organized resistance to white power structures

Characteristics

- Advocate of black revolution against white supremacy in the United States
- Insistence on representation of African influences on U.S. life and society
- Activist, editor, educator, and publisher who overcame political obstacles to broadcasting and promoting black voices

Questions

- More than fifty years after W. E. B. Du Bois articulated the concept of "double consciousness," Fuller contends in "Towards a Black Aesthetic" that "the two races are residents of two separate and naturally antagonistic worlds." In what ways does Fuller's essay echo and support Du Bois's theory? In what ways do Fuller's arguments about 1960s black and white life in the United States differ from Du Bois's turn-of-the-century theory? Where do Fuller and Du Bois stand in relation to Fuller's contemporary Addison Gayle Jr.?

Bibliography

Napier, Winston. "From the Shadows: Houston Baker's Move toward a Postnationalist Appraisal of the Black Aesthetic." *New Literary History* 25 (1994): 159–75.

Malcolm X (El-Hajj Malik El-Shabazz)

1925–1965

Works in the Anthology

The Autobiography of Malcolm X, Chap. 11 (1964)

Other Works

Malcolm X Speaks (1965)
The Speeches of Malcolm X at Harvard (1968)
By Any Means Necessary: Speeches, Interviews and a Letter (1970)
Malcolm X: The Last Speeches (1989)

Themes

- Power of literacy, reading, education, knowledge
- African American incarceration
- "Crimes against (black) humanity"
- Paradox of freedom through literacy while imprisoned
- White America as a nation of "devils"
- White supremacist intellectual and economic imprisonment of black America
- Elijah Muhammad, Black Muslims, and the Nation of Islam as sources of grace
- Mental anguish

Characteristics

- Vernacular storytelling, conversational tone
- Rhetorical and oratorical skills rooted in African American vernacular English

Teaching Strategies

- Have students listen to the recording of the speech by Malcolm X on the Audio Companion, and observe with them the traditional elements of African American vernacular English in terms of colloquialisms, rhythms, inflections, ideas, and so on.

Questions

- Review the selection by Marcus Garvey. In what ways do Garvey's ideas correspond to Malcolm X's? What influence did Garvey apparently have on Malcolm X?
- Compare the excerpt from Malcolm X's autobiography with the selection from Eldridge Cleaver's *Soul on Ice*. What features do the two texts share as autobiographies? Now compare and contrast the two men's life writings with Audre Lorde's "biomythology," *Zami: A New Spelling of My Name*. What gender-based differences do you find in these three texts? What ideological differences? What constructs, if any, do they share as contemporaneous texts?

Bibliography

Perry, Teresa, ed. *Teaching Malcolm X*. New York: Routledge, 1996.

Stull, Bradford. *Amid the Fall, Dreaming of Eden: Du Bois, King, Malcolm X, and Emancipatory Composition*. Carbondale: Southern Illinois UP, 1999.

John Alfred Williams

b. 1925

Works in the Anthology

The Man Who Cried I Am, Chaps. 1–3 (1967)

Other Works

The Angry Ones (novel, 1960)
Night Song (novel, 1961)
The Angry Black (editor, anthology, 1962)
Sissie (novel, 1963)
Beyond the Angry Black (editor, anthology, 1966)
Sons of Darkness, Sons of Light: A Novel of Some Probability (1969)
The King God Didn't Save: Reflections on the Life and Death of Martin Luther King, Jr. (biography, 1971)
Captain Blackman (novel, 1972)
Flashbacks: A Twenty Year Diary of Article Writing (1973)
Mothersill and the Foxes (novel, 1975)
The Junior Bachelor Society (novel, 1976)
!Click Song (novel, 1982)
The Berhama Account (novel, 1985)
Jacob's Ladder (novel, 1987)
If I Stop, I'll Die: The Comedy and Tragedy of Richard Pryor (co-author, 1990)
Bridges: Literature across Cultures (co-editor, 1994)

Themes

- The writer's life and moral code
- African American self-determination
- Condemnation of U.S. racism and race relations
- Fraternity of black male novelists
- Love and death
- Black male experience of racism and struggle as fatal illness
- Interracial and intercultural relationships
- Black expatriates in Europe

Characteristics

- Psychologically and philosophically complex prose
- Vernacular traditions invoked, especially black vernacular musical traditions
- "Hipster" discourse of the 1950s and 1960s

Questions

- Review the selections by Richard Wright and James Baldwin. What elements of their writings has Williams caught in his novel? What features of their life experiences has he borrowed for his plot? What is the significance of the appearance of these particular earlier novelists in Williams's work?
- Williams is as well-known for his hard-edged journalism as for his biting fiction. In what ways has his news writing influenced his fiction? Contrast the excerpt from *The Man Who Cried I Am* with selections by other African American journalists, including W. E. B. Du Bois and Pauline E. Hopkins.

Bibliography

Fleming, Robert. "John A. Williams: Writer Beyond -Isms." *Black Issues Book Review* 4 (2002): 46–49.

Martin Luther King Jr.

1929–1968

Works in the Anthology

"Letter from Birmingham Jail" (1963)

Other Works

Stride toward Freedom: The Montgomery Story (history chronicle, 1959)
Strength to Love (sermons, 1963)
Why We Can't Wait (historiography, 1964)
Where Do We Go from Here? (essays, 1967)
Trumpet of Conscience (lecture, 1968)
A Testament of Hope: The Essential Writings of Martin Luther King (ed. James M. Washington, 1986)

Themes

- Power of civil disobedience
- Faith in humanity and Judeo-Christian principles
- Resistance to racism and racialized subjugation
- White ignorance and complacency
- Police brutality
- Racial segregation

Characteristics

- Philosophical tone and invocation of historical and contemporary philosophers
- Eloquence through rhetorical features and devices
- Contemplative, passionate tone

Questions

- Compare and contrast the attitudes toward Christianity and the Bible that King asserts in his "Letter" with attitudes that Frederick Douglass asserts in the "Appendix" to his 1845 *Narrative*. Do you find one writer more persuasive than the other? If so, which one? What rhetorical features figure in your answer?

Bibliography

Murphy, John M. "Inventing Authority: Bill Clinton, Martin Luther King, Jr., and the Orchestration of Rhetorical Traditions." *Quarterly Journal of Speech* 83 (1997): 71–89.

Vander Lei, Elizabeth, and Keith Miller. "Martin Luther King Jr.'s 'I Have a Dream' in Context: Ceremonial Protest and African American Jeremiad." *College English* 62 (1999): 83–99.

Etheridge Knight

1931–1985

Works in the Anthology

"The Idea of Ancestry" (1968)
"Hard Rock Returns to Prison from the Hospital for the Criminal Insane" (1968)
"For Black Poets Who Think of Suicide" (1969)

Other Works

Poems from Prison (1968)
Belly Song and Other Poems (1973)
Born of a Woman: New and Selected Poems (1980)
The Essential Etheridge Knight (1986)

Themes

- Existential crisis, emptiness, fear, feelings of ineptitude and isolation
- Homelessness, dystopic black family
- Drug addiction as bondage versus poetry as salvation
- Prison as sociopolitical oppression, as physical incarceration, and as psychological state
- Paradox of prison as salvation from sociopolitical oppressions
- Death and resurrection
- Poetry as source of spiritual healing and rejuvenation for poet and audiences
- Poetry as source of sociopolitical advancement
- Ambivalence about the blues as (1) socially progressive or as (2) socially reductive

Characteristics

- Vernacular incorporation of African American traditional music forms
- Poetic digressions
- Rhythms of African American vernacular discourses and black southern regionalisms
- Reincarnation of various folk heroes

Questions

- In more than one interview Knight expressed a personal conviction that life and art cannot be separated. How do the selections of his poetry reflect this conviction?
- Review the chapter of Booker T. Washington's *Up From Slavery* from which Knight takes the title "The Idea of Ancestry." How does Knight revise Washington's concept? Do you perceive any similarity in the way the two writers use the title phrase?
- What debt to African American elders and African American progeny do Knight's poems posit? Do the speakers of his poems convince you of their capacity to fulfill their genealogical debt? On what do you base your answer?
- Situate Knight's "The Idea of Ancestry" among other poems from the tradition of prison literature. If you are unfamiliar with this subgenre of African American literature, research its trajectory. How is Knight's poem distinctive in this tradition? How is it representative?
- Research both mid-1960s and current statistics of African American men in prison for drug-related offenses. How do the statistics compare? Might Knight's poem have been written today with the same credibility as in its own day? Why or why not?

Bibliography

Anaporte-Easton, Jean. "Etheridge Knight, Poet and Prisoner: An Introduction." *Callaloo* 19 (1997): 941–46.

Rubeo, Ugo. " 'In the Inner Ear': Genealogy and Intertextuality in the Poetry of Etheridge Knight and Michael Harper." *GRAAT* 18 (1998): 23–31.

Seelow, David. "Loud Men: The Poetic Visions of Robert Bly, Ice Cube, and Etheridge Knight." *Journal of Men's Studies* 2 (1998): 149–69.

Addison Gayle Jr.

1932–1991

Works in the Anthology

The Black Aesthetic, "Introduction" (1971)

Other Works

Black Expression: Essays by and about Black Americans in the Creative Arts (editor, 1969)
The Black Situation (essays, 1970)
Bondage, Freedom, and Beyond: The Prose of Black Americans (editor, 1971)
Oak and Ivy: A Biography of Paul Laurence Dunbar (1971)
Claude McKay: The Black Poet at War (1972)
The Way of the New World: The Black Novel in America (1975)
Wayward Child: A Personal Odyssey (autobiography, 1977)
Richard Wright: Ordeal of a Native Son (1980)

Themes

- Celebration of African American literary accomplishments
- Role of black nationalism in African American literature and literary studies
- Usefulness of art in the development of a self-loving black nation
- Critique of white dominance in intellectual and artistic pursuits in the United States
- Origins of modern black rage and of blacks' "war" with white America

Characteristics

- Invocation of early African American writers to endorse 1960s and 1970s black art forms
- Historical chronicle of African American writings about black life in the United States
- Call for end to racial discrimination and racism
- Call of blacks to war with white supremacy, to end physical and psychological bondage

Questions

- Which ideas and contentions set forth in Gayle's introduction to *The Black Aesthetic* appear in the poetry, drama, and fiction selections in the Black Arts era section of *NAFAM*? Which of Gayle's ideas remain undeveloped in subsequent writings of the period?
- Comment on Gayle's representation of W. E. B. Du Bois and his theory of double consciousness. Do you find Gayle's contention that black writers should not attach honor to an identity as either an "American" or an "American writer" to be consistent, or inconsistent, with Du Bois's notion of double consciousness?

Bibliography

Napier, Winston. "From the Shadows: Houston Baker's Move toward a Postnationalist Appraisal of the Black Aesthetic." *New Literary History* 25 (1994): 159–75.

Audre Lorde

1934–1992

Works in the Anthology

"Equinox" (1973)
"Coal" (1976)
"Now That I Am Forever with Child" (1976)
"A Litany for Survival" (1978)
"Poetry Is Not a Luxury" (1977)
Zami: A New Spelling of My Name, Chaps. 3, 11, 31, Epilogue (1982)

Other Works

The First Cities (poems, 1968)
Cables to Rage (poems, 1970)
From a Land Where Other People Live (poems, 1973)
New York Head Shop and Museum (poems, 1974)
Between Ourselves (poems, 1976)
Coal (poems, 1976)
The Black Unicorn (poems, 1978)
Chosen Poems: Old and New (1982)
Our Dead behind Us (poems, 1986)
Undersong: Chosen Poems Old and New (1992)
The Marvelous Arithmetics of Difference (poems, 1994)
The Cancer Journals (diary, 1980)
Sister Outsider (essays, 1984)
I Am Your Sister: Black Women Organizing across Sexualities (theory, 1985)
A Burst of Light (essays and journals, 1988)

Themes

- Insistence on the right of oppressed peoples to express and define themselves
- Vernacular discourses, with emphasis on the power of speech acts, self-expression, and self-assertion
- Racial and sexual identities, complexly defined and articulated
- Political, sexual, and racial diversity/difference
- Beauty of human differences
- Critical need for human beings to discuss as well as embrace differences among themselves
- Feminist theory
- Black feminist spirituality
- International women's liberation movement
- Denunciation of racism, imperialism, and homophobia
- Critique of oppressive and imperialistic cultural norms

Characteristics

- Dialogues with other writers and leaders, especially across differences
- Penetrating critique of social systems
- Confessional but polemical style and tone
- Writes in several different genres (poetry, myth, autobiography, essay, epistle), sometimes creating generic hybrid texts

- Activist vision
- Dedication to pan-Africanism

Teaching Strategies

- Bring in one of the several films about Lorde's life, and view it with students. Discuss with students similarities and differences between the poet's life as represented in the film and the life of the protagonist of her fictionalized autobiography. Based on these life histories, what do students understand Lorde to mean by "biomythography"?

Questions

- Lorde professed to speak for those whose voices had been politically suppressed and to chronicle the triumphs, pains, and fears she observed in those she encountered. In what ways do the selections in *NAFAM* illustrate these particular poetic missions? Compare Lorde's work with that of other poets who assumed similar responsibilities, including Frances E. W. Harper, Nikki Giovanni, and Langston Hughes.
- One of the major themes of Lorde's writing is the "word" in all of its uses, including its function as the poet's tool and its power. She writes in "Coal" that words "are open / Like a diamond on glass windows." Summarize Lorde's definition of "the word." Consider the ways in which she uses this conceptualization in her essays as well as her poetry.
- Contrast "A Litany for Survival" with Claude McKay's "If We Must Die." What similarities do you find in these two poems by West Indian blacks of different eras?
- According to "Poetry Is Not a Luxury," what is the role of poetry in women's survival? Why must women write poems?
- In what ways do Lorde's ideas about the life-affirming quality of art and artistic expression in "Poetry Is Not a Luxury" resonate with Alice Walker's in "In Search of Our Mothers' Gardens"? With the theory implied in Ntozake Shange's *for colored girls who have considered suicide*?
- To what extent do Lorde's poems reflect the larger themes and concerns of the Black Arts era? Review other poems in this section and explain how Lorde's differ from these and how they are similar.
- In what ways do the selections from Lorde reflect the concerns of other African American women writers across the United States and African diasporic history?

Bibliography

Chinasole. "Audre Lorde and Matrilineal Diaspora: 'moving history beyond nightmare into structures for the future . . .'" In Joanne M. Braxton and Andrée Nicola McLaughlin, eds., *Wild Women in the Whirlwind*. New Brunswick, NJ: Rutgers UP, 1990. 379–94.

Dhairyam, Sagri. " 'Artifacts for Survival': Remapping the Contours of Poetry with Audre Lorde." *Feminist Studies* 18 (1992): 229–56.

Morris, Margaret Kissam. "Audre Lorde: Textual Authority and the Embodied Self." *Frontiers* 23 (2002): 168–90.

Wilson, Anna. "Audre Lorde and the African American Tradition: When the Family Is Not Enough." In Sally Munt, ed., *New Lesbian Criticism: Literary and Cultural Readings*. New York: Columbia UP, 1992.

Amiri Baraka

b. 1934

Works in the Anthology

"Preface to a Twenty Volume Suicide Note" (1961)
"In Memory of Radio" (1961)
"A Poem for Black Hearts" (1969)
"I don't love you" (1969)
"Three Movements and a Coda" (1969)
"SOS" (1969)
"Black Art" (1969)
"The Invention of Comics" (1971)
Dutchman (1964)
"The Revolutionary Theater" (1969)

Other Works

Home: Social Essays (1966)
The Dead Lecturer (poems, 1964)
The Slave (drama, 1964)
The Toilet (drama, 1966)
Tales (1967)
Black Fire: An Anthology of Afro-American Writing (co-editor with Larry Neal, 1968)
The Autobiography of LeRoi Jones (1984)

Thornton Dial: Image of the Tiger (essay, rpt. 1993)
Jesse Jackson and Black People (essay, 1996)

Themes

- Economic imperatives for black people
- African American history and culture
- Definitions of "the Black Aesthetic"
- Critique of bourgeois pretentiousness
- Faith in power of black vernacular music traditions to heal social evils

Characteristics

- Music critic and writer in many different literary genres
- Identified with the bohemian Beat poets of Greenwich Village
- Associated with writers and activists from third world countries, including Cuba and Mexico
- Developed an aesthetics highlighting socially conscious and politically aggressive expression
- In his birthplace (Newark, NJ), around 1966, he helped establish "Spirit House" and the National Black Political Assembly
- Juxtaposition, repetition, signification

Teaching Strategies

- *Dutchman* is a play rich in both historical and biblical signifiers. Most students will need to have the symbols identified for them. For instance, the title of the play refers both to the name of a slaver and to the *"Flying Dutchman"* myth. Working with students' thoughts about selected images of the play, guide them through a discussion that will illuminate the relationship between the story of the *Flying Dutchman*—a ship condemned to sail the seas until Judgment Day—and the play's setting on a hot, underground subway.
- Video versions of *Dutchman* might be used in tandem with the text to stimulate comparison and detailed discussion of genre/media conventions, production choices, and so on.
- You might also have students approach *Dutchman* through the theme of African American identity, especially as that concept was constructed by the black nationalist movement. Ask them to consider what happens when Clay begins to play Lulu's word game, to participate in her fantasy. Does he appear to have adequate self-awareness or self-knowledge? How familiar does he appear to be with his racial history? How does he present himself in relation to other African

Americans or to African American culture? What happens when he
begins to talk of Bessie Smith, Charlie Parker, and blues people? At
the end of the play has Clay changed? Has Lulu? Has their relationship? Why is he killed?

- To enhance a discussion of *Dutchman*, you might have students listen to the recording of Bessie Smith on the Audio Companion; then
  discuss how the figure of Bessie Smith functions in the play.

Questions

- Research the aesthetics of the Beat poets; then analyze the ways in
  which Baraka's poetry invokes that aesthetics and subverts it.
- Do the poems of Baraka and Bob Kaufman (who was of African
  American and Jewish American ancestry) differ from those of white
  Beat poets? If so, in what ways?
- Identify some of Baraka's usages of 1960s pop art imagery in his
  early poems. Do those images date the poems in disadvantageous
  ways? Why or why not?
- How does Baraka's attitude toward imagination, implicit in poems
  like "A Poem for Black Hearts," "Black Art," and "SOS," compare
  with tacit contentions about imagination developed in poems by Phil-
  lis Wheatley? In what ways does the eighteenth-century poet anticipate Baraka's aesthetics? What poets between Wheatley and Baraka
  assert similar notions of imagination and its function in African
  American life and culture?
- Compare "A Poem for Black Hearts" with Gwendolyn Brooks's and
  Margaret Walker's poems about Malcolm X. Or compare its clarion
  call to action with David Walker's *Appeal*, Claude McKay's "If We
  Must Die," and Margaret Walker's "For My People."
- "Black Art" is a manifesto for the era's black aesthetic, and the poem
  itself both theorizes and practices the tenets of the movement. How
  does this poem illustrate the ideas articulated in essays by Larry
  Neal, Hoyt Fuller, Maulana Karenga, and Addison Gayle Jr.? How
  does Baraka's poem present both aesthetic and political arguments?
- How does Baraka use the vernacular? What are the rhetorical effects
  of the particular language he uses throughout his writings?
- What rhetorical devices and stylistic features render "Black Art,"
  "SOS," and "A Poem for Black Hearts" poems for the education of
  black people? What is the relationship between the themes and form
  of these poems and the black power movement at large? What characteristics seem to be invoked when these three poems are read as
  "political"?
- How do the ideas in Baraka's essay manifesto "The Revolutionary
  Theatre" compare with those developed in his drama *Dutchman*?

- What does Baraka gain through the use of the name "Clay" for his main character in *Dutchman?* What other allusions to the biblical Eden—especially figures of Adam, the apple, and the temptress—seem significant to the play?
- What roles do Bessie Smith and Charlie Parker play in *Dutchman?* Is it important that they are black musicians? Are the specific music traditions they represent relevant?
- What faith does *Dutchman's* Clay place in the American Dream? To what extent does the character seem driven by efforts to take part in the dream?
- In what ways does Baraka construct images and ideas about colonization in *Dutchman?* Other than colonization, how else might the relationship between black and white America be imaged?
- Analyze gender relations in *Dutchman.* Explain how Baraka uses conventional gender identity as well as dominant attitudes about racial and sexual etiquette to develop the play's two main characters.

Bibliography

Lee, A. Robert. "Imamu Amiri Baraka." In Clive Bloom, ed., *American Drama.* New York: St. Martin's, 1995. 97–116.

Paek, Hwan Kie. "A Study on Myths in Plays of Imamu Amiri Baraka—*Dutchman* and *A Black Mass.*" *Journal of Modern British and American Drama* 14 (2001): 79–97.

Piggford, George. "Looking into Black Skulls: American Gothic, the Revolutionary Theatre, and Amiri Baraka's *Dutchman.*" In Robert Martin and Eric Savoy, eds., *American Gothic: New Inventions in a National Narrative.* Iowa City: U of Iowa P, 1998. 143–60.

Rahming, Melvin. " 'Goodbye to All That': Engaging the Shift of Sensibility between John Webster's *The White Devil* and Amiri Baraka's *Dutchman.*" *CLA Journal* 46 (2002): 72–97.

Reilly, Charlie, ed. *Conversations with Amiri Baraka.* Jackson: UP of Mississippi, 1994.

Thompson, Deborah. "Keeping Up with the Joneses: The Naming of Racial Identities in the Autobiographical Writings of LeRoi Jones/Amiri Baraka, Hettie Jones, and Lisa Jones." *College Literature* 29 (2002): 83–102.

Sonia Sanchez

b. 1934

Works in the Anthology

"homecoming" (1969)
"poem at thirty" (1969)
"for our lady" (1969)
"Summer Words of a Sistuh Addict" (1969)
A *Blues Book for Blue Black Magical Women*, Part Three, Present (1974)

Other Works

Homecoming (poems, 1969)
homegirls & handgrenades (poems, 1984)

Themes

- Womanhood, women's identity
- Birth, motherhood, women's fertility and fecundity, fertility rites
- Individual and collective (existential) transformations
- Critique of psychological violence against blacks

Characteristics

- Vernacular idioms and rhythms, vocal intonations and aphasia
- African American vernacular English
- Call and response performativity
- Contributor to African American literary advancement in various modes: poet, academic, essayist, playwright, memoirist

Questions

- In the 1960s and 1970s, Sanchez belonged to the Nation of Islam. What themes and aspects of that religious doctrine appear in her poems of the period?
- In the 1970s Sanchez was among black academic leaders who fought to preserve early incarnations of Afro-American Studies programs. Using her poems in *NAFAM*, construct an argument in support of the contributions that African American Studies makes to college curricula.

Bibliography

Davis, Eisa. "Lucille Clifton and Sonia Sanchez: A Conversation." *Callaloo* 25 (2002): 1038–75.

DeLancey, Frenzella. "Sonia Sanchez's *Blues Book for Blue Black Magical Women* and Sister Souljah's *The Coldest Winter Ever*: Progressive Phases amid Modernist Shadows and Postmodernist Acts." *BMA: The Sonia Sanchez Literary Review* 6 (2000): 147–79.

Kelly, Susan. "Discipline and Craft: An Interview with Sonia Sanchez." *African American Review* 34 (2000): 679–87.

Rampersad, Arnold. "Send for Langston." *PEN* 2 (2002): 88–115.

Spady, James, ed. "360 Degrees of Sonia Sanchez, Hip Hop, Narrativity, Iqhawe and Public Spaces of Being." *BMA: The Sonia Sanchez Literary Review* 6 (2000): 47–72.

Ed Bullins

b. 1935

Works in the Anthology

   Goin'a Buffalo: A Tragifantasy (1969)

Other Works

   Clara's Old Man (drama, 1965)
   Electronic Nigger (drama, 1969)
   The Gentleman Caller (drama, 1969)
   In the Wine Time (drama, 1969)
   Death List (drama, 1970)
   It Bees Dat Way (drama, 1970)
   Night of the Beast: A Screenplay (1970)
   In New England Winter (drama, 1971)
   The Hungered One (short stories, 1971)
   The Reluctant Rapist (novel, 1973)
   The Taking of Miss Janie (drama, 1975)
   I Am Lucy Terry: An Historical Fantasy for Young Americans (drama, 1976)
   The Mystery of Phyllis Wheatley: An Historical Play for Young Americans (drama, 1986)
   Storyville (musical, 1977)

Themes

- Life among the urban poor
- Life on the border of—sometimes crossing over the lines of—legality
- Impact of poverty and racism on African American love, faith, security, and violence
- Existential crises and emotional bondage
- Self-actualization and psychological constraints on personal freedom
- Moral choice

Characteristics

- Vernacular characteristics manifested in unexpurgated, raw language
- Alternates between dreams or fantasies and reality in time and setting
- Intensive, extended character study
- Reversals of expectation (e.g., African American migration east instead of west)

Teaching Strategies

- Clarence Major's and June Jordan's combinations of literary craft and experiments with political imperatives are, if not descendants of Bullins's vision, at least residents in his literary neighborhood. Other ideas that open Bullins's play beyond the obvious political and historical scope include his representation of love and sexuality; his use of names and symbols, such as Art, Pandora, and chess games; the blues; and the way in which he questions distinctions between reality and illusion.

Questions

- Compare Bullins's play with works by other writers of the Black Arts era. How do the structure, themes, and characters of Bullins's *Goin'a Buffalo* compare with those of Lorraine Hansberry's earlier play *A Raisin in the Sun*? With those of Amiri Baraka's later play *Dutchman*?
- How does Bullins's vision of outlaws and outcasts among poor urban blacks compare with James Baldwin's figures of poverty, (non)conformity, and reclusiveness in "Sonny's Blues"? With Bob Kaufman's versions of similar figures?

Bibliography

Canaday, Nicholas. "Toward Creation of a Collective Form: The Plays of Ed Bullins." *Studies in American Drama, 1945–Present* 1 (1986): 33–47.

DiGaetani, John L. "Ed Bullins." In John L. DiGaetani, ed., *A Search for a Postmodern Theater: Interviews with Contemporary Playwrights*. New York: Greenwood, 1991.

Elder, Arlene A. "Ed Bullins: Black Theater as Ritual." In Emmanuel S. Nelson, ed., *Connections: Essays on Black Literatures*. Canberra, Australia: Aboriginal Studies, 1988. 101–9.

Hay, Samuel A. *Ed Bullins: A Literary Biography*. Detroit: Wayne State UP, 1997.

Ratliff, Peggy S. "Ed Bullins (1935–)." In Emmanuel S. Nelson, ed., *Connections: Essays on Black Literatures*. Westport, CT: Greenwood, 1999. 64–68.

Sell, Mike. "Bullins as Editorial Performer: Textual Power and the Limits of Performance in the Black Arts Movement." *Theatre Journal* 53 (2001): 411–28.

Eldridge Cleaver

b. 1935

Works in the Anthology

Soul on Ice, Chap. 1 (1968)

Other Works

Soul on Fire (autobiography, 1978)

Themes

• Black male primitivism

Characteristics

• Incendiary, revolutionary rhetoric
• Crude, vulgar language

Questions

- What themes and aspects of the Black Muslim faith, to which Cleaver converted during the 1960s, seem significant in his writing?

Bibliography

Waldrep, Shelton. " 'Being Bridges': Cleaver/Baldwin/Lorde and African-American Sexism and Sexuality." *Journal of Homosexuality* 26 (1993): 167–81.

A. B. Spellman

b. 1935

Works in the Anthology

"Did John's Music Kill Him?" (1969)

Other Works

The Beautiful Days (1965)
Four Lives in the Bebop Business (biography, 1966)

Themes

- Power and beauty of African American vernacular and literary traditions

Characteristics

- Associated with the bohemian Beat poets of the United States
- Representative of diverse fields: influential as poet, editor, music critic, professor of African American studies
- Extensive musical knowledge
- Commitment to advancing African American literature

Teaching Strategies

- Listen with the students to the Audio Companion recording of John Coltrane's music. Discuss its effects on them as listeners and as readers of African American literature. Ask if the recording illuminates aspects of Spellman's poem for them and, if so, which aspects. Explore how this effect is achieved.

Questions

- Compare and contrast this poem with another tribute to master jazz musician John Coltrane, Michael S. Harper's "Dear John, Dear Coltrane." What qualities indicate that both poems are from the same era? In what ways do the two poets pay a different kind of tribute to Coltrane?
- Listen to the recording of John Coltrane's music on the Audio Companion. Now read Spellman's poem as a gloss on Coltrane's music. How does the poem teach you how to hear Coltrane's music (anew)?

June Jordan

1936–2002

Works in the Anthology

"In Memoriam: Martin Luther King, Jr." (1968)
"Poem about My Rights" (1980)
"Poem for Guatemala" (1989)
"Intifada" (1989)
From *Civil Wars* (1981)
From *Soldier: A Poet's Childhood* (2001)

Other Works

Who Look at Me (poems, 1969)
New Days: Poems of Exile and Return (1974)
Things That I Do in the Dark: Selected Poetry (1977)
Passion: New Poems (1980)
His Own Where (young adult novel, 1982)
Living Room: New Poems (1985)
Lyrical Campaigns: Selected Poems (1989)
Naming Our Destiny: New and Selected Poems (1989)
Haruko/Love Poems (1993)
On Call: Political Essays (1985)
Technical Difficulties: African American Notes on the State of the Union (nonfiction, 1992)
In the Spirit of Sojourner Truth (drama, 1979)
The Issue (drama, 1985)
I Was Looking for the Ceiling and Then I Saw the Sky: Earthquake/ Romance (opera, 1995)
Some of Us Did Not Die (poems, 2002)

Themes

- Oppression of women, children, the disadvantaged around the world
- Women's resistance to oppression
- Critique of U.S. imperialism
- Faith in power of poetry as a tool for self-determination
- Jamaican immigration/African diasporas
- Child/spousal/domestic violence
- Beauty of African cultural norms and values, especially as manifest in African American vernacular English
- African American self-identification and self-determination
- International activism for liberation

Characteristics

- Controversial, confrontational, confessional tone
- The power of African American vernacular English to resist dominance
- Explorations and writings in multiple literary and artistic genres

Questions

- Compare the relationship between the narrator and her father in the excerpt from Jordan's *Soldier* with the father-daughter relationship described in Harriet Jacobs's *Incidents*. In what ways does Jordan invoke, reconstitute, and revise Jacobs's autobiography?
- Parental relationships form the core of Dorothy West's *The Living Is Easy* and Jessie Redmon Fauset's *Plum Bun*. Review the excerpts from these two earlier fictions by African American women and identify rhetorical, structural, and thematic constructs they share with Jordan's *Soldier*.
- Compare the prose texts by Jordan and Audre Lorde, both of whom represent black families who immigrated to New York City.
- Trace the development of issues of dignity and integrity in Jordan's work. Where does Jordan suggest these human virtues originate?
- According to Jordan's poetry, how can individuals most effectively overcome oppression?
- Jordan has identified Richard Wright, James Baldwin, and Paule Marshall as her most significant literary influences. Review samples of their works to trace evidence of their rhetorical impact on Jordan's writing.

Bibliography

Brogan, Jacqueline V. "From Warrior to Womanist: The Development of June Jordan's Poetry." In Jeanne C. Reesman, ed., *Speaking the Other Self: American Women Writers*. Athens: U of Georgia P, 1997. 198–209.

Comfort, Juanita. "Becoming a Writerly Self: College Writers Engaging Black Feminist Essays." *College Composition and Communication* 51 (2000): 540–59.

Eagleton, Mary. "Working across Difference: Examples from Minnie Bruce Pratt and June Jordan." In Elizabeth Russell, ed., *Caught between Cultures: Women, Writing, and Subjectivities*. Amsterdam, Netherlands: Rodopi, 2002. 129–50.

Keating, Analouise. "The Intimate Distance of Desire: June Jordan's Bisexual Inflections." *Journal of Lesbian Studies* 4 (2000): 81–93.

MacPhail, Scott. "June Jordan and the New Black Intellectuals." *African American Review* 33 (1999): 57–71.

Lucille Clifton

b. 1936

Works in the Anthology

"the lost baby poem" (1972)
"malcolm" (1972)
"homage to my hips" (1980)
"wishes for sons" (1990)
"move" (1993)

Other Works

Good Times (poems, 1969)
Good News about the Earth (poems, 1972)
An Ordinary Woman (poems, 1974)
Two-Headed Woman (poems, 1980)
Good Woman: Poems and a Memoir, 1969–1980 (1987)
Next (poems, 1987)
Ten Oxherding Pictures (poems, 1988)
Quilting (poems, 1991)
The Book of Light (poems, 1993)
Generations (autobiography, 1976)

Themes

- Family, heritage, ancestry
- African American identity and collectivity
- African American creative legacies
- Spirituality, religious piety, personal devotion
- Hope
- Womanhood, feminist power
- Personal resistance to oppression
- Motherhood, matrilineage, daughterhood
- Physiological illness, loss, death
- Self-examination and self-scrutiny
- The role of art in psychological, spiritual, and emotional healing

Characteristics

- Spare, lean language
- Eschewing of conventional mechanics of standard American English
- Litotes, rhetorical questions, and other forms of understatement
- Internal rime
- Deft use of enjambment

Questions

- Discuss the effects of Clifton's eschewing of such formal adornments as punctuation and capital letters in her poetry. What correlations do you find, if any, between the appearance of Clifton's poems and the themes about which she writes?
- Compare Clifton's tribute to Malcolm X with other poets', including Margaret Walker's. What renders Clifton's tribute distinctive? What does this distinction imply about her poetry generally?
- Clifton is perhaps best known for her understated yet piercing representation of sociopolitical and economic issues affecting African Americans. Identify the series of particular issues deliberated in "the lost baby poem."
- Examine the recurrence and particularized treatment of the black female body in the selections by Clifton. What statement does she make about African American women and their corporeality? Would you describe these poems as feminist? Why or why not?

Bibliography

American Poetry Review 30 (Nov.–Dec. 2001) [Special section on Lucille Clifton].

Callaloo 22 (Winter 1999) [Special issue on Lucille Clifton].

Glaser, Michael. " 'I'd Like Not to Be a Stranger in the World: A Conversation/Interview with Lucille Clifton." *Antioch Review* 58 (2000): 310–24.

Holladay, Hilary. "Black Names in White Space: Lucille Clifton's South." *Southern Literary Journal* 34 (2002): 120–33.

———. " 'Our Lives Are Our Line and We Go On': Concentric Circles of History in Lucille Clifton's *Generations*." *Xavier Review* 19 (1999): 18–29.

———. "Song of Herself: Lucille Clifton's Poems about Womanhood." In Joanne Gabbin, ed., *The Furious Flowering of African American Poetry*. Charlottesville: U of Virginia P, 1999. 281–97.

Thyreen-Mizingou, Jeannine. "Grace and Ethics in Contemporary American Poetry: Resituating the Other, the World, and the Self." *Religion and Literature* 32 (2000): 67–97.

Wall, Cheryl. "Sifting Legacies in Clifton's *Generations*." *Contemporary Literature* 40 (1999): 552–74.

White, Mark Bernard. "Sharing and Living Light: Rhetorical, Poetic, and Social Identity in Lucille Clifton." *CLA Journal* 40 (1997): 288–304.

Jayne Cortez

b. 1936

Works in the Anthology

"How Long Has Trane Been Gone" (1969)

Other Works

Pisstained Stairs and the Monkey Man's Wares (poems, 1969)
Festivals and Funerals (poems, 1971)
Scarifications (poems, 1973)
Mouth on Paper (poems, 1977)
Firespitter (poems, 1982)
Merveilleux Coup de Foudre: Poetry of Jayne Cortez and Ted Joans (poems, 1982)
Coagulations: New and Selected Poems (1984)

Celebrations and Solitudes: The Poetry of Jayne Cortez (recording, 1975)
Unsubmissive Blues (recording, 1980)
There It Is (recording, 1982)
Poetry in Motion (film, 1982)
War on War (film, 1982)
Jayne Cortez in Concert I (multimedia, 1982)
Maintain Control (recording, 1986)
Life and Influences of Jayne Cortez (multimedia, 1987)

Themes

- Critique of imperialism, poverty, and other forms of sociopolitical oppression
- Power of public theater to transform social systems
- Economic inequity
- Cultural appropriation and theft of ethnic values
- African American vernacular traditions as source of pride and beauty
- Music as resistance to oppression and domination

Characteristics

- Precursor to hip hop performativity
- Jazz-inflected vocalizations

Teaching Strategy

- Play the recordings of both Cortez's "How Long Has Trane Been Gone" and Michael S. Harper's "Dear John, Dear Coltrane" from the Audio Companion. Ask students to observe differences between these two jazz-inflected tributes to the legendary saxophonist and composer.

Questions

- Examine the attitudes toward a biological or inherent African identity in Cortez's "How Long Has Trane Been Gone."

Bibliography

Bolden, Tony. "All the Birds Sing Bass: The Revolutionary Blues of Jayne Cortez." *African American Review* 35 (2001): 61–75.

Melham, D. H. "A *MELUS* Profile and Interview: Jayne Cortez." *MELUS* 21 (1996): 71–80.

Larry Neal

1937–1981

Works in the Anthology

"The Black Arts Movement" (1968)

Other Works

Black Fire: An Anthology of Afro-American Writing (co-editor, 1968)
Black Boogaloo: Notes on Black Liberation (poems, 1969)
Hoodoo Hollerin' Bebop Ghosts (poems, 1971)
Trippin': A Need for Change (co-author, 1969)
The Glorious Monster in the Bell of the Horn (drama, 1976)
In an Upstate Motel: A Morality Play (drama, 1981)

Themes

- Correlations between the Black *Arts* movement and the black *power* movement
- Influence of black vernacular musical traditions on African American literature
- Aspirations of the black middle class in the 1960s, '70s, and '80s
- Aspirations of African American artists
- African American collective responsibility
- (Black) existential crises and ethical responses to them
- Black literary and political aesthetics

Characteristics

- Allusions to African American vernacular musical traditions and other black vernacular figures and tropes
- Chronicles and preserves history of Black Arts and black power movements

Questions

- What roles for African American *women* are implicit in the various essays on black aesthetics developed by Neal, Amiri Baraka, Haki R. Madhubuti, and others? What contributions do they attribute to African American women, either implicitly or explicitly? What do you make of their relatively unstated acknowledgment of black women's contributions to the Black Arts era?

- In what ways does "The Black Arts Movement" differ from other essays on black aesthetics that emerged alongside it during the 1960s and 1970s? In what ways does it echo other theoretical and ideological positions?
- Consider a random selection of texts from the Harlem Renaissance included in *NAFAM* and assess the extent to which you agree with Neal's claim that the Harlem Renaissance "was essentially a failure." What does he say the Harlem Renaissance failed to do or to achieve? Reviewing the texts you've selected from that era, do you agree with Neal that the Harlem Renaissance "failed to link itself concretely to the struggles of [the black] community"?

Bibliography

Anadolu-Okur, Nilgun. *Contemporary African-American Theater: Afrocentricity in the Works of Larry Neal, Amiri Baraka, and Charles Fuller.* New York: Garland, 1997.

Ishmael Reed

b. 1938

Works in the Anthology

"I am a cowboy in the boat of Ra" (1972)
"Railroad Bill, a Conjure Man" (1972)
"Dualism" (1972)
"Chattanooga" (1973)
"Neo-HooDoo Manifesto" (1972)
Mumbo Jumbo, Chaps. 1–2 (1972)

Other Works

The Free-Lance Pallbearers (novel, 1967)
Yellow Back Radio Broke-Down (novel, 1969)
19 Necromancers from Now (editor, 1970)
Conjure: Selected Poems 1963–1970 (1972)
The Last Days of Louisiana Red (novel, 1974)
Flight to Canada (novel, 1976)
A Secretary to the Spirits (poems, 1978)
Shrovetide in Old New Orleans: Essays (1978)
Califa: The California Poetry (editor, 1979)
God Made Alaska for the Indians: Selected Essays (1982)

The Terrible Twos (novel, 1982)
Reckless Eyeballing (novel, 1986)
New and Collected Poems (1988)
Writing Is Fighting: Thirty-Seven Years of Boxing on Paper (essays, 1988)
The Terrible Threes (novel, 1989)
The Before Columbus Foundation Fiction Anthology (editor, 1992)
The Before Columbus Foundation Poetry Anthology (editor, 1992)
Japanese by Spring (novel, 1993)
Airing Dirty Laundry (essays, 1993)

Themes

- Satirical attack on white supremacy
- Satirical burlesque of leading African American writers, past and present
- Critique of U.S. feminism
- Exposé of race and class crimes committed by U.S. status quo

Characteristics

- Satirical perspective and thematics
- Seeks controversy in every literary endeavor
- Parody of canonical American literature and history
- Parody of various canonical American literary forms
- Parody of the fugitive slave narrative form
- Parody of diverse African American vernacular traditions and forms
- Bold, audacious critiques of diverse U.S. systems
- Writer/satirist as conjuror

Questions

- Compare and contrast Reed's "Chattanooga" with Nikki Giovanni's "Knoxville, Tennessee." How do these poems about southern cities differ? In what ways do they project a common African American sensibility about the U.S. South? What do they together reveal about Black Arts era poets and the U.S. South?
- To what extent do you find Reed's texts to be misogynist? In what ways is such a characterization unfair?
- How does Reed define *American*? What does his work suggest about the constructs of an "African American" identity?
- Based on "Dualism" do you understand Reed to be an admirer or literary descendant of Ralph Ellison? Why or why not?

Bibliography

Davis, Matthew R. " 'Strange History. Complicated, Too': Ishmael Reed's Use of African-American History in *Flight to Canada.*" *The Mississippi Quarterly* 49 (1996): 743–54.

Harde, Roxanne. " 'We Will Make Our Own Future Text': Allegory, Iconoclasm, and Reverence in Ishmael Reed's *Mumbo Jumbo.*" *Critique* 43 (2002): 361–77.

Swope, Richard. "Crossing Western Space, or the HooDoo Detective on the Boundary in Ishmael Reed's *Mumbo Jumbo.*" *African American Review* 36 (2002): 611–28.

Michael S. Harper

b. 1938

Works in the Anthology

"Dear John, Dear Coltrane" (1970)
"Deathwatch" (1970)
"Br'er Sterling and the Rocker" (1973)
"Grandfather" (1975)

Other Works

Dear John, Dear Coltrane (poems, 1972)
History Is Your Own Heartbeat (poems, 1971)
Photographs: Negatives: History as Apple Tree (poems, 1972)
Song: I Want a Witness (poems, 1972)
Debridgement (poems, 1973)
Nightmare Begins Responsibility (poems, 1975)
Images of Kin: New and Selected Poems (1977)
Rhode Island: Eight Poems (1981)
Healing Song for the Inner Ear (poems, 1984)
Songliness: Mosaics (poems, 1991)
Honorable Amendments (poems, 1995)
Songliness in Michaeltree: New and Collected Poems (2000)
The Collected Poems of Sterling Brown (editor, 1980)
Chant of Saints: A Gathering of Afro-American Literature, Art, and Scholarship (co-editor, 1979)
Every Shut Eye Ain't Sleep: An Anthology of Poems by African Americans Since 1945 (co-editor, 1994)
The Vintage Book of African American Poetry (2000)

Themes

- Double consciousness
- Black folk myths, mysteries, and recoveries
- History, African American ancestral past, intersection of past and present
- Black reconstruction and reintegration of a troubled, racist past
- Black redemption
- Black significations on white dominance
- African American familial love
- Intersection, blurred lines ostensibly separating myth or history and music
- Human possibility, combination, and diversity

Characteristics

- Personal and confessional tone
- Invocation of African American vernacular music traditions, especially through improvisational techniques and rhythms
- Poetry that consists of chants, hymns, musical allusions, and references to famous black musicians
- Poetic and rhetorical replications of musical instruments, sounds, and visions
- Use of secular music forms, especially jazz techniques, themes, artists
- Emphasis on the legendary jazz artist John Coltrane as inspiration for both poetic forms and subjects
- Appropriation of mythic poetic forms

Teaching Strategies

- Ask students to consider Harper's work alongside the first chapter of W. E. B. Du Bois's *Souls of Black Folk*. Perhaps begin a discussion of the two works by listening to Harper's reading of "Dear John, Dear Coltrane" on the Audio Companion or by reading aloud Harper's "Deathwatch." Then ask students to use additional poems by Harper to explicate Du Bois's theory of "double-consciousness."
- Play both Harper's reading of "Dear John, Dear Coltrane" and the recording of "Rock Me, Baby" from the Audio Companion and ask students to draw comparisons between the two folk traditions the songs represent.

Questions

- Compare and contrast Harper's use of black vernacular music traditions with W. E. B. Du Bois's use of the same traditions.
- Discuss ways that the selections by Harper support his statement elsewhere that "all great art is finally testamental, and its technical brilliance never shadows the content of the song. Deliver the melody, make sure the harmony's correct, play as long as you like, but play sweet, and don't forget the ladies. A final note on the blues is that they always say *yes* to life; meet life's terms but never accept them."
- Compare Harper's deployment of black folk music and other black vernacular materials with that of the earlier poets Langston Hughes and Sterling A. Brown, as well as that of his contemporaries Sherley Anne Williams and Ntozake Shange.
- Explore Harper's conceptualization of myth and its relation to folklore as implied in "Br'er Sterling and the Rocker."
- Compare Harper's use of myth with that of Robert Hayden. Can Harper be rightly said to create literary myths when he writes about or references Hayden, Ralph Ellison, Sterling A. Brown, and others? As you develop your response, refer to the poetry of these other black writers.
- Contrast Harper's representation of black familial love in "Grandfather" with other *NAFAM* authors, including Nikki Giovanni ("Nikki-Rosa") and Rita Dove (the "Thomas and Beulah" series). How are these poets' familial memories similar? How different?

Bibliography

Antonucci, Michael. "The Map and the Territory: An Interview with Michael Harper." *African American Review* 34 (2000): 501–8.

Harper, Michael S. "My Poetic Technique and the Humanization of the American Audience." In R. Baxter Miller, ed., *Black American Literature and Humanism*. Lexington: UP of Kentucky, 1981.

Meyer, Horst. "The Forms of Things Unseen: Photography as 'Poetic Reference' in the Poetry of Michael Harper." In Detlev Gordbandt, et al., eds., *Seeing and Saying: Self-Referentiality in British and American Literature*. Berlin: Lang, 1998. 131–46.

Pope, Jacquelyn. "Citizen Pilgrim Poet." *Harvard Review* 20 (2001): 52–56.

Share, Don. "Michael S. Harper: An Introduction, Seven Poems, and a Critique." *Harvard Review* 20 (2001): 39–52.

Toni Cade Bambara

1939–1995

Works in the Anthology

"Raymond's Run" (1971)
The Salt Eaters, Chap. 1 (1980)

Other Works

The Black Woman (editor and contributor, 1970)
Tales and Stories for Black Folks (editor and contributor, 1971)
Gorilla, My Love (stories, 1972)
The Sea Birds Are Still Alive (stories, 1977)
"Introduction" to *This Bridge Called My Back* (1981)
These Bones Are Not My Child (novel, 2000)

Themes

- African American girls' cultivation of moral intelligence, motherwit, interdependence, resistance to oppression and victimization, cultural pride, and familial survival
- Feminist solidarity
- Black women's individual and collective contributions to Black Arts era social, economic, and political advancements
- Women's resistance to various forms of dominance and subjugation
- Women's narrative authority
- African American vernacular English as a sign of communal consciousness and urban vernacular power
- Destabilization of myths about women's moral and mental weaknesses
- Collective ethnic pride

Characteristics

- Proto-feminist first-person singular (girl/child) narrators, usually pre-pubescent girls
- Vernacular: oral and aural story-telling strategies with emphasis on dialogue; characters (usually) speak in urban African American vernacular English; traditional patterns of storytelling; jazz improvisational elements (e.g., linear plot digressions); blues motifs (e.g., comedic exploration of grievous situations); didactic elements as precursor to hip hop

- Exposé of hypocrisy, especially as manifested in systems constructed by and/or endorsing white supremacy, capitalism, and other forms of race, gender, class, and age oppression
- Rejection of myths like those contained in *The Moynihan Report*, which pathologized mid-twentieth-century black families

Teaching Strategies

- You might ask students to view either Bambara's 1986 documentary about the Philadelphia police bombing of the radical group MOVE or her film *W. E. B. Du Bois—A Biography in Four Voices* to draw comparisons between her film work and her mastery of the short story form. Students who view the film on MOVE will likely find Lucille Clifton's poem "move" to be interesting as well.

Questions

- Compare and contrast Hazel's description of her typical dream at the onset of a race in "Raymond's Run" with other descriptions of African American dreams in texts like Martin Luther King Jr.'s "I Have a Dream" and Langston Hughes's "Montage of a Dream Deferred."
- In what ways does Hazel's epiphany compare to epiphanies typically experienced by blues (anti)heroes?
- What attitudes toward the African American past—especially the black power movement of the 1960s—does Bambara's narrator imply in the excerpt from *The Salt Eaters*?
- What seems to be the relationship between Minnie Ransom and Velma in the excerpt from *The Salt Eaters*?
- What is the rhetorical function of Minnie's humming in the excerpt from *The Salt Eaters*?
- What seems to have caused "amnesia" to "set in" to Velma's psyche in the excerpt from *The Salt Eaters*?

Bibliography

Collins, Janelle. "Generating Power: Fission, Fusion, and Post-Modern Politics in Bambara's *The Salt Eaters*." *MELUS* 21 (1996): 35–48.

Comfort, Mary. "Liberating Figures in Toni Cade Bambara's 'Gorilla, My Love.'" *Studies in American Humor* 3 (1998): 76–97.

Maierhofer, Roberta. "Bambara's 'My Man Bovanne.'" *The Explicator* 57 (1998): 57–60.

Muther, Elizabeth. "Bambara's Feisty Girls: Resistance Narratives in *Gorilla, My Love*." *African American Review* 36 (2002): 447–60.

Maulana Karenga

b. 1941

Works in the Anthology

"Black Art: Mute Matter Given Force and Function" (1968)

Other Works

Introduction to Black Studies (1982)

Kwanzaa: A Celebration of Family, Community and Culture (theology, 1996)

Selections from the Husia: Sacred Wisdom of Ancient Egypt (history, 1984)

Kawaida Theory: A Communitarian African Philosophy (philosophy, 1997)

"The Oppositional Logic of Malcolm X: Differentiation, Engagement, and Resistance" (essay, 1993)

The Million Man March/Day of Absence: A Commemorative Anthology (co-editor, 1996)

Themes

- Black separatism
- Functionality of African American art and culture
- Faith in power of black art to effect social and political advancement of black people
- Denunciation of the blues tradition as reactionary and outmoded

Characteristics

- Polemical, confrontational language
- Afrocentric ideology
- Critique of white racism

Questions

- What critiques of white people and/or institutions does Karenga's essay launch in its argument for a separate course of studies on black people and cultures?
- Discuss and assess the validity of Karenga's charge that white institutional ways of studying U.S. ethnic minority cultures have been inad-

equate or erroneous. To what extent, if any, does such a charge seem valid to you today?

- To what extent do you think the ideas in Karenga's essay may lead to greater distances among U.S. ethnic and racial groups? How might Americans benefit from applying Karenga's theory?

Bibliography

Ngozi-Brown, Scot. "The Us Organization, Maulana Karenga, and Conflict with the Black Panther Party: A Critique of Sectarian Influences on Historical Discourse." *Journal of Black Studies* 28 (1997): 157–71.

Haki R. Madhubuti

b. 1942

Works in the Anthology

"Back Again, Home" (1967)
Think Black, Introduction (1969)
"The Long Reality" (1967)
"Malcolm Spoke / who listened?" (1969)
"a poem to complement other poems" (1969)

Other Works

Black Pride Poems (1968)
Don't Cry Scream (poems, 1969)
Dynamite Voices I: Black Poets of the 1960s (editor, 1971)
To Gwen with Love: An Anthology Dedicated to Gwendolyn Brooks (1971)
Killing Memory: Seeking Ancestors (poems, 1987)
Black Men: Obsolete, Single, Dangerous (theory, 1988)
Confusion by Any Other Name: Essays Exploring the Negative Impact of "The Black Man's Guide to Understanding Women" (1990)
Claiming Earth: Race Rage, Rape, Redemption: Blacks Seeking a Culture of Enlightened Empowerment (essays, 1994)
GroundWork: New and Selected Poems of Don L. Lee/Haki R. Madhubuti from 1966–1996 (1996)

Themes

- Black pride and self-love
- Black self-awareness and self-actualization
- Urban intelligence
- Need for African Americans to perceive, honor, and attend to black visionaries

Characteristics

- African American vernacular English
- Humorous, street-wise, sardonic tone
- Direct, didactic, hortatory discourse
- Visions of African American sociopolitical future

Questions

- Compare and contrast Madhubuti's 1960s and 1970s poetry with more recent hip hop lyrics. In what ways do Madhubuti's poems anticipate the later works?
- Support or refute Madhubuti's claim in the "Introduction" to *Think Black* that "black art is created from black forces that live within the body." How do other poets of the Black Arts era support or refute this contention?
- What do you understand Madhubuti to mean by his claim in the Introduction to *Think Black* that "black art is reciprocal"?

Bibliography

Kazi-Ferrouillet, Kuumba. "Are Black Men Obsolete, Single, Dangerous? A Conversation with Haki R. Madhubuti." *Black Collegian* 21 (1990): 164–68.

Nikki Giovanni

b. 1943

Works in the Anthology

"For Saundra" (1968)
"Beautiful Black Men" (1968)
"Nikki-Rosa" (1968)
"Knoxville, Tennessee" (1968)
"From a Logical Point of View" (1968)

Other Works

Black Feeling (poems, 1967)
Black Judgment (poems, 1968)
Re: Creation (poems, 1970)
My House: Poems (1972)
Dialogue (with James Baldwin, theory, 1973)
Ego Tripping and Other Poems for Young People (1974)
A Poetic Equation: Conversations between Nikki Giovanni and Margaret Walker (1974)
Gemini: An Extended Autobiographical Statement on My First Twenty Years of Being a Black Poet (1974)
Cotton Candy on a Rainy Day (poems, 1978)
Conversations with Nikki Giovanni (ed. Virginia Fowler, 1992)
Racism 101 (essays, 1994)

Themes

- Politics and aesthetics of the Black Arts era, including black political militancy
- Denunciation of white racism and oppression
- Celebration and affirmation of African American beauty
- Vernacular music inflections as intrinsic to African American poetry
- Strength of African American familial love
- Resistance to whites' pathologies of African American family structure
- Heterosexual romantic love between blacks
- Racial discrimination, especially in U.S. higher education
- Critique of audacious and uninformed white assessment of black life as deprived, depraved, bleak, and barren

Characteristics

- Published works that were considered militant, political, and expressive of the revolutionary temperament of the Black Arts era
- Writes literature for readers of all levels and ages
- Cultivation of a unique, passionate black female voice
- Candid, plain-spoken, and conversational use of African American vernacular English
- Vernacular rhythms of African American speech
- Vernacular music inflections
- Affirmation of African American males who possess much pride, conventionally beautiful physiques, and joyous personal confidence

Teaching Strategies

- In addition to Giovanni's reading of "Nikki-Rosa" included on the Audio Companion, you might want to find and play for students other recordings of Giovanni reciting her own work. At least three of these recordings (which include *Truth Is on Its Way*, 1971) feature Giovanni reading her poetry in concert with gospel choirs. Outline for students the traditional doctrines and values of Afro-Protestant churches, and have them use the *NAFAM* selections to enumerate the doctrines and values of the Black Arts era. Then you might discuss expectations, responses, surprises, and so forth they experience on hearing the revolutionary secular poet backed by sacred black music.

Questions

- Read "For Saundra" and "From a Logical Point of View" along with Amiri Baraka's "Black Art" and Sonia Sanchez's "poem at thirty." In what ways are the four poems different from one another? How similar? What values of the Black Arts era do they collectively articulate and develop?
- Giovanni's use of the vernacular—in terms of both African American conversation and musical allusions—is often compared with Jayne Cortez's, Michael S. Harper's, and Sherley Anne Williams's. Read these four Black Arts era poets together and discuss the similarities and differences in their work.
- To what extent do you find in Giovanni's poetry echoes of the poetry of Frances E. W. Harper, who wrote a century before Giovanni?
- Use *NAFAM* to locate and analyze poems by the later poets Yusef Komunyakaa and Rita Dove and the earlier poet Gwendolyn Brooks that complement Giovanni's recurring theme of the gifts and beauty of black familial life, particularly as articulated in "Nikki-Rosa" and "Knoxville, Tennessee." What similarities in the four poets' techniques and styles reinforce the similarities of their themes?
- Compare and contrast Giovanni's characterization of "Beautiful Black Men" with Toni Morrison's description of Milkman in *Song of Solomon* and with Helene Johnson's "Sonnet to a Negro in Harlem." In what ways do these portraits of men by women correspond to figures in song, ballad, and folklore in the vernacular section of *NAFAM*?

Bibliography

"Conversation: Gloria Naylor and Nikki Giovanni." *Callaloo* 23 (2000): 1395–96.

Fowler, Virginia C. *Nikki Giovanni*. New York: Twayne, 1992.

————, ed. *Conversations with Nikki Giovanni*. Jackson: UP of Mississippi, 1992.

The Nikki Giovanni Poetry Collection. 2 cassettes. Caedmon: Harper-Collins. 2002.

Reid, Calvin. "Nikki Giovanni: Three Decades on the Edge [an interview]." *Publishers Weekly* 246 (1999): 46–50.

Walters, Jennifer. "Nikki Giovanni and Rita Dove: Poets Redefining." *Journal of Negro History* 85 (2000): 210–19.

James Alan McPherson

b. 1943

Works in the Anthology

"A Solo Song: For Doc" (1970)

Other Works

Hue and Cry (stories, 1969)
Elbow Room (stories, 1977)
Crabcakes (memoir, 1997)
Fathering Daughters (co-editor, essays, 1998)
"Reflections of Titus Basfield, April 1850" (story, 2000)
A Region Not Home: Reflections from Exile (essay, 2000)

Themes

- Interpersonal relationships and conflicts, especially between men
- Railroad culture
- Intergenerational conflicts
- U.S. political conflicts of the twentieth century

Characteristics

- Crude, racist, unexpurgated language
- Vernacular story-telling tradition

Questions

- A graduate of Harvard Law School, McPherson has been described as having a "lawyerly approach" to the craft of fiction. Support or refute this assessment using "A Solo Song: For Doc" as the basis for your conclusions.

Bibliography

Beavers, Herman. *Wrestling Angels into Song: The Fictions of Ernest J. Gaines and James Alan McPherson*. Philadelphia: U of Pennsylvania P, 1995.

Champion, Laurie. "Assimilation versus Celebration in James McPherson's 'The Story of a Dead Man' and James Baldwin's 'Sonny's Blues.'" *Short Story* 8 (2000): 94–106.

Masiki, Trent. "The Burden of Insight: Dramatic Irony and the Rhetoric of Illumination in Selections from *Elbow Room*." *Short Story* 9 (2001): 78–87.

Reid, Calvin. "James Alan McPherson: A Theater of Memory [interview]." *Publishers Weekly* 244 (1997): 36–38.

Quincy Troupe

b. 1943

Works in the Anthology

"In Texas Grass" (1975)
"Conversations Overheard" (1975)
"Impressions/of Chicago; For Howlin' Wolf" (1975)

Other Works

Embryo Poems, 1967–1971 (1972)
Snake-Back Solos: Selected Poems, 1969–1977 (1978)
Skulls along the River (poems, 1984)
Watts Poets: A Book of New Poetry and Essays (editor, 1968)
Giant Talk: An Anthology of Third World Writings (co-editor, 1975)
The Inside Story of TV's Roots (co-author, 1978)
Miles, the Autobiography (co-author, 1989)
James Baldwin: The Legacy (editor, biography, 1989)
"The Golden Griot: An Interview with Salif Keita" (2001)

Themes

- Defeated dreams and disappointments

Characteristics

- African American vernacular English
- Vernacular musical traditions and rhythms

Questions

- Troupe has identified two of his primary poetic influences as the Afro-Protestant church, particularly its sacred music tradition, and the basketball court, especially its vernacular rhythms of speech and movement. What evidence do you find of these influences in Troupe's poems?
- Although they raised him in a completely black neighborhood, Troupe's parents brought many Anglo and Latino cultural icons and aspects into their home. What evidence do you find of these influences in his poems? Do you think the self-characterization of his poetry as "hybrid" is an apt description? Why or why not?
- Looking back on his struggle to find his voice as a poet, Troupe has insisted that anyone wanting to write poetry must be courageous: "you just have to be fearless" (*Antioch Review* roundtable). What rhetorical risks do you perceive in Troupe's poetry? Do you see daring as a subtext in his work? If so, where?

Bibliography

Gonzalez, Ray. "An Avalanche of Language: An Interview with Quincy Troupe." *Bloomsbury Review* 17 (1997): 9–10.

"Language Invented, or What? A Panel on Poetry." *Antioch Review* 55 (1997): 192–206.

Turner, Douglas. "Miles and Me: An Interview with Quincy Troupe." *African American Review* 36 (2002): 429–34.

Carolyn M. Rodgers

b. 1945

Works in the Anthology

"Jesus Was Crucified" (1969)
"It Is Deep" (1969)
"For Sistuhs Wearin' Straight Hair" (1969)

Other Works

Paper Soul (poems, 1968)
Songs of a Black Bird (poems, 1969)
2 Love Raps (poems, 1969)
how i got ovah: New and Selected Poems (1975)
The Heart Is Ever Green (poems, 1978)

Themes

- African American maternal/filial love
- African American generational conflicts
- Language and experiences of mundane life
- African American religious and spiritual traditions
- Critique of white supremacy and capitalism

Characteristics

- African American vernacular English
- Vernacular storytelling traditions
- Wit, humor, earnestness

Questions

- Comment on the unconventional capitalization, punctuation, and spelling in Rodgers's poetry. What effects do those usages have on contemporary readers? Based on other texts written about and published during the Black Arts era, what effects do the features seem designed to produce?
- In what ways does the relationship between the speaker and the mother figure in Rodgers's poems differ from the relationships between mothers and daughters in other poems of the Black Arts era and in poems of earlier periods? How does it differ from portraits of fathers and sons in the Black Arts and/or other African American literary periods?

Teaching the Black Arts Era

Not all of the writers included in the "Black Arts Era" section of *NAFAM* adhered to the philosophies and ideologies generally associated with the time. Historical analysis, then, should begin with trying to understand why the diversity of the period is subsumed under such a rubric. Reading the manifestos and critical essays of the period included in the anthology will provide some background, and reviewing the introductions to other periods should be helpful as well.

From a historical perspective, it is clear that the Black Arts era is, in many ways, an echo of both Reconstruction and the Harlem Renaissance. Once again, African Americans questioned the terms of their identity, history, and future prospects as citizens of the United States. They were concerned with the meaning and purpose of art both as a factor in social change and as an economic enterprise. Relevant questions about stylistics, form, and discourse/language as well as intended audience and purpose were again debated. Yet the terms and circumstances of these questions and concerns were distinctly different, if for no other reason than writers of the Black Arts era were aware that their literary predecessors had raised similar issues during Reconstruction and the Harlem Renaissance. From that legacy dating back to one hundred years before, they determined that artists needed to exert more control over the production and marketing of their works. More so than Reconstruction and Harlem Renaissance authors, Black Arts era writers questioned both the personal and the communal significance of literary production and distribution. Many chose to be published by small (and often transitory) presses that allowed them greater freedom of expression, that targeted a particular readership, or that simply promised greater financial profit.

Another contrast between authors of the earlier periods and those of the Black Arts era can be seen in the ways that genres developed. Theorists such as Maulana Karenga, Addison Gayle Jr., Hoyt Fuller, and Larry Neal pushed the essay form into new and often vernacular directions, producing essays arguably more imaginative even than those by writers like Frances Harper in the nineteenth century and Zora Neale Hurston during the Harlem Renaissance. Some Black Arts era writers, including Fuller and Neal, created anthologies or edited periodicals to canonize particular kinds of literature. Dramatists such as Amiri Baraka and Ed Bullins found it desirable not only to write but to encourage, direct, produce, and create theater companies as well. With attention to historical differences, collaborations such as the one between Alex Haley and Malcolm X may be considered against those of the antebellum narratives quite profitably. Etheridge Knight's "Hard Rock Returns to Prison" and Sonia Sanchez's "Summer Words of a Sistuh Addict" bring another perspective to the combination of art and social protest seen in earlier periods. From some vantage points, a greater sense of separation and concern for viable black communities is evident. Whereas Langston Hughes had said in the 1920s that writers were going to create whether people liked or understood them or not, the proponents of the Black Arts era contended that their work *must* be understood by African Americans, that it *must* be both political and aesthetic, and that to be successful, it must *move* their audiences to action. Since the literature was to be for, by, and about African Americans, there were no specific—that is, no white-mandated—restrictions on language, setting, or subject matter. Adherence to conventional literary structures and subjects was neither particularly encouraged nor admired.

The Audio Companion should prove very helpful when approaching this period. "The Revolution Will Not Be Televised," by Gil Scott-Heron, offers an excellent example of the combination of sound and sense and the appropriation of diasporic language and rhythms that also characterized many of the written poems. Listening to the Audio Companion as part of the introduction to poems by Carolyn M. Rodgers, Haki R. Madhubuti, Etheridge Knight, Sonia Sanchez, and Amiri Baraka, for example, should help students "hear" what these writers were doing. Black Arts era writers' attempts to recognize, redefine, and emphasize those elements in African American culture that fostered African American survival are not only evident in the period's prose and poetry but also in its drama. *NAFAM* includes the entire texts of both Ed Bullins's *Goin'a Buffalo: A Tragifantasy* and Baraka's *Dutchman*, a version of which is available on videotape. Introducing students to relevant selections on the Audio Companion and/or pertinent visual resources will help them comprehend the growth of street or guerrilla theater during this period among African Americans and other groups pushing against the status quo. The War on Poverty and other such federal and state programs sometimes helped fund grass-roots participation in the creation of literature. Changes in the available electronic technology, which allowed for better and more portable sound systems as well as different formats for production and re-production, enhanced the development of the Black Arts era.

Genres

Poetry

Evans
Knight
Lorde
Baraka
Sanchez

Spellman
Jordan
Clifton
Cortez
Reed
Harper
Madhubuti

Fiction

Williams
Reed
Bambara

Autobiography

Malcolm X
Lorde
Cleaver
Jordan

Drama

Baraka
Bullins

Political/Literary/Aesthetic Theory

Fuller
King
Gayle
Lorde
Baraka
Jordan
Neal
Reed
Karenga
Madhubuti

Short Story

Bambara
McPherson

Bibliography

Bush, Harold K. Jr. "The Declaration of Independence and *Uncle Tom's Cabin*: A Rhetorical Criticism Approach." In Elizabeth Ammons and Susan Belasco, eds., *Approaches to Teaching* Uncle Tom's Cabin. New York: MLA, 2000. 172–83.

Dubey, Madhu. *Black Women Novelists and the Nationalist Aesthetic*. Bloomington: Indiana UP, 1994.

Glaude, Eddie Jr., ed. *"Is It Nation Time?" Contemporary Essays on Black Nationalism and Black Power*. Chicago: U of Chicago P, 2002.

Singh, Amritjit, and Peter Schmidt, eds. *Postcolonial Theory and the United States: Race, Ethnicity, and Literature*. Jackson: U of Mississippi P, 2000.

Ukpokodu, I. Peter. "African Heritage from the Lenses of African-American Theatre and Film." *Journal of Dramatic Theory and Criticism* 16 (2002): 69–93.

Worcester Review 19.1–2 (1998) [Special issue on Etheridge Knight].

Literature since 1975

Albert Murray

b. 1916

Works in the Anthology

  Train Whistle Guitar, "History Lessons" (1974)

Other Works

  The Omni-Americans (essays, 1970)
  South to a Very Old Place (novel, 1971)
  The Hero and the Blues (lectures, 1973)
  Stomping the Blues (music theory, 1976)
  The Autobiography of Count Basie as Told to Albert Murray (biography, 1985)
  The Spyglass Tree (novel, 1991)
  The Blue Devils of Nada (criticism, 1996)
  The Seven League Boots (novel, 1996)
  From the Briarpatch File: On Context, Procedure, and American Identity (essays, 2000)
  Trading Twelves: The Selected Letters of Ralph Ellison and Albert Murray (2000)
  Conjugations and Reiterations (poems, 2002)

Themes

- Improvisation
- Black jazz artists and their virtuosity
- Beauty of black folk heritage and traditions
- Blues defiance and resilience against oppression
- Southern folkways amid early-twentieth-century industrialization
- Black memory as oral history
- Black southern childhood
- Racial passing

Characteristics

- Modernist play with improvisational rhetoric
- Rapture of African American vernacular English
- Black vernacular music traditions, especially blues and jazz
- Blues rhetoric and sensibility
- Revision of U.S. history to include African American experiences
- Revision of the vernacular figure of the bluesman

Questions

- Read closely a selected paragraph to analyze Murray's nuanced use of southern speech and idioms in *Train Whistle Guitar*. Compare and contrast your findings of his rhetorical style and the effects of his poetics with the style and content of any one of the following writers whose works glorify southern black discourses and dialects: Jean Toomer's *Cane*, Zora Neale Hurston's *Mules and Men*, Rudolph Fisher's "The City of Refuge," or Maya Angelou's *I Know Why the Caged Bird Sings*.
- What attitudes about formal learning and literacy are communicated by Murray's description of Scooter's early academic experiences in *Train Whistle Guitar*?
- What informal "history lessons" does Scooter learn in the selection from Murray's *Train Whistle Guitar*? How do they differ from the lessons Scooter has at school? Do you understand Murray to privilege one type of history lesson over another? If so, which does he seem to esteem more? On what do you base your answer?
- What are the effects of the radical shift in the appearance of the text when the matter of "histry-book whitefolks" enters *Train Whistle Guitar*? Discuss Murray's gradual diminution of paragraph length and style, from Scooter's claim that "I didn't know very much about history then" through his pronouncement that "conjunction is membership; and interjection is the spirit of energy."

Bibliography

Breen, Nelson E. "To Hear Another Language [A conversation between Albert Murray, Romare Bearden, James Baldwin, Alvin Ailey]." *Callaloo* 24 (2001): 656–58.

Jones, Carolyn M. "Race and Intimacy: Albert Murray's *South to a Very Old Place.*" *Critical Survey* 12 (2000): 111–31.

Karrer, Wolfgang. "The Novel as Blues: Albert Murray's *Train Whistle Guitar* (1974)." In Peter Bruck and Wolfgang Karrer, eds., *The Afro-American Novel since 1960*. Amsterdam: Grüner, 1982. 237–62.

Maguire, Roberta S., ed. *Conversations with Albert Murray*. Jackson: UP of Mississippi, 1997.

Rowell, Charles H. "'An All-Purpose, All-American Literary Intellectual': An Interview with Albert Murray." *Callaloo* 20 (1997): 399–414.

Maya Angelou

b. 1928

Works in the Anthology

"And Still I Rise" (1978)
"My Arkansas" (1978)
I Know Why the Caged Bird Sings, Chaps. 15–16 (1970)

Other Works

Gather Together in My Name (autobiography, 1974)
Oh Pray My Wings Are Gonna Fit Me Well (poems, 1975)
And Still I Rise (poems, 1978)
The Heart of a Woman (autobiography, 1981)
All God's Children Need Traveling Shoes (autobiography, 1986)
I Shall Not Be Moved (poems, 1990)
Wouldn't Take Nothing for My Journey Now (poems, 1993)
The Complete Collected Poems of Maya Angelou (1994)
A Song Flung Up to Heaven (autobiography, 2002)

Themes

- Black women's self-esteem
- Survival and endurance
- Black vernacular strategies for triumph over oppression

- Healing power of writing
- Intergenerational dynamics in African American families
- Black motherhood
- Black aristocracy and *noblesse oblige*
- Rural life in the segregated U.S. South
- Assertion of black voices

Characteristics

- African American vernacular English and rural southern idioms
- Black vernacular narrative forms
- Revision of slave narrative conventions

Questions

- Review the tall tales in the vernacular section of *NAFAM*. Then compare and contrast the ballads of heroes there with Angelou's "And Still I Rise." What specific constructs does Angelou borrow from this earlier African American literary tradition? In what ways does her gender necessitate a revision of "bad *man*" types like Stackolee?
- Review the hip hop lyrics in the vernacular section of *NAFAM*. Then compare and contrast the development of the theme of bravado there with Angelou's development of that theme in "And Still I Rise." What specific constructs does Angelou share with this African American literary tradition? In what ways does her gender necessitate a revision of "bad *man*" rappers and DJs?
- Compare and contrast "My Arkansas" with other African American poems about lynching, including James Weldon Johnson's "Brothers," Paul Laurence Dunbar's "The Haunted Oak," and Angelina Weld Grimké's "The Black Finger" and "Tenebris." Then listen with your classmates to the Audio Companion recording of "Strange Fruit." What characteristics do these works share? What rhetorical features indicate that these writers strive to make clear that they are joining a specific protest tradition?
- Now that you are familiar with Maya Angelou's *I Know Why the Caged Bird Sings*, read Paul Laurence Dunbar's "Sympathy" to speculate about Angelou's reasons for borrowing from Dunbar's poem for her title. What kinds of intertextuality do you read in these two works?
- In his review of Angelou's 2002 autobiographical narrative *A Song Flung Up to Heaven*, Hilton Als suggests that *I Know Why the Caged Bird Sings* echoes the British *Bildungsroman* by Charlotte Brontë, *Jane Eyre*. Do you think Als's comparison is fitting? Why or why not?
- Compare and contrast the description of the beginning of literacy

that Angelou gives her narrator in *I Know Why the Caged Bird Sings* with Richard Wright's narrator's description of the same event in *Black Boy*. Is there any textual evidence that Angelou had read Wright's autobiographical account before she wrote Chapter 15 of *I Know Why the Caged Bird Sings*?

- What kinds of relations between black and white women does Angelou depict in Chapter 16 of *I Know Why the Caged Bird Sings*? Do you think such relations persist today? On what do you base your response?

Bibliography

Als, Hilton. "Songbird." *The New Yorker*, Aug. 5, 2002. 72–76.

Koyana, Siphokazi, and Rosemary Gray. "Growing Up with Maya Angelou and Sindiwe Magona: A Comparison." *English in Africa* 29 (2002): 85–100.

Walker, Pierre A. "'Racial Protest, Identity, Words and Form in Maya Angelou's 'I Know Why the Caged Bird Sings.'" *College Literature* 22 (1995): 91–108.

Paule Marshall

b. 1929

Works in the Anthology

"Reena" (1962)
"To Da-Duh, in Memoriam" (1967)
"The Making of a Writer: From the Poets in the Kitchen" (1983)

Other Works

Brown Girl, Brownstones (novel, 1959)
Soul Clap Hands and Sing (novellas, 1961)
The Chosen Place, the Timeless People (novel, 1969)
Reena and Other Stories (1983)
Praisesong for the Widow (novel, 1983)
Daughters (novel, 1991)
The Fisher King (novel, 2000)

Themes

- Feminist exploration of immigrant women's socioeconomic issues
- Transnational, postcolonial, and international women's political struggle
- "The triple-headed hydra of racism, sexism, and class bias" (Marshall's words)
- Repatriation as maturation
- Gender identity formation
- Tyranny of beauty standards for women
- Domesticity and/as women's spaces
- Power of African languages and idioms
- Metatexuality
- Women's social roles in U.S. capitalist society
- African ancestors as perpetual life influences
- Ancient wisdom versus New World urbanity
- Vitality of African diasporic oral traditions
- Harm of stereotypes of black women
- Intraracial color-caste system
- Interracial romance
- Friendships and kinships between black women

Characteristics

- West Indian *Bildungsroman, Kunstlerroman*
- Metatexuality
- Critique of capitalism and materialism
- Denunciation of stereotypes of African American women
- Challenge to myth of African America as monolithic community
- African American vernacular English and Afro-Caribbean discourses

Questions

- What does Marshall gain by using a first-person narrator who is not the eponymous hero to tell "Reena"? Discuss the rhetorical advantages of having Reena narrate her story to her cousin?
- Marshall has said that the theme of "Reena" can be understood as black women's "efforts to realize whatever talents we had and to be our own persons in the face of the triple-headed hydra of racism, sexism, and class bias we confronted each day." Analyze the central dialogue between the narrator and her cousin, in which they recite accusations typically leveled against socially assertive black women. To what extent do you think such accusations persist today? To what extent do you find the two cousins' litany of complaints sympathetic or unsympathetic?

- According to "Reena," what forces primarily destroyed the relationship between Reena and Bob? How—for what purposes—does Reena say she and Bob "used" each other? Based on this representation of interracial romance in the United States, debate whether it is possible for interracial lovers to "escape what our color had come to mean in this country."

- In Marshall's story "Reena," what ultimately destroys Reena's marriage to Dave? How do color and gender play out in their marriage? To what extent does Marshall imply that different cultural and national values—the Caribbean versus the United States—destroyed their marriage?

- In Marshall's story "Reena," for what reasons does Reena say she plans relocation—repatriation—in Africa? Does the tone of the story insinuate an authorial approval of this plan? On what do you base your answer?

- Compare Marshall's representation of sugar cane in "To Da-duh, in Memoriam" with Jean Toomer's throughout *Cane* in the generation before.

- Analyze the verbal sparring between grandmother and granddaughter in Marshall's "To Da-duh, in Memoriam" to determine whether she argues for or against a romanticization of postcolonial Barbadian life.

- What values do traditional elder and exiled child respectively espouse in Marshall's "To Da-duh, in Memoriam"? Do they have any values in common? What value of the grandmother does the last paragraph of the story assert?

- Locate and read the opening section of Virginia Woolf's 1925 book *A Room of One's Own*. Then review "The Making of a Writer" to discern ways in which Marshall signifies on what Woolf argues are essential conditions and fundamental motivations for women writers.

- In what ways is Marshall's "The Making of a Writer" a metatextual essay? Explain how its rhetorical tropes convey the argument at its thematic center.

Bibliography

Brondum, Lene. "'The Persistence of Tradition': The Retelling of Sea Islands Culture in Works by Julie Dash, Gloria Naylor, and Paule Marshall." In Maria Diedrich, Henry Louis Gates Jr., and Carl Pedersen, eds., *Black Imagination and the Middle Passage*. Oxford, UK: Oxford UP, 1999. 152–63.

Coser, Stelamaris. *Bridging the Americas: The Literature of Paule Marshall, Toni Morrison, and Gayl Jones*. Philadelphia: Temple UP, 1995.

DeLamotte, Eugenia C. *Places of Silence, Journeys of Freedom: The Fiction of Paule Marshall*. Philadelphia: U of Pennsylvania P, 1998.

Denniston, Dorothy Hamer. *The Fiction of Paule Marshall: Reconstructions of History, Culture, and Gender*. Knoxville: U of Tennessee P, 1995.

Francis, Donette A. "Paule Marshall: New Accents on Immigrant America." *The Black Scholar* 30 (2000): 21–26.

Hawthorne, Evelyn. "The Critical Difference: Paule Marshall's Personal and Literary Legacy." *The Black Scholar* 30 (2000): 2–7.

King, Rosamond S. "The Flesh and Blood Triangle in Paule Marshall's *The Fisher King*." *Callaloo* 26 (2003): 543–47.

Japtok, Martin. "Sugarcane as History in Paule Marshall's 'To Da-Duh, in Memoriam.'" *African American Review* 34 (2000): 475–82.

Lock, Helen. "'Building Up from Fragments': The Oral Memory Process in Some Recent African-American Written Narratives." *College Literature* 22 (1995): 109–20.

Pettis, Joyce Owens. *Toward Wholeness in Paule Marshall's Fiction*. Charlottesville: UP of Virginia, 1995.

Rogers, Susan. "Embodying Cultural Memory in Paule Marshall's *Praisesong for the Widow*." *African American Review* 34 (2000): 77–98.

Adrienne Kennedy

b. 1931

Works in the Anthology

A Movie Star Has to Star in Black and White (1976)

Other Works

Funnyhouse of a Negro (drama, 1964)
The Owl Answers (drama, 1985)
Adrienne Kennedy: In One Act (drama, 1988)
People Who Led to My Plays (autobiography, 1987)
Deadly Triplets: A Theater Mystery and Journal (novel, 1990)
Ohio State Murders (drama, 1992)
She Talks to Beethoven (drama, 1991)
The Alexander Plays (1992)

The Film Club: A Monologue (1992)
Sleep Deprivation Chamber (drama, 2001)
The Adrienne Kennedy Reader (2001)

Themes

- Interracial marriage
- Amalgamation, miscegenation, and madness
- Race, gender, and social ostracism
- Vexed relationships between Africans and African Americans
- Blurred line between reality and fantasy
- Fragmented, irreconcilable identities—split personalities
- Double consciousness
- Historical memory as reconstructive process
- Motherhood and daughterhood
- Home and hearth as women's space
- Existential crisis
- Death, murder, suicide
- Whiteness as hegemonic dominance and national obsession
- Hollywood iconography as imperialism, oppression, and national obsession

Characteristics

- Structural distortions to reflect interior chaos
- Dramatic monologues
- Repetition
- Verbal and dramatic irony
- Sexual double entendre
- Dreamscape, nightmare, and transmogrifications
- Revision of the figure of the tragic mulatta
- Distortion of black subjectivity
- Dominant white imagery, especially in costumes and stage props
- Autobiographical details
- Development of a unique mythology of the mind

Questions

- Written a quarter of a century after Lorraine Hansberry's better known *A Raisin in the Sun*, Kennedy's *A Movie Star Has to Star in Black and White* depicts late-twentieth-century African American life very differently from its predecessor. Compare and contrast these two versions of black life and values in (post)modern urban settings.
- What theatrical and thematic values does *A Movie Star Has to Star in*

Black and White share with its dramatic descendant *Joe Turner's Come and Gone*, by August Wilson?

- Review some of the more theoretical essays published during the Black Arts era, that is, in the decade before Kennedy published *A Movie Star Has to Star in Black and White*. To what extent is Kennedy's play truly "black art," as defined by theorists like Larry Neal, Hoyt Fuller, and Addison Gayle Jr.?

- Read W. E. B. Du Bois's theory of double consciousness as articulated in *The Souls of Black Folk*. To what extent does that theory operate in Kennedy's *A Movie Star Has to Star in Black and White*?

- What values does Kennedy ascribe to the black middle class in *A Movie Star Has to Star in Black and White*? How do these values intersect with larger social and political issues?

- What does Kennedy imply about the psychological development of black women in *A Movie Star Has to Star in Black and White*?

- Why, according to Kennedy's play, must Hollywood stars perform in "black and white"? Or do you think Kennedy means something other than "perform" when she asserts that a movie star must "star" in "black and white"?

- What role does U.S. history play in *A Movie Star Has to Star in Black and White*? How do the various Hollywood icons, portrayed by Clara, undermine the images and ideologies of the American entertainment industry and of the spectators who support it?

Bibliography

Brown, E. Barnsley. "Passed Over: The Tragic Mulatta and (Dis)Integration of Identity in Adrienne Kennedy's Plays." *African American Review* 35 (2001): 281–95.

Bryant-Jackson, Paul K., and Lois More Overbeck, eds. *Intersecting Boundaries: The Theatre of Adrienne Kennedy*. Minneapolis: U of Minnesota P, 1992.

Wilkerson, Margaret. "Diverse Angles of Vision: Two Black Women Playwrights." In Bryant Jackson and Overbeck, eds., *Intersecting Boundaries: The Theatre of Adrienne Kennedy*. Minneapolis: U of Minnesota P, 1992. 58–72.

Toni Morrison

b. 1931

Works in the Anthology

Song of Solomon, Part 2 (1977)
"Rootedness: The Ancestor as Foundation" (1984)
"The Site of Memory" (1987)
"Unspeakable Things Unspoken: The Afro-American Presence in American Literature" (1988)

Other Works

The Bluest Eye: A Novel (1970)
Sula (novel, 1974)
The Black Book (editor, 1974)
Tar Baby (novel, 1981)
Beloved: A Novel (1987)
Jazz (novel, 1991)
Playing in the Dark: Whiteness and the Literary Imagination (essays, 1991)
Race-ing Justice, En-gendering Power: Essays on Anita Hill, Clarence Thomas, and the Construction of Social Reality (editor, 1992)
Lecture and Speech of Acceptance, Upon the Award of the Nobel Prize for Literature (1993)
To Die for the People: The Writings of Huey P. Newton (editor, 1995)
The Dancing Mind: Speech upon Acceptance of the National Book Foundation Medal (1996)
Birth of a Nation'hood: Gaze, Script, and Spectacle in the O. J. Simpson Case (editor, 1997)
Paradise: A Novel (1998)
Love: A Novel (2003)

Themes

- Migration, flight, journey
- African American self-determination
- Legacy of chattel slavery on mid-twentieth-century U.S. life and society
- Friendships among African American men
- Impact of past on present and future
- Familial relationships
- Black heterosexual romantic love

- African American community and cultural history
- Intraracial economic class issues among African Americans
- Intersection of race, class, gender, power, and imperialism

Characteristics

- Extensive use of black vernacular folklore and folktales
- Biblical, mythological, and philosophical allusion
- Revision of hegemonic histories and ideologies
- Critique of capitalism, greed, avarice, especially as manifest in chattel slavery and its legacies
- Critique of bigotry, racialized hatred, and misogyny

Questions

- Discuss Morrison's fictive radical group called the Days, of which Guitar is a member in *Song of Solomon*. Paraphrase the group's goals and methods. What is the narrator's attitude toward the group? According to the novel's ethos and ethics, how valid or effective is this group likely to be in correcting the social ills that plague mid-twentieth-century African Americans?
- Along with flight, figures of hunt and chase function as a leitmotif in Morrison's *Song of Solomon*. Discuss the author's integration of these figures such that the search for history, identity, and treasure are bound up with material and metaphysical pursuits throughout Part 2 of the novel.
- Milkman's odyssey in Part 2 of Morrison's *Song of Solomon* in several respects parallels the Western myth of the sojourner-searcher, including a Cyclops figure and a siren. Research Homer's *Odyssey*, and compare and contrast Morrison's revision of it in *Song of Solomon*. In a novel so dedicated to African mythology, do you find the Western mythology distracting or otherwise ill-advised? Why or why not?
- In all of Morrison's novels, proper names are rich with significance. Analyze her designations of major and minor characters in *Song of Solomon*. Review the Old Testament story of Hagar to analyze its pertinence to that of Morrison's Hagar. How does Morrison achieve a shift in your interpretation when Milkman realizes that he has mistaken *Solomon* for "Sugarman" in the Virginia children's ring game?
- How do the events of *Song of Solomon* reflect on the national events and racial history of the period in which Morrison sets them? How, if at all, do the fictive events reshape your understanding of this historical era?
- Review the male identities implied or expressed in the folktales and ballads in the vernacular section of *NAFAM*. Are there "Milkman"

figures in these texts? How does *Song of Solomon*'s hero in the pale beige suit compare or contrast with John Henry, Railroad Bill, Brer Rabbit, Stackolee, the Flying Fool, the signifyin' monkey, and others?

- Morrison uses black vernacular music forms for her title *Song of Solomon* and later for *Jazz*. Her reliance on antebellum spirituals is further apparent in her deployment of themes and moods from what W. E. B. Du Bois calls in *The Souls of Black Folk* the "sorrow songs." Trace the use of black vernacular music throughout Part 2 of *Song of Solomon*, beginning perhaps with Guitar's nickname.

- In "Rootedness," Morrison celebrates the black sermonic tradition as an important influence on her novels to date. What evidence is there in *Song of Solomon* that Morrison strives to "make [readers] feel something profoundly in the same way that [any one] Black preacher [in the vernacular section of *NAFAM*] requires his congregation to . . . join him in the sermon"?

- In "Rootedness," Morrison grieves the "discrediting" of African (American) ways of knowing, and explains that she wrote *Song of Solomon* in part to sustain the place of the supernatural in African American literature and epistemology. Identify specific passages or episodes in the novel that seem designed to reclaim "discredited knowledge."

- What is the role of the ancestor in black fiction, according to Morrison in "Rootedness"? Summarize the power of this figure, as Morrison details it. Assess her identification of Pilate as the/an ancestor in *Song of Solomon* by deciding whether Part 2 of the novel supports the author's claim that Hagar's "difficulty" is a lack of positive male nurturance in her early life.

- Are you surprised by Morrison's recitation in "The Site of Memory" of Western patriarchs who have been very explicit about their low estimation of African intellectuality? What impact did men such as Thomas Jefferson, David Hume, and Immanuel Kant have on African American history?

- In "The Site of Memory," Morrison laments the lack of "mention of their interior life" among narrators of slavery autobiographies. Review some of the antebellum slave narratives included in *NAFAM* to decide whether or not you agree with Morrison that these texts do not represent slaves' interiority.

- Morrison laments the lack of "mention of [slave narrators'] interior life" in antebellum black autobiographies. One contemporary novel that, like Morrison's fiction, tries to "fill in the blanks that the slave narratives left" in their accounts of individual lives is Caryl Phillips's *Crossing the River*. Summarize Morrison's description of her strategy for inscribing slaves' interiority. Then read the excerpt from Phillips's novel to assess both the tenability of Morrison's critical principles in "The Site of Memory" and Phillips's literary achievement.

- Morrison asks in "Unspeakable Things Unspoken" about that which renders a text "black," and concludes that the "most fraught" point of entry is the culturally distinctive language of a text. Select one or two of your favorite works in *NAFAM* and analyze their language to determine whether the language is what renders the work an African American text in your mind. Do your selected texts bear up to the scrutiny of Morrison's suggestion that "it does not 'go without saying' that a work written by an Afro-American is automatically subsumed by an enforcing Afro-American presence"?

- Research critical literary essays on any one of Morrison's novels published before her October 1988 Tanner Lecture, "Unspeakable Things Unspoken," to determine whether or not her strategy of examining her own novels up to that year—rather than a strategy of reading fiction by another African American writer—is the most effective for arguing the thesis of her lecture.

- How does the gloss on the opening sentence of *Song of Solomon* that Morrison provides in "Unspeakable Things Unspoken" help you contextualize and appreciate textual details of Part 2 of the novel?

- In "Unspeakable Things Unspoken" Morrison writes about the "journalistic" style for which she worked in the opening sentence of *Song of Solomon*. Earlier, in "The Site of Memory," she admits that she likes "the feeling of a told story . . . a guiding voice [that] doesn't know what's going to happen next" any more than its readers do. Do these two narrative/voice theories conflict with one another? Why or why not?

- In "The Site of Memory" Morrison insists that she writes to "fill in the gaps that the slave narratives left," and in "Unspeakable Things Unspoken" she expressly describes the spaces she is "filling in, and can fill in because they were planned." Are these spaces the same in each essay? How did you determine your answer?

Bibliography

Bryant, Cedric Gael. "'Every Goodbye Ain't Gone': The Semiotics of Death, Mourning, and Closural Practice in Toni Morrison's *Song of Solomon*." *MELUS* 24 (1999): 97–110.

Deans, Gary, dir. *Toni Morrison Uncensored* [videorecording. 30 min. sd., col.] Princeton, NJ: Films for the Humanities and Sciences, 1998.

Dussere, Erik. *Balancing the Books: Faulkner, Morrison, and the Economies of Slavery*. New York: Routledge, 2003.

Furman, Jan. *Toni Morrison's* Song of Solomon: *A Casebook*. New York: Oxford UP, 2003.

McKay, Nellie Y., and Kathryn Earle, eds. *Approaches to Teaching the Novels of Toni Morrison*. New York: MLA, 1997.

Randle, Gloria T. "Lady Sings the Blues: Toni Morrison and the Jazz/Blues Aesthetic." In James Conyers, ed., *African American Jazz and Rap*. Jefferson, NC: McFarland, 2001. 131–44.

Roberson, Gloria G. *The World of Toni Morrison: A Guide to Characters and Places in Her Novels*. Westport, CT: Greenwood, 2003.

Thompson, Betty Taylor. "Common Bonds from Africa to the U.S.: Africana Womanist Literary Analysis." *The Western Journal of Black Studies* 25 (2001): 177–85.

Tidey, Ashley. "Limping or Flying? Psychoanalysis, Afrocentrism, and *Song of Solomon*." *College English* 63 (2000): 48–69.

Wang, Chih-ming. "The X-Barred Subject: Afro-American Subjectivity in Toni Morrison's *Song of Solomon*." *Studies in Language and Literature* 9 (2000): 269–88.

Young, John. "Toni Morrison, Oprah Winfrey, and Postmodern Popular Audiences." *African American Review* 35 (2001): 181–204.

Ernest J. Gaines

b. 1933

Works in the Anthology

"The Sky Is Gray" (1963)

Other Works

Catherine Carmier (novel, 1964)
Bloodline (short stories, 1968)
The Autobiography of Miss Jane Pitman (novel, 1971)
In My Father's House (novel, 1978)
"Home: A Photo Essay" (1978)
A Gathering of Old Men (novel, 1983)
A Lesson Before Dying (novel, 1993)

Themes

- Southern plantation life and culture
- Moral and ethical dilemmas
- Black motherhood
- African American family dynamics and interdependence
- Material poverty
- Education and literacy as challenge to illiteracy and ignorance
- Impact of U.S. military on black families

Characteristics

- Sparse descriptions of rural Louisiana landscape
- Analysis of charged emotional situations
- Cultivation of an idiosyncratic mythology
- Black vernacular traditions, especially blues music
- African American vernacular English and southern regional dialects
- Extensive use of dialogue
- Exploration of mythological southern community
- Oral storytelling techniques
- Flashback

Teaching Strategies

- Arrange a viewing of the televised version of "The Sky Is Gray" for your students. Discuss with them the genre differences between the original story and the televised production. What qualities and features does each form of media emphasize? What is gained or lost in the translation from print text to visual?

Questions

- Identify particular elements of Gaines's unique mythology. What are some aspects of the specific tone and time, history and landscape, collectivity and religious concepts that the author develops for/within his mythological community?
- Contrast Gaines's mythological landscape in "The Sky Is Gray" with that Octavia Butler develops in "Bloodchild."
- How do the rural southern setting and characters in the excerpt from Maya Angelou's autobiography compare and contrast with Gaines's southern rural setting and characters in "The Sky Is Gray"?
- Like Richard Wright's "The Ethics of Living Jim Crow, an Autobiographical Sketch," Gaines's "The Sky Is Gray" narrates a black boy's coming of age. Read these pieces together to examine differences in

how the two authors represent the segregated South as well as how they document the incipient dismantling of Jim Crow racism.

• Comment on the conflict between the black youth and the white preacher in the dentist's waiting room in "The Sky Is Gray." What does the story gain through the representation of the white political reactionary as a violent Christian minister?

• Compare the respective scenes in which an older black woman compels a young black man to kill a songbird in Gaines's "The Sky Is Gray" and Michelle Cliff's "Columba." Do the two scenes ultimately illustrate similar—or different—ideas? In what ways, if any, is each story gendered? Is there any textual evidence that Cliff consciously drew on Gaines's earlier story for her own fiction?

• In *Contemporary Novelists,* Gaines is quoted as saying, "My characters are usually poor, mostly uneducated, and almost always very independent. The conflict in which they usually find themselves is *how to live as a man* in that short period of time." Compare Gaines's perspective on manhood with that offered in Walter Mosley's "Equal Opportunity."

• Analyze Gaines's representation of the necessity of sacrifice, action, and social responsibility in a small town. How does his depiction of social sacrifice compare with Gwendolyn Brooks's consideration of family, duty, and responsibility in *Maud Martha*?

Bibliography

Beavers, Herman. *Wrestling Angels into Song: The Fictions of Ernest J. Gaines and James Alan McPherson.* Philadelphia: U of Pennsylvania P, 1995.

Brown, Dale. "A Lesson for Living: For Louisiana Writer Ernest Gaines, Home Is the Place Where You're Torn between the Difficulty of Leaving and the Terror of Staying." *Sojourners* 31 (2002): 30–34.

Clark, Keith. *Black Manhood in James Baldwin, Ernest J. Gaines, and August Wilson.* Urbana: U of Illinois P, 2002.

Doyle, Mary-Ann. "Erasure and Identity in Ernest Gaines's Louisiana." *Educational Studies* 32 (2001): 452–70.

Doyle, Mary Ellen. *Voices from the Quarters: The Fiction of Ernest J. Gaines.* Baton Rouge: Louisiana State UP, 2002.

Estes, David C., ed. *Critical Reflections on the Fiction of Ernest J. Gaines.* Athens: U of Georgia P, 1994.

Lowe, John, ed. *Conversations with Ernest Gaines.* Jackson: UP of Mississippi, 1995.

Vinson, James, ed. "Gaines, Ernest." *Contemporary Novelists*. New York: St. James, 1972.

Wardi, Anissa J. "Inscriptions in the Dust: *A Gathering of Old Men* and *Beloved* as Ancestral Requiems." *African American Review* 36 (2002): 35–54.

Clarence Major

b. 1936

Works in the Anthology

"Swallow the Lake" (1970)
"Round Midnight" (1984)
"On Watching a Caterpillar Become a Butterfly" (1994)
"Chicago Heat" (1994)

Other Works

The Fires That Burn in Heaven (chapbook, 1954)
Love Poems of a Black Man (chapbook, 1965)
Human Juices (chapbook, 1966)
Man Is Like a Child: An Anthology of Creative Writing by Students (editor, 1968)
All-Night Visitors (novel, 1969)
Swallow the Lake (poems, 1970)
The New Black Poetry (editor, 1970)
Private Line (poems, 1971)
Symptoms and Madness (poems, 1972)
The Cotton Club: New Poems (1972)
No (novel, 1973)
The Dark and Feeling: Black American Writers and Their Work (1974)
The Syncopated Cakewalk (poems, 1974)
Reflex and Bone Structure (novel, 1975)
Emergency Exit (novel, 1979)
The Other Side of the Wall (poems, 1982)
Inside Diameter: The France Poems (1985)
My Amputations (novel, 1986)
Painted Turtle: Woman with Guitar (novel, 1988)
Surfaces and Masks (poems, 1988)
Some Observations of a Stranger in Zuni in the Latter Part of the Century (poems, 1989)

Fun and Games (stories, 1990)
Parking Lots (poems, 1992)
Calling the Wind: Twentieth-Century African American Short Stories
    (editor, 1993)
Juba to Jive: A Dictionary of African American Slang (editor, 1994)
Configurations: New and Selected Poems, 1958–1998 (1998)
Come by Here: My Mother's Life (prose, 2002)
Waiting for Sweet Betty (poems, 2002)

Themes

- Shifting denotations and connotations of English lexicon and
  language
- African American ties to the natural world
- Double consciousness
- Transnational and international African American experiences
- Artistic freedom and metafictiveness
- Costs of black assimilation of Euro-American values
- Subversion and reversal
- Race, gender, and madness
- African Americans and the U.S. judicial and penal systems

Characteristics

- Extensive use of visual, painterly imagery
- Fragmented subjectivity
- Metatextuality
- Postmodern stylistics and thematics, especially nonlinearity
- Trickster speaker
- Revision of traditional dramatic monologue

Questions

- While the speaker of Major's "Swallow the Lake" overtly expresses a
  sense of alienation from various tropes of civilization—the "Things
  I could not give back"—as well from other human beings—those
  "Blank monkeys of the hierarchy"—assertions of his relationship to
  nature are perhaps more oblique. Isolate the assertions that reveal
  why the poem ends with a lament that "I could not swallow the
  lake."
- Consider Major's "Swallow the Lake" as a meditation on the travesty
  of the Middle Passage.
- The speaker of Major's "Round Midnight" insists that "you" are familiar with his story. Paraphrase his story; then identify the "you" he

addresses in the poem. Do you think the speaker correctly asserts that "you" know his story? Why or why not?

- Review the Brer Rabbit folktales in the vernacular section of *NAFAM*. Then read them alongside Major's "On Watching a Caterpillar Become a Butterfly." Compare the element of subversion that you find in the folktales with the caesura at the center of Major's poem.

Bibliography

African American Review 13 (1979) [special issue on Clarence Major].

African American Review 28 (1994) [special issue on Clarence Major].

Bell, Bernard, ed. *Clarence Major and His Art: Portraits of an African American Postmodernist*. Chapel Hill: U of North Carolina P, 2001.

Selzer, Linda Furgerson. "Reading the Painterly Text: Clarence Major's 'The Slave Trade: View from the Middle Passage.'" *African American Review* 33 (1999): 209–33.

Leon Forrest

1937–1997

Works in the Anthology

From *There Is a Tree More Ancient than Eden* (1973, 1988)

Other Works

Theatre of the Soul: A Three-Act Play (1967)
The Bloodworth Orphans (novel, 1977)
"Luminosity at the Lower Frequencies: An Essay on Ralph Ellison's *Invisible Man*" (1980)
"Oh Say Can You See" (story, 1982)
Two Wings to Veil My Face (novel, 1984)
"In the Light of Likeness—Transformed" (essay, 1988)
Divine Days (novel, 1992)
"A Solo Long-Song for Lady Day" (essay, 1993)

Themes

- Failure of the Lyndon Johnson presidency
- Persistence of race and gender discrimination

- Religiocultural diversity among African Americans
- Segregated twentieth-century Chicago as African American homeland
- Power of black sermonic tradition
- Legacy of chattel slavery
- White economic racism
- Double consciousness and Afro-Anglo-American tradition

Characteristics

- Integration of multiple and diverse literary traditions
- Epistolary tradition
- Intertextuality and heavy use of literary allusion
- Black vernacular traditions, especially folklore and jazz, bebop, and blues forms
- Inventive, innovative rhetorical structures and prose
- Satire, humor, irony, double entendre

Teaching Strategies

- Discuss Forrest's allusion to "We Shall Overcome" in "The Epistle of Sweetie Reed."

Questions

- Summarize Sweetie Reed's primary concerns about President Lyndon Johnson's 1960s War on Poverty in Forrest's *There Is a Tree More Ancient Than Eden*. What evidence does the character offer for the legitimacy of her concerns?
- What does Forrest gain—or lose—by constructing a hundred-year-old black woman for his correspondent in *There Is a Tree More Ancient Than Eden*? What are the rhetorical effects of Sweetie Reed's self-designation as a "freed-up lady of color"?
- Review "The Wonderful Tar-Baby Story" to explain the multiple allusions in Sweetie Reed's parenthetical remark about President Lyndon Johnson: "Why rumor even has it you could pull a rabbit out of tarbaby, without tipping your hand."
- What do you make of the minstrel show at play during Sweetie Reed's university address in Forrest's *There Is a Tree More Ancient Than Eden*?
- Reread the lyrics to "Run, Nigger, Run" to explain Forrest's allusions to it in *There Is a Tree More Ancient Than Eden*.
- Research the numbers racket as a folk phenomenon in African American communities and explain Forrest's derision of it in *There Is a*

Tree More Ancient Than Eden. Compare Forrest's use of the numbers game with Edwidge Danticat's in *Breath, Eyes, Memory*.

- Trace Forrest's use of news media in *There Is a Tree More Ancient Than Eden.* What role does television news coverage play in the letter from Sweetie Reed?

Bibliography

Williams, Dana. "Preachin' and Singin' Just to Make It Over: The Gospel Impulse as Survival Strategy in Leon Forrest's *Bloodworth Trilogy*." *African American Review* 36 (2002): 475–85.

John Edgar Wideman

b. 1941

Works in the Anthology

Brothers and Keepers, "Robby's Version" (1984)
Damballah (1981)

Other Works

A Glance Away (novel, 1967)
Hurry Home (novel, 1970)
The Lynchers (novel, 1973)
Hiding Place (novel, 1981)
Sent for You Yesterday (novel, 1983)
Reuben (novel, 1987)
Fever: Twelve Stories (1989)
Philadelphia Fire (novel, 1990)
The Stories of John Edgar Wideman (1992)
All the Stories Are True (stories, 1993)
Fatheralong: A Meditation on Fathers and Sons, Race and Society (autobiography, 1994)
The Cattle Killing (novel, 1996)
Two Cities: A Love Story (novel, 1998)
Hoop Roots (nonfiction, 2001)

Themes

- African American vernacular English and regional dialects
- African American family relationships and dynamics

- Roots of black vernacular culture
- African epistemologies
- Relationships between black men
- Black masculinity
- Impact of poverty and drug culture on black urban communities
- Black sermonic tradition
- Black oral storytelling tradition
- Subversion and defiance
- Antebellum slavery and its modern incarnations

Characteristics

- Experimentation with representations of black speech
- Hybrid text that blends memory, history, interpretation, subjectivity, imagination
- Journalistic preoccupation with truth and fact
- Autobiographical details
- Black sermonic tradition
- Dreamscape and stream of consciousness

Questions

- Compare Wideman's multigeneric explorations in *Brothers and Keepers* with those by his contemporaries Ntozake Shange and Rita Dove, and in earlier texts by Frances E. W. Harper and W. E. B. Du Bois.
- Wideman has said that his writing "experiments with language, experiments with form, bringing to the fore black cultural material, history, archetypes, myths, the language itself, the language that black people actually speak and trying to connect that with the so-called mainstream." In what ways does "Robby's Version" in *Brothers and Keepers* validate this claim? Contrast Wideman's representation of black speech forms with that of another contemporary author in *NAFAM*, one who also experiments with black vernacular discourses, for example, Sherley Anne Williams, Ernest J. Gaines, and Gayl Jones.
- Compare and contrast Wideman's exploration of psychological and sociopolitical differences between two brothers in *Brothers and Keepers* with James Baldwin's in "Sonny's Blues." What textual details reveal that Wideman writes much later than does Baldwin?
- What rhetorical qualities in *Brothers and Keepers* indicate that, for Wideman, the phenomenon, process, or act of memory is individual, familial, and communal?
- What does Wideman's *Brothers and Keepers* argue about the ways and reasons that autobiography and biography, public and private history merge?

- Discuss ways that in *Damballah* Wideman suggests slavery as a continuing legacy for urban black neighborhoods, as a source of both social problems and strategies of resistance.
- Analyze *Damballah* as a neoslave narrative in the tradition of Gayl Jones's *Corregidora*, Charles Johnson's "The Education of Mingo," and Robert Hayden's "Runagate Runagate." Support or refute the idea that Wideman himself parallels *Damballah*'s Orion, transmitting vital history and culture to his audience.
- Support or refute the contention that Wideman exoticizes Orion's black skin in *Damballah*.
- Summarize the epistemology of enslaved people that Wideman theorizes in *Damballah*.
- Identify the highest authority in Wideman's *Damballah*. How did you determine your answer?
- What parallels does Wideman suggest in *Damballah* between the process of identity formation and the transmission of black culture? Are you persuaded by his argument?
- What does Aunt Lissy's condemnation of Orion's message as "heathen talk" reveal about her assessment of black vernacular traditions in Wideman's *Damballah*? What does it reveal about Wideman's attitude toward women?
- What significance do you attribute to Wideman's simile descriptions of Lissy as "shiny blue-black like a *crow's* wing" with a "voice like *chicken's* cackle" (italics added) in *Damballah*? Compare and contrast Wideman's portrait of Lissy with Richard Wright's portrait of Aunt Sarah in "Long Black Song."
- What is the function of the formal letter that Wideman incorporates into *Damballah*?

Bibliography

Byerman, Keith E. *John Edgar Wideman: A Study of the Short Fiction.* New York: Prentice Hall, 1998.

Callaloo 22.3 (Summer 1999) [special issue on John Edgar Wideman].

Hoem, Sheri I. "'Shifting Spirits': Ancestral Constructs in the Postmodern Writing of John Edgar Wideman." *African American Review* 34 (2000): 249–62.

Lustig, Jessica. "Home: An Interview with John Edgar Wideman." *African American Review* 26 (1992): 453–57.

Mbalia, Doreatha D. *John Edgar Wideman: Reclaiming the African Personality.* Selinsgrove, PA: Susquehanna UP, 1995.

Samuel R. Delany

b. 1942

Works in the Anthology

From *Atlantis: Model 1924* (1995)

Other Works

The Jewels of Aptor (novel, 1962)
Captives of the Flame (1963, rev. as *Out of the Dead City*, novel, 1968)
The Towers of Toron (novel, 1964, 1968)
The Ballad of Beta-2 (novel, 1965)
City of a Thousand Suns (novel, 1965, 1969)
Babel-17 (novel, 1966)
Empire Star (novel, 1966)
Nova (novel, 1968)
The Fall of the Towers (novel, 1970)
The Tides of Lust (novel, 1973)
Dhalgren (novel, 1975)
Distant Stars (novel, 1981)
Stars in My Pocket Like Grains of Sand (novel, 1984)
The Complete Nebula Award–Winning Fiction (stories, 1986)
They Fly at Ciron (novel, 1993)
Hogg (novel, 1994)
Silent Interviews on Language, Race, Sex, Science Fiction and Some Comics (nonfiction, 1994)
Atlantis: Three Tales (1995)
Shorter Views: Queer Thoughts & the Politics of the Paraliterary (essays, 1999)
1984: Selected Letters (2001)

Themes

- Sexuality, erotics, race, and culture
- Homosexuality
- African American literary history: homage to literary ancestors
- Excess and indulgence
- Impact of the human psyche and libido on memory
- Great migration
- Entrée into urban life and cultures
- 1920s New York City literati
- Race relations

Characteristics

- Experimental fictional forms and themes
- Explorations of human appetites and desires
- Autobiographical details
- Symbolic language, extensive use of metaphors and tropes
- Development of mixed-race characters
- Explorations of human sexuality

Teaching Strategies

- Listen with students to Stevie Wonder's "Living for the City" and ask them to contrast the experiences of Wonder's southern immigrant in New York with Delany's.

Questions

- Compare and contrast "The City of Refuge," Rudolph Fisher's earlier satire of black male southern immigration into New York City, with Delany's "Atlantis: Model 1924."
- Note that Delany's "Atlantis: Model 1924" opens with an allusion to Jean Toomer's *Cane*. Review *Cane* and explain why the allusion is particularly suited to "Atlantis."

Bibliography

The Review of Contemporary Fiction 16 (Fall 1996) [special issue on Samuel R. Delany].

Steiner, K. Leslie. "An Interview with Samuel R. Delany." *The Review of Contemporary Fiction* 16 (1996): 97–103.

Sherley Anne Williams

1944–1999

Works in the Anthology

"The Peacock Poems: 1" (1975)
"I Want Aretha to Set This to Music" (1982)
"Tell Martha Not to Moan" (1967)

Other Works

The Peacock Poems (as Shirley Williams, 1975)
Some One Sweet Angel Chile (poems, 1982)
Dessa Rose (novel, 1986)
Give Birth to Brightness: A Thematic Study in Neo-Black Literature (1972)

Themes

- Labor in the rural South
- Economic exploitation of black workers
- African American family
- African American womanhood and motherhood
- African American Christianity
- Rural versus urban sensibilities

Characteristics

- African American vernacular English and regional discourses
- Traditional quatrains with unconventional content
- Lyric experimentation
- Black vernacular music as source of healing and survival
- Blues rhythms and resilience
- Celebration of black artistic foremothers

Teaching Strategies

- Listen with students to Alberta Hunter's recording of "Handy Man" on the Audio Companion. Discuss with them the poet's reconstruction/revision of the singer's style and voice.

Questions

- Compare and contrast the representation of African American vernacular English and of poor black women's attitudes in Williams's "The Peacock Poems: 1" and the excerpt from Alice Walker's The Color Purple.
- What qualities are shared by the mother figures in Williams's "The Peacock Poems: 1" and Ernest J. Gaines's "The Sky Is Gray"? What can we infer about black motherhood in impoverished conditions in the South from these two texts?
- Read the blues lyrics in the vernacular section of NAFAM alongside Williams's "I Want Aretha to Put This to Music." Comment on

Williams's success in capturing and revising such classic blues rhythms and conventions as those in "Handy Man."

- Read Williams's "I Want Aretha to Put This to Music" along with Ntozake Shange's *for colored girls*. Can the latter text rightly be proclaimed a blues lyric similar to Williams's poem?
- Summarize the ideological issues that Williams explores in "Tell Martha Not to Moan." In terms of black masculinity, what does the story ultimately assert? What does it assert about black motherhood?

Bibliography

Basu, Biman. "Hybrid Embodiment and an Ethics of Masochism: Nella Larsen's *Passing* and Sherley Anne Williams's *Dessa Rose.*" *African American Review* 36 (2002): 383–402.

McKible, Adam. "'These Are the Facts of the Darky's History': Thinking History and Reading Names in Four African American Texts." *African American Review* 28 (1994): 223–35.

Williams, Sherley Anne, and Deborah McDowell. "Conversation." In Joanne V. Gabbin, ed., *The Furious Flowering of African American Poetry.* Charlottesville: UP of Virginia, 1999. 194–205.

Alice Walker

b. 1944

Works in the Anthology

"Women" (1970)
"Outcast" (1973)
"On Stripping Bark from Myself" (1979)
"'Good Night, Willie Lee, I'll See You in the Morning'" (1979)
"In Search of Our Mothers' Gardens" (1974)
"Everyday Use" (1973)
"Advancing Luna—and Ida B. Wells" (1981)
From *The Color Purple* (1982)

Other Works

Once: Poems (1968)
The Third Life of Grange Copeland (novel, 1970)
Revolutionary Petunias (poems, 1972)
In Love and Trouble: Stories of Black Women (1973)

In Search of Our Mothers' Gardens: The Legacy of Southern Black Women (essays, 1974)

Looking for Zora (essays, 1975)

Meridian (novel, 1976)

I Love Myself When I Am Laughing . . . (editor, 1979)

Living by the Word (essays, 1988)

You Can't Keep a Good Woman Down (stories, 1991)

Possessing the Secret of Joy (novel, 1992)

Warrior Marks: Female Genital Mutilation and the Sexual Blinding of Women (co-author, 1993)

The Same River Twice: Honoring the Difficult (essays, 1997)

Anything We Love Can Be Saved: A Writer's Activism (essays, 1997)

The Way Forward Is with a Broken Heart (stories, 2000)

Sent by Earth: A Message from the Grandmother Spirit: After the Bombing of the World Trade Center and Pentagon (stories, 2001)

Absolute Trust in the Goodness of the Earth: New Poems (2003)

Themes

- African Americans in the U.S. Southeast
- Black women's (unfulfilled) artistic abilities
- Psychic, domestic, and/or sexual violence against women
- Relationships across lines of color/class/gender/authenticity
- African American romantic love
- Southern black folkways as survival strategies
- 1960s southern voter registration movement
- Matrilineage and matrilineal power
- African American family relationships
- Impact of nature on black life and culture
- African American folk spirituality
- Creativity and imagination
- Metatextuality
- Dignity of economically impoverished southern blacks

Characteristics

- Love
- Conciseness
- Intertextuality and reverence for African American artistic/literary ancestors
- Autobiographical details
- Critique of fraudulence of every sort
- Innovative experimentation in literary forms
- Critique of gendered subjugation and dominance

- Critique of white supremacist capitalism
- Philosophical and theological explorations into the divine
- Investigations into African American experiences of a broad range of human emotion, including anguish, elation, loss, serenity, remorse, pity, compassion, and hope

Questions

- Compare and contrast the excerpts from Walker's *The Color Purple* and Ntozake Shange's *for colored girls*. Both texts were severely criticized by African American men at the time of their near-simultaneous publication. Research some of the negative critical reviews of these texts and use the excerpts to support or refute their validity.
- Notice that the longest line in Walker's lyric "'Good Night, Willie Lee'" contains only nine words. Explicate the three poems by Walker, paying closest attention to the density of their diction and their use of enjambment.
- Feminist literary scholars have canonized Walker's "In Search of Our Mothers' Gardens" and "Everyday Use" as fundamental interdisciplinary texts, especially for the coining of the term *womanist* in the former. Discuss the ideas in these works to ascertain why they have appealed to feminists across a broad, complex spectrum of ideology.
- What does Walker gain by beginning "In Search of Our Mothers' Gardens" with an allusion to Jean Toomer's *Cane?*
- Walker's works have been read as casting and recasting particular themes in increasing degrees of nuanced interpretation. Select three texts to read in chronological order and analyze any one theme that the later two texts revise in greater depth.
- "In Search of Our Mothers' Gardens" establishes that artistic expression enables African American women's survival even as the essay redefines "art." Analyze the text to discern Walker's theory of the relation of art and language to mental health and physical survival.
- What connections, if any, do you read between Walker's "In Search of Our Mothers' Gardens" and "Everyday Use"? Does "Everyday Use" conform to the ideas her essay argues about literacy, art, identity, black female interiority, and cultural heritage?
- Walker cites Zora Neale Hurston as a major influence on her own literary production. Read one or more of Hurston's texts to uncover elements that Walker seems to have revised in her own work. Besides the southern locale and the similar characterization of women, what ideas about healing and harm, history and myth, silence and articulation do the two authors share?
- Debate the theological issues that both underpin and are explicit in

the conversation between Celie and Shug in Walker's *The Color Purple*. Comment on Shug's comparison of the deity to an orgasm (and vice versa).

- What implications do you read in the protagonist's prayer to and dialogue with Ida B. Wells in Walker's "Advancing Luna"?
- Review Ida B. Wells-Barnett's *A Red Record*. How does Wells-Barnett's essay inform your interpretation of Walker's story? To what extent do you find Walker's use of "Ida B. Wells" more figurative than literal?
- Given that Walker's "Advancing Luna–and Ida B. Wells" intently challenges social mores on a number of fronts, what (dis)advantages do you find in the story's multiple endings? Based on your knowledge of the racialized complexity of the 1960s civil rights movement, to what extent do these multiple endings rightly represent the historical truths of the era?

Bibliography

Christian, Barbara, ed. *Alice Walker: "Everyday Use."* New Brunswick, NJ: Rutgers UP, 1994.

Fraile Marcos, Ana-Maria. "'As Purple to Lavender': Alice Walker's Womanist Representation of Lesbianism." In Michael J. Meyer, ed., *Literature and Homosexuality*. Amsterdam: Rodopi, 2000. 111–34.

Gates, Henry Louis Jr., and K. A. Appiah, eds. *Alice Walker: Critical Perspectives Past and Present*. New York: Amistad, 1993.

Jenkins, Candice M. "Queering Black Patriarchy: The Salvific Wish and Masculine Possibility in Alice Walker's *The Color Purple*." *Modern Fiction Studies* 48 (2002): 969–1000.

Smith, Pamela A. "Green Lap, Brown Embrace, Blue Body: The Ecospirituality of Alice Walker." *Cross Currents* 48 (1998–99): 471–87.

Warhol, Robyn R. "How Narration Produces Gender: Femininity as Affect and Effect in Alice Walker's *The Color Purple*." *Narrative* 9 (2001): 182–87.

Winchell, Donna Haisty. *Alice Walker*. New York: Twayne, 1992.

August Wilson

b. 1945

Works in the Anthology

  Joe Turner's Come and Gone (1988)

Other Works

  Ma Rainey's Black Bottom (drama, 1985)
  Fences (drama, 1986)
  The Piano Lesson (drama, 1988)
  Testimonies: Four Monologues (1991)
  Two Trains Running (drama, 1992)
  Seven Guitars (drama, 1995)
  Jitney (drama, 2001)
  King Hedley II (drama, 2001)
  Gem of the Ocean (drama, 2003)
  How I Learned What I Learned (autobiographical monologue, 2003)

Themes

- Impact of slavery on African American families and kin communities
- Centrality of conjure traditions to black folk life
- African (American) healing and recovery rituals
- (Apparently) conflicting spiritual and religious belief systems among blacks
- Early-twentieth-century Great Migration
- Black rootlessness, displacement, and survival
- Tyranny of white patrollers *cum* "people finders"
- Exploitation of black workers
- Black imprisonment and incarceration
- Black economic self-determination
- Intergenerational legacies of loss and search among (formerly) enslaved peoples

Characteristics

- African American vernacular English
- Invocation of black vernacular traditions, especially musical forms and genres
- Celebration of black folk life through representation of community (and) rituals

Teaching Strategies

- Listen with students to a few of the vernacular selections on the Audio Companion that reinforce the spirituality themes and vernacular conventions in Wilson's *Joe Turner*. The most pertinent selections include such spirituals as "Steal Away to Jesus" and such juke-house songs as Zora Neale Hurston's "You May Go But This Will Bring You Back."
- Stress the significance of Wilson's position as the second African American playwright to have a dramatic text performed on Broadway since the 1959 production of *A Raisin in the Sun* by asking students to research the history of blacks on Broadway. Ask them to focus as well on other winners of Pulitzer Prizes, whom Wilson, a two-time winner, joins. What characteristics and themes does his work share with those other (white) winners?

Questions

- Why does Seth oppose Bynum's spirituality in Wilson's *Joe Turner*? What values are implied in Seth's rejection of Bynum's practices?
- Analyze the scene in Wilson's *Joe Turner* that involves only the two children and ends with their kissing. How does this scene relate to other scenes of romantic or sexual attraction in the play? What does it contribute to the whole structure?
- Discuss the names Wilson gives his characters in *Joe Turner*. In what ways does each live up to his or her name? Which names, if any, do you find ironically deployed?
- Several characters in Wilson's *Joe Turner* reference their fathers. What seems to be the role of the patriarch in this play? Do you find this focus and portrayal ironic or earnest?
- How do you understand the events with which Wilson's *Joe Turner* culminates? Does Loomis assume Bynum's role as savior and healer, or not? On what do you base your response?
- Discuss Selig's function in *Joe Turner*. What comment do you understand Wilson to make by rendering Selig a descendant of antebellum slave nappers?

Bibliography

Bogumil, Mary L. "'Tomorrow Never Comes': Songs of Cultural Identity in August Wilson's *Joe Turner's Come and Gone*." *Theatre Journal* 46 (1994): 463–76.

Elam, Harry J. Jr. "August Wilson, Doubling, Madness, and Modern African-American Drama." *Modern Drama* 43 (2000): 11–34.

Elkins, Marilyn, ed. *August Wilson: A Casebook*. New York: Garland, 2000.

Harris, Trudier. "August Wilson's Folk Traditions." In Kimball King, ed., *Modern Dramatists: A Casebook of Major British, Irish, and American Playwrights*. New York: Routledge, 2001. 369–82.

Heard, Elizabeth. "August Wilson on Playwriting: An Interview." *African American Review* 35 (2001): 93–103.

Keller, James R. "The Shaman's Apprentice: Ecstasy and Economy in Wilson's *Joe Turner*." *African American Review* 35 (2001): 471–79.

Nadel, Alan. "Boundaries, Logistics, and Identity: The Property of Metaphor in *Fences* and *Joe Turner's Come and Gone*." In Alan Nadel, ed., *May All Your Fences Have Gates: Essays on the Drama of August Wilson*. Iowa City: U of Iowa P, 1994. 86–104.

Taylor, Regina. "That's Why They Call It the Blues." *American Theatre* 13 (1996): 18–24.

Michelle Cliff

b. 1946

Works in the Anthology

"Within the Veil" (1985)
"Columba" (1990)

Other Works

Claiming an Identity They Taught Me to Despise (poetry, 1980)
Abeng (novel, 1984)
The Land of Look Behind: Prose and Poetry (1985)
No Telephone to Heaven (novel, 1987)
Bodies of Water (stories, 1990)
Free Enterprise (novel, 1993)
The Store of a Million Items: Stories (1998)

Themes

- Race, class, and gender issues for women of color
- Caribbean immigrant identities
- African diasporas

- Border crossings, cultural and sexual differences
- Speech and voice as sources of power/empowerment
- Life and culture in postcolonial Jamaica
- Color-caste systems
- Racism
- Resistance to oppression
- Double consciousness and racial passing
- Impact of entertainment industry on Western youth

Characteristics

- Explorations of voice, voicelessness, self-expression, and self-assertion
- Critique of colonialism and imperialism throughout the world
- African American vernacular rhythms and idioms
- Innovations with classic blues structure
- Irony, understatement, satire

Teaching Strategies

- Listen with students to "Rock Me, Baby" on the Audio Companion. Engage students in a discussion of the basic conventions of classic blues; then compare and contrast those conventions with the ones Cliff deploys in "Within the Veil."

Questions

- Review some of the classic blues lyrics in the vernacular section of *NAFAM*. What fundamental conventions of this tradition does Cliff appropriate for "Within the Veil"? In what ways does she revise the tradition?
- Cliff takes her title from W. E. B. Du Bois's famous description of African American double consciousness. Discuss Cliff's use of the image of the veil in "Within the Veil" and the implications of her application of the symbol as an international or universal figure.
- Whom do you understand Cliff to mean by the "us" and "them" in the final stanzas of "Within the Veil"?
- What is the source of the amity between the narrator and Columba in Cliff's "Columba"?
- Review the folk ballads of Stackolee in the Vernacular section of *NAFAM*. Explain why you think Cliff has Columba give this name to one of the doves in the wrecked Rover in her "Columba."
- What do you make of the suggestion of the narrator of Cliff's "Columba" that her home is "a colony within a colony"?

Bibliography

Aegerter, Lindsay Pentolfe. "Michelle Cliff and the Paradox of Privilege." *College English* 59 (1997): 895–98.

Hakkarainen, Marja Leena. "The Death of Marilyn Monroe: Myth and Countermyth in Michelle Cliff's 'Columba.'" In Jopi Nyman and John A. Strotesbury, eds., *Postcolonialism and Cultural Resistance*. Joensuu, Finland: Faculty of Humanities, U of Joensuu, 1999. 102–9.

Octavia Butler

b. 1947

Works in the Anthology

"Bloodchild" (1984)

Other Works

Patternmaster (novel, 1976)
Mind of My Mind (novel, 1977)
Survivor (novel, 1978)
Kindred (novel, 1979)
Wild Seed (novel, 1980)
Clay's Ark (novel, 1984)
Adulthood Rites: Xenogenesis (novel, 1988)
Imago (novel, 1989)
Parable of the Sower (novel, 1993)
Bloodchild and Other Stories (1996)

Themes

- Slavery and slave trade
- Race and species preservation
- Lesbian sexualities
- Motherhood
- Narcotic addiction as race control
- Relationships between women
- Familial relationships
- Symbiosis of life, death, and birth cycles
- Interdependence of various species
- Sexual violation versus sexual consent

Characteristics

- Rejection of hegemonic beauty standards
- Horrific, grotesque detail of slaughter and murder
- Allegory of Western and African experiences
- Critique of hegemonic dominance and force

Questions

- Review one or more slave narratives in the "Literature of Slavery and Freedom" section of *NAFAM*. What rhetorical and thematic conventions of antebellum slave narratives does Butler deploy for "Bloodchild"? Why do you suppose she draws so heavily on the U.S. past to imagine a future?
- To what does the title of Butler's "Bloodchild" refer?
- Examine the confrontation between the two brothers in Butler's "Bloodchild." What role does fraternal love play in their dispute? How much of their fight seems based on fraternal jealousy? Do you read this scene as a revision of the biblical story of Cain and Abel? Why or why not?
- In Butler's "Bloodchild," why does Gan ultimately decide to sacrifice himself for his sister?
- In Butler's "Bloodchild," why do Terrans live within a cage?
- In "Bloodchild," to what extent do you understand Gan's revulsion at the idea of "red worms" of human embryos inside his sister to form Butler's argument against the perpetuation of human life?
- In Butler's "Bloodchild," why do you think Gan ultimately tries to convince T'Gatoi that Terrans should be shown the "birth" process he witnessed? What seems to be the basis of his conjecture that Terrans should observe this process?

Bibliography

Helford, Elyce Rae. "'Would You Really Rather Die Than Bear My Young?' The Construction of Gender, Race, and Species in Octavia E. Butler's 'Bloodchild.'" *African American Review* 28 (1994): 259–72.

Mitchell, Angelyn. "Not Enough of the Past: Feminist Revisions of Slavery in Octavia E. Butler's *Kindred*." *MELUS* 26 (2001): 51–77.

Potts, Stephen W. "'We Keep Playing the Same Record': A Conversation with Octavia E. Butler." *Science-Fiction Studies* 23 (1996): 331–39.

Raffle, Burton. "Genre to the Rear, Race and Gender to the Fore: The Novels of Octavia E. Butler." *The Literary Review* 38 (1995): 454–62.

Yusef Komunyakaa

b. 1947

Works in the Anthology

"February in Sydney" (1989)
"Facing It" (1988)
"Sunday Afternoons" (1992)
"Banking Potatoes" (1992)
"Birds on a Powerline" (1993)

Other Works

Lost in the Bonewheel Factory (poems, 1979)
Copaceti (poems, 1984)
I Apologize for the Eyes in My Head (poems, 1986)
Dien Cai Dau (poems, 1988)
Magic City (poems, 1992)
The Jazz Poetry Anthology (co-editor, 1991)
Neon Vernacular (poems, 1992)

Themes

- Homecoming
- Familial loyalty
- Power of black occult
- Integration of African spiritual traditions and Western Christianity
- Violence of racialized social ostracism
- Migration, flight, escape
- Commingling of mundane and sacred rituals
- War, loss, death, memorial, grief
- Power of a shard of light to alter reality

Characteristics

- Traditional, classical stanza forms
- Bird imagery
- Irony, paradox
- Literary and vernacular allusions
- Black vernacular traditions, especially jazz and folktales
- Flashback

Questions

- Do the jazz musicians whom the speaker conjures up in Komun-
  yakaa's "February in Sydney" truly provide the comfort he seeks?
  How did you determine your answer?
- What is the source of the speaker's "old anger" in Komunyakaa's
  "February in Sydney"? Why does it seem to recur there?
- What seems to be the message of the crows in Komunyakaa's "Birds
  on a Powerline"?
- Besides the figure of Jim Crow (as symbol not of racist discrimina-
  tion but rather of the common sense of black people), what other el-
  ements of black vernacular tradition does Komunyakaa cite in "Birds
  on a Powerline"?
- What does the allusion to poet Frances E. W. Harper contribute to
  Komunyakaa's "Birds on a Powerline"?
- Analyze Komunyakaa's commingling of ordinary and holy gestures in
  "Facing It," "Sunday Afternoons," and "Birds on a Powerline." Start
  with exterior versus interior spaces as you describe the contrasts in
  these two poems.
- Analyze Komunyakaa's use of bird and flight imagery in "Facing It,"
  "Sunday Afternoons," and "Birds on a Powerline." Do you find these
  images connected to such folktales as "All God's Chillen Had Wings"
  and/or "A Flying Fool"? If so, how? If not, how do the flight symbols
  in Komunyakaa's poems differ from those in the folktales?
- What do "they" seem to be latching inside in Komunyakaa's "Sunday
  Afternoons"? What figures in the poem, besides the "dresser mirror,"
  seem "Held prisoner in the house"?

Bibliography:

Salas, Angela M. "'Flashbacks through the Heart': Yusef Komunyakaa and
   the Poetry of Self-Assertion." In Joanne V. Gabbin, ed., *The Furious
   Flowering of African American Poetry*. Charlottesville: UP of Virginia,
   1999. 298–309.

Suarez, Ernest. "Yusef Komunyakaa." *Five Points: A Journal of Literature
   and Art* 4 (1999): 15–28.

Nathaniel Mackey

b. 1947

Works in the Anthology

"Falso Brilhante" (1985)
"Song of the Andoumboulou: 8" (1994)
From "Djbot Baghostus's Run" (1986)

Other Works

Four for Trane (poetry chapbook, 1978)
Septet for the End of Time (poetry chapbook, 1983)
Eroding Witness (poems, 1985)
From a Broken Bottle Traces of Perfume Still Emanate: Atet A.D. (prose, 1986)
From a Broken Bottle Traces of Perfume Still Emanate: Bedouin Hornbook (prose, 1988)
Outlandish (poetry chapbook, 1992)
Moment's Notice: Jazz in Poetry and Prose (co-editor, 1993)
From a Broken Bottle Traces of Perfume Still Emanate: Djbot Baghostus's Run (prose, 1993)
Discrepant Engagement: Dissonance, Cross-Culturality and Experimental Writing (1993)
Song of the Andoumboulou 18–20 (poetry chapbook, 1994)
Strick: Song of the Andoumboulou 16–25 (recording, 1995)

Themes

- Influence of black art and popular culture on production of new art
- Narcotic-induced visions
- Ambiguity, complexity, (un)certainty
- Metatextuality
- African mystical traditions and spiritualities
- Jazz and the inherent jazziness of English language idioms

Characteristics

- Irreverence and high esteem for English language idioms and forms
- Improvisation
- Metatextuality
- Irony, ambiguity, and subversion
- Black vernacular musical forms, especially jazz and bebop

- Multigeneric literary forms
- Representation of diverse cultures from among peoples of color
- Reciprocity of diverse cultures from among peoples of color
- Hybrid, experimental formalistic innovations
- Postmodern stylistics
- Strong visual, aural, and oral conventions

Questions

- What roles do popular media play in Mackey's "26.IX.81"? What relationships do the narrator and his art have with popular culture? Given these connections, what can we infer about the "Angel of Dust" to whom the letter is addressed?
- Compare and contrast the representation of the power of jazz to influence human choices in Mackey's "26.IX.81" and any poems by his contemporary Yusef Komunyakaa. Now compare and contrast works by these contemporary poets with the 1950s and 1960s jazz-inflected poetry of Bob Kaufman.
- What seems to be the source of the speaker's disillusionment and ennui in Mackey's "Falso Brilhante"?
- Can Mackey's "Song of the Andoumboulou: 8" rightly be called a dirge? If so, what sorrows does the speaker express? If not, what particular kind of lyric is this song?

Bibliography

Callaloo 23 (Spring 2000) [special issue on Nathaniel Mackey].

Gysin, Fritz. "Double-Jointed Time in Nathaniel Mackey's Jazz Fiction." *Amerikastudien/American Studies* 45 (2000): 513–18.

Hreha, A. Sarah, and Scott Hreha. "Nathaniel Mackey's *Bedouin Hornbook*: An Annotated Discography of Specific Musical References." *Callaloo* 25 (2002): 321–38.

O'Leary, Peter. "An Interview with Nathaniel Mackey." *Chicago Review* 43 (1997): 30–47.

Charles Johnson

b. 1948

Works in the Anthology

"The Education of Mingo" (1986)

Other Works

Black Humor (prose, 1970)
Half-Past Nation Time (prose, 1972)
Faith and the Good Thing (novel, 1974)
Oxherding Tale (novel, 1982)
The Sorcerer's Apprentice (short stories, 1986)
Being and Race: Black Writing Since 1970 (essays, 1988)
Middle Passage (novel, 1990)
In Search of a Voice: Charles Johnson and Ron Chernow (1991)
Black Men Speaking (co-editor, 1997)
Dreamer: A Novel (1998)
King: The Photobiography of Martin Luther King, Jr. (co-editor, 2000)

Themes

- African educability and intelligibility
- Double consciousness
- Hegemonic intellectual pretensions
- Ironies of white supremacist patriarchy
- Homoeroticism between slavers and slaves

Characteristics

- Regional dialects
- Black vernacular tropes, especially from folktales
- Revision of theories of Western enlightenment
- Critique of white supremacist patriarchy
- Irony, humor, double entendre
- Queer critique of homoerotic tensions between slavers and slaves

Teaching Strategies.

- Watch and discuss with your students the short PBS video about Charles Johnson.

Questions

- Compare and contrast Moses's description of Mingo's refusal to kill chicken hawks in Johnson's "The Education of Mingo" to black men's resistance to killing birds of flight in Michelle Cliff's "Columba" and Ernest J. Gaines's "The Sky Is Gray."
- Review the folktales in the vernacular section of *NAFAM* to determine the origins of the now obliquely, now overtly expressed kinship between blacks and birds in Johnson's "Education of Mingo."
- Review W. E. B. Du Bois's notion of double consciousness, and support or refute the idea that despite his "education" from Moses, Mingo both experiences and exhibits this racialized phenomenon in Johnson's story.
- Research fundamental principles of Buddhism; then trace Johnson's deployment of them as subtext in "The Education of Mingo."
- Explain the associations implied in Johnson's allusion to Mary Shelley's *Frankenstein* in his "Education of Mingo."
- Discuss Johnson's ironic revision, in his "Education of Mingo," of the implications of the 1850 Fugitive Slave Law in Moses's fantasy that he and Mingo must "[run] forever, across all space, all time . . . like fugitives with no fingers, no toes, like two thieves or yokefellows."

Bibliography

Byrd, Rudolph P., ed. *I Call Myself an Artist: Writings by and about Charles Johnson*. Bloomington: Indiana UP, 1999.

Charles Johnson [videorecording, 30 min.]. Alexandria, VA: KCTS Television and PBS Video, 1996.

Levasseur, Jennifer, and Kevin Rabalais. "An Interview with Charles Johnson." *Brick* 69 (2002): 133–44.

Nash, William R. *Charles Johnson's Fiction*. Urbana: U of Illinois P, 2003.

———. "'I Was My Father's Father, and He My Child': The Process of Black Fatherhood and Literary Evolution in Charles Johnson's Fiction." In Keith Clark, ed., *Contemporary Black Men's Fiction and Drama*. Urbana: U of Illinois P, 2001. 108–34.

Selzer, Linda. "Master-Slave Dialectics in Charles Johnson's 'The Education of Mingo.'" *African American Review* 37 (2003): 105–15.

Ntozake Shange

b. 1948

Works in the Anthology

From *for colored girls who have considered suicide / when the rainbow is enuf* (1977)
"Nappy Edges" (1978)
"Bocas: A Daughter's Geography" (1983)

Other Works

Nappy Edges (poems, 1978)
Melissa and Smith (prose, 1978)
Spell #7: A Theater Piece in Two Acts (drama, 1981)
A Photograph: Lovers in Motion: Poemplay (1981)
A Daughter's Geography (poems, 1983)
Sassafras, Cypress, and Indigo: A Novel (1983)
See No Evil: Prefaces, Essays and Accounts, 1976–1983 (1984)
Betsy Brown: A Novel (1985)
Three Pieces (drama, 1982)
Matrilineal Poems (1983)
From Okra to Greens: A Different Kind of Love Story (poems, 1984)
Ridin' the Moon in Texas (poems, 1987)
The Love Space Demands (drama, 1991)
I Heard Eric Dolphy in His Eyes (drama, 1992)
I Live in Music (poems, 1995)
The Beacon Best of 1999: Creative Writing by Women and Men of All Colors (editor, 1999)

Themes

- African American heterosexual romantic relationships
- Geopolitics
- Conflicts in and among postcolonial African nations
- Cultural and political connections between Africa and its diasporas
- Power of international solidarity of disenfranchised people
- African American women's culture
- Black women's self-definition and self-actualization

Characteristics

- Postmodern rhetorical structure
- Rhythms of jazz, blues, and other black vernacular discourses

- Critique of international politics
- Critique of colonialism and Western imperialism
- Celebration of international (feminist) struggle for human rights
- Popular culture iconography
- Unexpurgated language

Questions

- One of the most controversial of the poems in Shange's *for colored girls*—all of which drew intense collective criticism from African American men—is the one in which the lady in green proclaims that "somebody almost walked off wid alla my stuff." Identify passages that you think might have aroused men's ire, and support or refute the feminist principles they espouse.
- What argument does the lady in green finally assert about the extent to which she has been victimized in Shange's poem that begins "somebody almost walked off wid alla my stuff"? Does she imply or assert a degree of complicity in the near theft of her "stuff"?
- What connections does the speaker of Shange's "Bocas: A Daughter's Geography" insist on between Chicago and such international cities as Cape Town and Johannesburg? What is the nature of the "new world" she describes? Whom do you understand her to reference in the phrase the "same old men"?
- Consider the title *Bocas*, which is the Spanish word for "mouths." Then characterize the tone of "Bocas: A Daughter's Geography." Is it a lament, dirge, or elegy? Or is it a threat or imperative? What relationship does the poem establish between the symbol of a mouth and its own tone?
- Why do you think Shange casts the speaker of "Bocas: A Daughter's Geography" as a mother figure? What is gained—or lost—by this choice?
- What connection does Shange establish between black women's hair and physical/geographical movement in "Nappy Edges"?
- Trace the images of lynching in Shange's "Nappy Edges" and discuss their relationship to songs like "Strange Fruit" on the Audio Companion. Are you persuaded of the validity of these images in a poem about the U.S. Midwest? Why or why not?

Bibliography

Damon, Maria. "Kozmic Reappraisals: Revising California Insularity." In Jacqueline Vaught Brogan and Cordelia Chavez Candelaria, eds., *Women Poets of the Americas: Toward a Pan-American Gathering*. Notre Dame, IN: U of Notre Dame P, 1999. 254–71.

O'Connor, Mary. "Subject, Voice, and Women in Some Contemporary Black American Women's Writing." In Lois Parkinson Zamora, ed., *Contemporary American Women Writers: Gender, Class, Ethnicity*. London: Longman, 1998. 32–50.

Splawn, P. Jane. "'Change the Joke[r] and Slip the Yoke': Boal's 'Joker' System in Ntozake Shange's *for colored girls . . .* and 'spell #7.'" *Modern Drama* 41 (1998): 386–99.

————. "New World Consciousness in the Poetry of Ntozake Shange and June Jordan: Two African-American Women's Response to Expansionism in the Third World." *CLA Journal* 39 (1996): 417–32.

Gayl Jones

b. 1949

Works in the Anthology

From *Corregidora* (1975)

Other Works

Chile Woman (drama, 1974)
Eva's Man (novel, 1977)
White Rat (short stories, 1978)
Liberating Voices: Oral Tradition in African American Literature (editor, 1991)
Song for Anninho (poems, 1981)
The Hermit Woman (poems, 1983)
Xarque and Other Poems (1985)
The Healer (novel, 1998)
Mosquito (novel, 2000)

Themes

- Power of song, lyricism, art, black vernacular music forms, all beauty
- Preservation of African American history through memory, orality, and storytelling
- Capacity of blues to heal physical and emotional maladies
- Madness, psychic distortions, emotional anguish, and other legacies of slavery
- Matrilineage and black motherhood
- Incest, forcible prostitution, and other sexual assaults on black women

- Importance of oral and written documentation of sociopolitical history
- Sexual slavery in African diasporas
- Intraracial color-caste system

Characteristics

- African American vernacular English and southern dialects
- Unexpurgated language, sexual idioms
- Black vernacular art forms, especially jazz and blues
- Qualities and constructs of African American orality and speech patterns
- Italics to indicate temporal, narrative, or emotional shifts
- Flashback, dreamscape

Teaching Strategies

- Discuss with students the implications of the 1970 Kentucky ratification of the Thirteenth Amendment on *Corregidora* (see Crouther). In addition, you might want to require them to research historical and sociopolitical conditions throughout twentieth-century Kentucky that manifest the lack of protection of African Americans resulting from the state's failure to ratify the Thirteenth Amendment until 1970.
- Consider the complexities of Lou-Ann Crouther's teaching of *Corregidora*. Crouther explains that she must confront her "distaste" for

  the state song, "My Old Kentucky Home, Good-Night!," written by Stephen Collins Foster (1826–1864) in 1853. It is commonly said that the line about "darkies being gay" was changed in the 1960s and was replaced with "the folks" or "the people" are gay. Of course, many are sometimes brought to tears when this song is sung before the Kentucky Derby each May, a horse race in which the first jockeys were African American men. The word changes do little to change the song's nostalgic sentiments for antebellum days when "darkies" knew their place. And that "place" was not in a state university teaching English! (223)

Questions

- Describe the relationship between Ursa and her mother in Jones's *Corregidora*. Why does Ursa say that what the two of them would have considered prying, outsiders would deem "ridiculous"?
- Why does Mama speak in Great Gram's voice in Jones's *Corregidora*? Summarize the story Mama tells. Could Mama have witnessed the events she narrates?

- To what extent does Jones's *Corregidora* argue that "Palmares was now"—i.e., that Jones's day represents the fulfillment of a black freedom struggle?
- Contrast the story that Great Gram tells in Jones's *Corregidora* with events narrated by Linda Brent in Harriet Jacobs's *Incidents in the Life of a Slave Girl*. Does your contrast illuminate why Jones tells a story of slavery—tells this particular story of slavery—more than a hundred years after Emancipation? If so, why? If not, why not?
- Compare and contrast Jones's *Corregidora* with other *NAFAM* stories of fugitive slaves, including Frederick Douglass's account of his desire for freedom in his 1845 *Narrative*. What tropes of Jones's revision of slave escape, if any, mark her narrative as written in the twentieth century rather than during the Fugitive Slave Act era?
- Describe the dynamic between Ursa's parents, Mama and Martin, as Mama narrates it in Jones's *Corregidora*. What seems to cause the sexual dysfunction in their marriage?

Bibliography

Cognard-Black, Jennifer. "'I Said Nothing': The Rhetoric of Silence and Gayl Jones's *Corregidora*." *NWSA Journal* 13 (2001): 40–60.

Crouther, Lou-Ann. "'Results Matter': When the Other Teacher Teaches English in the Bluegrass State." In Lucila Vargas, ed., *Women Faculty of Color in the White Classroom*. New York: Lang, 2002. 219–35.

Fraile Marcos, Ana Ma. "Lady Sings the Blues: Gayl Jones' *Corregidora*." In Michael J. Meyer, ed., *Literature and Music*. Amsterdam: Rodopi, 2002. 203–27.

Hardack, Richard. "Making Generations and Bearing Witness: Violence and Orality in Gayl Jones's *Corregidora*." *Prospects* 24 (1999): 645–61.

Nishida, Mieko. *Slavery and Identity: Ethnicity, Gender, and Race in Salvador, Brazil, 1808–1888*. Bloomington: Indiana UP, 2003.

Rushdy, Ashraf H. A. "'Relate Sexual to Historical': Race, Resistance, and Desire in Gayl Jones's *Corregidora*." *African American Review* 34 (2000): 273–315.

Simon, Bruce. "Traumatic Repetition: Gayl Jones's *Corregidora*." In Judith Jackson Fossett, ed., *Race Consciousness, African-American Studies for the New Century*. New York: New York UP, 1997. 93–111.

Jamaica Kincaid

b. 1949

Works in the Anthology

Annie John, Chap. 2 (1985)

Other Works

At the Bottom of the River (short stories, 1983)
A Small Place (nonfiction, 1988)
Lucy (novel, 1990)
The Autobiography of My Mother (novel, 1996)
My Brother (memoir, 1998)
My Favorite Plant: Writers and Gardeners on the Plants They Love (editor, 1998)
My Garden (Book) (memoir, 2001)
Talk Stories (essays, 2002)
Mr. Potter: A Novel (2003)

Themes

- Growing up female in the West Indies
- West Indian family life and culture
- Relationships between parents and daughters
- Gender identity development
- Difficulty of the onset of adolescence for girls and their parents

Characteristics

- West Indian female *Bildungsroman*
- Sparse, minimalist sentence structure
- Densely detailed paragraph development
- Repetition of words and phrases

Questions

- Contrast Kincaid's description of her early life with Nikki Giovanni's in her poem "Nikki-Rosa" and Edwidge Danticat's in the novel *Breath, Eyes, Memory*. Then contrast Kincaid's autobiographical story with Harriet Jacobs's slave narrative *Incidents in the Life of a Slave Girl* from the century before. What common characteristics do you find in each black woman writer's account of the relationship between a daughter and her (surrogate) mother?

- As you read the excerpt from Kincaid's *Annie John*, what aspects of familial relationships, if any, surprise you? If you experience surprise, in what ways are your expectations challenged?
- Do you understand the final paragraphs of the excerpt from Kincaid's *Annie John* to describe a budding lesbian relationship between the narrator and her new school buddy, Gweneth? Why or why not?
- What do the details about the narrator's father's loss of his parents and grandparents contribute to the excerpt from Kincaid's *Annie John*?

Bibliography

Perry, Donna. "Initiation in Jamaica Kincaid's *Annie John*." In Lois Parkinson Zamora, ed., *Contemporary American Women Writers: Gender, Class, Ethnicity*. London: Longman, 1998. 128–37.

Simmons, Diane. "Jamaica Kincaid and the Canon: In Dialogue with *Paradise Lost* and *Jane Eyre*." *MELUS* 23 (1998): 65–85.

David Bradley

b. 1950

Works in the Anthology

From *The Chaneysville Incident* (1981)

Other Works

South Street (novel, 1975)

Themes

- Black manhood, masculinity, and misogyny
- African American homophobia
- Relationships among African American men
- Father-son relationships
- Black family dynamics
- Multiple accounts/theories of American history
- African influences on U.S. life and society
- Power of African American memory as history
- Pursuit of literacy

Characteristics

- Scriptural allusion
- Flashback technique
- African American vernacular English and regional dialects

Questions

- How do you understand Jack's statement that the narrator's father in Bradley's *The Chaneysville Incident* beseeched Jack "to make sure [the narrator] learned how to be a man"? According to Jack, what values and actions constitute manhood?
- In Bradley's *Chaneysville Incident* Jack's reiteration of Moses's suggestion that it is possible for a young boy to have "too much woman" within him is arguably homophobic and misogynist. Research recent theories of homophobia and misogyny as well as African American masculinity to determine the extent to which Moses and Jack may espouse antigay ideas. Discuss your conclusions with your classmates.
- In Bradley's *Chaneysville Incident* Jack's account of Moses's unwillingness to correct false information about his life situates Moses within the tradition of African American tricksters. Review the folktales in the vernacular section of *NAFAM* and trace rhetorical features there that apparently influenced Bradley.

Bibliography

Egan, Phillip J. "Unraveling Misogyny and Forging the New Self: Mother, Lover, and Storyteller in *The Chaneysville Incident*." *Papers on Language and Literature* 33 (1997): 265–88.

Kubitschek, Missy Dehn. "'So You Want a History, Do You?': Epistemologies and *The Chaneysville Incident*." *Mississippi Quarterly* 4 (1996): 755–75.

Lock, Helen. "'Building Up from Fragments': The Oral Memory Process in Some Recent African-American Written Narratives." *College Literature* 22 (1995): 109–21.

Pavlic, Edward. "Syndetic Redemption: Above-Underground Emergence in David Bradley's *The Chaneysville Incident*." *African American Review* 30 (1996): 165–85.

Gloria Naylor

b. 1950

Works in the Anthology

The Women of Brewster Place, "The Two" (1982)

Other Works

Linden Hills (novel, 1985)
Mama Day (novel, 1988)
Bailey's Café (novel, 1992)
The Men of Brewster Place (novel, 1998)

Themes

- African Americans in urban settings
- Homosexual/lesbian romantic love
- Women's community
- Gossip
- Intraracial oppression, especially color-caste discrimination
- Befuddled black memory in a politically and economically diseased society
- Homophobia—palpable, malodorous, and killing
- Misogyny
- Sexual violence against African American women
- Maternal abuse

Characteristics

- Verbal irony
- Jaundiced point of view
- Invocation of antebellum spirituals

Questions

- Naylor uses a multigeneric hybrid structure to develop The Women of Brewster Place that is similar to the one Jean Toomer uses in Cane. Review the Harlem Renaissance text to appraise Toomer's influence on Naylor not only for the rhetorical development of her novel but also for the thematic content and rhetorical style of "The Two."
- Compare the portrait of black homophobia in Naylor's "The Two" and in Essex Hemphill's Conditions. According to the two authors,

what are the roots of this malady? What implicit suggestions do the two authors make about antidotes to it?

- In what ways does Naylor's "The Two" answer such homophobic 1960s black writers as Addison Gayle Jr., Hoyt Fuller, and Larry Neal? In what ways does it anticipate later such critiques of misogyny as Toni Morrison's *Song of Solomon* and Caryl Phillips's "West"?
- Summarize arguments by Naylor, Essex Hemphill, and Audre Lorde about the impact of homophobia on black families. Are you surprised that this social disease can disrupt the deep bond that African American writers like Lorraine Hansberry have collectively cited as a key characteristic of black families? Why or why not?
- Use Naylor's own textual evidence throughout "The Two" to support or refute Tee's definition of lesbianism as an intrinsic sexual orientation, a lá chocolate chip cookie.
- Use Naylor's own textual evidence throughout "The Two" to support or refute Lorraine's definition of lesbianism as a normative human condition—"a lousy human being who's somebody's daughter or somebody's friend or even somebody's enemy."
- What does Naylor's invocation of the antebellum spiritual "Swing Low Sweet Chariot" contribute to her story? What is the function of the song in "The Two"?

Bibliography

Cox, Karen C. "Magic and Memory in the Contemporary Story Cycle: Gloria Naylor and Louise Erdrich." *College English* 60 (1998): 150–73.

Henderson, Carol E. "In the Shadow of Streetlights: Loss, Restoration, and the Performance of Identity in Black Women's Literature of the City." *Alizes: Revue Angliciste de la Reunion* 22 (2002): 23–34.

Kelley, Margot Anne, ed. *Gloria Naylor's Early Novels.* Gainesville: UP of Florida, 1999.

Lattin, Patricia H. "Naylor's Engaged and Empowered Narrator." *CLA Journal* 41 (1998): 452–70.

O'Connor, Mary. "Subject, Voice, and Women in Some Contemporary Black American Women's Writing." In Lois Parkinson Zamora, ed., *Contemporary American Women Writers: Gender, Class, Ethnicity.* London: Longman, 1998. 32–50.

Puhr, Kathleen. "Healers in Gloria Naylor's Fiction." *Twentieth-Century Literature* 40 (1994): 518–28.

Rowell, Charles H. "An Interview with Gloria Naylor." *Callaloo* 20 (1997): 179–92.

Stave, Shirley A., ed. *Gloria Naylor: Strategy and Technique, Magic and Myth*. Newark: U of Delaware P, 2001.

Wardi, Anissa J. "The Scent of Sugarcane: Recalling *Cane* in *The Women of Brewster Place*." *CLA Journal* 42 (1999): 483–85.

Wilson, Charles Jr. *Gloria Naylor: A Critical Companion*. Westport, CT: Greenwood, 2001.

Rita Dove

b. 1952

Works in the Anthology

"David Walker (1785–1830)" (1980)
"Parsley" (1983)
"Receiving the Stigmata" (1983)
From *Thomas and Beulah* (1986)
"Pastoral" (1989)
From *Mother Love* (1995)

Other Works

Ten Poems (1977)
The Only Dark Spot in the Sky (poems, 1980)
The Yellow House on the Corner (poems, 1980)
Museum (poems, 1983)
Fifth Sunday (short stories, 1985)
The Other Side of the House (prose, 1988)
Grace Notes (poems, 1989)
Through the Ivory Gate (novel, 1992)
Mandolin (prose, 1982)
Selected Poems (1993)
The Darker Face of the Earth: A Verse Play in Fourteen Scenes (1994)

Themes

- African American history and experience
- Motherhood for African American women
- African American literary heritage
- African American familial lineage
- Recovery of African American history
- Black romantic love, sexual desire, and marriage

- Costs of African American self-assertion and self-expression
- Suppression of black women's sexual and social desires
- Great Migration
- Death, loss, transition, change as existential crises
- African American women's negotiations of the Cult of True Womanhood

Characteristics

- Revision of the traditional sonnet cycle
- Exploration and reimagining of autobiographical details
- Celebration of African American abolitionists
- Devotion to ancestors and an African American historical past
- Irony
- Subversion of classic literary texts

Teaching Strategies

- You might want to ask students to discuss the extent to which they think Dove's poetry validates a statement she has made about her interest in the sonnet and her experimentation with its conventions. In the forward to *An Intact World,* she explains:

  "Sonnet" literally means "little song." The sonnet is a *heile Welt,* an intact world where everything is in sync, from the stars down to the tiniest mite on a blade of grass. And if the 'true' sonnet reflects the music of the spheres, it then follows that any variation from the strictly Petrarchan or Shakespearean forms represents a world gone awry. Or does it? Can't form also be a talisman against disintegration? . . . I like how the sonnet comforts even while its prim borders (but what a pretty fence!) are stultifying; one is constantly bumping up against Order. The Demeter/Persephone cycle of betrayal and regeneration is ideally suited for this form since all three—mother-goddess, daughter-consort and poet—are struggling to sing in their chains.

- Listen with students to Dove's reading from *Thomas and Beulah* on the Audio Companion. Ask them to articulate and discuss their reactions to the poet's oral interpretation of her own poems.

Questions

- Trace the influence of Langston Hughes, Gwendolyn Brooks, and Claude McKay in Dove's poetry. What evidence is there in the *NAFAM* selections that Dove draws on the work of these poets?
- What is the effect of Dove's use of text from David Walker's *Appeal* on her "David Walker"? Review Walker's *Appeal* and identify the

common themes in the *Appeal* and Dove's poem. How does Dove's poem pay homage to Walker?

- Review the selections by Maria W. Stewart, who like Dove was a black woman highly influenced by Walker. What common features of the work by Stewart and Dove suggest their gendered revision of Walker's *Appeal*?

- Dove's "Parsley" addresses the issue of politicized speech: natives who could not or did not pronounce the "*r*" in *perejil*, the Spanish word for "parsley," were identified as Haitian and consequently massacred by Dominican dictator Rafael Trujillo. In addition, the poem denounces racialized oppression by imaginatively exploring the motivations for Trujillo's tyranny. Consider the effect of splitting the poem into sections (the cane fields and the palace), the way in which the rhythm and imagery of the first section changes in the second, and ways the two sections inform one another.

- What aspects of Dove's "Daystar," if any, link it to the tradition of African American literature about bondage and freedom?

- If readers are aware that Dove is African American, how does the absence of racial markers in "Receiving the Stigmata" affect readings of her poem? What are the effects of this—or any—poem without explicit racial designations?

- Compare Dove's "Receiving the Stigmata" to other poems by African Americans about lynching, including Angelina Weld Grimké's "Tenebris" and "The Black Finger," James Weldon Johnson's "Brothers," and Paul Laurence Dunbar's "The Haunted Oak."

- What particular fears of motherhood and childrearing do the poems in Dove's cycle *Mother Love* enumerate? What coping strategies does Dove imply black mothers use for their own sanity and survival as well as that of their children?

- How has the trope of the American Dream shaped the lives at the center of Dove's *Thomas and Beulah*? What images in the poem "The Oriental Ballerina" from that cycle most overtly capture the effect of the myth of the American Dream on the protagonists? Do the poems in *Thomas and Beulah* ultimately suggest that (black) men and women lead essentially separate lives, that there is little or no possibility of connection? On what do you base your response?

- How does the perspective in Dove's "Pastoral" affect your understanding of the significance of gender in that poem?

- How do Dove's sonnets compare with those by Claude McKay and Countee Cullen in terms of structure, imagery, and theme?

- Trace the development of the trope of the black family in the poems from Dove's *Thomas and Beulah* and *Mother Love*.

- If you are unfamiliar with it, research the Greek myth featuring Demeter and Persephone. Then review Dove's revision of the myth in lyric and sonnet form. How does Dove revise the myth? What are the effects of her translation of it into contemporary lyrics from the particular version you've researched?

- Compare Dove's use of Greek mythology to Phillis Wheatley's. What changes in African American women's revision of the ancient lore have occurred in the centuries between Wheatley's writing and Dove's?
- Discuss the effects of Dove's use of irony and subversion in the image of a (male) baby roasting on a spit like a "Virginia ham" in "Mother Love."
- Compare Dove's "Mother Love" with Gwendolyn Brooks's "the mother" and Lucille Clifton's "wishes for sons." What rhetorical strategies do the poets deploy to circumvent, critique, and/or revise stereotypes of African American mothers?

Bibliography

Cavalieri, Grace. "Rita Dove: An Interview." *The American Poetry Review* 24 (1995): 11–15.

Pellegrino, Joe. "Moving through Color: Rita Dove's *Thomas and Beulah*." *Kentucky Philological Review* 14 (1999): 27–31.

Pereira, Malin. *Rita Dove's Cosmopolitanism*. Urbana: U of Illinois P, 2003.

———. "'When the Pear Blossoms / Cast Their Pale Faces on / the Darker Face of the Earth': Miscegenation, the Primal Scene, and the Incest Motif in Rita Dove's Work." *African American Review* 36 (2002): 195–211.

Stefen, Therese. "Rooted Displacement in Form: Rita Dove's Sonnet Cycle *Mother Love*." In Joanne V. Gabbin, ed., *The Furious Flowering of African American Poetry*. Charlottesville: U of Virginia P, 1999. 60–76.

Walter Mosley

b. 1952

Works in the Anthology

"Equal Opportunity" (1998)

Other Works

Devil in a Blue Dress (novel, 1990)
A Red Death (novel, 1991)
White Butterfly (novel, 1992)
Black Betty (novel, 1994)
A Little Yellow Dog (novel, 1996)
Gone Fishin' (novel, 1997)
Always Outnumbered, Always Outgunned (short stories, 1998)
Black Genius: African American Solutions to African American Problems (editor, 1999)
Six Easy Pieces (short stories, 2000)
Workin' on the Chain Gang: Shaking Off the Dead Hand of History (nonfiction, 2000)
Futureland: Nine Stories of an Imminent World (2001)
Bad Boy Brawly Brown (novel, 2002)
What Next: A Memoir toward World Peace (2003)
Fear Itself (novel, 2003)

Themes

- Race discrimination in the U.S. work force
- Intersection of race, class, ethnicity, literacy, and economics
- Impact of inequitable and unjust penal system on African American workers
- Discrimination against black ex-felons in capitalist society
- Rehabilitation endeavors of black ex-felons in the United States
- African American manhood and masculine identities
- Black self-determination
- Black rage against bigotry
- Economic deprivation of blacks in South-Central Los Angeles
- African American male friendships and intimacies

Characteristics

- African American vernacular English and urban idioms
- Jazz idioms and rhythms influencing sentence structure

- Extensive use of dialogue between characters
- Short, terse sentences and paragraph structure
- African American male subjectivity and interiority
- Critique of socioeconomic injustices against African Americans

Questions

- Compare and contrast the hero of Mosley's story "Equal Opportunity" with the heroes in the ballads, folktales, and hip hop texts included in the vernacular section of *NAFAM*. What qualities do these heroes share?
- Isolate and analyze various passages in which Mosley describes Socrates' rage against the unjust treatment he experiences in "Equal Opportunity." Discuss your response to sentences such as "He was so mad that he balled his fists in his sleep twenty-five years after the fact."
- Analyze Mosley's concise, brusque rhetoric by reading closely the opening paragraphs of section 3 of "Equal Opportunity," ending before the space break with "His dream blared until dawn." Characterize Mosley's rhetorical style by paying attention to the section's visual imagery and textured details, to the active verbs, and to the mood and diction.
- What does the paragraph in which "a mouse in the kitchen jumped up and out of the potato pan" reveal about Mosley's sense of perspective in "Equal Opportunity"?
- In "Equal Opportunity," what evidence does Mosley provide to support Socrates' hunch that "some kind of joke was being played on this Connie Rodriguez," whose surname suggests that he is, like Socrates, an ethnic minority/man of color?

Bibliography

Berger, Roger A. "'The Black Dick': Race, Sexuality, and Discourse in the L.A. novels of Walter Mosley." *African American Review* 31 (1997): 281–95.

Jablon, Madelyn. "'Making the Faces Black': The African-American Detective Novel." In Larry E. Smith and John Rieder, eds., *Changing Representations of Minorities East and West*. Honolulu: College of Languages, Linguistics and Literature, U of Hawaii P, 1996. 26–40.

Lock, Helen. "Invisible Detection: The Case of Walter Mosley." *MELUS* 26 (2001): 77–87.

Pepper, Andrew. "Bridges and Boundaries: Race, Ethnicity, and the Contemporary American Crime Novel." In Kathleen Gregory Klein, ed., *Di-*

versity and Detective Fiction. Bowling Green, OH: Popular, 1999. 240–59.

Thompson, Clifford. "The Mystery Man of the Harlem Renaissance: Novelist Rudolph Fisher was a Forerunner of Walter Mosley." *Black Issues Book Review* 5 (2003): 63–65.

Wesley, Marilyn C. "Power and Knowledge in Walter Mosley's *Devil in a Blue Dress*." *African American Review* 35 (2001): 103–21.

Young, Mary, "Walter Mosley, Detective Fiction, and Black Culture." *Journal of Popular Culture* 32 (1998): 141–50.

Harryette Mullen

b. 1953

Works in the Anthology

From *Muse & Drudge* (1995)

Other Works

Tree Tall Woman (poems, 1981)
Trimmings (poems, 1991)
S*PeRM**K*T (poems, 1992)
Sleeping with the Dictionary (poems, 2002)

Themes

- Race and representation
- Gender issues
- African American identity formation
- Language, linguistics, rhetoric, and wordplay
- U.S. ethnic diversity
- Popular culture and American icons
- Black women as blues artists

Characteristics

- Innovative, experimental poetic style
- Revision of traditional lyric forms
- Hip hop revisions of Western traditions
- African American vernacular English and regional idioms

- Representations of orality
- Double entendre and sexual innuendo
- Postmodern popular culture allusions
- Engagement with other poets; intertextuality

Questions

- Research the visual art and iconography by Kara Walker, and compare and contrast the effects of Walker's use of the silhouette with the effects of Mullen's rhetorical manipulations of the hip hop lyric.
- Review the blues lyrics in the "Vernacular" section of *NAFAM* to identify the sources of Mullen's witty revisions. How do you characterize this particular poetic intertextuality?
- Compare the use of flight and bird imagery in Mullen's poetry to the deployment of similar images in Toni Morrison's *Song of Solomon*.
- Mullen has identified Zora Neale Hurston as a primary influence on her poetry. Review *Mules and Men* to determine the ways in which Mullen's poetry bears Hurston's mark.
- After reading the selections from Mullen's work, analyze the title *Muse & Drudge*. To what do you think it alludes?

Bibliography

Frost, Elisabeth. "An Interview with Harryette Mullen." *Contemporary Literature* 41 (2000): 397–422.

Hogue, Cynthia. "Beyond the Frame of Whiteness: Harryette Mullen's Revisionary Border Work." In Laura Hinton and Cynthia Hogue, eds., *We Who Love to Be Astonished: Experimental Women's Writing and Performance Poetics*. Tuscaloosa: U of Alabama P, 2002. 81–89.

Mullen, Harryette, and Stephen Yenser. "Theme and Variations on Robert Hayden's Poetry." *Antioch Review* 55 (1997): 160–75.

Williams, Emily Ann. "Harryette Mullen, 'The Queen of Hip Hyperbole': An Interview." *African American Review* 34 (2000): 701–9.

Essex Hemphill

1957–1995

Works in the Anthology

From *Conditions* (1986)

Works

Earth Life (poems, 1985)
Ceremonies (poems and prose, 1992)
Brother to Brother: Writings by Black Gay Men (co-editor, 1991)

Themes

- Racialized and gendered violence as social disease
- Intraracial relations and internalized racism
- Irony of homophobia in the United States
- Celebration of gay romantic commitment and union
- "The blind leading the blind" as critique of white patriarchy

Characteristics

- African American vernacular English and postmodern black slang
- Literary allusion to key iconic texts
- Normalization of gay romantic love
- Formalistic and structural critique of race and gender hegemony

Questions

- Note the use of the first and second person in *Conditions* XXI. To whom is Hemphill's speaker referring when he uses "you" and "we"?
- What stereotypes of African American women does *Conditions* XXI reference? To what extent does Hemphill undercut these stereotypes?
- If Hemphill's *Conditions* XXI is a riddle, what is its answer or resolution? What connection does it make between deafness and unfulfilled or impractical promises? Between deafness and unawareness? Why must the "seven blind men" be blind? How can one determine whether the speaker of the poem is one of its "seven blind men"?
- Research recent scholarly and critical discussions of gay and lesbian marriage; then reread Hemphill's *Conditions* XXIV. Discuss your responses to the readings and the poem with your classmates.
- Hemphill's *Conditions* XXIV alludes to several iconic texts, including

the Judeo-Christian Bible and Martin Luther King Jr.'s "I Have a Dream" speech. Identify these allusions, and comment on Hemphill's use of them. Is his usage ironic? Why or why not?

Bibliography

Glave, Thomas. "(Re-) recalling Essex Hemphill: Words to Our Now." *Callaloo* 23 (2000): 278–84.

McBride, Dwight A. "Can the Queen Speak? Racial Essentialism, Sexuality and the Problem of Authority." *Callaloo* 21 (1998): 363–80.

Sharpe, Christina Elizabeth. "Racialized Fantasies on the Internet." *Signs* 24 (1999): 1089–96.

Caryl Phillips

b. 1958

Works in the Anthology

Crossing the River, "West" (1993)

Other Works

The Final Passage (novel, 1985)
A State of Independence (novel, 1986)
The European Tribe (travelogue, 1987)
Higher Ground (novel, 1989)
Cambridge (novel, 1991)
The Nature of Blood (novel, 1997)
Atlantic Sound (memoir, 2000)
A New World Order: Selected Essays (2001)

Themes

- Shifting identities
- Impact of the past on the present
- Integration of African and African American histories
- Longevity of Middle Passage
- African diaspora and the experiences of Africans outside Africa
- Antebellum Great Migration westward
- Racism in U.S. economics

- Heterosexual romantic love
- Relationships between women
- Cross-cultural and interracial relations
- Intersections of imperialism, racism, and slavery
- Slave families, slave kinships
- Black survival and self-determination

Characteristics

- Multiple perspectives and voices to convey cross-culturalism and polyvocality
- Dreamscape
- Nonlinear representations of space, time, memory, and reality
- Interior monologue and stream of consciousness
- Conventions of "Wild West" and frontier literature

Questions

- Review slave narratives written by other authors in *NAFAM*. What rhetorical and thematic conventions does Phillips's "West" share with such antebellum narratives as Harriet Jacobs's *Incidents in the Life of a Slave Girl* and William Wells Brown's *Clotel*? What expectations do you have of similarities between Phillips's fiction and Jacobs's *Incidents*, given the authors' gender and genre differences? To what extent are your expectations fulfilled?
- What similarities and differences do you observe between the slave-woman's narrative at the center of Phillips's *Crossing the River* and Toni Morrison's *Song of Solomon* as two stories that analyze the effect of slavery on former slaves and/or descendants of slaves? Do you think Phillips and Morrison ultimately say similar—or different—things about the persistence of the memory of slavery?
- Examine the representation of the commodification of enslaved people through Martha's interior narrative in *Crossing the River*. What rhetorical conventions does Phillips deploy to portray this "peculiar" socioeconomic institution?
- Identify Martha's recurring memories in "West." What criteria did you use to identify them? How does Phillips use these memories to comment on the nature of slavery and the nature of enslaved women? What comment do the memories make about slaves and slavery?
- Analyze the points of view offered in "West." What does Phillips gain by narrating some sections from a third-person omniscient perspective and other sections in first-person singular?

- Phillips has cited James Baldwin and Baldwin's mentor Richard Wright as two key influences on his fiction. Review the *NAFAM* selections by Baldwin and Wright to determine traces of their influence in Phillips's "West."
- In "The Site of Memory" Toni Morrison laments the lack of "mention of [slave narrators'] interior life" in black antebellum autobiographies. Caryl Phillips, like Morrison, tries to "fill in the blanks that the slave narratives left" in their accounts of their lives. Read both "West" and "The Site of Memory" to evaluate Morrison's critical principles and Phillips's literary achievement.

Bibliography

Goddard, Horace I. "Travel Discourse in Caryl Phillips' *The Final Passage* and *A State of Independence*." *Kola* 14 (2002): 39–52.

Julien, Claude. "Surviving through a Pattern of Timeless Moments: A Reading of Caryl Phillips's *Crossing the River*." In Henry Louis Gates, Jr. and Carl Pedersen, eds., *Black Imagination and the Middle Passage*. Oxford, UK: Oxford UP, 1999. 86–95.

Ledent, Benedicte. "'Overlapping Territories, Intertwined Histories': Cross-Culturality in Caryl Phillips's *Crossing the River*." *Journal of Commonwealth Literature* 30 (1995): 55–63.

Low, Gail. "'A Chorus of Common Memory': Slavery and Redemption in Caryl Phillips's *Cambridge* and *Crossing the River*." *Research in African Literatures* (Dec. 1998): 122–42.

Edwidge Danticat

b. 1969

Works in the Anthology

Breath, Eyes, Memory, Chaps. 1, 35 (1994)

Other Works

Krik?Krak! (novel, 1995)
The Farming of Bones (novel, 1998)
The Butterfly's Way: Voices from the Haitian Diaspora in the United States (editor, 2001)

The Beacon Best of 2000: Great Writing by Women and Men of All Colors and Cultures (editor, 2000)
After the Dance: A Walk Through Carnival in Jacmel, Haiti (travelogue,
2002)

Themes

- Haitian-American cultural beliefs, values, and ways
- African spirituality and sacred traditions
- Afro-Caribbean communal relations
- Material poverty
- Immigration blues
- Border crossings
- Power and necessity of storytelling
- Memory in African diasporas
- Bicultural and bilingual *Bildungsroman*
- Matrilineage and mother love
- Mother-daughter relationships
- Intergenerational family conflicts
- Socioeconomic class consciousness
- Existential freedom

Characteristics

- Exploration and evaluation of the costs of geographical and cultural migration
- Chronicle of difficulty of "personal translation" into English language
- Critique of past and present sociogeographical locations
- Bilingual discourse
- Structural and thematic repetition, echo, and reiteration

Questions

- The *NAFAM* headnote to Danticat suggests that the Haitian-American author's "fusion of celebration and critique" of her native culture is comparable to a similar fusion found in texts by such African American women writers as Zora Neale Hurston, Toni Morrison, and Alice Walker. Choose one of these writers, and review one of her works to assess the validity of this comparison. Identify passages in both Danticat's work and the second author's that illustrate their appreciation and analysis of the cultures that shaped them.
- What does Danticat achieve by opening her first novel, *Breath, Eyes, Memory*, with the regular visit of a shape-shifting numbers runner?

What readerly expectations does she set up with her description of the lottery agent's stop at the home of Sophie and Tante Atie?

- Analyze Danticat's use of communication media in the first and last chapters of *Breath, Eyes, Memory*. What are the effects of centering Chapters 1 and 35 on audiocassettes with messages from or about Sophie's mother?

- Comment on circularity in the first and last chapters of *Breath, Eyes, Memory*, paying particular attention to the narrator's repetition of the idea that "people die here everyday." What are the effects of this repetition?

- The final chapter of *Breath, Eyes, Memory* describes the narrator's rush into a canebrake. Review Jean Toomer's multigeneric work *Cane*, searching for any influences on Danticat's novel.

- The final chapter of *Breath, Eyes, Memory* echoes two phrases closely associated with the novelist Toni Morrison: "to pass on" and "unspeakable acts." Certainly, Danticat invokes these phrases to honor her literary elder. Review the *NAFAM* excerpts from *Song of Solomon* to determine other, more subtle traces of Morrison's work in Danticat's novel.

Bibliography

Gerber, Nancy F. "Binding the Narrative Thread: Storytelling and the Mother-Daughter Relationship in Edwidge Danticat's *Breath, Eyes, Memory*." *Journal of the Association for Research on Mothering* 2 (2000): 188–99.

Herndon, Gerise. "Returns to Native Lands, Reclaiming the Other's Language: Kincaid and Danticat." *Journal of International Women's Studies* 3 (2001): 1–10.

Lyon Johnson, Kelli. "Both Sides of the Massacre: Collective Memory and Narrative on Hispaniola." *Mosaic* [Winnipeg] 36 (2003): 75–92.

N'Zengou Tayo, Marie Jose. "Rewriting Folklore: Traditional Beliefs and Popular Culture in Edwidge Danticat's *Breath, Eyes, Memory* and *Krik?Krak!*" *MaComere: Journal of the Association of Caribbean Women Writers and Scholars* 2 (2000): 123–40.

Shemak, April. "Remembering Hispaniola: Edwidge Danticat's *The Farming of the Bones*." *Modern Fiction Studies* 48 (2002): 83–113.

Colson Whitehead

b. 1969

Works in the Anthology

From *John Henry Days* (novel, 2001)

Other Works

The Intuitionist (novel, 1999)

Themes

- Superficiality, fraudulence, banality, and insecurity
- African American masculinity
- Gluttony
- The nature of the hero
- The African American heroic quest
- Disparagement of black folk traditions
- Trivialization of black oral histories
- Speciousness of newspaper culture and journalistic truth

Characteristics

- Satire, irony, and sarcasm
- Postmodern hybrid of autobiography, folk legend, and historical fact
- Black vernacular folktales
- Critique of racism and white supremacy
- Exposé of mass media, especially print and news media

Questions

- Review the folktale of John Henry in the vernacular section of *NAFAM*. In what specific ways has Whitehead revised the story's hero in *John Henry Days*? What does his novel ultimately contend about the notion of heroism at the heart of the legend?
- In *John Henry Days*, the lives of fictive John Henry and the fictional protagonist J. Sutter merge. What does Whitehead gain by using a young black male folk singer as the pivot on which these two lives intersect?
- Does the excerpt from *John Henry Days* suggest that the legendary John Henry triumphed in his struggle to outdo the machine—or

rather that he lost? What kind of struggle does Whitehead create for his postmodern protagonist?

- How do you think Whitehead would position his (anti)hero of *John Henry Days* vis-à-vis W. E. B. Du Bois's Talented Tenth?
- Reviews of Whitehead's novels favorably compare them with Toni Morrison's. A more apt comparison, however, perhaps lies in the satire of such writers as Wallace Thurman of the Harlem Renaissance and Ishmael Reed of the Black Arts era. Review the *NAFAM* selections by these ironists to determine whether *John Henry Days* perpetuates the black satire of these earlier authors.

Bibliography

"Eavesdropping (A Conversation Between Colson Whitehead and Walter Mosley)." *Book* (May 2001): 44–51.

Mari, Christopher. "Colson Whitehead." *Current Biography* 62 (2001): 86–89.

Sherman, Suzan. "Colson Whitehead." *BOMB* 76 (2001): 74–80.

Teaching Literature since 1975

What should be apparent almost immediately about this period is that many of the writers included here were highly influenced and/or affected by the Black Arts era. This period invites emphases such as postcoloniality, intertextuality, metatextuality, and literature as history. You might want to launch your students' investigation of the last three decades of African American literature with a summary of the academic debates about the advantages and disadvantages of literary historical periodization. This grounding might prove especially helpful to students for whom "past history" is more alien than the relevant facts of the recent past.

On its own historical terms, a salient feature of literature since 1975 is its preoccupation with the impact of the past on the present and, moreover, the simultaneity of time, the redundancy of notions of "past" in considerations of "the present." The excerpts from John Edgar Wideman's *Damballah*, Gayl Jones's *Corregidora*, and Caryl Phillips's *Crossing the River*, as well as such shorter texts as Charles Johnson's "The Education of Mingo" and Rita Dove's "David Walker (1785–1830)," all revisit slavery for their settings. Other texts—perhaps chief among them Toni Morrison's *Song of Solomon* and Edwidge Danticat's *Breath, Eyes, Memory*—focus on the more immediate, personal pasts of individual coming-of-age experiences, of family and ancestral relations. The poetry of Rita Dove and Maya Angelou and the stories of Jamaica Kincaid and Albert Murray as well as the dramas by Adrienne Kennedy and August Wilson are relevant here. Many writers, like Gloria Naylor and Essex Hemphill, interrogate ideas of community, gender and sexual politics, and strategies of survival. One unifying pattern for considering these very diverse writers is their representation of time as cyclical, as more spiral than linear—as developed, too, in Samuel Delany's "Atlantis: Model 1924" and Nathaniel Mackey's *Djbot Boghostus's Run*.

Besides Jones and Mackey, Clarence Major and Sherley Anne Williams also deliberately use music for both rhetorical form and subject matter. Select recordings on the Audio Companion to engage students in discussions about the particular deployment of music in this period, about the ways it complements or deviates from the use of music in literature of the Harlem Renaissance or the Black Arts era. In addition, ask students to research other recordings from the earlier periods to present and analyze in additional class discussions. What relationships do they find in both African American *written* literature since 1975 and black *vernacular* traditions since 1975?

In literature since 1975, African American women writers have emerged in number and in force, essentially (re)defining the tradition. From the 1970s until very recently, more African American women writers were being published by more publishers for a larger and more varied reading public than ever before in U.S. history. To understand this phenomenon, we must consider it and the women's writing as an outgrowth of the Black Arts era as well as within the context of the late-twentieth-century struggles for women's rights, international peace, and other empowering concepts. Many of the women writers in the closing section of *NAFAM* began their public lives in these movements and began asserting their literary voices through increased educational opportunities as well as changes in school curricula, in the publishing industry, and in reading tastes across the nation. These women opened up ways of viewing African American life even as they challenged these and other movements to recognize their exclusive tendencies and to live up to their potential and rhetoric. Often they were addressing issues and themes that were new and that challenged many of the long-held beliefs concerning relationships, sexuality, or community. For instance, both Paule Marshall in "Reena" and Gayl Jones in *Corregidora* develop women characters who question the centrality of men and marriage to black women's lives.

Similarly, relationships between black mothers and their children—indeed, matrilineal relationships of various sorts—are the focus of works by Maya Angelou, Ernest Gaines, Jamaica Kincaid, and Alice Walker. Lucille Clifton makes "wishes for sons" and pays "homage to my hips" while Ntozake Shange titles her work *Nappy Edges* to challenge beauty and health myths heretofore spoken (about) only in private, intraracial settings. Angelou, Dove, Walker, Shange, Naylor, Danticat: the list is rich and ripe for broadening students' understanding of African American women writers' contributions to black literature and to revisions of the many ways in which they, like their brother writers, view themselves and assume themselves to be viewed by others as artists, interpreters, reporters, and contributors to the United States and its literature.

Genres

Poetry

Angelou
Major
Williams
Walker
Cliff
Komunyakaa
Mackey
Dove
Mullen
Hemphill

Drama

Kennedy
Wilson

Prose Narrative/Critical Theory

Marshall
Morrison
Walker

Autobiography

Angelou
Wideman

Short Story

Marshall
Gaines
Major

Delany
Williams
Walker
Cliff
Butler
Johnson
Mosley

Novel

Murray
Morrison
Forrest
Wideman
Walker
Mackey
Jones
Kincaid
Bradley
Naylor
Phillips
Danticat
Whitehead

Bibliography

Clark, Keith, ed. *Contemporary Black Men's Fiction and Drama*. Urbana: U of Illinois P, 2001.

Dawahare, Anthony. *Nationalism, Marxism, and African American Literature between the Wars: A New Pandora's Box*. Jackson: UP of Mississippi, 2003.

In Black and White: Conversations with African American Writers [video; 151 min.]. San Francisco: California Newsreel and SSR-RTSI Swiss Television, 1992.

Kiuchi, Toru, Robert J. Butler, and Yoshinobu Hakutani, eds. *The Critical Response in Japan to African American Writers*. New York: Lang, 2003.

Levin, Amy K. *Africanism and Authenticity in African-American Women's Novels*. Gainesville: UP of Florida, 2003.

Major, Clarence, ed. *The Garden Thrives: Twentieth-Century African-American Poetry*. New York: HarperCollins, 1996.

Metting, Fred. "The Possibilities of Flight: The Celebration of Our Wings in *Song of Solomon, Praisesong for the Widow*, and *Mama Day*." *Southern Folklore* 55 (1998): 145–67.

Mitchell, Angelyn. *The Freedom to Remember: Narrative, Slavery, and Gender in Contemporary Black Women's Fiction*. New Brunswick, NJ: Rutgers UP, 2002.

Monteith, Sharon. *Advancing Sisterhood?: Interracial Friendships in Contemporary Southern Fiction*. Athens: U of Georgia P, 2000.

Taylor, Carole Anne. *The Tragedy and Comedy of Resistance: Reading Modernity through Black Women's Fiction*. Philadelphia: U of Pennsylvania P, 2000.

Thomas, Lorenzo. *Extraordinary Measures: Afrocentric Modernism and Twentieth-Century American Poetry*. Tuscaloosa: U of Alabama P, 2000.

Vendler, Helen. *The Given and the Made: Recent American Poets*. Cambridge, MA: Harvard UP, 1995.

Vickroy, Laurie. *Trauma and Survival in Contemporary Fiction*. Charlottesville: U of Virginia P, 2002.

Walters, Wendy W. "'One of Dese Mornings, Bright and Fair, / Take My Wings and Cleave de Air': The Legend of the Flying Africans and Diasporic Consciousness." *MELUS* 22 (1997): 3–30.

Wolff, Janice M. "Teaching in the Contact Zones: The Myth of Safe Houses." In Janice M. Wolff, ed., *Professing in the Contact Zone: Bringing Theory and Practice Together*. Urbana: National Council of Teachers of English, 2002. 240–56.

Essay and Exam Questions

Many of the questions provided throughout the course guide have been designed for easy translation into research projects and essay or exam questions. Ideas for examination questions can also be gleaned from the "Teaching" sections for each literary period in this guide.

1. For courses with a postcolonial or diasporic emphasis, Giselle Anatol suggests:

   > To [provide a] lesson on stereotypes, during the second class meeting I require first-year students to write short essays on what they think of when they hear the word 'Caribbean.' The images elicited from this exercise are not difficult to predict: palm tress swaying in balmy breezes [etc.] After sharing the lists, I ask the students to consider where these images come from and why these scenes might be the most popular. Recognizing the tourist economy, U.S. political races, and other factors starts to open some of their eyes to reasons for the generation of these stereotypes (62–63).

   See Anatol, "'Passing/Out' in the Classroom: Eradicating Binaries of Identity," in *Women Faculty of Color in the White Classroom*, edited by Lucila Vargas.

2. Trace the subversion of the Anglo-American epistolary tradition in African American literature by drawing on such texts as the folktale

"How to Write a Letter," "The Epistle of Sweetie Reed" in Forrest's *There Is a Tree More Ancient Than Eden*, the slaveholder's letter in Wideman's *Damballah*, and Celie's letter about God in Walker's *The Color Purple*.

3. Trace the development of the figure of the orator/preacher, beginning with the earliest African American sermons and orations, including the folktale "Big Talk" and the speech by the nineteenth-century preacher-activist Sojourner Truth and ending with a monologue by Bynum in Wilson's *Joe Turner's Come and Gone* or with Robby's oral history of his own speechmaking in Wideman's *Brothers and Keepers*.

4. In Williams's "Tell Martha Not to Moan," the bluesman Time tells his lover: "'When a woman take the blues, She tuck her head and cry. But when a man catch the blues, he grab his shoes and slide.'" Analyze the blues lyrics and other texts in *NAFAM*, including Jones's *Corregidora* and Mullen's poems in *Muse & Drudge,* to determine whether or not a woman can also "grab [her] shoes and slide" away from/with the blues.

5. What evidence does *NAFAM* provide in pre-1970s vernacular and written traditions that rap and hip hop are not new?

6. The plots of two important novels, Morrison's *Song of Solomon* and Whitehead's *John Henry Days*, center on the trope of the quest. What do these post–civil rights movement texts posit as worthy quests for black people today? What do they imply African Americans *should be* seeking in the twenty-first century?

7. Professor Bertram Ashe asks students about ways that Hurston's "How It Feels to Be Colored Me" and Hughes's "The Negro Artist and the Racial Mountain" answer these questions about black self-actualization:

   • How should we improve our condition? Accommodation or resistance? Nonviolence or self-defense? Integration or separation?
   • How should we attain our freedom, both during and after slavery?

   Where does each essay come down, in terms of these questions? How do the points made in each essay move the text closer to one set of possible "improvements" than the other? What do your efforts to situate the text within this context say about the questions?

8. Literary critics often treat African American male figures in oppositional pairs: for example, John Henry versus Stackolee, Douglass versus Delany, Washington versus Du Bois, Wright versus Ellison, and Martin Luther King Jr. versus Malcolm X. Use *NAFAM* texts by one of these pairs to reevaluate the conventional critical assessment of the authors as ideologically opposed. What ideological forces seem to drive their juxtaposition as antagonists?

9. Brown's *Clotel* is based in part on the legendary sexual relationship of Thomas Jefferson and his slave Sally Hemings. Since Jefferson was one of the writers of the Declaration of Independence and a president of the United States, this story was particularly appropriate for Brown's argument that slavery thrived *because* of the complicity of the country's leaders and that moral degeneracy was not limited to overseers and slaveholders. According to the selections in "Literature since 1975," what moral debates ensuing from the slavery issue remain significant in U.S. life and race relations today? What moral questions have recently arisen in the wake of DNA tests on Jefferson's and Heming's descendants?

10. Use *NAFAM* texts to support or refute the current arguments for slavery reparations.

11. In "What to the Slave Is the Fourth of July?" Douglass states, "Oppression makes a wise man mad." Working across or within historical periods, analyze texts in *NAFAM* that support Douglass's claim. What do short stories like Chesnutt's "The Wife of His Youth" and Walker's "Everyday Use" suggest about class oppression among African Americans? What do poems by Lorde and Hemphill suggest about sexual-orientation oppression among African Americans?

12. Trace the representation of economic disparity and the economic exploitation of black labor in texts throughout *NAFAM*, from *A Narrative of the Life and Adventures of Venture* to Dove's poems in *Thomas and Beulah*. Analyze the texts you select through the lens of the folktale "'Ah'll Beatcher Makin' Money.'"

13. In June 2003 the Supreme Court ostensibly upheld affirmative action in the U.S. academy. What do the most recent literary works in *NAFAM*—by Danticat and Whitehead—suggest about the impact of traditional academic pursuits on black sociopolitical advancement? What problematic issues do other texts that more directly address ed-

ucation and literacy issues, such as Mosley's "Equal Opportunity" and Naylor's "The Two," define as complexities of blacks and "book-learning"?

14. August 2003 marked the fortieth anniversary of the 1963 March on Washington and the oration that Martin Luther King Jr. delivered there. Use the selections in "Literature since 1975" to assess the fulfillment of King's dream. According to these texts, has King's dream been fulfilled? What setbacks have there been to black citizenship and civil rights since 1963? Since the Clinton administration elevated several ethnic minorities to key leadership positions in national government?

15. Professor Kristin Herzog poses these questions about violence against blacks and about war as a concept and trope in African American literature:

> How does racial location affect authorial attitudes toward violence and nonviolence? How are we to determine what violence is or is not? Are whites justified in the violent suppression of 'insurrections,' whereas blacks are commanded to be nonviolent? Would it have been wrong . . . for Linda Brent to kill Dr. Flint, whereas governments can authorize massive killing to keep order or to win a war? (140).

> See "*Uncle Tom's Cabin* and *Incidents in the Life of a Slave Girl*: The Issue of Violence," in *Approaches to Teaching Stowe's* Uncle Tom's Cabin, edited by Ammons and Belasco. Trace definitions and declarations of war across African American literature, from *David Walker's Appeal* through the Black Arts era to Komunyakaa's "Facing It." How do women writers insinuate the twin themes of war and violence in such texts as Terry's "Bars Fight," Marshall's "Reena," Butler's "Bloodchild," and Walker's "Advancing Luna"?

16. Specify ways that details about a writer, such as class and gender, affect your expectations of that writer as well as affect technique or content. For example, with what readerly expectations do you begin a text that opens by asserting, "I was born a slave, but I never knew it till six years of happy childhood had passed away"? Identify texts in *NAFAM* to which you had a particular initial response that altered significantly as you continued reading.

17. Moral and psychological conflicts that arise out of racial discrimination or class differences concern many writers of African American literature, including Chesnutt, J. W. Johnson, Larsen, and Kennedy. Discuss

the representation of black emotional anguish in texts by these authors and others in *NAFAM*, such as Fauset, West, and Wright. Then contrast these texts with others by authors like Hughes and Hurston, who seem purposely to represent black interiority quite differently.

18. Analyze the rhetorical risks taken by African American writers whose texts reconstruct madness or psychic trauma. What racialized responsibility do writers insinuate in such texts as Séjour's "The Mulatto," Walker's "In Search of Our Mothers' Gardens," Morrison's *Song of Solomon*, and Major's "Chicago Heat"?

19. What risks do women writers run in depicting the anger of African American women? Consider the overt representation of gender, womanhood, and fury by Stewart, Keckley, Wilson, Cooper, Hopkins, Petry, Jordan, and Clifton. What alternative strategies are deployed by such women writers as Bonner, Brooks, Hansberry, and Sanchez? Or *are* their strategies different?

20. Trace the recurring figure of Emmett Till as a trope of violence against African Americans in literature produced after 1959.

21. Trace the public library as a recurring figure in African American literature after Richard Wright. Read back to slave narratives by Equiano and Douglass to analyze the intersection of the acquisition of literacy by slaves and the patronage of public libraries by descendants of slaves.

22. Joycelyn Elders, an African American, was dismissed from her position as U.S. Surgeon General during the Clinton administration in part for her efforts to publicize issues of sexual activity and sexual safety. Long before Elders, African American women were victimized by sexual stereotypes. Analyze issues of sexual assault or proscription in *NAFAM* texts, including Jacobs's *Incidents in the Life of a Slave Girl*, Dunbar Nelson's "Violets," Petry's "Like a Winding Sheet," Walker's "Advancing Luna," and Naylor's "The Two."

23. Analyze rhetorical conventions of postmodern literature by African American writers. Begin with an exploration of metatextuality and hybridity in texts by Reed, Mackey, Mullen, and Cortez. Identify ways that texts by these authors are anticipated and foregrounded in Du Bois's *The Souls of Black Folk* and in Toomer's *Cane*.

24. Morrison's essay "The Site of Memory" and her Tanner Lecture argue that the role of whiteness in the study of black literature has been

greater than critics and scholars have admitted. What *NAFAM* texts suggest, conversely, that whiteness *has* been central to black letters before Morrison's pronouncement? What *NAFAM* texts argue that whiteness has *no* place in the study of African American life and literature? On which side of the issue do you fall? Use *NAFAM* texts to determine and explain your position.

Multimedia Resources for Teaching African American Literature

African-American Sheet Music: 1850–1920. Available at: memory.loc.gov/ ammem/award97/rpbhtml/aasmhome.html.

Angelou, Maya. *Even the Stars Look Lonesome* [read by author]. New York: Random House, 2001.

Bambara, Toni Cade. *The Bombing of Osage Avenue* [documentary; 58 min.]. Philadelphia: WHYY/Scribe Video, 1986.

bell hooks: Cultural Criticism and Transformation [videorecording; 62 min.]. Northampton, MA: Media Education Foundation, 1997.

Davis, Zeinabu Irene. *Mother of the River* [film on slavery; 28 min.]. New York: Women Make Movies, 1995.

God's Trombones: A Trilogy of African American Poems [live sound recording]. New York: 1993.

God's Trombones: A Trilogy of African American Poems [videorecording; 30 min.]. Tapeworm Video. Valencia, CA. Distributed by billy budd films, 1994.

Hansberry, Lorraine. Audio Collection: *A Raisin in the Sun* and *To Be Young, Gifted, and Black* [read by author]. New York: Harper Audio, 2001.

Hunte, O. D., and Extreme Music Library. *Hip Hop* [CD]. Princeton, NJ: Films of the Humanities and Sciences, 1998.

Hurston, Zora Neale. *Every Tongue Got to Confess* [500 folktales, read by Ruby Dee and Ossie Davis]. New York: Harper Audio, 2001.

Katz, Joel. *Strange Fruit* [video; 57 min.]. San Francisco: Oniera Films, dist. by California Newsreel, 2003.

Mekuria, Salem. *As I Remember It* [videorecording on Dorothy West; 56 min.]. New York: Women Make Movies, 1991.

Raimist, Rachel. *Nobody Knows My Name* [videotape of women who love hip hop; 58 min.]. New York: Women Make Movies, 1999.

Royals, Demetria. *Conjure Women* [documentary film of four black women artists; 85 min.]. New York: Women Make Movies, 1995.

Shaman, William, and Peter G. Adamson, comp. and ed. *Voices of Black America: Historical Recordings of Speeches, Poetry, Humor and Drama.* Williamsville, NY: Naxos AudioBooks, 2001.

Voice of the Poet: Langston Hughes. New York: Random House, 2001.

Wade in the Water: African American Sacred Music Tradition [26 segments]. Smithsonian Folkways Recordings, National Public Radio, 1993.

Selected Bibliography

Multimedia

Bates, Randolph. "Teaching Film and *A Raisin in the Sun*." *Louisiana English Journal* 4 (1997): 62–67.

[*J.D.B.*] *DeBow's Review: Agricultural, Commercial, Industrial Progress and Resources*. New Orleans, 1846–52; New Orleans and Washington, D.C., 1853–60; New Orleans and Charleston, SC, 1861–62; Columbia, SC, 1864; New Orleans, etc., 1866–80. Available at www.hti. umich.edu/m/moajrnl/browsejournals/debo.html.

Emerson, Rana A. "'Where My Girls At?' Negotiating Black Womanhood in Music Videos." *Gender and Society* 16 (2002): 115–36.

Hudson, Shawna. "Re-Creational Television: The Paradox of Change and Continuity within Stereotypical Iconography." *Sociological Inquiry* 68 (1998): 242–58.

McCarthy, Cameron. *Sound Identities: Popular Music and the Cultural Politics of Education*. New York: Lang, 1999.

Paris, Peter J. "Basic African American Values: Gifts to the World." *Soundings* 81 (1998): 553–70.

Sotiropoulous, Karen. "African-American Sheet Music: 1850–1920." *Journal of American History* 88 (2001): 1225–26.

Visual

Kimball, Robert, and William Bolcom. *Reminiscing with Noble Sissie and Eubie Blake*. New York: Cooper Square, 2000.

Turner, Patricia A. *Ceramic Uncles and Celluloid Mammies: Black Images and Their Influence on Culture*. New York: Anchor, 1994.

Vernacular

Brown, Fahamisha Patricia. *Performing the Word: African American Poetry as Vernacular Culture*. New Brunswick, NJ: Rutgers UP, 1998.

Butler, Jerry, with Earl Smith. *Only the Strong Survive*. Bloomington: Indiana UP, 2000.

Campbell, Kermit. "'Real Niggaz's Don't Die': African American Students Speaking Themselves into Their Writing." In Carol Severine, Juan C. Guerra, and Johnnella E. Butler, eds., *Writing in Multicultural Settings*. New York: MLA, 1997. 67–78.

Forman, Murray. *The 'Hood Comes First: Race, Space, and Place in Rap and Hip-Hop*. Middletown, CT: Wesleyan UP, 2002.

Jablon, Madelyn. "Womanist Storytelling: The Voice of the Vernacular." In Julia Brown, ed., *Ethnicity and the American Short Story*. New York: Garland, 1997. 47–62.

Keyes, Cheryl Lynette. *Rap Music and Street Consciousness*. Urbana: U of Illinois P, 2002.

Kimball, Robert, and William Bolcom. *Reminiscing with Noble Sissie and Eubie Blake*. New York: Cooper Square, 2000.

Light, Alan, ed. *Vibe: The Vibe History of Hip Hop*. New York: Three Rivers, 1999.

Major, Clarence. *Juba to Jive: A Dictionary of African-American Slang*. New York: Penguin, 1994.

Nelson, Angela M. S., ed. *This Is How We Flow: Rhythm in Black Culture*. Columbia: South Carolina UP, 1999.

Perry, Theresa, and James W. Fraser, eds. *Freedom's Plow: Teaching in the Multicultural Classroom*. New York: Routledge, 1993.

Scanlon, Larry. "News from Heaven: Vernacular Time in Langston Hughes's *Ask Your Mama*." *Callaloo* 25 (2002): 45–65.

Smitherman, Geneva. *Black Talk: Words and Phrases from the Hood to the Amen Corner*. Boston: Houghton Mifflin, 2000.

Pedagogical

Anatol, Gizelle L. "'Passing/Out' in the Classroom: Eradicating Binaries of Identity." In Vargas, *Women Faculty of Color*. 55–72.

Berlin, James A. *Rhetorics, Poetics, and Cultures: Refiguring College English Studies*. Urbana, IL: National Council of Teachers of English, 1996.

Brown, Kimberly Nichele. "Useful Anger: Confrontation and Challenge in the Teaching of Gender, Race, and Violence." In Vargas, *Women Faculty of Color*. 89–107.

Carson, Diane, and Lester D. Friedman, eds. *Shared Differences: Multicultural Media and Practical Pedagogy*. Urbana: U of Illinois P, 1995.

Crouther, Lou-Ann. "'Results Matter': When the Other Teacher Teaches English in the Bluegrass State." In Vargas, *Women Faculty of Color*. 219–35.

Dastenell, Louis A. Jr., and William F. Pinar, eds. *Understanding Curriculum as Racial Text: Representations of Identity and Difference in Education*. Albany: State U of New York P, 1993.

Downing, David B., ed. *Changing Classroom Practices: Resources for Literary and Cultural Studies*. Urbana, IL: National Council of Teachers of English, 1994.

Goebel, Bruce A., and James C. Hall, eds. *Teaching a "New Canon"?: Students, Teachers, and Texts in the College Literature Classroom*. Urbana, IL: National Council of Teachers of English, 1995.

Haile, Barbara J., and Audreye E. Johnson. "Teaching and Learning about Black Women: The Anatomy of a Course." *Sage: A Scholarly Journal on Black Women* 6 (1989): 69–73.

Haymes, Stephen Nathan. *Race, Culture, and the City: A Pedagogy for Black Urban Struggle*. Albany: State U of New York P, 1995.

hooks, bell. *Teaching to Transgress: Education as the Practice of Freedom*. New York: Routledge, 1994.

———. "Whiteness in the Black Imagination." In Ruth Frankenberg, ed., *Displacing Whiteness: Essays in Social and Cultural Criticism*. Durham, NC: Duke UP, 1997. 165–79.

Johnson, Cheryl L. "Participatory Rhetoric and the Teacher as Racial/Gendered Subject." *College English* 56 (1994): 409–19.

Johnson-Feelings, Dianne. *Telling Tales: The Pedagogy and Promise of African American Literature for Youth.* New York: Greenwood, 1990.

Kafka, Phillipa. "A Multicultural Introduction to Literature." In James M. Cahalan and David B. Downing, eds., *Practicing Theory in Introductory College Literature Courses.* Urbana, IL: National Council of Teachers of English, 1991. 179–88.

Lappas, Catherine. "Building Multicultural Bridges with Literature." *Readerly Writerly Texts: Essays on Literature, Literary Textual Criticism, and Pedagogy* 1 (1994): 151–70.

Lee, Carol D. *Signifying as a Scaffold for Literary Interpretation: The Pedagogical Implications of an African American Discourse Genre.* Urbana, IL: National Council of Teachers of English, 1993.

Lee, Valerie. "Strategies for Teaching Black Women's Literature in a White Cultural Context." *Sage: A Scholarly Journal on Black Women* 6 (1989): 74–76.

Linkon, Sherry. "Gender, Race, and Place: Teaching Working-Class Students in Youngstown." *Radical Teacher* 46 (1995): 27–32.

Luthra, Rashmi. "Negotiating the Minefield: Practicing Transformative Pedagogy as a Teacher of Color in a Classroom Climate of Suspicion." In Vargas, *Women Faculty of Color.* 109–24.

Maitino, John R., and David R. Peck, eds. *Teaching American Ethnic Literatures: Nineteen Essays.* Albuquerque: U of New Mexico P, 1996.

Miller, Suzanne M., and Barbara McCaskill, eds. *Multicultural Literature and Literacies: Making Space for Difference.* Albany: State U of New York P, 1993.

Murdy, Anne-Elizabeth. "Teach the Nation: Public School, Racial Uplift, and Women's Writing in the 1890's." New York: Routledge, 2003.

Myrsiades, Kostas, and Linda S. Myrsiades, eds. *Margins in the Classroom: Teaching Literature.* Minneapolis: U of Minneapolis P, 1994.

Neumann, Bonnie H., and Helen M. McDonnell, eds. *Teaching the Short Story: A Guide to Using Stories from Around the World.* Urbana, IL: National Council of Teachers of English, 1996.

Ng, Roxana, Pat Staton, and Joyce Scane, eds. *Anti-Racism, Feminism, and Critical Approaches to Education.* Westport, CT: Bergin & Garvey, 1995.

Onyekwuluje, Anne B. "Guess Who's Coming to Class: Teaching through the Politics of Race, Class, and Gender." In Vargas, *Women Faculty of Color.* 237–56.

Simawe, Saadi A., ed. *Black Orpheus: Music in African American Fiction from the Harlem Renaissance to Toni Morrison.* New York: Garland, 2000.

Sleeter, Christine E., and Peter L. McLaren, eds. *Multicultural Education, Critical Pedagogy, and the Politics of Difference.* Albany: State U of New York P, 1995.

Sullivan, Patricia A., and Donna J. Qualley, eds. *Pedagogy in the Age of Politics: Writing and Reading (in) the Academy.* Urbana, IL: National Council of Teachers of English, 1994.

Swartz, Ellen. "Multicultural Education: Disrupting Patterns of Supremacy in School Curricula, Practices, and Pedagogy." *Journal of Negro Education* 62 (1993): 493–506.

Vargas, Lucila, ed. *Women Faculty of Color in the White Classroom.* New York: Lang, 2002.

Valade, Roger M. III. *The Essential Black Literature Guide.* Detroit: Visible Ink, 1996.

Criticism

Beaulieu, Elizabeth Ann. *Black Women Writers and the American Neo-Slave Narrative: Femininity Unfettered.* Westport, CT: Greenwood, 1999.

Bryant, Jacqueline K. *The Foremother Figure in Early Black Women's Literature: Clothed in My Right Mind.* New York: Garland, 1999.

Diggs, Marylynne. "Surveying the Intersection: Pathology, Secrecy, and the Discourses of Racial and Sexual Identity." *Journal of Homosexuality* 26 (1993): 1–19.

Grasso, Linda M. *The Artistry of Anger: Black and White Women's Literature in America, 1820–1860.* Chapel Hill: U of North Carolina P, 2002.

Harris, Trudier. *Saints, Sinners, Saviors: Strong Black Women in African American Literature.* New York: Palgrave, 2001.

James, Joy, and T. Denean Sharpley-Whiting, eds. *The Black Feminist Reader.* Malden, MA: Blackwell, 2000.

Johnson, Yvonne. *The Voices of African American Women: The Use of Narrative and Authorial Voice in the Works of Harriet Jacobs, Zora Neale Hurston, and Alice Walker.* New York: Lang, 1998.

Marsh Lockett, Carol P., ed. *Black Women Playwrights: Visions on the American Stage.* New York: Garland, 1999.

Martin, Charles D. *The White African American Body: A Cultural and Literary Exploration.* New Brunswick, NJ: Rutgers UP, 2002.

Okur, Nilgun Anadolu. "Afrocentricity as a Generative Idea in the Study of African American Drama." *Journal of Black Studies* 24 (1993): 88–108.

Pagnattaro, Marisa Anne. *In Defiance of the Law: From Anne Hutchinson to Toni Morrison.* New York: Lang, 2001.

Patton, Venetria K. *Women in Chains: The Legacy of Slavery in Black Women's Fiction.* Albany: State University of New York P, 2000.

Ripley, C. Peter, and Jeffrey S. Rossbach, eds. *The Black Abolitionist Papers.* Chapel Hill: U of North Carolina P, 1985–92.

Spillers, Hortense J. *Black, White, and in Color: Essays on American Literature and Culture.* Chicago: U of Chicago P, 2003.

Twagilimana, Aimable. *Race and Gender in the Making of an African American Literary Tradition.* New York: Garland, 1997.

Index

This index covers authors and works in *The Norton Anthology of African American Literature*, Second Edition. **Boldface page numbers indicate major discussion of authors.**